WITHDRAWN
UTSA LIBRARIES

The Soviet
Union and the
Middle East
in the 1980s

The Soviet Union and the Middle East in the 1980s

Opportunities, Constraints, and Dilemmas

Edited by
Mark V. Kauppi
University of Colorado

R. Craig Nation
University of Southern California

LexingtonBooks
D.C. Heath and Company
Lexington, Massachusetts
Toronto

Library of Congress Cataloging in Publication Data

Main entry under title:
  The Soviet Union and the Middle East in the 1980s.

  Includes bibliographical references and index.
  1. Near East—Foreign relations—Soviet Union—Addresses, essays,
lectures. 2. Soviet Union—Foreign relations—Near East—Addresses, essays,
lectures. I. Kauppi, Mark V. II. Nation, R. Craig.
DS63.2.S65S66   1983   327.47056   82-48097
ISBN 0-669-05966-8

LIBRARY
The University of Texas
At San Antonio

*Copyright © 1983 by D.C. Heath and Company, with the exception
of chapter 2, for which copyright is claimed by J.C. Hurewitz.*

All rights reserved. No part of this publication may be reproduced or trans-
mitted in any form or by any means, electronic or mechanical, including
photocopy, recording, or any information storage or retrieval system, without
permission in writing from the publisher.

Published simultaneously in Canada

Printed in the United States of America

International Standard Book Number: 0-669-05966-8

Library of Congress Catalog Card Number: 82-48097

To our parents

Contents

                 Dynamics of Involvement**   *Richard Ned Lebow*
                 with *Jonathan Cooper*   265

                 Index   281

                 About the Contributors   291

                 About the Editors   293

Acknowledgments

We would like to express our appreciation to our friend and colleague, Dr. Douglas T. Stuart, director of the University of Southern California's School of International Relations German Graduate Program, for giving us the opportunity to organize the April 1982 USC-U.S. Army Russian Institute (USARI) symposium on the Soviet Union and the Middle East. A number of the chapters appearing in this book were first presented at the symposium. Special thanks also goes to Lois Galpert of USC for assuring a smooth-running conference. We also wish to acknowledge the aid, encouragement, and support of Captain Joseph Tullbane of USARI, and Ray Russell, Annette Reiserer, Coleen Walters, Linda Koenig, William Tow, and Lawrence Whetten of USC. We also thank Carol Tifft Nation for her timely editorial assistance.

1

Introduction: The Soviet Union and the Middle East

Mark V. Kauppi

Over the past five years the topic of the Soviet Union and the Third World has been the subject of a number of books and a multitude of articles and monographs. The Middle East has been a particularly popular area of investigation given its proximity to the Soviet Union, Moscow's activities in the area, the Arab-Israeli dispute, and the importance of Persian Gulf oil to the Western world.[1] One may well ask, therefore, why another book on the topic? An obvious initial response is that the region is highly unstable and events outpace published analyses, requiring a continual updating and reassessment of Soviet involvement in the region. In a little over three years the world has witnessed the Soviet military occupation of Afghanistan, the assassination of Egypt's President Sadat, the Iran-Iraq war, and the Israeli invasion of Lebanon. Such events require constant evaluation of Soviet intentions and policies in the region as part of an overall assessment of Western security policy in the 1980s. This is particularly true following the death of Leonid Brezhnev and the potential for Soviet policy to move in new directions.[2]

But there are other reasons as well, which deal less with the problem of topicality and more with the questions of scope and perspective. First, much of the recent work concerning Soviet involvement in the Middle East is country specific and therefore generally has excluded an overall analysis of Soviet involvement throughout the region. Studies on Egypt and Afghanistan immediately come to mind.[3]

Second, there traditionally has been a tendency for scholars of the Middle East and the Soviet Union to emphasize the Arab-Israeli struggle as the epicenter around which conflict in the area revolves. Given the recurrent Arab-Israeli wars and the 1982 invasion of Lebanon, this is understandable. No other dispute in the Middle East is as likely to lead to a Soviet-U.S. confrontation, transforming a regional conflict into an international one. The ramifications of the Arab-Israeli problem can also be felt in the bilateral relations between a superpower and its erstwhile allies in the region. Washington's close association with Israel, for example, is one reason Arab regimes such as in Saudi Arabia are hesitant to become too closely identified with the United States.[4] But the diverse nature of the region—stretching

It should be noted that in an attempt at consistency, we have generally followed the transliteration style of the *Middle East Journal*.

from Morocco to Afghanistan and from the Horn of Africa to Turkey—
is the source of a number of other intense rivalries based on religious, ethnic,
historical, and political cleavages. Some are intrasocietal (the current domestic Iranian situation), some transnational (the Kurdish and Palestinian
struggles for homelands), and several of the most dangerous conflicts
threatening the tenuous stability in the region are interstate and driven in
part by nationalism (Iran and Iraq, Ethiopia and Somalia).

Third, much of the literature generated on the topic of the security of
the Persian Gulf suffers from a rather narrow military perspective. Until
recently, the Persian Gulf quite often was viewed as simply an object of
superpower attention. Little analysis was devoted to either the views of the
Arab states in the region concerning the use of such U.S. military options as
the Rapid Deployment Force or the domestic sources of conflict that are
more likely than a Soviet invasion to threaten the political survivability of
members of the Gulf Cooperation Council.[5]

Finally, there is a tendency for much of the literature and discussion
within the Western foreign-policy establishment to be preoccupied almost
exclusively with the Kremlin's opportunities and successes and Washington's
problems and failures in the region; all U.S. setbacks are deemed disas-
trous, while those of the Soviets apparently are never permanent. Such
preoccupation is understandable. A preliminary assessment reveals that by
invading Afghanistan, Soviet forces are now within tactical aircraft range
of the oilfields throughout the Persian Gulf. President Sadat of Egypt is
assassinated and his successor hints at establishing closer ties with Moscow.
The Soviet-supported Ethiopian regime defeats the U.S.-backed Somali
government. The only self-proclaimed Marxist Arab state in the region,
South Yemen, poses a continual threat to Oman and to the leftist but non-
Marxist government in North Yemen. Libya is a constant unsettling factor
in the Middle East, and the Soviets continue to build their naval strength in
the Indian Ocean.[6]

From the U.S. point of view, however, the United States over the past
four years has lost two of its major supporters (the shah of Iran and President Sadat). The Camp David peace process has verged on collapse as
Israeli relations with both the United States and Egypt take a turn for the
worse following the invasion of Lebanon. President Reagan has been un-
able to forge what Washington has termed a strategic consensus among
Israeli and moderate Arab leaders to deter possible Soviet activity in the
Persian Gulf and has been further disappointed at the reluctance of the
Saudis to play an assertive security role in the region. By the end of 1982 the
United States found itself trying to prevent the return of civil war to
Lebanon while hoping for movement on the issue of some form of Pales-
tinian autonomy, as well as an end to the Iran-Iraq war. Furthermore, the
United States is faced with a number of perplexing policy dilemmas: arms

and Airborne Warning and Control Systems (AWACS) for the Saudis to increase the security of the Persian Gulf disturbs the Israelis; identifying closely with the Saudi royal family brings forth images of the U.S. experience with the shah; the inability of Washington to influence the Begin government on the issue of Palestinian autonomy causes friction between Washington and Jerusalem as well as between the United States and moderate Arab governments; hoping to reestablish some sort of relationship with Iran, Washington decides to resist Iraqi requests for more military aid; deference to the Saudis leads U.S. administrations to treat North Yemen as an extension of our interests in Saudi Arabia, contributing to an incoherent policy toward the government in Sana'a; and support for King Hassan of Morocco alienates the Polisario Front. All in all, 1982 was a trying year for U.S. foreign policy in the Middle East.[7]

But it can be argued that the reason the United States appears to be facing so many problems in the Middle East is because its presence and influence in the region simply is greater than that of the Soviet Union. A case could be made that the beginning of 1983 witnessed Soviet influence in the Middle East at its lowest point since 1955: it is distrusted by virtually all the states throughout the area, largely excluded from the Arab-Israeli peace process, passively watched as the Palestine Liberation Organization (PLO) was dealt a devastating military blow in Lebanon, and has lost Iraqi support by supplying arms to Iran without receiving any encouraging signs from the Khumayni regime. South Yemen and Syria usually are viewed as the Soviet Union's only reliable allies in the region, but there have been signs that after the war in Lebanon the regime of Hafiz al-Asad, disappointed with Soviet military equipment and lack of political support, might be gradually distancing itself from Moscow.[8] Evidence seems to suggest that Arab regimes have turned to the Soviet Union for aid not because of compatible political goals but rather because of weakness and lack of alternative sources of external support.

Underlying Themes

This book does not claim to cover comprehensively all aspects and prospects of Soviet involvement in the Middle East. Such a task would require a project of greater length and would be more ambitious in scope. Furthermore, the contributors to this book are a highly diverse, international group of scholars and policymakers, and the perspectives presented are often quite divergent. Nevertheless, several themes reoccur. First, while the opportunities presented to the Soviets in the Middle East in the 1980s are discussed, equal emphasis is given to the constraints and dilemmas they face in this turbulent part of the world. Consider some of the problems faced by Moscow. In supporting Ethiopia, it lost its foothold in Somalia. By backing the radical government in South Yemen, the Soviets have had problems in convincing

North Yemen and Saudi Arabia of its supposedly innocent intentions. In tilting toward Khumayni in the Iran-Iraq war, the trade-off has been a cooling of relations with Baghdad. By invading Afghanistan to bolster a flagging pro-Moscow regime, Moslems throughout the Middle East view Soviet activities in the region with increasing alarm. Furthermore, the dispatching of Soviet, Cuban, and East European advisors and military personnel to countries such as Ethiopia and South Yemen simply has encouraged reciprocal action on the part of the United States, as evidenced by its securing of limited naval facilities in Somalia and Oman and its increased aid to friendly regimes.

A second underlying theme found in a number of chapters in this book is that the constraints and dilemmas faced by Moscow are not due simply to actions taken by the United States but also to the regional and internal dynamics of the area. Rivalries between the Arabs and Israelis, Iraqis and Iranians, Egyptians and Libyans, Ethiopians and Somalis, as well as between the factions in Lebanon, cannot be traced simply to the superpowers; they have their own historical roots. In their search for allies, however, Moscow and Washington have been prone to lavish their clients with arms, aggravating indigenous instability and contributing their share to ever-costly and destructive wars.

Finally, in discussing Soviet involvement in the region, it is obviously necessary to address the role of its principal competitor, the United States. What emerges is the general observation on the part of a number of authors that the superpowers have been frustrated in their attempts to shape developments in the region to their satisfaction. Intentions are not translated always into desired outcomes. Growing interest, involvement, and attention in the Middle East on the part of the United States and the Soviet Union have not necessarily resulted in a commensurate amount of political influence. Even those governments that turn to the United States for help tend to maintain an underlying suspicion of outside powers. The acceptance of foreign aid and arms does not mean necessarily a common perspective on political and military policies between donor and recipient. Furthermore, such ties always have the potential to draw the superpowers into a regional quarrel that they would perhaps prefer to avoid.[9] In sum, despite the varying perspectives of the authors, the reader will find throughout this book references not only to the opportunities that events in the Middle East have presented to the Soviet Union in the 1980s but also to the constraints, dilemmas, paradoxes, and unintended consequences of involvement in this part of the world.

This does not suggest that the Soviet Union poses no threat to the vital (or even not so vital) interests of the West in the Third World. What is being argued is that if one's primary concern is preventing an expansion of Soviet global influence, this goal is best served by realistic assessments of the domestic and regional constraints in the Third World faced by the Soviets as well as by the West. Similarly, if one is primarily concerned with crisis prevention and the avoidance of superpower confrontation, such as in the Middle East in October 1973, it is also necessary to recognize the circumstances under which the Soviets and Americans may be inadvertently drawn into a conflict neither wishes to see escalate.[10]

The Contributors

Professors Hurewitz, Nation, Freedman, and Steinbach discuss in general terms the sources and nature of Soviet involvement in the Middle East. Professor Hurewitz opens with a careful description of the interaction of global and regional dynamics in the area using the Israeli invasion of Lebanon and the Iran-Iraq conflict as case studies. He notes the continuing inability of the superpowers to control effectively events in the region and the persistence of their policies of mutual denial. Dr. Nation attempts to investigate systematically the sources of Soviet involvement in the area and concludes that although the Soviets may be perceived to have a long-term interest in maintaining a regional presence, the degree to which this presence directly threatens Western interests might be questioned. Professor Freedman's contribution is a case study intended to demonstrate the style of Soviet diplomacy in the Middle East, using the first year of the Reagan administration as a framework for analysis. Udo Steinbach takes issue with the popular image of the Islamic Middle East as an infertile ground for communist expansionism and suggests that as totalitarian ideologies both communism and Islam have common features that might provide a ground for radical political alternatives should the current wave of Islamic fundamentalism lead to widespread political disillusionment.

Brigadier Kenneth Hunt, in considering Soviet threats to the Middle East, emphasizes the need for a political strategy to complement any military strategy. Mamoun Kurdi presents an analysis of how threats to the Arabian Gulf are best dealt with, particularly emphasizing the role of the states within the region.

Mohammed Anis Salem discusses Soviet-Egyptian relations in the wake of the Sadat assassination. In drawing up a balance sheet of forces encouraging and discouraging a realignment of Egyptian policies toward Moscow, he foresees a cautious and pragmatic orientation emerging from Cairo. Galia Golan focuses on the Soviet relationship with the PLO, which she characterizes as ''tactical'' and also unstable, particularly given the lack of support for the organization during its war in Lebanon. In his discussion of Soviet policy in the Bab al-Mandab area, Paul Viotti stresses the constraints regional dynamics place upon Soviet initiatives.

Malcolm Yapp and Henning Behrens discuss Soviet policy toward, respectively, Iran and Afghanistan. Yapp downplays the long-term threat to Iran posed by the Soviets despite Moscow's concerns over the disruptions of the Khumayni revolution. Behrens presents a balanced overview of the Soviet Union's Afghanistan intervention and concludes by considering potential contexts for a negotiated resolution of the problem. In his conclusion, Richard Ned Lebow describes the tension created by attracting and stymieing forces that have drawn both superpowers into the Middle East but make it impossible for them to control effectively the terms of their involvement.

This book augments the already substantial literature devoted to Soviet policy in the Middle East—both by updating events as well as by airing fresh and sometimes controversial perspectives and interpretations.

Notes

1. For brief overviews, see Henry Trofimenko, "The Third World and U.S.-Soviet Competition, *Foreign Affairs* 59 (Summer 1981):1012-1040; Donald Zagoria, "Into the Breach: New Soviet Alliances in the Third World," *Foreign Affairs* 57 (Spring 1979):733-754; Steven R. David, "The Superpower Competition for Influence in the Third World," in Samuel P. Huntington, ed., *The Strategic Imperative: New Policies for American Security* (Cambridge, Mass.: Ballinger, 1982), pp. 229-252; and in the same volume, Bruce D. Porter, "Washington, Moscow, and Third World Conflict in the 1980s," pp. 253-300.

2. For recent statements on the problems of discerning the Soviet decision-making process and intentions, see William Zimmerman, "What Do Scholars Know about Soviet Foreign Policy?" *International Journal* 37, 2 (Spring 1982):198-219; Keith A. Dunn, "'Mysteries' about the Soviet Union," *Orbis* 26, 2 (Summer 1982):361-379.

3. See selected bibliography for citations.

4. William B. Quandt, *Saudi Arabia in the 1980s* (Washington, D.C.: The Brookings Institution, 1981); Fouad Ajami, "The Shadows of Hell," *Foreign Policy* 48 (Fall 1982):94-110.

5. For an analysis of the circumstances under which the Soviets have threatened or actually used combat forces in the Middle East, see Francis Fukuyama, "Nuclear Shadowboxing: Soviet Intervention Threats in the Middle East," *Orbis* 25, 3 (Fall 1981):579-605. The four-volume series edited by Shahram Chubin, *Security in the Persian Gulf* (Montclair, N.J.: Allanheld, Osmun and Co., 1981-1982), covers domestic, regional, and international sources of instability. See also Hermann F. Eilts, "Security Considerations in the Persian Gulf," *International Security* 5, 2 (Fall 1980):79-113.

6. For disturbing analyses of these trends, see George Lenczowski, "The Soviet Union and the Persian Gulf: An Encircling Strategy," *International Journal* 37, 2 (Spring 1982):307-327; John G. Merriam, "Egypt After Sadat," *Current History* 81, 471 (January 1982):5-8, 38-39; Christopher Van Hollen, "North Yemen: A Dangerous Pentagonal Game," *Washington Quarterly* 5, 3 (Summer 1982):137-142; Dov S. Zakheim, "Towards a Western Approach in the Indian Ocean," *Survival* 22 (January/February 1980):7-14. A particularly alarming book concerning Soviet actions is Kurt London, ed., *The Soviet Union in World Politics* (Boulder: Westview Press, 1980).

7. "Although the Soviets do not explicitly say this to Americans, their behavior and propaganda clearly demonstrate that they are cheered by the continuing bitterness and recurring violence between Arabs and Israelis, the mounting anger among the Palestinians, and the growing disillusionment of many Middle Eastern people toward the United States. They see the United States progressively weakened throughout the region, even absent Soviet propaganda or action." Landrum R. Bolling, "A Realistic Middle East Policy, *Orbis* 26, 1 (Spring 1982):6. Reprinted with permission.

8. "Moscow Vexed Over US Mideast Plan," *Christian Science Monitor*, 15 September 1982, p. 3; "Iraq Says Its Treaty with Soviet Hasn't Worked," *New York Times*, 17 November 1982, p. 3; "Soviet Influence in Iran Shows a Sharp Decline," *New York Times*, 14 November 1982, p. 12; "Lebanon War Transforms Syria from Radical to Moderate," *Christian Science Monitor*, 29 September 1982, p. 6; "Soviet Arms Come in Second in Lebanon," *New York Times*, 19 September 1982, p.E2.

9. "America Faces Credibility Gap in Arab World," *Christian Science Monitor*, 20 September 1982, p. 10; "Arabs Grow Disillusioned with White House, Kremlin," *Christian Science Monitor*, 9 November 1982, p. 4. When 1,200 U.S. Marines returned to Beirut at the end of September 1982 following the massacre of Palestinians in the refugee camps, the United States accepted the role of policeman. The danger was that the United States was given more responsibility but, perhaps, no more influence to shape events. See Barry Rubin, "The Hope of Lebanon," *New York Times*, 25 October 1982.

10. Alexander L. George, et al., *Managing U.S.-Soviet Rivalry: Problems of Crisis Prevention* (Boulder: Westview Press, 1983); Joanne Gowa and Nils H. Wessell, *Ground Rules: Soviet and American Involvement in Regional Conflicts*, Philadelphia Policy Papers (Philadelphia: Foreign Policy Research Institute, 1982); I. William Zartman, *Ripe for Resolution: Conflict and Intervention in Africa* (New Haven: Yale University Press, 1982.

8

Selected Bibliography

6

4

USSR and the Third World

Albright, David E., ed. *Communism in Africa*. Bloomington: Indiana University Press, 1980.

Donaldson, Robert H., ed. *The Soviet Union in the Third World: Successes and Failures*. Boulder: Westview Press, 1981.

Duncan, W. Raymond, ed. *Soviet Policy in the Third World*. New York: Pergamon Press, 1980.

Feuchtwanger, E.J., and Peter Nailor, eds. *The Soviet Union and the Third World*. London: Macmillan, 1981.

Heldman, Dan C. *The USSR and Africa: Foreign Policy under Khrushchev*. New York: Praeger, 1981.

Hosmer, Steven T., and Thomas W. Wolfe. *Soviet Policy and Practice toward Third World Conflicts*. Lexington, Mass.: Lexington Books, D.C. Heath and Co., 1982.

Katz, Mark N. *The Third World in Soviet Military Thought*. Baltimore: Johns Hopkins University Press, 1982.

Nogee, Joseph L., and Robert H. Donaldson. *Soviet Foreign Policy since World War II*. New York: Pergamon Press, 1981.

Weinstein, Warren, ed. *Chinese and Soviet Aid to African Nations*. New York: Praeger, 1975.

USSR and the Middle East

Dawisha, Adeed, and Karen Dawisha, eds. *The Soviet Union in the Middle East*. London: Heineman, 1982.

Freedman, Robert O. *Soviet Policy toward the Middle East since 1970*. 3d ed. New York: Praeger, 1982.

Golan, Galia. *Yom Kippur and After: The Soviet Union and the Middle East Crisis*. Cambridge: Cambridge University Press, 1977.

Halliday, Fred. *Soviet Policy in the Arc of Crisis*. Washington, D.C.: Institute for Policy Studies, 1981.

Hurewitz, J.C., ed. *Soviet-American Rivalry in the Middle East*. New York: Praeger, 1969.

Klieman, Aaron S. *Soviet Russia and the Middle East*. Baltimore: Johns Hopkins University Press, 1970.

Laqueur, Walter. *The Soviet Union and the Middle East*. New York: Praeger, 1959.

Lederer, Ivo J., and Wayne S. Vucinich, eds. *The Soviet Union and the Middle East: The Post-World War II Era*. Stanford: Hoover Institution Press, 1974.

Leitenberg, Milton, and Gabriel Sheffer, eds. *Great Power Intervention in the Middle East*. New York: Pergamon Press, 1979.

McLaurin, R.D. *The Middle East in Soviet Policy*. Lexington, Mass.: D.C. Heath and Co., 1975.

Mangold, Peter. *Superpower Intervention in the Middle East*. New York: St. Martin's Press, 1978.

Ottaway, Marina S. *Soviet and American Influence in the Horn of Africa*. New York: Praeger, 1982.

Pennar, Jaan. *The U.S.S.R. and the Arabs: The Ideological Dimension*. New York: Crane, Russak, 1973.

Rabinovich, Itamar. *The Soviet Union and Syria in the 1970's*. New York: Praeger, 1982.

Rezun, Miron. *The Soviet Union and Iran*. Rockville, Md.: Sijthoff and Noordhoff, 1981.

Ro'i, Yaacov. *From Encroachment to Involvement: A Documentary Study of Soviet Policy in the Middle East, 1945-1973*. New York: Wiley; Jerusalem: Israel Universities Press, 1974.

_____., editor. *The Limits to Power: Soviet Policy in the Middle East*. New York: St. Martin's Press, 1979.

Sella, Amnon. *Soviet Political and Military Conduct in the Middle East*. New York: St. Martin's Press, 1981.

Smolansky, Oles M. *The Soviet Union and the Arab East under Khrushchev*. Lewisberg: Bucknell University Press, 1974.

_____. *The Soviet Union and Iraq, 1968-1979*. New York: Praeger, 1982.

Egypt and Afghanistan

Arnold, Anthony. *Afghanistan: The Soviet Invasion in Perspective*. Stanford, Calif.: Hoover Institution Press, 1981.

Aspaturian, Vernon, Alexander Dallin, and Jiri Valenta. *The Soviet Invasion of Afghanistan: Three Perspectives*. ACIS Working Paper no. 27. Los Angeles: University of California at Los Angeles, Center for International and Strategic Affairs, 1980.

Bradsher, Henry S. *Afghanistan and the Soviet Union*. Durham: Duke Press Policy Studies, 1982.

Dawisha, Karen. *Soviet Foreign Policy towards Egypt*. New York: St. Martin's Press, 1979.

Griffiths, John C. *Afghanistan: Key to a Continent*. Boulder: Westview Press, 1981.

Heikal, Mohamed. *The Sphinx and the Commissar: The Rise and Fall of Soviet Influence in the Middle East*. New York: Harper and Row, 1978.

Hyman, Anthony. *Afghanistan under Soviet Domination, 1964-1981*. New York: St. Martin's Press, 1982.

Misra, K.P., ed. *Afghanistan in Crisis*. New York: Advent Books, 1981.

Monks, Alfred L. *The Soviet Intervention in Afghanistan*. Washington and London: American Enterprise Institute for Public Policy Research, 1981.

Newell, Nancy Peabody, and Richard S. Newell. *The Struggle for Afghanistan*. Ithaca and London: Cornell University Press, 1981.

Rubinstein, Alvin Z. *Red Star on the Nile: The Soviet-Egyptian Influence Relationship since the June War*. Princeton: Princeton University Press, 1977.

Persian Gulf and Saudi Arabia

Cottrell, Alvin J., and Frank Bray. *Military Forces in the Persian Gulf*. The Washington Papers no. 60. Beverly Hills: Sage Publications, 1978.

Dunn, Keith A. "Constraints on the USSR in Southwest Asia: A Military Analysis." *Orbis* 25, 3 (Fall 1981):607-629.

El Mallakh, Ragaei. *Saudi Arabia: Rush to Development*. Baltimore: Johns Hopkins University Press, 1981.

Epstein, Joshua M. "Soviet Vulnerabilities in Iran and the RDF Deterrent." *International Security* 6, 2 (Fall 1981):126-158.

Helms, Christine Moss. *The Cohesion of Saudi Arabia*. Baltimore: Johns Hopkins University Press, 1980.

Kemp, Geoffrey. "Military Force and Middle East Oil." In *Energy and Security*, edited by David A. Deese and Joseph S. Nye, 365-387. Cambridge, Mass.: Ballinger, 1981.

Niblock, Tim, ed. *State, Society and Economy in Saudi Arabia*. New York: St. Martin's Press, 1981.

Quandt, William B. *Saudi Arabia in the 1980s*. Washington, D.C.: The Brookings Institution, 1981.

Ross, Dennis. "Considering Soviet Threats to the Persian Gulf." *International Security* 6, 2 (Fall 1981):159-180.

Tucker, Robert. "Oil: The Issue of American Intervention." *Commentary* (January 1975).

Lebanon

Bulloch, John. *Death of a Country: The Civil War in Lebanon*. London: Weidenfeld and Nicolson, 1977.

Deeb, Marius K. *The Lebanese Civil War*. New York: Praeger, 1980.

Faris, Hani A. *Beyond the Lebanese Civil War: Historical Issues and the Challenges of Reconstruction*. Georgetown: Center for Contemporary Arab Studies, 1982.

Gordon, David C. *Lebanon: The Fragmented Nation*. Stanford: Hoover Institution, 1980.

Haley, P. Edward, and Lewis W. Snider, eds. *Lebanon in Crisis: Participants and Issues*. Syracuse: Syracuse University Press, 1979.

Khalidi, Walid. *Conflict and Violence in Lebanon: Confrontation in the Middle East*. Cambridge, Mass.: Harvard University, Center for International Affairs, 1980.

Iran

Abrahamian, Ervand. *Iran between Two Revolutions*. Princeton: Princeton University Press, 1982.

Bonine, Michael E., and Nikki R. Keddie. *Modern Iran: The Dialectics of Continuity and Change*. Albany: State University of New York Press, 1981.

Fischer, Michael M.J. *Iran: From Religious Dispute to Revolution*. Cambridge, Mass.: Harvard University Press, 1980.

Heikal, Mohamed. *Iran: The Untold Story*. New York: Pantheon Books, 1981.

Ismael, Tareq Y. *Iraq and Iran: Roots of Conflict*. Syracuse: Syracuse University Press, 1982.

Jabbari, Ahmad, and Robert Olson, eds. *Iran: Essays on a Revolution in the Making*. Lexington, Ky.: Mazda Publishers, 1981.

Keddie, Nikki R. *Roots of Revolution: An Interpretive History of Modern Iran*. with a section by Yann Richard. New Haven: Yale University Press, 1981.

Koury, Enver, and Charles MacDonald, eds. *Revolution in Iran: A Reappraisal*. Hyattsville, Md.: Institute of Middle Eastern and North African Affairs, 1982.

Looney, Robert E. *Economic Origins of the Iranian Revolution*. Elmsford, N.Y.: Pergamon Press, 1982.

Rubin, Barry. *Paved with Good Intentions: The American Experience and Iran*. New York: Penguin Books, 1981.

Saikal, Amin. *The Rise and Fall of the Shah*. Princeton: Princeton University Press, 1980.

Zabih, Sepehr. *Iran since the Revolution*. Baltimore: Johns Hopkins University Press, 1982.

2 The Interplay of Superpower and Regional Dynamics

J.C. Hurewitz

I

Domestic disputes in the Middle East often inflate into regional and then into global disputes, for in the Middle East the strategic interests of the United States and the Soviet Union intersect. As the concentration of the media on crises in the Middle East in recent years amply confirms, domestic and regional conflicts in which the superpowers become tangled multiply faster than diplomats and politicians can cope with them. A comprehensive analysis of the interplay of superpower and regional dynamics in the sprawling, diversified Middle East could hardly overlook any drawn-out regional disputes. These would include, as a minimum, the Moroccan war with the Algerian-backed Polisario guerrillas in Western (former Spanish) Sahara, Libya's edgy relations with all its immediate neighbors save Algeria, the Soviet-supported Ethiopian conflicts with Somalia and with the Eritrean resistance, the on-again-off-again fighting between the two Yemens, the intractable Arab quarrel with Israel, the Iraq-Iran war at the head of the vulnerable Persian Gulf, and the Soviet invasion of Afghanistan and Moscow's inability to legitimate its chosen regime.

Such inclusive treatment lies beyond the scope of a necessarily brief evaluation. Rather than skim the surface, it would be more instructive to focus on two issues—Israel's invasion of Lebanon in hot pursuit of the Palestine Liberation Organization and the Iraq-Iran war—and their interaction with Soviet-U.S. rivalry. At the time of writing, the PLO has been evacuated from Beirut and the outcome of the Iran-Iraq war remains inconclusive. Despite the uncertainty, there is ample evidence to illustrate the interplay of world and regional dynamics in the Middle East.

In the prevailing view of each superpower, its rival and the rival's Middle East clients are responsible for the many recurrent and abiding crises. As the regional insiders see it, the interstate quarrels basically center on local issues and are aggravated by the interference of either the United States or the Soviet Union or both. Clearly, the superpower and regional rivalries mesh, for the superpowers stir up as much trouble by their competitive behavior as do the Middle East disputants. Yet even if this assumption is

---

This chapter was completed on 1 September 1982; the evidence on the Lebanese war was limited to media coverage.

13

accepted, the patterns of U.S. and Soviet relations with regional governments are changeable, for politics in the Middle East tends to be fluid. The reasons for the instability can be explained, but such explanations hardly diminish the difficulties of sound assessment.

In an inquiry into international and regional politics in the Middle East, the start of analytical wisdom lies in the recognition that the region is defined variably even by the experts. As my listing of major disputes suggests, I favor a broad construction reaching from Morocco to Afghanistan, encompassing an area that is easily twice the size of the continental United States. Often in academia as in the media, however, the Middle East is treated essentially as the areal equivalent of Israel and the adjacent Arab states. The region so defined would omit some of the most resonant claimants to a voice in the Arab-Israeli dispute such as Algeria, Libya, and the People's Democratic Republic of Yemen (PDRY), which along with Syria and the PLO have constituted the Steadfastness and Confrontation Front. The front rejected any dealings whatsoever with Israel. Moreover, all Arab League states from Morocco to Oman and from Iraq to Somalia (which by any criteria other than membership in the league would be disqualified as an Arab country) have become involved at intervals in the controversy with Israel.

Even the narrow constructionists often indiscriminately couple the Arab-Israeli conflict and the issues of the Persian Gulf. Actually, the ties between the two are limited and intermittent. Before we explore them, it should be noted that many Arabs have been calling it the Arabian or the Arab Gulf. The date for the popular adoption of the change of name was roughly 1970. It has been the energy crisis in the industrial states in the past decade that leads the concerned governments, media, and public to associate developments in the Gulf and the Arab-Israeli zone.

Undeniably, the selective oil embargos and production cutbacks by the Arab oil-producing governments during the Arab-Israeli war of October 1973 influenced the policies of the United States and its Organization for Economic Cooperation and Development (OECD) partners. It also made feasible the initial doubling and redoubling of the price of crude oil by the Organization of Petroleum Exporting Countries (OPEC) during and soon after the war. The October War and its aftermath, however, were the only times that the Arab governments used the oil weapon effectively in support of their diplomacy toward Israel. On closer scrutiny, it becomes clear that the relationship between the energy crisis and the Arab-Israeli dispute is much more subtle. As late as 1977 the Gulf supplied Japan with nearly 75 percent of its daily oil needs, Western Europe with roughly 60 percent, and the United States with less than 14 percent. Yet it should be noted that U.S. oil imports from the Gulf had almost quintupled since 1972, when it represented less than 3 percent of daily consumption. The further trebling of the price of crude in 1979-1980 resulted from the overturn of the shah and the outbreak of the Iraq-Iran war.

To put it differently, the oil crisis of the importing countries turned into the exporters' bonanza. So long as the price of crude remained high and threatened to go higher, as was still the case in the spring of 1981, all importers were vulnerable to the exporters' political caprice. A year later, the glutted world oil market, to which declining demand in the major industrial states had largely contributed, softened the price of crude and weakened the political influence of the Gulf producing countries, which accounted then as before for approximately two-thirds of OPEC's global sales. On the rising price curve, when the consumers are most vincible, the Arab producers might be tempted to use the oil weapon in support of the Palestine cause, as they did in 1973-1974. But on the declining price curve, as in the spring of 1982, the Arab oil exporters lost most of their potential leverage. A few months later, however, during the Israeli invasion and occupation of Lebanon, even if the demand in the industrial states had risen sharply and their stocks of crude had run down, Iraq and the peninsular oil states were too preoccupied with their own defense against threats from Iran to be able to give concerted attention to the use of the oil weapon. In a word, the effective relationship between the continuing oil and Arab-Israeli crises is inconstant. Thus the Iraq-Iran war, whose origins had nothing objectively to do with the Arab-Israeli question, produced in the industrial states an abiding concern over its impact on the oil industry and its implications for the future.

Or take the case in December 1979 of the Soviet invasion of Afghanistan, which is physically removed from the Gulf and seems remote from its problems. Nevertheless, the moment Russian forces crossed into Afghanistan, anxiety sped through the Gulf and the Arab and Islamic worlds as well as Western Europe and the United States. The Kremlin's action was strategic and left the concerned extraregional powers wondering whether it had established a precedent for future Soviet policy toward Middle East countries—Iraq, the People's Democratic Republic of (South) Yemen, and Syria—with which it had concluded treaties of friendship and cooperation. The Soviet military occupation of Afghanistan, even if identified as a Gulf problem, as President Carter did in January 1980, had no direct bearing on the Arab-Israeli dispute.

The United States and the Soviet Union pay close attention to the Middle East, and each is sensitized to regional changes attributable to the other. Whenever a perceived advantage accrues to one superpower, the adversary may be expected to try to check its growth or seek compensation. Thus, by agreeing to direct negotiations for a political settlement, President Anwar al-Sadat of Egypt in November 1977 broke Arab solidarity on the denial of legitimacy to Israel. The United States did a double take at the time by abandoning altogether the proposed joint-superpower sponsorship of such negotiations, announced a few weeks earlier. The Carter administration then offered its unilateral mediation to the two Middle East governments, leading to an Egyptian-Israeli agreement at Camp David in September 1978 and the signing of formal instruments of peace in March 1979. Throughout this period, the Soviet Union played a spoiler role by discouraging the extension of the Camp David process and even the execution of the Egyptian-Israeli peace terms. Through diplomacy and propaganda the Kremlin aided and abetted the Steadfastness and Confrontation Front of Arab states, which had been formed in December 1977 expressly to frustrate Sadat's plans for direct talks with Israel.

The opportunity for a U.S. riposte came at the turn of 1980, immediately after the Soviet invasion of Afghanistan. On U.S. initiative the UN Security Council convened to consider a draft resolution, sponsored by five of its Third World members, condemning the USSR. Following the Soviet veto of the draft, the five, with applause from the United States, convoked the General Assembly in emergency session, which adopted in mid-January—by a resounding majority—an exact replica of the failed draft. Soon thereafter comparable action was taken at Islamabad (Pakistan) by the Islamic Conference, an organization of forty-two countries, at its first emergency meeting. This decision too, was reached with encouragement from the United States. By then the Carter Doctrine had stipulated that the United States would forcibly resist any attempted Soviet penetration of the Gulf. To make the doctrine credible the administration in Washington imposed economic sanctions on the Soviet Union and gave wide publicity to accelerated plans for laying down the infrastructure of the Rapid Deployment Force in the Indian Ocean approaches to the Arabian peninsula.

If *detente* means the deliberate, structured, mutually agreed relaxation and removal of the causes of tension, the United States and the Soviet Union have never reached such an understanding on the Middle East. Here the Soviet-U.S. competition has been characterized by the politics of mutual denial in defense of perceived strategic interests. The Soviet Union regards the Middle East states along its southwest frontier as its backyard and views with deep suspicion intimate relations between these states and major powers. To exclude such relations it tried in 1945-1947 to assimilate Turkey and Iran into a Soviet sphere of influence, comparable to the sphere that the Kremlin was creating in Eastern Europe. The Soviet initiatives had exactly the opposite effect of the one it had sought, bringing the United States into the region as the declared defender of Russia's southern neighbors. By the same token, the United States has regarded the Middle East as an area from which Russian influence had been excluded ever since the nineteenth century and has viewed any attempted Soviet political and economic penetration as threatening Western interests, particularly access to Gulf oil. The

United States also sees the Arab-Israeli dispute and the recurrent wars to which it has given rise as destabilizing the region. For this reason, and because the United States developed over the years a moral commitment to the survival of Israel, successive U.S. administrations have consistently taken the lead in promoting a peaceful settlement. The United States and its allies reacted with alarm to the Soviet entry into the Arab Middle East in 1955-1956 as arms purveyor to Egypt, Syria, and Yemen, adding Iraq and Algeria by 1963.

Since then, each superpower has sustained favorite friends in the region with generous diplomatic material and technical assistance. In the six Arab-Israeli wars, the United States and the Soviet Union have tended to avoid active entanglement. When they have not—as in Russia's assumption of the air defense of Egypt in its war of attrition with Israel in 1969-1970 and in the rival Soviet and U.S. airlifts to the opposing sides in the Yom Kippur or Ramadan War of October 1973—superpower tensions have threatened to escalate beyond control. Until now both governments have acted as if in clear recognition of the need to escape a replay of August 1914 by disallowing their respective regional friends to exercise in effect the right of declaring a superpower war. The United States and the USSR have remained firm in their determination to prevent a nuclear confrontation, sparked by a Middle East war over regional issues.

Short of this invariable rule that the superpowers have so far honored, there is ample scope for maneuver, which both have exploited with only momentary interludes of cooperation and relaxation of pressures but without abatement of mutual suspicion. Despite Soviet-U.S. agreements on the avoidance of a nuclear war (the hot line, the test ban and nonproliferation treaties, and Strategic Arms Limitation Talks (SALT) I), on the promotion of commerce, and on shoring up security in Europe (if Helsinki may be so described), only incidental benefits have accrued to the Middle East. Washington and Moscow have used the hot line to frame guidelines for their behavior in the 1967 and 1973 Arab-Israeli wars. They have also cooperated, at times, in defining the terms of ceasefire resolutions. But they can point to very few, if any, other concrete measures for the reduction of superpower rivalry in and over the Arab-Israeli and other regional disputes. If the United States and the Soviet Union have failed to adopt restraints on their diplomatic behavior in the Middle East as a whole, it follows that the superpower Cold War in the region has continued without interruption. This in turn implies no diminution of mutual suspicion and the regional tensions that such a superpower relationship generates. The Soviet Union and the United States have kept up their mutually abrasive propaganda and continue to try to outwit each other in specific situations of crisis and opportunity.

The Soviet Union manifestly lost no chance after the October War to dissuade its Arab friends from resuming diplomatic relations with the United

States. In the same period, Secretary of State Henry A. Kissinger verbally upheld superpower cooperation, while proceeding unilaterally to help negotiate Israel's separation-of-forces agreements with Egypt and Syria. By definition, cold warriors favor strategies of containment. Each superpower has appeared bent on keeping the other out of areas and activities in which it does not already have a secure footing—and preferably on easing them out of positions of economic, political, and military advantage. When U.S.-Turkish relations chilled after the reopening of the Cyprus crisis in August 1974 and by 1975-1976 the United States lost access to a complex of military and intelligence facilities in Turkey, the USSR was able to reciprocate the applause of the United States on the souring of Soviet-Egyptian relations after July 1972, culminating less than four years later in Egypt's repudiation of its treaty of friendship with Russia. Containment has also been reflected in the spirited superpower naval competition in the Mediterranean, the Indian Ocean, the Arabian Sea, and even for a while in the Gulf where modern naval vessels do not have elbow room to maneuver. Similar considerations also condition Soviet and U.S. arms-transfer policies.

The two sets of belligerents in the Israeli invasion of Lebanon and the Iraq-Iran war, which will be considered subsequently, have practiced diplomacy comparable to that of the superpowers. In both regional instances, they have pushed mutual denial to its logical extreme of mutual regime destruction. Moreover, the two wars share this in common: the weapons of the combatants have come primarily from the superpowers or their allies, and the suppliers have used arms to compete for political influence in the region. The Soviet Union has been the paramount supplier to Syria and the PLO, and the United States, to Israel. The United States also impressively built-up Iran's arsenal in the final half-dozen years of the shahdom. After the outbreak of the war with Iraq, the *ulama* or religious leaders, forgetting about the "tainted" past, rehabilitated the armed forces for the defense of the homeland. In the process, they also discovered massive stores of weaponry and parts that the shah had accumulated. Similarly, the Iraqi republic for more than two decades had come to lean heavily on the Soviet Union as its principal source of munitions, although for supplementary procurement, it continued to turn to Western powers, chiefly Britain and France. As Soviet-Iraqi relations began cooling in the later 1970s, the proportions changed, with enlarging amounts imported from the West but the Soviet items still predominating.

Without the flow of arms from the superpowers, neither war could have been fought on a grand scale. Yet regardless of the military consequences of either contest, the political benefits, if any, to the military victors and their superpower patrons were certain to be short-lived. Despite the risks of such wars, fought with increasingly sophisticated equipment, there is no evidence to show that the superpowers or their regional friends are about to modify their practices in the arms-transfer game. To understand and evaluate the conditions in which the self-defeating politics thrive, we have to take a closer look at regional and international politics in the postwar Middle East.

II

The international and regional systems in the postwar Middle East have been transformed, but neither has yet found its level of durable accommodation. As late as 1945 the Middle East still fell under British and French hegemony, built up step by step in the preceding century and a half. World War II had undermined the positions in the region of the two European powers; however, neither showed any inclination to surrender them lightly. The primary challenge came at first from the Soviet Union, whose aims were largely strategic, to ease out of the area the extraregional powers and to prevent the United States from replacing them, so as to assimilate at least the adjacent Middle East states into a Soviet sphere of influence. To check the Soviet advance, Britain relinquished the responsibility in 1947 to the United States, which declared its intention to contain the Soviet Union at the international borders. Under the Truman Doctrine of 1947 the United States built up positions of preponderant influence initially in Turkey and, after the restoration of the shah to full authority in 1953, also in Iran.

The Soviet and U.S. strategies of mutual exclusion in the Middle East were thus first put to work in what John Foster Dulles in the 1950s dubbed the region's "northern tier." To its south and west, in the Arab states and Israel, where in the first postwar decade Soviet-U.S. competition was marginal, the United States eschewed direct responsibilities, preferring instead to accept the leadership of Britain and France. While endorsing the principle of national self-determination for the European dependencies in Arab Asia and North Africa, the U.S. administrations favored negotiated arrangements for imperial withdrawal, which they occasionally mediated. Washington also lent its prestige to collective policies, such as the Tripartite Declaration of May 1950, under which the three allies jointly regulated arms exports to the independent Arab states and Israel and guaranteed interstate boundaries and armistice lines against forcible change.

After more than one stillborn project to integrate the Atlantic allies and Middle East states into a single defense system in the cause of blocking Soviet expansion, Britain and the United States alone formed the Baghdad Pact in 1955 with Turkey, Iraq, Iran, and Pakistan. The creation of the pact infuriated the Soviet Union and upset existing alignments in the Middle East. Omitted because they were seen as liabilities in plans to enlarge Arab participation in the security scheme, France and Israel were drawn together in their own tacit alliance. The inclusion of Iraq and Pakistan alienated Egypt and Afghanistan, opening the way in both countries to the Kremlin's use, for the first time, of arms sales to weaken Western influence and enhance its own. The Soviet penetration of the arms market in the Arab interior ended the Western monopoly and contributed to the 1956 Suez crisis. The failure of the British-French expedition at the Suez Canal, largely because of U.S. condemnation, left the United States in the position of paramount custodian of allied interests west and north of the canal. East of it the United States preserved the partnership with Britain and accepted the latter's superior responsibility.

The Pax Americana, which was intended to simplify crisis management in safeguarding Western interests in the Mediterranean Middle East, lasted for more than a decade. One of its early instruments, the Eisenhower Doctrine, in a bid to outdo the Soviet Union, advertised that any state in the Arab East desiring U.S. economic and military aid in its own defense against ''international communism'' need no longer enroll in a Western security system. The doctrine was first applied to Jordan in April 1957, when it looked as if the Arab unity nationalists in the kingdom were about to topple the monarchy. U.S. marines landed peaceably in Lebanon in July 1958 to suppress an incipient civil war and did not leave until after the inauguration of a newly elected president, with the unanimous endorsement of the Arab League Council, assured the survival of the regime. To the success of both ventures, the U.S. Sixth Fleet, then unopposed in the Mediterranean, proved indispensable. Even after the USSR began to develop its rival squadron in the Mediterranean in 1964, the Soviet naval vessels on deployment there were no match for the U.S. Sixth Fleet, although its commander took the necessary precautions to observe closely the Soviet naval—particularly submarine—movements.

Largely because of Vietnam, the United States became reluctant after the Arab-Israeli war of June 1967 to continue carrying alone the burdens of curbing the further growth of Soviet influence in the Middle East. For the first time, the United States agreed in 1968 to admit the USSR to a role in the Arab-Israeli peaceseeking process outside the United Nations, along with Britain and France in four-power talks and in bilateral superpower talks over the next two years. While the cumbersome exchanges were under way, the United States carried out its commitment to sell Israel F-4 Phantom jets and other sophisticated equipment. In Egypt's war of attrition with Israel in 1969-1970, the Soviet Union installed and manned surface-to-air missile batteries on the west bank of the Suez Canal. It also deployed Soviet pilots for double reconnaissance duty, on behalf of Egypt over Israeli-occupied Sinai and in its own interest in the Mediterranean, to keep track of the movements of the Sixth Fleet. The Kremlin, in short, was using Egypt as a substitute for aircraft carriers in the Mediterranean Squadron, since the Soviet navy did not add carriers to its inventory until the 1970s. Little wonder that the parallel four-power and two-power talks on an Arab-Israeli settlement yielded no practical results. For all intents and purposes Moscow was opting itself out of the peaceseeking process by its failure to restore diplomatic relations with Israel, which it had severed in June 1967, thereby signaling its preference for a partisan rather than a mediatory role in the Arab-Israeli dispute.

Many observers of superpower behavior in the October 1973 war believed that the Soviet airlift to the Arab belligerents had virtually demolished U.S. influence in the Arab world for our generation. Yet no sooner had the war ended than Egypt turned to the United States, which had airlifted supplies to Israel, as the sole acceptable mediator. Moreover, Egypt and Syria restored diplomatic relations with the United States, after an interruption of seven years. The Soviet Union could hardly have welcomed these developments. It stood to lose prestige and influence and to endanger political, strategic, and economic interests in the Arab world that it had so carefully cultivated at such great expense in the preceding two decades. Such an unexpected outcome may be awaited only in a condition of unsettled relations. The inventive U.S. leadership in 1973-1974 was limited to the Arab-Israeli dispute. Because of congressional opposition and the Watergate crisis, the Nixon and Ford administrations failed to do the same in the renewed fighting on Cyprus in 1974 and the Greek-Turkish strife it rekindled. Similarly, the continuing domestic distractions and public uncertainty precluded U.S. leadership from trying to end the civil war that broke out in Lebanon a year later.

The Carter administration in 1977 resumed the U.S. initiative in attempting to set the stage for a comprehensive Arab-Israeli settlement by seeking, with the help of Saudi Arabia, to entice Egypt, Jordan, Syria, and the PLO to the conference table with Israel. But the PLO backed away under pressure from internal opposition. Besides, the administration in Washington, in its effort to deal the Soviet Union into the process, did so too casually. Its failure to consult in advance the regional parties, notably Israel and Egypt, elicited the hostility of both. At the superpower level, the failed Carter demarche intensified the Soviet-U.S. cold war in the Arab-Israeli zone, once the United States became the sole mediator in the direct negotiations between Egypt and Israel.

Meanwhile, for the defense of Western interests in the Gulf after Britain laid down its primary responsibilities in 1971, the Nixon administration had framed the twin-pillar policy to circumvent congressional resistance to a U.S. replacement of Britain as the custodian of Gulf security. The twin pillars, Iran and Saudi Arabia, it was held, would keep unwanted intruders out of the strategic inland sea; in return, the United States would provide the essential diplomatic and implied military backup. Saudi Arabia's oil revenues overtopped those of all other OPEC members, including Iran; but its population did not exceed one-ninth that of Iran's. Moreover, the ruling Saudi family was much more cautious than the shah. It invested heavily in military and economic modernization, but most of it went into infrastructure.

In Iran, however, the United States applied the Nixon Doctrine, which called for U.S. military assistance to those governments that were willing and able to take care of their own defense. For the shah this meant, after 1972, an opportunity to buy the most advanced conventional equipment from the United States. At the time there was no way of knowing that by the end of 1973 the sharp rises in the price of crude oil would funnel to Iran monumental revenues, luring the shah to implement a strategy of instant military and economic modernization. The overall size of Iran's armed forces had moderately declined in the dozen years ending in 1972, from 202,000 to 191,000 officers and men, even taking into account the expansion of the air force to more than 10 percent of the total military manpower. Over the next five years, the armed forces more than doubled in size to 413,000: the ground forces increasing by nearly 80 percent to 285,000, the navy trebling to 28,000, and the air force growing by more than 450 percent to about 100,000. The investment in military hardware outpaced by far the growth in military manpower. The shah had spent an estimated $1.2 billion on arms imports between 1945 and 1972. In the next six years, he entered into commitments for the purchase of weapons valued at more than $18 billion, among the items some of the most highly developed systems in the United States and Western Europe.

The overturn of the shah early in 1979 brough to an inglorious end the U.S. twin-pillar strategy. For lack of an alternative plan to defend Western interests in the Gulf, the United States shifted course yet again by deploying on regular duty in the Indian Ocean two carrier battle groups. The Soviet invasion of Afghanistan at the end of the year convinced many Americans in and out of Washington that the policy planners in the Kremlin had not changed by an iota their perception, going back at least to the mid-1940s, of the prerequisites for the security of the Soviet Union: the conversion of the Middle East into a community of states friendly to itself, in the image of post-Yalta Eastern Europe. Early in 1980 President Carter warned the Soviet Union that any attempt "to gain control of the Persian Gulf region" would "be repelled by any means necessary, including military force."[1] To make the Carter Doctrine credible, the United States generously advertised the development of the infrastructure for the Rapid Deployment Force (RDF) in the Indian Ocean and its Red Sea and Gulf extensions. Far from repudiating the doctrine of the RDF, the Reagan administration in 1981-1982 accelerated the build-up and mounted joint maneuvers with the armed forces of the cooperating governments in the neighborhood.

III

A postwar phenomenon, regional politics in the Middle East also grew out of the progressive disappearance of European imperialism. As late as 1945 regional politics in the Middle East was nothing more than a continuation of European politics, since the whole region had been assimilated into the European system, chiefly the British and French empires. Even the handful of sovereign states—Afghanistan, Saudi Arabia, and Yemen, to be sure, but even Turkey and Iran—conducted their external affairs in the shadow of Europe, avoiding the pursuit of policies that might suggest defiance of the concerned great powers. Those who might argue that Iraq and Egypt had attained full independence on admission to membership in the League of Nations in the 1930s should note that the leaders of the two Arab states were still protesting strongly in the early postwar years against the lingering British military presence and diplomatic preference under the terms of the unequal treaties of alliance. Only after the replacement of the preferential treaty in October 1954 did the Egyptian nationalists feel that their country had been liberated. The Iraqi nationalists had to wait four years longer, until the overturn of the monarchy and the repudiation of their country's membership in the Baghdad Pact.

Indeed, four of every five of the twenty-five states in the Middle East, at a rate of one every fifteen months, realized sovereignty between 1946 and 1971, when European disimperialism finally ran its course. Relations among so many new polities, with little or no prior experience in the conduct of domestic and external affairs, often puzzled the best-informed observers. Even the new Arab states, with their shared hatred of Israel and their abiding suspicion of alien dominance, have rarely been able to rise above local rivalries and tensions. The Arab League, created in 1945, constituted for many of its founders the first practical step toward Arab unity. The league could take major credit for hastening the British and French surrender of Arab dependencies. By contrast, it demonstratively failed to develop machinery for conflict resolution to help its members resolve differences over boundaries, natural resources, water, and ideology. Equally unproductive have been attempts by Arab states, outside the league, to agree on the relinquishment of elements of local independence in the cause of larger unity. The one serious experiment in merger, the formation of the United Arab Republic by Egypt and Syria in February 1958, was abandoned less than four years later, leaving a legacy of misunderstanding. From end to end the Arab world in the next two decades became punctuated by divisive quarrels and occasional wars.

From the birth of Israel, the frontline states, in effect as agents of the Arab League, assumed the primary custodianship of the Palestine Arab interest in a strategy to bring the Jewish state to its knees through diplomatic, political, and economic blockade. The Arab leaders must have expected that, by withholding legitimacy from the undesired state, they would win the cooperation of the world community inchmeal, transform Israel into a pariah, and eventually compel its disestablishment. Until 1967 pragmatists governed Israel. They had received with enthusiasm the original UN General Assembly's 1947 partition proposal. Because of Arab resistance, Israel had to fight a war of independence against the frontline states. Its pragmatic leaders, who had no difficulty in accepting the armistice lines of 1949, which enlarged the de facto area of the country by 45 percent, devoted themselves to state and nation building. The unorganized Palestinians continued leaning on the Arab League, which after 1954 was dominated by Gamal Abd al-Nasir, the leader of the military junta that had overthrown the monarchy in Egypt. Abd al-Nasir, who came by the mid-1950s to personify the popular aspiration for Arab unity, breathed new life into the crusade for the isolation of Israel. The lack of formal relations intensified the mutual fear, suspicion, and hatred on both sides of the armistice lines and gave high priority to arms build-up, with the Soviet Union becoming the sole—and generous—provider of Egypt and Syria, and France of Israel. The position of Israel at the time was primarily defensive, for the Arab leaders hardly let a day pass without announcing in the media that Israel would be driven into the sea and Palestine restored to the Palestinians.

The 1956 Suez war did not truly test the military capabilities of the regional enemies, for Britain and France had joined the fray. But tensions kept rising over the next decade; so, too, did the levels of military preparation. The withdrawal of the UN Emergency Force from Sinai in May 1967, at Egypt's request, violated Abd al-Nasir's pledge of a decade earlier to UN Secretary General Dag Hamarskjold. It was accompanied by the closure to Israeli shipping of the straits of Tiran and followed by Egypt's formation of what were termed defensive alliances with Syria and Jordan. Given the excitement on both sides, there was little need for deepening the mutual mistrust. But for reasons that are still obscure, the Soviet ambassador early in May 1967 "informed" the government at Damascus about alleged troop concentrations along the Syrian border. His counterpart at Tel Aviv protested to the Israeli government but rejected Prime Minister Levi Eshkol's invitation to visit the Syrian frontier to see for himself that the allegation was false. This conveyed to security planners in Israel a sense of Soviet-Arab collusion in a plan of encirclement. Since the United States and the international community did not go to the rescue, Israel mounted a preemptive strike, defeating its foes in six days. The ceasefire terminated the 1949 armistice regime and left Israel in occupation of the Golan Heights, the West Bank, the Gaza Strip, and Sinai. Israel made an initial generous gesture: for full peace the occupied districts would be returned to Syria, Jordan, and Egypt. There were no takers. Instead a summit council of the Arab

League, reflecting the pervasive humiliation of its members, adopted a con-
clusively negative response to Israel: no reconciliation, no recognition, no
negotiation.

In the prolonged stalemate that followed, subtle political changes occurred in Israel. The pragmatists steadily lost ground to the ideologues. The
pace quickened after the Yom Kippur War of October 1973 and hardened in
1977 after the toppling of Labor as the dominant party in Israel's multiple-
party system. Likud, Labor's successor, under the leadership of Menahem
Begin, measured national security by depth of territorial holding and ra-
tionalized it by religious and historical symbolism. The second Begin
government, installed in 1981, even more firmly than the first, let it be
known that Israel would not give up a single fragment of former Palestine.
If the Arab League states, in the first nineteen years of the contest with
Israel, had sought an accommodation to the evolving political realities, instead of digging their heels in deeper after each defeat, there might have
been a negotiated settlement. They kept insisting that they were seeking
nothing but justice, which required the restoration of all of Palestine to the
Palestinians. As the 1969 Palestine National Charter put it: the Palestinians
claimed no more than the transformation of former Palestine into a secular,
democratic state, in which Jews as well as Christians and Muslims would
live as full citizens. This, however, was a concealed call for the disestablishment of Israel. Since Israel had no intention of committing political suicide,
its anxiety about national security mounted.

By then the Arab-Israeli dialectic, that has governed the emotional relations between the Arab states and Israel and has frustrated efforts at
peaceseeking, was shaping the frenzied arms-procurement policies of the
adversaries. Arabs everywhere became convinced that Israel is expansionist.
To prove their contention they noted the piecemeal outward thrust of
Israel's boundaries from the UN General Assembly proposal of November
1947 through the armistice lines of the 1949 agreements to the ceasefire lines
of 1967. Israel on its side claimed that the Arab states had consistently supported the Palestine Arabs in their efforts to destroy Israel. It is the fear of
political extinction that has propelled Israel into focusing on the growth and
increasing sophistication of its arsenal, so as to cling to military superiority
over any combination of Arab enemies. In the doctrine of immutable Arab
military inferiority, the corollary of Israel's insistence on immutable
military superiority, no self-respecting Arab government can acquiesce.

In acknowledgment of their adversary's military power, the Arab states
from the outset inclined toward tightening their isolation of Israel while
striving to invent ways of becoming militarily more powerful than it. This
was the solidarity that President Anwar al-Sadat of Egypt disrupted in
November 1977 when he flew to Jerusalem for direct negotiations. The first
reaction of the Arab anti-Israel diehards—Algeria, Libya, and the PDRY,

along with Syria and the PLO—was the creation of the Steadfastness and Confrontation Front, which in 1979 persuaded a summit council of the Arab League to punish Egypt along with Israel by blockading both. To burst the ring of isolation and the PLO violence it encouraged across the de facto borders, Israel for its part has been prone—as in the invasions of Lebanon in 1978 and 1982—to mount preemptive strikes against its menacing neighbors. Israel and the Arab states have thus locked themselves into a vicious circle that interested outsiders have so far been unable to break.

Meanwhile, to understand the frustration of the United States, the only irrepressible searcher for an Arab-Israeli peace since the expiry of the mandate, one does not have to dig very deep. Peace with justice, as the Palestinians and their Arab partners define it, would give Israel no security. On the contrary, it would require the destruction of the Jewish state. Peace with security, as the Israeli ideologues and their champions abroad construe it, would deprive the Palestinians of political justice and of ever realizing self-determination on even a moiety of former Palestine. Reduced to the simplest terms, Israel and the PLO since 1967 have engaged in the politics of mutual destruction, which is the logical extreme of mutual denial. The act was being played out in Lebanon in mid-1982.

IV

Israel's invasion of Lebanon on 6 June 1982, touched off by an attempt three days earlier on the life of the Israeli ambassador to Britain, seemed at first a replay of the action in 1978 when the Israel Defense Forces (IDF) occupied southern Lebanon for three months. The government at Jerusalem announced that the aim of the latest strike was limited: the removal of the *fidai* or commando concentrations of the PLO from southern Lebanon to a depth of twenty-five miles from the Israeli border, thus pushing them beyond rocket and artillery range of the towns and villages of northern Galilee. At the start of the campaign, informed observers also speculated that the IDF might seek to smash the nineteen Syrian batteries of surface-to-air (SAM) missile launchers in the Biqa' valley of eastern Lebanon. The Israel Air Force put an end to the speculation on the fourth day of combat, when it destroyed the entire Soviet-supplied launcher complex in the Biqa'.

By then, the Israel offensive was rolling northward, well beyond the announced twenty-five-mile limit, toward the outskirts of the Lebanese capital and the main highway linking Beirut and Damascus. This was no massive retaliation. It was a full-scale war, the sixth in the Arab-Israeli series. At first it looked like a replica of the 1967 lightning war that ended in six days. Within nine days, the IDF locked in west Beirut the PLO leaders and their guerrillas, variously estimated at 5,300 to 9,000, ostensibly with no alternative but surrender. But there the advance stalled, as the IDF tightened the ring around the besieged Palestinians without forcing its way into the heavily populated districts where the PLO had established its headquarters and its commandos were taking their stand. The pause of the IDF was attributable not to the lack of firepower or to the declining willpower of General Ariel Sharon, Israel's minister of defense, as shown in the massive bombing of west Beirut after the resumption of fighting in August, but to the decision of the Israeli cabinet because of political pressure at home and in the international community, particularly in the United States.

The ceasefires, recurrently broken by artillery, machinegun, and rocket exchanges and restored by U.S.-orchestrated diplomacy, accompanied the convoluted, many-sided, direct and indirect talks for the withdrawal from Beirut of "All the P.L.O. leadership, offices and combatants . . . for prearranged destinations," to use the terminology of the text of the agreement that Ambassador Philip C. Habib stitched together by August 19, the seventy-fifth day of the war.[2] In the six weeks of stalemate Yasir Arafat, the chairman of the PLO executive, seemed on the verge of converting a military disaster into a political victory. He tried to maneuver the diplomatic exchanges and the plans for a multinational force into U.S. recognition of the PLO. But his shifting conditions for withdrawal were unacceptable to Israel, which insisted on unconditional withdrawal. Early in August the Israeli cabinet, persuaded that the PLO was not negotiating in good faith, ran out of patience and authorized Sharon to move into the international airport and the southern approaches to west Beirut, while keeping up the devastating barrage by land, air, and sea. The lightning war had already stretched out into a war of attrition, resembling the Egyptian-Israel war of 1969-1970.

The main explanation for the war's unfolding from a punitive expedition to a war of attrition was found in the tactics of the belligerents. As a guerrilla organization, the PLO did its thing in the style of guerrillas by establishing an infrastructure in the heart of Lebanese society, largely in west Beirut and in the area south of the Beirut-Damascus highway. Here the PLO set up shop—arsenals, command centers, redoubts, public-relations offices—in the Palestine refugee camps and amid the civilian Lebanese population in large towns and small. Schools, hospitals, mosques, and churches as well as high-rise apartment buildings in west Beirut were the favorite spots.

To destroy the PLO infrastructure, the Israel Defense Forces had to ignore, or at least to accept, high civilian casualties. This posed a major problem for the IDF, a citizen army that has prided itself on a humanitarian record in past wars expressly limiting civilian casualties wherever possible. It also explained Israel's tactics of trying to frighten the concerned civilian population into leaving targeted areas by showering warning leaflets before dropping bombs. In Tyre and Sidon in the opening days of the war (unlike west Beirut), the tactics worked after a fashion, as they did also in the smaller towns. But in the Palestinian refugee camps, the civilians were as desperate as the guerrillas. This was their struggle for survival and, by and large, they stayed put, many suffering martyrdom. Some, who sought refuge in the eastern or Christian sector of the capital, were denied entry. The fighting in west Beirut must be evaluated in this light, as backdrop to the prolonged negotiations for a durable ceasefire.

As a citizen army of a small country, the IDF could not afford high losses or sustained fighting, for an attritional war with even a few casualties each week was unacceptable. The PLO meanwhile was preparing for street-to-street fighting, converting roads into minefields, sandbagging buildings, taking defensive positions for the climactic shootout. In such an encounter, the PLO could reasonably expect to inflict on the enemy the highest toll. This was the only way for it to win the war. But General Sharon, an Israeli incarnation of General George S. Patton, was a brilliant field commander who hardly showed the same concern for public sensibilities, or human life, as for his reputation as a soldier. Clearly, he was chafing at the bit, when held back at the outskirts of west Beirut from taking full advantage of his initial momentum by domestic opposition and by U.S. and international public and official opinion. The IDF tightened the ring around west Beirut by air, land, and sea; prevented large-scale arms resupply; slowed down to a trickle, with total stoppages, the flow of water, food, and electricity; and tried recurrently to persuade the civilians to leave. Some did. Most did not. Sharon's response in the end was the saturation bombing of the PLO-dominated enclave.

Understandably, the Arabs exaggerated the number of civilian casualties; the Israelis understated them. As most Palestinians and many other Arabs saw it, the invasion merely confirmed Israel's unrestrained expansionism, designed this time to enlarge the Jewish state at Lebanon's expense. Moreover, the preemptive invasion was genocidal, some charged, because it aimed at the total destruction of the Palestinians. Prime Minister Menahem Begin, on his side, reiterated his public assurance that Israel did not seek one inch of Lebanese territory but only the expulsion of the PLO—and the Syrian occupation forces—from Lebanon. To the IDF, the fidai command centers, bases, and redoubts equipped with artillery and rockets that honeycombed south Lebanon represented a threat to the security of Israel. The very presence of Katiusha launchers and 130-mm and 155-mm howitzers that could target urban and rural settlements in northern Israel, was found to be aggressive and unacceptable by most Israelis. No less intolerable were the missile batteries, which were intended to inhibit, if not preclude, reconnaissance by the Israel Air Force of possibly hostile Syrian military movements. To the government at Damascus, the SAM launchers in Lebanon were indispensable for the strategic defense of Syria against a potential assault by Israel.

The latest Arab-Israeli war hardly caught the superpowers by surprise. Both had engaged in brisk rivalry as arms purveyors to the regional adversaries, the United States supplying Israel and from time to time Lebanon; and the Soviet Union, the PLO and Syria. Still, unlike the October War, the superpowers mounted no rival airlifts. So far as is publicly known, Moscow sent its supplies to the PLO and handled a miniscule airlift to Syria so discreetly that it went almost unnoticed. One implication seemed clear—and ominous: the superpowers had deposited enough equipment with their friends before the war to diminish the need for emergency resupply. On the other hand, the mild, almost indifferent, response of the Soviet Union to the 1982 war puzzled the partisans and the experts alike, for the Kremlin did little more, at least visibly, than uphold the PLO and Syria by diplomacy at the United Nations and by a steady stream of anti-Israel and anti-U.S. propaganda, which, perhaps because unaccompanied by practical actions, sustained a high level of shrillness and abuse.

The United States, as mediator, placed its prestige on the line by committing its presidential influence to the withdrawal from Lebanon of the PLO, the Syrian troops, and the IDF and helping Lebanon restore its territorial integrity, and the Lebanese government, its authority. Even the total evacuation of foreign military units, however, would still leave behind the Lebanese National Movement, which could, if unchecked, keep the civil war going. Whether by design or incapability, the Soviet Union, as a partisan in the Arab-Israeli dispute and a patron of the PLO and Syria in the utterly confused contest in Lebanon, seems to be betting that neither Israel nor the United States can clean up the mess in Lebanon. The policy planners in Moscow must therefore have concluded that both are bound to make more than one serious mistake, from which the Kremlin could hardly fail to benefit. In a word, according to this line of reasoning, the Soviet Union, even by doing nothing, stood to gain over time from whatever mistakes Washington might make in its diplomatic initiatives. This would far outweigh the risks of an immediate Soviet spoiler role, which might invite a confrontation with the United States.

The Reagan administration worked hard to prevent the war from raging out of control, to arrange for the stoppage of the fighting, and to promote the negotiation of durable conditions, if not of peace, at least of nonbelligerency. Uncommonly, in the opening days of the 1982 hostilities and again in August after General Sharon outdid himself in lack of sensitivity to destruction of civilian life and property, the United States joined the other members of the U.N. Security Council in unanimous approval of resolutions that Israel rejected, or abstained, and allowed their passage, calling for an immediate ceasefire or its restoration and unconditional withdrawal of Israeli troops from Lebanon. But when the Soviet Union joined thirteen other Security Council members in reinforcing a projected resolution that recommended coercive measures if Israel failed to heed the request, the United States vetoed the draft, as it did again a Soviet replica after the IDF entry into west Beirut early in August. Yet when it came to the negotiation of the ceasefires and a more lasting arrangement, it was the United States that served as the crisis manager, not the United Nations or the Soviet Union. The U.S. mediator, Ambassador Philip C. Habib, accepted as a starting point the terms laid down by the Begin government: the total withdrawal from Lebanon of the PLO—political leaders, guerrillas, and their military stores—and of the Syrian occupying forces and the resumption of responsibility for the country's security—lost seven years earlier on the outbreak of the civil war—by a freely elected Lebanese government, as prerequisites to Israel's terminating its own occupation in the country.

How does one account for the confusion? An examination of the antecedents of Israel's intervention in Lebanon should provide a partial explanation. By June 1982, Lebanon had been wracked by a civil war that after seven years of carnage and chaos still defied negotiated settlement. After the mid-1970s Lebanon developed into a flash point of violence where many destabilizing regional and international disputes intertwined. The civil war had already replaced the only functioning democracy in the Arab world with a nonregime lacking authority. Those who exercised power did so with the barrel of a gun. Even then, the armed sector of the country had been atomized into perhaps as many as eighty rival militarized groups ranging from well-trained, disciplined communal militias or budding armies to teenage street gangs. The Lebanese National Movement, a cluster of a dozen or so ideological factions, continued the inconclusive struggle for changing the confessional polity into a secular one. Moreover, starting in 1970, Lebanon served as unwilling host to the headquarters of the PLO and most of its eight—and at times more—constituent groups, which steadily intensified its terrorist crusade against Israel.

As the civil war unfolded into permanency, the Maronite Christians, the chief custodians of the old regime, began despairing of its restoration and thinking of partition as a possible alternative. Yet they, too, split into three factions: one collaborated openly with Syria, and the others quietly with Israel. Moreover after mid-1978, Major Sa'd Haddad, a Greek Catholic who commanded a militia in the south with the acknowledged support of the Begin government, administered a district bordering directly on Israel. This district formed, together with the adjacent United Nations Interim Force in Lebanon (UNIFIL) zone, a twin-layered buffer between Israel and its adversaries in Lebanon. The largest sectarian community in the country and, before the civil war, bunched in the south, the Shi'is were substantially uprooted with many living as refugees in Beirut and its suburbs. Perhaps a majority of the Shi'is came to share the Maronite hostility toward the Palestinians and the Syrians; some of this group welcomed Israel's intervention. Many others looked for inspiration to the Ayatallah Ruhallah Khumayni's non-Arab revolutionary Islamic republicans in Iran.

Syria sent troops into Lebanon in June 1976 for the declared purpose of ending the civil war. In October Egypt and Saudi Arabia mediated, and in November the Arab League Council legitimated, the conversion of the Syrian military presence in Lebanon into a nominal Arab Deterrent Force by the addition of token units from Kuwait, Qatar, Saudi Arabia, Sudan, and the United Arab Emirates. By 1982 the Arab Deterrent Force, which had proved incapable of restructuring a viable regime in Lebanon, was reduced once again to a wholly Syrian entity and the government at Damascus seemed incapable of evacuating its troops, who had become more and more unpopular with important segments of all communities. Meanwhile, Iraq and Libya as well as Syria, each for its own private reasons, had selected rival factions of the Lebanese National Movement and the PLO for the exercise of influence through patronage, thereby bracing the factionalism of both. The Arab oil states in the Gulf—which basically mistrusted and, Kuwait apart, did not even exchange diplomatic relations with Moscow—were financing, with occasional interruptions, much of the reimbursable arms procurement of the PLO and Syria from the Soviet Union.

The Begin government accused the PLO of organizing violent opposition to Israel's settlement policies and autonomy scheme for the West Bank. In an alleged attempt to destroy the PLO headquarters, the Israel Air Force bombed west Beirut in July 1981. With Saudi cooperation, Ambassador Habib contrived to cobble together a ceasefire that brought to a halt "all hostile military actions between Lebanese and Israeli territory." The calculated ambiguity concealed the fact that the arrangement, which the mediator negotiated in part through third parties, nevertheless committed Israel and the PLO to observe mutually binding terms, even though neither one recognized the legitimacy of the other. The vagueness yielded conflicting interpretations. Israel contended that the ceasefire prohibited the fidai reappearance and accumulation of arms in the UNIFIL zone and fidai actions in Israel-administered territory or against Israeli or pro-Israeli targets in the world at large. The PLO, for its part, argued that the ceasefire merely banned armed raids across Israel's northern border and nothing more, certainly not the thickening or upgrading of fidai positions in south Lebanon or the freedom of operation beyond the Lebanon-Israel frontier either within Israel or its occupied territories or anywhere else.

In the opening months of 1982 the domestic, regional, and international crises in Lebanon began heating up once again. Israel accused the PLO of violating the ceasefire by spiriting below the Litani River artillery pieces, rockets, and tanks. Following the failure of the UN Security Council to discourage PLO or Israeli incursions into the conflicted zone of south Lebanon, the United States took unilateral steps to shore up the shaky ceasefire or, perhaps more accurately, to preclude its total breakdown. Habib returned to the field more than once in the spring and, while there, also sought to reinforce plans for the sexennial presidential election in Lebanon later in the year. To cope with a perceived security threat, Israel meanwhile reserved the right to take action against the PLO. Before April 25, the date for the completion of Israel's evacuation of Sinai and the accompanying loss of leverage over Egypt, the Begin government fell under strong domestic pressure—which its hardline strategy had largely generated—to mount a preemptive strike against PLO positions in Lebanon. In the aftermath of the Sinai evacuation, which included the dismantling of Jewish settlements, pressure in Israel did not subside. The Begin government sought to distract the domestic opponents of its return of the peninsula to Egypt by reassurances of inflexibility on the residual occupied territories and on Lebanon.

While Israel-PLO tension rose, the Begin government warned Syria more than once to remove the missile batteries it had deployed in the Biqa' valley in 1981 or face their forcible removal. To Israel's warnings Syria turned a deaf ear, for the beleaguered regime of President Hafiz al-Asad had lost most of its options. The leveling of a good part of Hamah in February 1982 and the killing and wounding of thousands of its residents undermined Asad's legitimacy at home and among the Arab states at large. Syria's isolation in the Arab world widened after it reaffirmed in May its endorsement of non-Arab Iran in the continuing war with Arab Iraq. Even Asad's relations with the PLO were cooling. In this overcharged atmosphere, the spark that ignited the explosion was the serious wounding on June 3 of the Israeli ambassador in London. The PLO denied responsibility but failed to repudiate the action, thus furnishing Israel the pretext to invade Lebanon three days later.

V

No less perplexing than the situation in and around Lebanon was that enveloping Iran. Even before the consolidation of gains deriving from the seizure of power in February 1979, the Islamic republicans in Tehran launched a campaign to export their revolution to the Arab states of the Gulf by exhorting the Shi'i communities to overturn their Sunni rulers. Iraq and Bahrain, with Shi'i majorities, proved vulnerable. Such provocation, mingled with assertive personal ambitions to become the towering leader in the

Gulf and in the Arab world at large, went far to explain the decision of Saddam Husayn, the president of Iraq, to invade Iran in September 1980 for the obvious purpose of destroying the disruptive imamate that had replaced the overbearing shahdom.

Saddam Husayn must have expected that the preoccupation of the *ulama* or religious leaders with the protracted crisis of the U.S. hostages (November 1979-January 1981) would prevent the Iranians from mounting an effective defense; that in any case Iran's armed forces, originally built by the shah, could hardly be revived after the slaughter of its top officers; that Iran's multi-ethnic society would fall apart, starting in the tribal areas that appeared to be relishing their newly recovered autonomy; that the Arabs of Khuzistan, which the regime in Baghdad kept calling Arabistan as it had been known a half-century earlier, would rebel against the republican imamate and flock to the invaders' banner; and that Iran's rundown economy, with its substantial loss of oil revenues, could not endure a long war. In all these and other respects, Saddam Husayn's expectations turned out to be grossly exaggerated.

The political-economic cost of the attritional war to Iraq, as to the Arab world at large, kept rising. The Iraqi president tried to assuage the public by guns and butter. Despite the inflated wartime budget, Baghdad and its suburbs became a large construction site, with imposing new buildings rising all over the lot, and consumer goods from abroad bulging on the capital's store shelves. As the hostilities dragged on, the government pushed its public-works program into the provinces, especially those with large Shi'i population. The frantic pace of construction in the capital included extravagant conference facilities, modern hotels, roads, and parks as elaborate preparation for the summit meeting of the nonaligned movement in September 1982. Because of the stepped-up fighting it was announced in August that the meeting would be transferred to New Delhi. War and life as usual were heavily, yet quietly and reluctantly, subsidized by Saudi Arabia and the oil-producing city states of the Gulf—Kuwait, Bahrain, Qatar, and the United Arab Emirates as well as Oman. An often-cited monthly subsidy average of one billion dollars in the first twenty-two months may have been high; but whatever the true figure, it was high enough to pinch the finances of even the rich oil states, always excepting Saudi Arabia, in a glutted world oil market.

Iraqis grew more and more demoralized, first by an inconclusive war and then, in the spring of 1982, by Iran's dramatic reversal of fortunes. The Islamic republican army and the ragtag *pasdaran* or religious militia reached Iraq's frontier in the south, after retaking Khurramshahr late in May. They captured massive amounts of equipment and thousands of Iraqi prisoners. Saudi Arabia and the other Gulf oil states had taken advantage of Iraq's distraction, as early as the spring of 1981, to form the Gulf Cooperation Council (GCC) for coordinated economic and military planning. The GCC members above all sought to keep the war from spreading and the superpowers from meddling. As of mid-August 1982 neither had happened, but the degree to which this might have been attributed to the GCC initiatives remains debatable.

In the Islamic republic there was only one voice of authority with many voices of advocacy. The record shows that in the long intervals of Khumayni's silence, however, the advocates often take matters in their own hands. So it transpired in Iran's war with Iraq. Between the opening of Iran's triumphant counteroffensive in March 1982 and the recapture of Khurramshahr in May, it appeared that the slow-motion hostilities had taken a decisive turn in Iran's favor, that the Iraqis would not be able to stop the Islamic republican juggernaut. Saddam Husayn's offers of a negotiated ceasefire and Iraqi withdrawal proved nonstarters. On June 20 he finally reaffirmed a unilateral end to the fighting, first disclosed by the Revolutionary Command Council of the Ba'th party ten days earlier and the prompt evacuation of Iraqi troops from their remaining Iranian positions. But Iran did not reciprocate.

Instead, on July 13, the estimated equivalent of eight divisions or more than 100,000 soldiers and religious militia reportedly crossed the international border, heading as a first objective for the capture in the south of Basrah, second in size only to Baghdad. The Iranians remained adamant in their demand for the resignation of Saddam Husayn and hardly concealed their preference for the replacement of what they termed the atheist Ba'thi regime by an Islamic republic. In exuberant encouragement of the invaders Khumayni announced that, following the defeat of Iraq on Iranian terms, the next target would be the "liberation" of Jerusalem. Iran, meanwhile, stepped up its appeals to the Shi'is in the Arabian peninsular states to overturn their Sunni regimes and warned these governments to stop aiding the enemy. But soon the Iranian invaders bungled the campaign. Six attacks on Iraq's southern metropolis in the first five weeks of the invasion failed. The awaited insurgence of the almost solid Shi'i population of the district did not take place. The war in mid-August 1982 appeared once again to have entered a stage of inconclusiveness.

In more than twenty-two months of fighting, neither superpower managed to get a handle on either belligerent. The Islamic republic had pulled itself free from all ties to the United States without moving into a Soviet embrace, even though it was accepting Soviet diplomatic, military, and economic favors. Iraq, meanwhile, was continuing to wriggle itself loose from the once-tight Soviet hug but was still remote from normalizing its relations with the United States. It did not even restore diplomatic relations, severed in 1967, let alone establish a favored position for U.S. support. The continued uncertainty, many observers felt, helped the Soviets; if so, only in the psychological sense of threatening the future production of oil in the Gulf; but in an oversupplied world market, it did not evoke a sense of urgency. Lacking formal relations with either belligerent, the United States could at least take satisfaction in the self-containment of the Gulf war, even though U.S. offers of joint maneuvers with one or more of the peninsular states, as a deterrent to Iran, found no takers.

Further afield, the war added yet another fracturing factor to the Arab world. Jordan took Iraq's side from the outset, affording it a secure harbor at Aqabah for the import of military and civilian goods and their onward transport to Iraq by Jordanian vehicles. Publicly neutral until Israel finally evacuated Sinai, Egypt privately and on a relatively modest scale began sending to Iraq in mid-1981 Soviet weapons and spare parts, which had been deactivated in the Egyptian inventory. Egypt stepped up its support as soon as Iran made known its plans militarily to replace the regime of Saddam Husayn.

On the other hand, the dispute between the governments of Syria and Iraq, which had reerupted about the time that Saddam Husayn seized power in the summer of 1979, grew steadily more virulent after the invasion of Iran a year later. Syria, with Libya in tow openly, backed the imamate. For well over a year Syria's action weakened the otherwise durable Arab coalition, the Steadfastness and Confrontation Front. The front, to which Iraq briefly adhered in 1978-1979, was just a new name for the earlier Rejectionist Front, founded a year after the Arab-Israel war of October 1973, when its members declared themselves implacable opponents of accommodation with Israel.

The long-lived Arab alliance nearly broke up after the onset of the Iraq-Iran war, as the PLO and Algeria took pains to establish their neutrality and, if possible, mediate a ceasefire. The Steadfastness Front nominally closed ranks, once more, at a meeting in Algiers late in May 1982, when it announced the coalition's endorsement of Iran as a true friend of the Arabs and appealed to all Arab governments to stop aiding Iraq.

But the reunion did not long persist. Within a fortnight the front's two primary authors again fell apart. After the start of Israel's intervention in Lebanon, Syria did not link up with the PLO. Even when the Asad regime on the fourth day of the war resisted Israel's advance into the Biqa' valley and the destruction of the missile batteries, the Syrian action proved too little and too late, ending two days later in a unilateral ceasefire with Israel. In the hour of the PLO's greatest need, Mu'ammar al-Qadhdhafi advised the Palestinian guerrillas to commit mass suicide to demonstrate devotion to their nationalist cause. Algeria remained passive during the war but offered an asylum to a part of the guerrillas in Habib's package settlement, as did also the PDRY (South Yemen). The many contradictory pressures of the two wars had pulled the Steadfastness Front apart. But even the coalition's visible unhelpfulness in the PLO's hour of urgent need in Lebanon and its inability to agree on the Gulf war did not necessarily rule out its future resurgence as a regional and international diplomatic lobby.

In the meantime, Israel and Syria, though resolute enemies in the lingering Lebanese crisis and the even more prolonged Palestine question and bitter antagonists over violations of their mutual armistice line before 1967 and over the Israel-occupied Golan Heights thereafter, had nevertheless been funneling arms and spare parts to Iran. However, after Israel's deep penetration into Lebanon and its declared intent to destroy the PLO and bring an end to the Syrian occupation, the republican imamate proclaimed its fidelity to the Palestinian and Muslim struggle against "Zionism and American imperialism." The utter confusion arising from the wars in Lebanon and at the head of the Gulf epitomizes the pervasive instability in the Middle East.

VI

The superpower Cold War in the Middle East in mid-1982, as reflected in the two regional wars, showed no signs of early abatement. A contrary judgment might be suggested by the relative Soviet passivity in Lebanon and the unilateral U.S. crisis management. But these were no more than appearances. Behind the scenes the superpowers were engaged in their accustomed rivalry and might be expected to continue, visibly and invisibly, their politics of mutual exclusion. In the Arab-Israeli dispute, the United States and the Soviet Union have both been partisans. The United States has refused to talk with the PLO since 1975, and the Soviet Union with Israel since 1967. Nonetheless, Washington has enjoyed a significant advantage over Moscow in the mediatory process since it has been able to negotiate with concerned Arab governments no less than with Israel, as reaffirmed in the Habib missions of 1981-1982.

The agreed-upon Habib plan, which related exclusively to the Beirut area, stipulated a ceasefire in place, charged the PLO leaders with responsibility for organizing and managing the evacuation—to be carried out in daylight only—of its guerrillas, and empowered a small observer group already stationed in the capital to remain in service, as the only and undeclared link to the United Nations. Each guerrilla was permitted to take with him only a single personal "side weapon (pistol, rifle, or machine gun) and ammunition." The PLO undertook to transfer to the Lebanese armed forces "as gifts all remaining weaponry in their possession, including heavy, crew-served and spare weaponry and equipment, along with all munitions" abandoned in the capital and its environs. All Palestinian civilians left behind, the evacuees' families included, were made "subject to Lebanese laws and regulations," with "appropriate guarantees" of the governments of Lebanon and the United States that they had procured "assurances (of nonmolestation) . . . from the Government of Israel . . . and from the leadership of certain Lebanese (and other armed) groups," especially the Maronite Phalangists, though not mentioned by name. An estimated total number of evacuees approaching 15,000—11,000 to 12,000 PLO guerrillas and some 2,700-3,600 associated Syrian troops (among the latter a majority were assumed to be Palestinians attached to Syria's Arab Deterrent Force)—were relocated (between August 21 and 31, some days ahead of schedule) in eight Arab states: Algeria, Iraq, Jordan, Sudan, Syria, Tunisia, and the two Yemens. Some 230 guerrillas, mostly wounded and in need of further hospitalization, were ferried to Greece and Cyprus. A Multinational Force, outside the jurisdiction of the United Nations, consisting of some 2,000 troops from France, Italy, and the United States, monitored the PLO departure. Together with the Lebanese armed forces, they appointed from their own ranks a Liaison and Coordination Committee to "carry out close and effective liaison with, and provide continuous and detailed information to," the IDF. On behalf of the committee, the Lebanese armed forces maintained "close and effective liaison with the P.L.O., and other armed groups" in and around Beirut.[3]

The PLO's claim that it had kept the war with Israel going longer than any Arab government had been able to do was an exaggeration. Egypt's war of attrition lasted from April 1969 to August 1970. Nonetheless, the Palestine resistance movement proved its mettle by bringing effectively to bear its political influence and its propaganda in the international community, which together with the guerrillas' courage and defiance, held the IDF at bay for seventy-five days. Thus, the Habib plan was not dictated by Israel. Rather did it represent an accommodation of the positions of Israel, Lebanon, and the PLO.

Beyond the greater Beirut area south of the Beirut-Damascus highway, the IDF, without accountability to other authority than its own government, presumably made the final arrangements for the removal of the PLO personnel, infrastructure, and possessions. There still remained the unresolved problems of north Lebanon and the Biqa' valley, where the future was yet to be decided of the residual PLO units and particularly of the bulk of the Syrian occupation forces. Speculation on such questions would be idle, since much depended on whether or not the U.S. crisis manager might reach a negotiated arrangement with the concerned parties, with or without further fighting. Nor could the possibility of some other form of mediation than the unilateral U.S. effort be dismissed entirely.

The inability of either the Soviet Union or the United States, as of the time of writing, to persuade the belligerents at the head of the Gulf to accept mediation, after twenty-three months of war, confirms the inability of the two superpowers to shape developments in this contest. The pace of the Iraq-Iran war, however, clearly differed from that in Lebanon, and it appeared more likely that regional, Islamic, or UN diplomacy in the end might prove more acceptable to both parties than direct superpower brokerage.

The low superpower arms-transfer profile in both wars, as contrasted with the high profile of rival airlifts during most of the October War nine years earlier, was misleading. All the belligerents in the Gulf and Lebanon had stockpiled massive amounts of sophisticated equipment, most of it manufactured by the superpowers or under their license. Without the steady and generous flow of equipment from Russia over the preceding four years, the PLO could hardly have held out as long as it had, lobbing artillery rounds and releasing Katiusha rockets in such volume even after the Israeli blockade of west Beirut had interrupted major resupply. Nor could Israel have kept up its coordinated heavy assaults by land, air, and sea on the targets in Lebanon in June and August without the prior accumulation of matériel from the United States to supplement its own domestic arms production. Even in the more leisurely Gulf war, Iraq and Iran had benefited from the swollen arsenals built-up over the preceding decade, although both sides found it necessary, and possible, to replace their diminishing stocks through purchases in the open international arms market. On the basis of the past record, it would be realistic to assume that, with the continuance of the Cold War, the belligerents would not have to wait too long after the end of the wars to replenish depleted supplies and to add new weaponry of even higher sophistication than those used in the past.

The PLO fought the war in Lebanon essentially unaided by the Arab states. None of the hardline partners of the PLO—not even Syria, which faced the same enemy—went to the rescue of the Palestinians. The steadfastness coalition, it became apparent, had already been shattered by its inability to develop a viable consensus on the Iraq-Iran war. Nor could the nonbelligerent Gulf oil states be immediately helpful to the PLO because they were distracted by common fears of Iran and political impotence in a glutted world oil market. Still, after the war the PLO might reasonably expect a resumption of generous financial and diplomatic assistance from its wealthy patrons in the Arabian peninsula, but whether the latter would, in turn, be able to infuse a measure of pragmatism into Arab diplomacy in the quarrel with Israel remained much less certain. Undeniably triumphant at least as far as the war had gone by mid-August, Israel could claim only a pyrrhic victory. The political price in the international community and the economic price at home were steep. The long-term political consequences were hardly likely to be as decisive as the Begin government was seeking. The latest Arab-Israeli war, like the five that preceded it, had already created more problems than it solved. In the Gulf, in mid-August 1982, it appeared that neither side would be capable of eliminating its opponent's regime by resorting to an inconclusive, drawn-out, costly war. So, here too, new difficulties were compounding their troubled legacy.

It would thus seem that politics as usual in the exercise of mutual denial in the regional and international systems and their interconnections in the Middle East would persist into the postwar future of the Arab-Israeli zone and the Gulf.

Notes

1. "Transcript of State of the Union Address," *Facts on File*, 40, 2046 (January 25, 1980):42.

2. "Text of the Agreement on Withdrawal of Palestinian Forces From West Beirut," *New York Times*, 21 August 1982, p. 5. Reprinted with permission.

3. Ibid.

3 The Sources of Soviet Involvement in the Middle East: Threat or Opportunity?

R. Craig Nation

The Soviet Union has been intimately involved in the affairs of the Middle East since at least 1955, when arms sales to Egypt propelled it into the politics of the region. Over more than a quarter-century Soviet initiatives have led to both successes and failures, but there has been no slackening of will or commitment to a forward policy. In an area dominated by the European colonial powers up to the Second World War, and by U.S. influence subsequently, the Soviet pursuit of a regional presence has often been perceived as a direct challenge to Western interests. A large and diverse scholarly literature (in both the West and the USSR) has been generated in an attempt to characterize Soviet involvement. But Western scholarship, often preoccupied with the tactical dimensions of Soviet conduct, has not achieved anything resembling a consensus concerning the underlying sources of Soviet policies.[1] What factors have motivated the Soviet Union, often at great expense and risk, to pursue an ongoing involvement in the affairs of the Middle East? How is the apparent permanence and high-prioritization of the Soviet commitment best explained? What is the current status of Soviet policy and what, if any, are its long-term goals? These important questions deserve more careful and systematic attention than they have received in the past.[2]

The factors that motivate the international behavior of states are complex and elusive at best. The closed nature of the Soviet political system makes this particularly the case for Soviet international conduct, but this should not be allowed to frustrate the search for functional definitions bringing us closer to the sources of Soviet initiatives. Despite the (relative) obscurity of the Soviet decision-making process, it is possible to analyze Soviet behavior in a systematic manner. Such an analysis should be sensitive to the various levels on which Soviet policies unfold and to the multidimensionality of Soviet interests. In the case of the Middle East it should further take into account the radical instability that has characterized the politics of the region, and to which the involvement of extraregional actors has in measure contributed. In the analysis that follows I use broad categories, subjectively defined but intended to provide the widest possible context for uncovering a diversity of motivations. Sources of Soviet involvement are described as *geographical, economic*, and *political* and an attempt is made to explore the implications of each category extensively. I also make frequent reference to Soviet sources, both academic and policy oriented, on the assumption (admittedly challengeable) that cumulatively such sources provide a reliable image of Soviet motivations and priorities. I assume that an appropriate characterization of the sources of Soviet policy in the Middle East should be complex and nuanced, developed conditionally, and flexible enough to allow for revision and redirection.

Sources of Involvement—Geographical Proximity

The USSR has reacted to virtually every event of significance in the Middle East over the past twenty-five years with the ritual phrase "the Near East is a region located in immediate proximity to the southern borders of the Soviet Union, and events there cannot help but affect the interests of the USSR."[3] The sheer persistence with which such explanations are offered virtually requires that they be taken seriously. Physical proximity does in fact impact upon Soviet policy toward the Middle East in diverse and important ways.

Regional Contiguity

Definitions of what constitutes the Middle East vary widely. The term itself is a legacy of colonialism and has never achieved descriptive clarity.[4] A narrow definition emphasizing geographical contiguity could limit the region to the strategic triangle formed by Egypt, the Levant, and Anatolia. A broader definition, placing more emphasis upon cultural, linguistic, and ethnic interlinkages, could extend the region westward to include the Maghrib, southward to include the Sudan, Somalia, and the Muslim peoples of the Horn of Africa, and eastward to include the Gulf region and Iran.

The Soviet Union itself distinguishes between a Near East focused upon the Arab-Israeli conflict area, and a Middle East including the so-called southern-tier nations (I prefer this term, expressing as it does a Soviet perspective, to the northern-tier designation) bordering the USSR's southern flank. By some definitions, however, the region could be extended even further to include Afghanistan, Pakistan, and the six predominantly Muslim Soviet Union Republics of Azerbaidzhan, Kazakhstan, Turkmenistan, Uzbekistan, Kirgizistan, and Tadzhikistan. These Soviet Republics share in the most important unifying factor in the region as a whole, the cultural context of Islam. They are populated dominantly by Turkic, Persian, and other peoples that constitute parts of larger Middle Eastern ethnic and linguistic families. Historically, their identity as part of a broad Central

Asian Islamic civilization is much more deeply rooted than the more recent association with the Slavic north. Soviet Azerbaidzhan and Central Asia are culturally, historically, linguistically, and racially a composite of the Middle East as it is commonly defined.[5]

Perhaps the most important effects of regional contiguity upon Soviet policy in the Middle East lie in the realm of perception. Soviet commentary is infused with the conviction that the Soviet Union *is* a Middle Eastern power by right of history and geography, with an unchallengeable claim to a voice in local affairs. Moscow has been continuously involved in the area throughout the modern period, and this has arguably left a legacy of attitudes and impulses, including a latent sense of cultural superiority, that continue to condition policy today. The experience of absorbing and administering the predominantly Muslim Central Asian Republics has given the Soviet leadership a tutorial attitude toward many of the problems of the region.[6] Historically conditioned perceptions might at least help to account for a certain continuity in czarist and Soviet policy, for the defensiveness of Soviet assertions of a legitimate regional role, and for the persistence of the Soviet search for influence despite obstacles and risks.

Strategic Exposure

For a number of reasons the Russian state has always been hypersensitive to the security of its borders. This has led in the past to a policy of extending influence into the southern tier: to a sequence of wars between the czarist, Persian, and Ottoman empires during the eighteenth and nineteenth centuries; to the colonization of large, predominantly Muslim areas to the south; and to the refusal of demands for political autonomy in the Caucasus and Central Asia after 1917. Soviet attempts to assert influence in the region continued through the 1920s and 1930s despite preoccupations elsewhere (for example, the Baku Conference of 1920 and the anti-imperialist thrust of Comintern agitation and propaganda with which it was linked; the cultivation of friendship treaties with Turkey, Iran, and Afghanistan;[7] the transformation of Outer Mongolia into a Soviet protectorate; and active participation in the shaping of the Montreux Straits Convention in 1936). These attempts carried over into the post-World War II period in the form of the pressures placed upon Turkey and Iran during 1945-1947.[8]

The strategic redefinitions occasioned by World War II saw the emergence of the United States as the dominant power in the region. The Truman Doctrine in 1947 was the first enunciation of the U.S. intention to assume a leading role and was accompanied by U.S. intervention in the Greek civil war; the Central Intelligence Agency (CIA) induced fall of Muhammad Musaddiq's government in Iran and subsequent U.S. backing for the shah;

increasing support for the state of Israel; and the creation of the North Atlantic Treaty Organization (NATO) in 1949 (eventually to include Greece and Turkey) and the Baghdad Pact in 1955, as U.S.-sponsored regional alliances in the spirit of containment. The emerging U.S.-Soviet global rivalry was rapidly superimposed upon the Middle East, which became an area of primary Western strategic attention. Of the four doctrines proclaimed by U.S. presidents in the postwar era, three (the Truman Doctrine of 1947, the Eisenhower Doctrine of 1957, and the Carter Doctrine of 1980) dealt specifically with the Middle East, and the fourth (the Nixon Doctrine of 1969) had important implications for the area.[9] For its part, and given U.S. strategic predominance, the Soviet Union was drawn almost inevitably into a posture of strategic denial, very much in character with its historical approach to the region, which it has substantially maintained ever since.[10]

The problem of maintaining an acceptable regime in the Turkish straits has preoccupied Russian diplomacy ever since the 1774 treaty of Kuchuk Kainardji.[11] Likewise the insurance of strategically secure borders traditionally has dominated Russian policy in the southern-tier area. With the deployment in 1963 of the USS *Lafayette* and *Alexander Hamilton*, the first nuclear, missile-launching Polaris submarines, the Soviet Union was, however, confronted with a challenging new strategic dilemma.[12] In order to confront the Polaris, deployed in the Mediterranean as a component of the U.S. Sixth Fleet and with a range of 1,600 miles (and the enhanced strike capacity of U.S. carrier groups with onboard, nuclear-capable aircraft), the Soviet navy was required to venture beyond the protection of land-based aircraft. The result was a new concern for basing and support facilities capable of sustaining a naval presence away from home ports.[13]

The Soviet Union had maintained a modest naval presence in the Mediterranean from 1958 to 1961 based near Vlorë, Albania, on the Strait of Otranto. In 1961, as a result of the rift with Albania occasioned by the Sino-Soviet split, the Soviets lost access to this facility and withdrew all naval combatants. But in 1964 the Soviet navy returned with the creation of a Mediterranean squadron attached to the Black Sea Fleet. The deployment of the squadron was accompanied by an antisubmarine program that corresponded to its primary task, including alterations in ship construction programs, emphasis upon more sophisticated air-defense systems, the increasing use of the helicopter as an antisubmarine weapon, and an expansion of the auxiliary fleet capable of refueling, rearming, and repair work at sea or in foreign ports.[14]

A similar logic of involvement may be defined in regard to the Indian Ocean, where a permanent Soviet naval presence, projected from the Pacific Fleet based in the Soviet Maritime Province, dates to 1968. Soviet motives are somewhat more opaque here, but certainly included the perceived need to counter the possible use by the United States of the Indian Ocean as a launching area for sub-launched ballistic missiles (by the 1970s this may have included the Polaris and the Poseidon, and during the 1980s will definitely include the Trident system, with a range of 6,000 miles); the desire to project power into an area adjacent to the Gulf with its increasing strategic vulnerability after British withdrawal from Aden and the Gulf region in 1967 and 1971; and the desire to neutralize a growing U.S. presence in the Indian Ocean, signaled by the decision made in the early 1970s to build up the Diego Garcia naval facility.[15] (See table 3-1.)

The growing importance of a naval presence in the eastern Mediterranean and the Indian Ocean in turn enhanced the importance of the strategic waterway extending from the Black Sea through the Turkish straits, eastern Mediterranean, Suez Canal, Red Sea, Bab al-Mandab Strait, and into the Indian Ocean.[16] This represents the shortest naval connection between European Russia and the Soviet Far East, Siberia, and Central Asia—areas linked overland to the west only by the exposed and comparatively much less efficient trans-Siberian railway lines. The growing importance of these areas for the Soviet domestic economy, in terms of both resources and population growth, reinforces the strategic logic of the Soviet attempt to project itself into adjacent areas.

Cumulatively, strategic motives have drawn the Soviet Union inexorably into the region in search of port facilities, basing rights, military special privileges such as overflight, and the political relationships necessary to sustain them. The means the Soviets have used to accomplish these goals have varied and the degree of success attained has been irregular, but the underlying strategic logic has remained relatively constant.

Strategic rivalry between the superpowers in the Middle East and its watery flanks is of course quite dynamic. Since the early 1970s the Soviet navy has altered its ship-construction programs again, apparently seeking a more balanced force, although the antisubmarine function continues to dominate.[17] The search for political influence via demonstrative displays of military power has also become a more important aspect of Soviet deployments in recent years. Dependence upon land-based support facilities to retain naval credibility remains, however, a reality for Soviet strategic planners for the foreseeable future, with the alternative of a conventional carrier force perhaps programmed but still far away.[18] The difficulties of detection and antisubmarine warfare make the professed goal of neutralizing Trident highly problematic, but the nature of superpower strategic rivalry dictates that such efforts will most likely be sustained. The Soviet Union will also continue to have an interest in preventing an absolute U.S. strategic domination of the region, whether accomplished via regional gendarmes supplied with advanced U.S. arms and strategic *special relationships* (such as the shah's Iran, the Turkish military junta, or the state of Israel),[19] or via the emerging infrastructure of the Rapid Deployment Force.[20]

Table 3-1
The Soviet Navy

Soviet Navy Order of Battle	
Category	Quantity
Submarines—Nuclear-Powered	
SSBN[a] Ballistic-missile submarines (YANKEE, DELTA classes)	62
SSBN Ballistic-missile submarines (HOTEL class)	7
SSGN[a] Cruise-missile submarines	50
SSN[a] Torpedo-attack submarines	60
Submarines—Diesel-electric-powered	
SSB Ballistic-missile submarines	18
SSG Cruise-missile submarines	20
SS[a] Torpedo-attack submarines	160
Aviation Ships	
CVHG VSTOL aviation ships (KIEV class)	2
CHG Helicopter aviation ships (MOSKVA class)	2
Cruisers	
CGN[a] Guided-missile cruiser (nuclear) (KIROV class)	1
CG[a] Guided-missile cruisers (SAM/SSM)	26
CL Light-cruisers (SVERDLOV class)	9
Destroyers	
DDG[a] Guided-missile destroyers (SAM/SSM)	38
DD Destroyers	30
Frigates (Escorts)	
FFG[a] Guided-missile frigates (KRIVAK class)	28
FF/FFL Frigates/small frigates	140
Small Combatants	
Missile craft[a]	145
Patrol/ASW/torpedo craft[a]	395
Minesweepers[a]	395
Amphibious Ships	
LPD[a] Amphibious-assault transport dock (IVAN ROGOV class)	1
LST Amphibious-vehicle landing ships (ALLIGATOR, ROPUCHA classes)	25
LSM Medium landing ships (POLNOCNY/MP-4 classes)	60
Auxiliary Ships	
Mobile logistics ships[a]	150
Other auxiliaries[a]	605

Soviet Navy Aircraft	
Category	Quantity
Strike/Bombers	390
Backfire	
Badger	
Blinder	
Fighter/Fighter Bombers	70
Fitter	
Forger	
Reconnaissance/Electronic-Warfare Aircraft	180
Badger	
Bear D	
Blinder	
Antisubmarine Aircraft	400
Bear F	
Haze A	
Hormone A	
Hound	
Mail	
May	
Tanker	70
Badger	
Transport/Training Aircraft	330

Source: "Soviet Military Power," U.S. Department of Defense, 1981, as appeared in Joseph M.A.H. Luns, "Political-Military Implications of Soviet Naval Expansion," *NATO Review* 1 (February 1982):6.
[a]Indicates additional units under construction in these categories.

To accomplish strategic denial the Soviet Union requires its own military infrastructure capable of projecting power into the region and solid political relationships with strategically placed regional actors. The search for these prerequisites has importantly characterized Soviet policy in the area since 1955. Effective strategic denial would give the Soviet Union several obviously desirable advantages, including: (1) an improved posture adjacent to NATO's southern theater; (2) the ability to protect the southern routes of access to the USSR; (3) a degree of interdictive or retaliatory capacity against a sub or carrier-based nuclear threat in the Mediterranean and Indian Ocean; (4) the ability to maintain a containment, or encirclement, posture in relation to the People's Republic of China; (5) enhanced ability to project power into the region with the aim of influencing regional conflicts in such a way as to improve the Soviet strategic position to the detriment of the United States; (6) an enhanced ability to neutralize, subvert, or intimidate U.S. clients or allies, when possible at acceptable cost and risk; and (7) in general, an improved strategic posture in the region as a counter to the U.S. presence.

Is there a more aggressive and assertive thrust to the Soviet strategic attitude toward the Middle East? The inherent strategic value of the region, some would argue, transcends the predominantly defensive motives described above. The Middle East is the land bridge linking the European, African, and Asian continents. It encompasses the bulk of the Western world's petroleum reserves and the vital sea lanes through which these reserves are transported. Because of its geostrategic centrality the Middle East represents a prize, the strategic domination of which could lead to a decisive shift in the global balance of power. Given such high stakes, Soviet strategic motives have been described as increasingly expansionist, representing cumulatively an emerging threat to the region's dominant state system and geostrategic orientation.[21]

The bulk of evidence does not support such alarmist contentions. Given the balance of forces in the area, Soviet strategic attitudes are likely to be dominated by defensive concerns for the foreseeable future, at least in areas not directly contiguous to the Soviet frontier. Apart from its general weaknesses and strategic overexposure elsewhere, the Soviet Union confronts several basic strategic deficiencies that constrain its ability to intervene militarily in the Middle East. First, both the Black Sea and Pacific fleets must pass through exposed choke points to approach the region (the Bosporus/Sea of Marmara/Dardenelles passage and the Straits of Malacca, respectively). Furthermore the two boundary complexes of water are themselves linked only by the Suez/Red Sea/Bab al-Mandab passage, also an easily obstructed choke point. Geography has dictated the need for the Soviet Union to forward deploy forces drawn from two distinct naval commands on either flank of the region. The implictions of the geographical dispersion of the Soviet fleets must be taken into account in weighing Soviet options. Second, the Soviet navy lacks adequate air cover. Air-defense systems are not enough by themselves to protect shipping from land-based aircraft, and the aircraft carriers required to address effectively this lack are not in sight. Third, the Soviets lack adequate amphibious and airborne lift to massively and decisively project forces into areas not contiguous with their borders.[22]

Beyond these tactical limitations, the political base upon which the Soviet strategic infrastructure rests has proven highly volatile and unstable. Chronic regional instability has brought with it a constant threat of unexpected consequences. The Soviet Union has not always been able to control effectively its regional clients. The search for influence often has been a frustrating one, and the Soviets have repeatedly been exploited for their own ends by regional actors over whom they sought to exert control. Shifting political winds have carried the constant threat of expulsion and the loss of carefully cultivated strategic acquisitions. The unstable political context of the Middle East has made the Soviet strategic presence precarious at best and serves as an important barrier to a policy aiming at regional hegemony. Most of all, strategic involvement has brought with it the threat of an escalating regional conflict drawing the USSR into a clash with the United States. There is every indication that the highest single priority of Soviet policy in the region, as elsewhere, has been to avoid direct confrontation with its superpower rival.

In sum, the Middle East is today the most exposed of the major land flanks ringing the USSR, and it is a region where the USSR's key global rival has been and remains strategically dominant. Russian forces conducted campaigns in the Middle East in both prior world wars and would undoubtedly be called upon to do so in a third.[23] The region's strategic vitality, in Moscow's eyes, is determined by inalterable geostrategic realities.

Demographic Communality

Most of the major ethnic, cultural, and linguistic groups that constitute the Middle Eastern mosaic of peoples are represented within the boundaries of the USSR. The Soviet Union contains a large and growing Muslim community, in large part Sunni but with a Shi'a minority as well. Ethnically, the community is predominantly Turkic, speaking related languages and with a potentially pan-Turkic identity, but there is also a Farsi-speaking community (the Tadzhiks), plus Kurdish, Uighur, and other minorities.[24] Also, the Soviet Union contains the world's third largest (after the United States and Israel) Jewish community. I will focus on the Muslim and Jewish interlinkages, although it is worth noting that there are other areas where demographic communality affects the Soviet Union's involvement in the region (for example, by potentially facilitating manipulation of Azeri, Kurdish,

Turkmen, or other separatist tendencies in Iran, Iraq, Chinese Xinjiang, and other areas).

The rise of Islamic fundamentalism as a real political factor in the Muslim world at large has led to widespread speculation concerning the potential for a revival of Islamic identity within the Soviet Union itself. It has been suggested, for example, that the desire to control or contain Islamic revivalism was a major factor motivating the Soviet Union to occupy Afghanistan militarily, with all of the attendant regional and global ramifications.[25] Dramatic conclusions concerning the problem have been widely accepted despite the lack of hard evidence to support them.

It certainly is possible to identify sources of potential instability within the Soviet Central Asian Republics.[26] First, the Central Asian peoples are experiencing a birth rate that is dramatically higher than that of other groups in the Soviet population. If trends continue (and there are indications that they are beginning to moderate), within several generations the Muslim peoples of Central Asia will displace the traditionally dominant Slavs as the majority of the Soviet population, posing major problems of adaptation for an unrepentently Great Russian power elite.[27] Second, although plagued by a labor shortage nationwide, the USSR confronts a potential labor surplus in the Central Asian Republics. The economy of the region remains predominantly agricultural, diversification will be costly, and the potential for economic frustration to develop is high.[28] Third, the increasing proportion of the Soviet armed forces' conscripted manpower drawn from Central Asia poses problems of morale and control. Recruits are reportedly often ill-equipped to function in Russian, the official language of command, and Central Asian soldiers apparently have not always performed well in Afghanistan.[29] Finally, with higher levels of educational achievement and increasing urbanization the potential for enhanced national consciousness to lead to anti-Russian or anti-Soviet sentiments is very real. Islam would be, at a minimum, the cultural context within which a challenge to Russian hegemony would be posed. The existence of underground Sufi religious sects with traditionalist attitudes has been documented,[30] Soviet Central Asian communities remain relatively closed with low rates of intermarriage and internal mobility,[31] and religious affiliation appears to remain pervasive. At the republic-level party congress in Turkmenistan, which preceded the Twenty-sixth Party Congress of the Communist Party of the Soviet Union (CPSU) in January 1981, the phenomenon of party members simultaneously pursuing religious activities was formally criticized, and the "false rumors" supposedly emanating from "self styled" local holy men were ominously denounced.[32] Given these various potential sources of tension the USSR must, at a minimum, be concerned with how events and trends in the Muslim world across its borders might impact upon its own Islamic population.

This said, however, it should also be noted that there are very convincing reasons why major unrest in Soviet Central Asia is not highly probable in the foreseeable future. First, there is no indication that the diverse problems mentioned here (in many cases typical dilemmas for multinational states and developing regions and by no means unique to the USSR) will not be manageable in the long term. Levels of literacy and educational achievement, health services, and general development are distinctly higher within the Soviet Caucasian and Central Asian Republics than in the immediately adjacent states of Turkey, Iran, and Afghanistan. One could persuasively argue that the social and cultural dynamics that have produced the wave of Islamic fundamentalism elsewhere are to a large extent absent within the USSR. Limited but real channels for upward mobility do exist, and the Soviet hierarchy would be foolish indeed if it did not attempt to coopt local elites into the established structure of power. The Islamic hierarchy in the USSR consists of authentic Islamic *ulama*, is firmly linked to the state via four bureaucratized religious administrations (for Central Asia, the North Caucasus, the Transcaucasus, and European Russia-Siberia), and is entirely supportive of Soviet policies. Finally, the Soviet Muslim population is itself internally divided, with the elements of a broad populist consensus presently lacking.

In fact, the impact of Soviet Islam upon the regime's policies in the Middle East has been in many ways positive.[33] The Soviets have described their successes in developing and modernizing Central Asia as a model for development in the region as a whole. The Soviet ideological image of Islam, especially in the wake of the Iranian revolution and given Soviet attempts to develop a positive relationship with the Khumayni regime, has been carefully nuanced, emphasizing the "progressive," "socialist," and "humanist" dimensions of the faith.[34] Muslim delegations from the Middle East and elsewhere regularly visit the Soviet Caucasian and Central Asian Republics, and the Soviets also send Muslim delegations abroad in the role of cultural ambassadors.[35] Radio broadcasts in a gamut of Middle Eastern languages, including statements by spiritual leaders, are beamed daily throughout the region. The cumulative image that is produced, of a culturally distinct Islamic community, prospering economically and coexisting with Soviet power, has certainly not been without effect.[36] It has been noted, for example, that resistance to the Soviet occupation of Afghanistan has been less intense in the predominantly Uzbek areas adjacent to the Soviet border.[37] It is sometimes forgotten that by far the most visible and disruptive cultural influence upon the contemporary Middle East has been that of the West, with its presumed materialism and moral depravation. The Iranian revolution has made clear that in comparison with Western materialism, Soviet communism is very much a lesser Satan in the eyes of many people in the area. Soviet Islam, then, represents both a potential source of domestic instability and exposure and a policy asset, which conditions Soviet involvement in the affairs of the Middle East in complex and potentially contradictory ways.

Soviet relations with Israel have also been affected by the existence of an important Jewish minority within the USSR. The Soviet Union has been outspokenly critical of what it calls the reactionary and expansionist ideology of Zionism. Since the early 1950s it has consistently sided with the Arab states in the Arab-Israeli dispute, and in 1967 following the Six Day War broke diplomatic relations with Israel altogether. Antisemitism has deep cultural roots within eastern Europe as a whole, and some analysts in the West have argued that Soviet policy toward Israel has been importantly shaped by antisemitic attitudes.[38]

There is a large and ever-growing Soviet literature devoted to Zionism, and some of it certainly does verge upon antisemitic formulations.[39] However, to attribute Soviet policy toward Israel directly to antisemitic motives seems extreme. The Soviet Union originally supported the creation of a Jewish state in a part of the former British mandate of Palestine, was the first state to formally accord diplomatic recognition to Israel, and supplied Israel militarily during its war of independence.[40] The Soviets have consistently supported the right of Israel to exist and have condemned extremist elements in the Arab world calling for Israel's destruction or disestablishment.[41] Soviet criticism of Israel has focused upon its expansionist aims, its opposition to "progressive" trends in the Arab world, its intransigence on the Palestinian issue, and its close strategic relationship with the United States. Each of these areas has enough objective substance to make it a legitimate point of Soviet concern without factoring antisemitism into the equation.[42]

There are ways in which the status of Soviet Jewry does affect Soviet attitudes toward Israel. Soviet leaders have been wary concerning the political appeal of Zionism to their own Jewish community, especially given its high educational level, visibility, and links to groups abroad. This wariness was perhaps sparked by the large, spontaneous demonstrations of Moscow Jews that greeted the arrival of Golda Meir as the first Israeli ambassador to the USSR in 1948, and has been revived by the politicization of the issue of Jewish emigration from the USSR during the 1970s with its high levels of attendant publicity. Soviet analysts have always been sensitive to the role of what they call the "Zionist lobby" in the shaping of U.S. policies and priorities in the Middle East—and hence to the U.S. public image of the status of Soviet Jews.[43] These motivations, however, should not be exaggerated. Soviet officials are aware that the appeal of the state of Israel is limited and that only a minority of the Soviet Jewish emigration permanently settles there, and recent commentary has emphasized the lack of consensus concerning Israel and its goals that characterizes U.S. opinion.[44]

The sources of Soviet opposition to Israeli policies are best sought elsewhere. The Soviet break with Israel has sometimes been described as a tactical choice, reflecting a sense of the greater long-term viability of the anti-Israel position and the emerging regional predominance of the Arab forces. In describing Israel as a pawn of U.S. imperial interests, as the primary threat to peace and stability in the Middle East, and as a bastion of international reaction the Soviet Union is aligned with the mainstream of regional opinion (at least on the popular level). Despite its democratic institutions Israel is closely aligned economically, particularly in the area of arms sales, with a number of repressive military regimes, and its own armed forces have assumed a disproportionate domestic political role to which the Soviets have expressed sensitivity.[45] The summer 1982 Israeli invasion of Lebanon left the United States alone in international forums as the Begin government's sole supporter, and the subsequent massacres of Palestinians at the Chatila and Sabra refugee camps in Israeli-occupied west Beirut reinforced Israel's international isolation. The USSR has an ideological image to guard, and though ideology has proven a highly flexible guide to the pursuance of state-to-state relations, it dictates at least a prudent distancing from Israeli policies in the Middle East.

The Soviet Union's support for Israel's right to exist, based upon a realistic assessment of Israel's strengths and the implications of alternatives, has been reiterated in a variety of forums over many years and appears sincere. At the same time, Israel's isolation, unpopularity, and total dependence upon U.S. backing, coupled with its own regional ambitions, make it a logical target for Soviet criticism. Fear of the domestic impact of the Zionist appeal upon its own Jewish minority; sensitivity to Jewish opinion in the United States as a source of support for Israel; Israel's role as a kind of regional policeman whose goals clash directly with the Soviet regional presence; Israel's international unpopularity and isolation; and Israel's special strategic relationship with the United States all provide adequate foundations for the anti-Israel tenor of Soviet policies—and may be expected to continue to do so.

Sources of Involvement—Economic Factors

One of the key dimensions of the purported Soviet threat to the Middle East that recurs in Western analysis is a presumed desire to gain control over the region's vital resources, particularly oil, either as an alternative to cresting or declining domestic production, or to deny them to the West. The influence of the CIA's 1977 misestimates concerning impending oil shortages in the USSR,[46] since revised by the CIA itself and rejected by nearly every independent investigatory source, has created widespread misperceptions concerning this critical issue that are just beginning to dissipate. The Soviet Union does have an economic interest in maintaining or developing access to Middle Eastern energy reserves to allow for the continued exportation of a portion of its own production, but it is not being compelled onto the world market and does not confront an imminent energy crisis.[47]

Does the desire to dominate and potentially to deny Middle Eastern resources to the West play a role in Soviet policy calculations?[48] Here again, the assumptions upon which such arguments are based deserve careful analysis. On the one hand the Soviet Union does rhetorically support nationalizations, is a champion of OPEC, and has encouraged the use of the oil weapon by the Arab states. OPEC is described as an objectively anti-imperialist organization whose successes are linked to the advance of socialism worldwide. In the words of a leading Soviet commentator:

> OPEC is an organization of former colonies and semicolonies, which in the context of a changing correlation of forces in the world in favor of socialism has been able to break the front of colonial-monopolistic exploitation and in a series of questions to impose its will upon imperialism.[49]

Soviet analysis also identifies an increase in the role of "progressive" forces within OPEC and links the organization's impact to a democratization of international relations insuring local control over natural resources and expanded opportunities for independent economic development.[50] As the world's largest oil producer and an active exporter, the Soviet Union does stand to benefit in purely monetary terms from OPEC-induced price hikes. Also, Soviet analysis scathingly attacks the role of U.S. oil monopolies as a primary determinant of Washington's imperial ambitions in the area, a role the rise of OPEC is presumed to mitigate.[51]

On the other hand, Soviet discussions of the problem of control over Middle Eastern oil reserves are generally balanced. A good case can be made to the effect that the political and economic advantages to the Soviet Union derived from the oil price hikes of the 1970s have been disappointing.[52] The impact of oil wealth upon the Arab monarchies has been contradictory and in some cases has bound them closer to the West, and the prospects for OPEC to develop beyond its current ambiguous status are recognized to be limited.[53]

Moreover it is difficult to define an objective Soviet interest in a major disruption of world energy markets. One of the most visible structural trends within the Soviet economy as a whole in recent years (and some would argue since 1917) has been the search to broaden mutually advantageous agreements linking the Soviet economy more closely to world markets.[54] This trend also characterizes the Soviet economic relationship with the nations of the Middle East, and a survey of relevant statistics indicates that during the 1970s the volume of Soviet trade with the Middle East demonstrated a consistent growth, and the foreign-trade surplus derived from exchanges (including revenues derived from arms sales) has become increasingly important.[55] A stable context for developing economic interactions relates much more directly to immediate Soviet interests than the apocalyptic image of challenging the West for control. On the global level, the Soviet Union must be sensitive to the degree of Western dependence upon the resources of the area, and apart from the risks of a holocaust that it would entail, does not itself stand to benefit from the catastrophic impact on the world economy that a major disruption of oil supplies would occasion. The more limited argument that leverage over Middle Eastern resources could provide the Soviets with a means for manipulating Western dependency is also unconvincingly abstract. Studies of economic dependence indicate that to a large extent such dependence does not imply high levels of political compliance.[56]

The Soviet Union is in fact increasingly interdependent with the world capitalist market that it rhetorically decries. Recent Soviet scholarship devoted to the problem of development has been pessimistic about the possibility of autarkic development in isolation from the world market. Gradual, balanced economic growth and a progressive role for free enterprise, foreign investment, and even the multinational corporation are cited as positive alternatives.[57] A recent Western study by Vladimir Treml and Barry Kostinsky has posited a much higher degree of Soviet economic interdependence with world markets than had previously been supposed,[58] and although the methodological premises of the report are controversial the general commitment by Soviet planners to achieve higher levels of economic interdependence is clear. The Soviet Union has no objective interest in sabotaging an international economic system with which it is increasingly involved.

Economic interests do tie the Soviet Union closely to the Middle East, and as the relative weight of Soviet Central Asia and the Far East grows within the domestic economy these interests are likely to increase.[59] The Soviet Union has an interest in maintaining access to Middle Eastern oil and gas reserves, in improving its commercial position, and in preventing its own exclusion from the area. The potentiality of a U.S. seizure of Middle Eastern oil fields must also be considered, and U.S. forces have maintained contingency plans for such an eventuality for many years.[60] The increasing degree to which the Soviet Union is interdependent with regional and global markets, however, seems to indicate that Soviet interests are best served by prudent policies allowing for the development of conventional economic relations, sensitivity to vital Western interests, and acceptance of a substantial amount of Western involvement. The USSR attempts to exploit economic tensions and injustices in the region to enhance its own image, and it seeks political influence to improve its commercial standing, but this hardly constitutes the threat that some have perceived. In fact, the overall weakness of the Soviet economy, reflected in its inability to supply regional clients with technologically sophisticated equipment and sustained foreign aid, is also a major constraint upon the Soviet pursuit of influence.[61]

The true threat to international stability emerging from the Middle East relates not so much to Soviet designs as to dynamics at work within the region itself. The impact of oil wealth upon the economies of the Middle East, the division of the region into wealthy and impoverished states that it has created, demographic restructuring and the emergence of a younger generation with heightened expectations, and attendant problems of development and modernization have been immensely disruptive. Both superpowers have sought to exploit the resultant regional tensions, but neither has succeeded in mastering them. The impact of arms transfers upon the region, fed by petrodollars and unrestrained superpower competition, has become an independent variable with tremendously destabilizing potential. Oil price increases, excessive levels of military spending, and international recession have combined to create a threat to the viability of the entire regional order, with important global implications as well. The Soviet Union does not stand to gain—quite the contrary, in fact—from major economic dislocations, but the nature of superpower rivalry superimposed upon the Middle East may yet help to provoke them.

Sources of Involvement—Political Motives

Political motivation is a vague formulation that may encompass a large number of variables, including conventional diplomatic priorities, ideological factors, and institutional dynamics. In this regard increasing attention has been devoted recently in academic literature to the role of cognitive and organizational factors in the shaping of Soviet foreign policy.[62] These approaches assume that the sources of a state's international behavior include not only relatively permanent geostrategic and economic factors but also the perceptions of policy elites and decision-making processes themselves. A further distinction may be made between the policy process during relatively stable periods and crisis diplomacy, when under the stress of heightened responsibility and limited time for deliberation a special dynamic of decision is presumed to operate.[63]

Unfortunately, the closed nature of Soviet politics militates against a consistent application of cognitive and organizational perspectives. We know that Soviet decision making is highly centralized and that the General Secretary plays a dominant role in policy formulation, although since Stalin a collective leadership concept has limited the General Secretary's absolute preeminence. We may presume that bureaucratic and interest-group interactions characterize Soviet decision making and that various bureaucratic entities do develop relatively distinct institutional perspectives. We can discern a dynamic of crisis behavior with its own special structures and processes.[64] Beyond these generalities, however, one treads on thin ice in an effort to specify the effects of policy process upon decisions.

There have been occasional signs of individual dissent within the Soviet power elite regarding policy choices and priorities in the Middle East, but no clear manifestations of widespread and deeply rooted differences. Western analysts have attempted via a systematic reading of Soviet press organs to define distinct institutional perspectives within the spectrum of Soviet bureaucratic politics, but conclusions have often been vague and disappointing.[65] The presumably more aggressive strategic perspective emanating from the Ministry of Defense has not been clearly manifest in the Middle East, and some observers have claimed to detect signs of resistance within the high command to strategic overexposure in the region.[66] A proper investigation of these difficult but important themes, however, transcends the scope of this chapter.

There is also no consensus concerning how the various integrating values and legitimizing principles presumably shared by Soviet elites might impact upon international behavior. The ideological character of the Soviet state and the political culture inherited from the Russian past often are defined as elements of a world outlook unique to Soviet leaders, but one is forced to speculate concerning the way in which these presumed attributes influence policy choices. Certainly the USSR does need, for reasons of domestic legitimacy, to guard its professed ideological commitments and to appear as the champion of what are viewed as "progressive" forces in the developing world. Soviet elites take seriously the USSR's claim to great power status and for reasons of prestige are compelled to pursue their commitments in the Middle East in order to guard their presumed right to a regional role and to avoid humiliation. Soviet political culture is harshly authoritarian and in the Middle East, as in Eastern and central Europe, Soviet decision makers appear wary of authentically popular and democratic forces and tend to project their own autocratic manners onto regional clients. Authoritarian elements in Middle Eastern political tradition have to a degree overlapped with Soviet authoritarianism and created a political foundation for patron-client state relationships. There are ways, then, in which Soviet elite attitudes and perceptions may be said to affect Middle Eastern policy, but it is difficult to define these relationships in more than general terms.

Important political manifestations of Soviet involvement in the Middle East include (not necessarily in order of importance): (1) support for the Arab states in their confrontation with Israel and of "Arab unity" as the means to achieve long-term goals;[67] (2) support for the Palestinian national movement, culminating with the accordance of diplomatic status to the Palestine Liberation Organization in October 1981; (3) linkage to a local infrastructure of Communist parties and organizations dependent upon Soviet backing and capable of acting as agents of Soviet policies; (4) the attempt to construct a loose confederation of area states around the principle of anti-imperialism and directed against U.S. regional predominance; (5) the pursuit of stable state-to-state relations under the general rubric of peaceful coexistence; and (6) ideological formulations such as the *noncapitalist path of development* or the *state with socialist orientation* defining a progressive role for Arab nationalism and other powerful regional forces.[68] The Soviet Union apparently also uses unconventional diplomacy as a means of penetrating the region, including selective support for terrorist organizations; but this aspect of Soviet activity has been exaggerated in the Western mass media. The bulk of Soviet diplomatic activity in the region has been cautious and subdued.

Soviet definitions of what constitutes progressive forces have varied, and with the declining popularity of the noncapitalist-path scenario the label *progressive* is being applied to a hodge-podge of Islamic states (Algeria, Iran, Libya), repressive military dictatorships (Ethiopia, Iraq, Syria), and pseudo-Marxist regimes (Afghanistan, the People's Democratic Republic of Yemen). The *Treaty of Friendship and Cooperation* continues to define special relationships with favored clients, and the bulk of the treaties of this kind that the Soviet Union has negotiated have involved the states of the Middle East. At present treaties exist with Iraq (1972), Ethiopia (1978), Afghanistan (1978), the PDRY (1979), and Syria (1980), the treaties with Egypt (1971) and Somalia (1974) having been subsequently abrogated. But the exact nature of the obligations that these treaties entail remains eminently vague.

Communist parties have not struck deep roots in the Middle East, anticommunist policies have been no barrier to the Soviet pursuit of diplomatic relations, and the Soviets seem to place no great stock in indigenous Communist forces as an instrument of policy in the short term. At present Soviet diplomacy is particularly marked by an effort to stabilize relations with the Khumayni government in Tehran,[69] and to improve the climate of relations with the increasingly important Saudi monarchy.[70] Thus ideological flexibility, an infinitely malleable definition of what constitutes progressive forces, and tactical caution allow the Soviets to maintain an ideological image necessary for purposes of legitimacy, to champion locally potent causes such as Arab unity or Palestinian statehood, and to pursue a conventional and nonthreatening diplomacy suitable for courting reluctant potential partners such as the Saudis.

Sino-Soviet rivalry has also been an aspect of the Soviet desire for presence in the Middle East—and one often ignored by Western (though not Soviet) commentators.[71] Although initiatives taken by the Twelfth Congress of the Chinese Communist Party in September 1982 and conciliatory responses from the USSR have given rise to a softening of the feud at present,

Sino-Soviet competition is deeply rooted and will not be easily overcome. The rivalry in the past has been projected upon the Middle East in the form of competition for clients and influence in much the same way as the U.S.-Soviet rivalry. The Soviet occupation of Afghanistan represents a major barrier to an ongoing Sino-Soviet rapprochement, and China has been outspoken in condemning Soviet hegemonism in the region.[72] Sino-Soviet competiton in the Middle East may well remain latent for the foreseeable future, but if the foreign-policy adjustment presently in progress in Beijing moves China back toward a more genuine nonalignment, the Chinese example might once again become a relevant model in the eyes of area states.

A description often applied to the USSR and its political role in the Middle East is that of a *non status quo power*. According to this characterization the Soviet impact upon world politics has been essentially subversive, predicated upon a restructuring of the international political order in the Soviet image. In pursuit of its goals the Soviet Union encourages instability, "stirs up trouble," and favors a climate of insecurity. As a rising superpower seeking to expand its strategic domain it stands to benefit from a disruption of the current order, and this is particularly true in the Middle East where Soviet proximity coupled with U.S. strategic domination and regional instability provide an excellent context for meddling.

There is an element of truth to this characterization of Soviet motives but also a large element of oversimplification. Soviet diplomatic interactions in the Middle East are overwhelmingly conventional. The USSR has proposed comprehensive security plans covering the entire region (the Geneva conference format for a Middle Eastern settlement as elaborated upon by Brezhnev during September 1982, a Persian Gulf security plan to include the Afghanistan question, and a Indian Ocean security proposal).[73] Though perhaps not acceptable in their present form, these plans need not be dismissed as diplomatic ploys or sinister plots. They provide a potential context for diplomatic initiatives moving toward mutually acceptable settlements. The Soviet Union has not armed its local clients to the point of providing them with regionally disruptive military potential and has demonstrated some degree of responsibility in avoiding direct superpower conflict in the region. Non status quo is too broad a characterization of Soviet motives, which are diverse but lean toward a gradual extension of influence via conventional diplomatic bargaining.

The USSR also stands to lose from an uncontrollable eruption of regional tension. The Iranian revolution, for example, by disrupting gas supplies from Iran, caused the Soviets temporarily to reduce their own natural-gas deliveries to Western Europe by 20 percent.[74] The disintegration of the domestic situation in Afghanistan was probably the primary factor motivating the costly and protracted Soviet military occupation. The Arab-Israeli conflict repeatedly has threatened to drag the USSR into an unwanted superpower confrontation, and the Iran-Iraq war has left the USSR on the horns of a dilemma, seeking to maintain an acceptable relationship with both antagonists simultaneously. In fact the Middle East does not require non status quo powers to destabilize it from without. The legacy of colonialism with its frustrated national ambitions, ethnic resentments, and patterns of dependence and underdevelopment has created an intolerable and unsustainable status quo. The political fragility of many area states, with their isolated, corrupt, and inefficient ruling elites, is by itself a source of imminent concern. Rising popular dissatisfaction, interrupted modernization, and the brutal repression of popular movements all provide a context for approaching political storms. The USSR must be no less wary of the explosive brew than the United States and does not inevitably stand to gain from it.

Images of Soviet Involvement

The sources of Soviet policy in the Middle East are obviously multiform and complex. The combination of geostrategic, demographic, economic, and political interrelationships that bind the Soviet Union to the region substantially explain the intensive and persistent character of Soviet involvement over several decades. They also indicate that Soviet policies need not be viewed as uniformly offensive, calculated, aggressive, or imperial—but are in measure the logical outgrowth of a pattern of interdependencies that Soviet leaders could ignore only at their peril. It is above all the superimposition of the global U.S.-Soviet rivalry upon the region that has transformed what might otherwise be viewed as a positive involvement into one of the most volatile and dangerous realities in contemporary international politics.

Assuming that the Soviet Union does have a long-term interest in maintaining and extending its presence in the Middle East, to what degree has its search for influence succeeded, and what is the current status of Soviet policy? Several partially contradictory images of Soviet involvement may be identified in current academic literature.

Soviet Exclusion

According to one widespread view the highpoint of Soviet success in the region corresponds to the years 1967-1973 and was based above all upon the Soviet-Egyptian relationship. Since the October War, however, the dynamic of Soviet involvement has lost its momentum. Sadat's break with Soviet tutelage and engagement in the Camp David process has effectively expelled the Soviets from the core of the region, where their severance of diplomatic relations with Israel in 1967 has denied them effective influence over peace initiatives. Since Camp David, Soviet influence has been relegated to actors standing outside the dominant regional state system and to areas peripheral to the nerve centers of Middle Eastern politics. And, the Israeli invasion of Lebanon, despite its short-term disruptions, may eventually have the effect of pushing the Camp David process further.[75] Increasing Soviet reliance upon arms transfers as a means of penetrating the region may be interpreted as more a sign of weakness than strength, especially given the problematic character of the influence so obtained. Even the arms option has been tarnished by the poor showing of Soviet weapons in the brief but decisive encounters between Syrian and Israeli forces in the first stages of the war in Lebanon. Soviet quiescence during the war and unwillingness or inability to assist meaningfully its PLO and Syrian allies, coupled with its lack of adequate backing for Iraq in its protracted war along the Shatt al-Arab, reveal a decisive weakening of the USSR's regional role.[76]

Soviet Advances

A contrasting image argues that there has been in fact a shift in the strategic center of gravity within the region as a whole, away from the Arab-Israeli conflict and toward the Persian Gulf. The Soviet Union is less interested in the interminable Arab-Israeli dispute than in the past, as its strategic horizons have broadened. The creation of pro-Soviet regimes in the PDRY and Ethiopia astride the Bab al-Mandab Strait, the occupation of Afghanistan, and client-state relationships with strategically placed states such as Syria and Libya do not indicate a marginalized Soviet presence but rather signal advances into some of the region's most critical potential flashpoints. The Middle East is in the midst of a chaotic process of change from which the Soviet Union is well placed to benefit. The region's single most important political reality is the ongoing Iranian revolution, and here the West finds itself effectively devoid of influence and in a no-win situation. No matter what course the Iranian revolution takes in the years ahead the Soviet Union—with geographical proximity, an intervention option, and a loyal local client in the Tudeh party—is in a position to benefit disproportionately.[77] Even in the Arab-Israeli conflict the effects of Israeli overreaching may yet provoke a reaction in the Arab world from which the Soviet Union stands to gain. In an even more alarmist vein, trends in the region have been described as holding forth the promise of a Finlandized Middle East under Soviet hegemony leading to the subversion of the oil-dependent NATO alliance to the north.[78] Overall the Soviet position in the region has improved, not declined, and the fate of Iran contains the threat of a dramatic shift in the regional balance to Soviet advantage.[79]

Soviet Engagement

Both of the above images tend to view Soviet striving for influence in the Middle East as predominantly offensive, zero sum,[80] and non status quo in character. Both define Soviet policies in the idioms of the Cold War, as a threat to the region and the vital interests of the West. The arguments developed in this chapter suggest that the problem might well be posed somewhat differently. Given the weight of factors virtually compelling Soviet involvement in the affairs of the Middle East, one could argue that the attempt to exclude them from the reigon—whether via diplomatic maneuvering or *coup de main* in the Arab-Israeli zone or via financial and strategic interlinkages in the Gulf—has itself been a primary source of the irresponsible behavior with which the Soviets are often charged.

In many ways the perceptions of Soviet policy as zero sum and non status quo are analytically imprecise and misleading. The Soviet Union is not responsible for the radical instability that plagues the politics of the Middle East.[81] Though it is too exposed, involved, and committed in the region to passively accept a collapse of its influence and leverage, its ambitions and capacities are not unlimited, and when evaluated objectively Soviet policy choices seem to tend toward caution and pragmatism. One need not idealize Soviet motives in concluding that the USSR often has as much interest as the United States in managing and containing regional tensions.

"The world of the Arabs" writes Fouad Ajami, "has become too pivotal to be left alone,"[82] and, his observation applies as much to Soviet interests and priorities as it does to those of the United States. The death of Leonid Brezhnev on 10 November 1982 has created the preconditions for a major reassessment of Soviet policy in the Middle East, coming as it does on the heels of the USSR's apparent humiliation during the war in Lebanon. There is virtually no likelihood, however, that the Soviet commitment to maintaining an important regional presence will be reduced. More likely, Brezhnev's immediate successor Iurii Andropov will be presiding over an extended interregnum during which most substantial issues in Soviet foreign and domestic policy will be broadly debated and new options and approaches posed. Both Malcolm Toon and W.W. Rostow have recently criticized U.S. attempts to pursue a unilateralist course as crisis manager in the Middle East, arguing that it has encouraged the Soviets to adopt a spoiler role and has aggravated local dilemmas.[83] In the post-Brezhnev era, without a clear stake in Middle Eastern arrangements that respect its interests and concerns in the area, the Soviet Union may be expected to continue to pursue antagonistic policies that contain the seeds of confrontation.

In an address before the Chicago Council on Foreign Relations on 26 May 1982, on the eve of the Israeli invasion of Lebanon, then Secretary of State Alexander Haig lauded the dawning of "America's moment" in the Middle East.[84] In subsequent months Haig's own resignation and the destructive chaos have made clear the risks attached to the U.S. attempt to pursue unilateralist policies. More sensitivity to the graduated nature of Soviet interests in the Middle East, the constraints Soviet policymakers confront, and the opportunities for mutually acceptable arrangements that could begin to engage the Soviet Union constructively in the affairs of the region might well be a desirable corrective.

Notes

1. Recent literature is reviewed in John C. Campbell, "Soviet Policies in the Middle East: Western Views," *Studies in Comparative Communism* (Summer/Autumn 1981):219-232; and Karen Dawisha, "Moscow in the Middle East," *Problems of Communism* (May/June 1982):56-59.

2. Among attempts to address systematically the sources of Soviet conduct in the Middle East, see Helène Carrère d'Encausse, *La politique soviétique au Moyen-Orient 1955-1975* (Paris: Presses de la Fondation Nationale des Sciences Politique, 1975); Karen Dawisha, *Soviet Foreign Policy toward Egypt* (London: Macmillan, 1979), pp. 91-130; Galia Golan, *Yom Kippur and After: The Soviet Union and the Middle East Crisis* (Cambridge: Cambridge University Press, 1977), pp. 1-20; and Helmut Hubel, *Die Sowjetische Nah- und Mittelost Politik: Bestimmungsfaktoren und Ziele sowie Ansatzpunkte für Konfliktregelung zwischen West und Ost* (Bonn: Europa Union Verlag, 1982). Rather good Soviet accounts are provided by L.I. Medvedko, *K vostoku i zapadu ot Suetsa (Zakat kolonializma i manevry neokolonializma na Arabskom Vostoke)* (Moscow: Izd. politicheskoi literatury, 1980); and E.M. Primakov, *Anatomiia blizhnevostochnogo konflikta* (Moscow: Mysl', 1978).

3. The citation, a recent example in a long series, is taken from a front-page editorial commenting upon the Israeli invasion of Lebanon. "Mir—Blizhnemu Vostoku," *Pravda*, 6 July 1982, p. 1.

4. A description of the evolution of the term is provided by Roderic H. Davison, "Where is the Middle East?," *Foreign Affairs* (July 1960):665-675.

5. See Alec Nove and J.A. Newth, *The Soviet Middle East* (London: Allen & Unwin, 1967).

6. See Alexandre Bennigsen and Chantal Lemercier-Quelquejay, "L'expérience soviétique en pays musulmans: les leçons du passe et l'Afghanistan," *politique étrangère* 4 (1980):881-890.

7. Stable state-to-state relations were often pursued at the expense of indigenous Communist forces, as in 1924 when the USSR effectively ignored Ataturk's attacks upon Turkish communists. Adam Ulam correctly

calls Ataturk the predecessor of Nasir and Sukharno. Adam Ulam, *Expansion and Coexistence: The History of Soviet Foreign Policy 1917-1973* (New York: Praeger, 1974), p. 123.

8. Soviet-U.S. rivalry in Greece, Turkey, and Iran in the postwar period is described in Bruce Robellet Kuniholm, *The Origins of the Cold War in the Near East* (Princeton: Princeton University Press, 1980). The author interprets Soviet initiatives as part of an emerging imperial design upon the region.

9. Iu. A. Shvedkov, "Ot 'Doktriny Trumena' k 'Doktrine Kartera': retsidiv politiki sily," *SShA: politika, ekonomika, ideologiia* 8 (1980):3-14.

10. Soviet analysis of Middle Eastern problems is dominated by the image of a United States that is striving for strategic hegemony. For examples see V.L. Avakov, "SShA i blizhnevostochnaia problema," *Voprosy istorii* 9 (1979):79-92; O. Kovtunovich and V. Nosenko, "Blizhnevostochnaia problema i strategiia amerikanskogo imperializma," *Mirovaia ekonomika i mezhdunarodnye otnosheniia* 7 (1980):33-42; and E. Primakov, "Blizhnii Vostok: dal'neishaia militarizatsiia politiki SShA," *Kommunist* 9 (June 1980):105-115.

11. I.F. Chernikov, *V interesakh mira i dobrososedstva (o Sovetsko-Turetskikh otnosheniiakh v 1935-1970 gg.)* (Kiev: Naukova Dumka, 1977) provides a description of Soviet attitudes toward the problem of the Straits since the Montreux Convention.

12. After the Cuban missile crisis in 1962 and the removal of U.S. Jupiter missiles based in Turkey, President Kennedy was careful to note that it was the Polaris that would be assuming their strategic role. John F. Kennedy, *The Public Papers of the Presidents of the United States, 1963* (Washington, D.C.: U.S. Government Printing Office, 1964), p. 98.

13. See Robert G. Weinland, "Land Support for Naval Forces: Egypt and the Soviet Escadra 1962-1976," *Survival* (March/April 1978):73-79; and Alvin Z. Rubinstein, "The Soviet Union and the Eastern Mediterranean, 1968-1978," *Orbis* 3 (1979):299-316.

14. Jean Labayle Couhat, ed., *Combat Fleets of the World, 1982/83* (Annapolis: Naval Institute Press, 1982), pp. 615-640.

15. See Geoffrey Jukes, *The Indian Ocean in Soviet Naval Policy* Adelphi Paper No. 87 (London: International Institute for Strategic Studies, 1972); and Oles M. Smolansky, "Soviet Entry Into the Indian Ocean: An Analysis," in Michael MccGwire, ed., *Soviet Naval Developments: Capability and Context* (New York: Praeger, 1973), pp. 407-422. For an example of the large Soviet literature addressing the problem of security in the Indian Ocean see D. Nikolaev, "Za mir i bezopasnost' v Indiiskom Okeane," *Mezhdunarodnaia zhizn'* 8 (1982):50-58.

16. Nimrod Novik, *On the Shores of Bab al-Mandab: Soviet Diplomacy and Regional Dynamics* (Philadelphia: Foreign Policy Research Institute,

1979), pp. 1-3. Novik suggests that Soviet use of the Suez Canal in supplying North Vietnam during the Indo-Chinese conflict reinforced their awareness of its strategic importance. For a strong Soviet comment upon the significance of the Red Sea see *Izvestiia*, 16 April 1977. One might also note that approximately 20 percent of the Soviet fishing harvest comes from the Indian Ocean and Red Sea.

17. The much discussed Kiev, officially classified as an *antisubmarine cruiser*, is the prototype for the new orientation. Couhat, *Combat Fleets*, p. 595. For a critique of the Soviet emphasis upon antisubmarine warfare see Eric Morris, *The Russian Navy: Myth and Reality* (New York: Stein and Day, 1977).

18. On carrier construction see Jan S. Breemer, "The New Soviet Aircraft Carrier," *U.S. Naval Institute Proceedings* (August 1981):30-35.

19. Soviet sources particularly emphasize the threatening nature of the U.S.-Israel connection and Israel's nuclear potential. For examples see V.F. Davydov, "Iadernye ambitsii Tel'-Aviva i Vashington," *SShA: politika, ekonomika, ideologiia* 9 (1981):51-56; I. Riabinov, "Izrail'skii militarizm i politiki agressii," *Mirovaia ekonomika i mezhdunarodnye otnosheniia* 5 (1978):53-62; and G. Sukhachev, "Iadernye ambitsii Tel'-Aviva," *Aziia i afrika segodnia* 9 (1981):20-21.

20. For critiques of rapid deployment see A. Stepanov, "Zachem zazhzhena 'Iarkaia Zvezda'," *Novoe vremia*, 13 November 1981, pp. 12-13; and the TASS commentary on the "Global Shield" exercise in Oman in *Foreign Broadcast Information Service Daily Reports, Soviet Union*, 13 February 1981, p. H1.

21. Soviet commentary echoes this evaluation of the area's inherent strategic importance. A recent scholarly description of the sources of U.S. policy in the Middle East emphasizes the "military-strategic and economic significance" of the region in U.S. global strategy as follows. "The proximity of the region to the borders of the Soviet Union, its location at the junction of three continents and the intersection of two oceans, its massive energy resources—such are the basic factors shaping the approach of the American administration." N.V. Osipova and S.M. Rogov, "SShA i blizhnevostochnyi uzel: vnutripoliticheskie aspekty," *SShA: politika, ekonomika, ideologiia* 4 (1982):17.

22. For an analysis of the Soviet ability to intervene militarily in a Middle Eastern conflict see Amnon Sella, *Soviet Political and Military Conduct in the Middle East* (London: Macmillan, 1981), pp. 56-65. Sella describes Soviet intervention in a local war in the Middle East as technically feasible but unlikely.

23. Fred Halliday, *Soviet Policy in the Arc of Crisis* (Washington, D.C.: Institute for Policy Studies, 1981), p. 37.

24. Background is provided by Alexandre Bennigsen and Chantal Lemercier-Quelquejay, *Islam in the Soviet Union* (New York: Praeger,

1967); and Geoffrey Wheeler, *The Modern History of Soviet Central Asia* (Westport: Greenwood Press, 1964).

25. "Moskaus Moslems: Sprengstoff für das Sowjet-reich," *Der Spiegel*, 31 March 1980, pp. 150-153.

26. Helène Carrère d'Encausse, *Decline of an Empire* (New York: Newsweek Books, 1979) provides an influential but perhaps overstated account of the Soviet Union's nationality problem.

27. Population estimates are based upon the census of 1979. *Naselenie SSSR: po dannym vsesoiuznoi perepisi naseleniia 1979 g.* (Moscow: Politizdat 1980).

28. Michael Rywkin, "Central Asia and Soviet Manpower," *Problems of Communism* (January/February 1979):1-13.

29. Edmund Brunner, *Soviet Demographic Trends and the Ethnic Composition of Draft Age Males, 1980-1995* (Santa Monica: Rand, 1981); Dallace Meehan, "Ethnic Minorities in the Soviet Military," *Air University Review* (May/June 1980):67-73; and Ellen Jones, "Manning the Soviet Military," *International Security* (Summer 1982):105-131.

30. Alexandre Bennigsen, "Muslim Conservative Opposition to the Soviet Regime: The Sufi Brotherhoods in the North Caucasus," in Jeremy R. Azrael, ed., *Soviet Nationality Policies and Practices* (New York: Praeger, 1978).

31. Ethel Dunn and Stephen Dunn, "Ethnic Intermarriage as an Indicator of Cultural Convergence in Soviet Central Asia," in Edward Allworth, ed., *The Nationality Question in Soviet Central Asia* (New York: Praeger, 1973).

32. See the remarks by the First Secretary of the Communist Party of Turkmenistan M.G. Gapurov to the Party's twenty-second congress in *Turkmenskaia iskra*, 17 January 1982, pp. 2-5. For a similar emphasis see the editorial statement "Ateisticheskaia rabota—nerazryvnaia chast' kommunisticheskogo vospitaniia," *Sovetskaia Kirgizia*, 27 December 1981, p. 3.

33. See particularly Martha Brill Olcott, "Soviet Islam and World Revolution," *World Politics* (July 1982):487-504.

34. Diverse examples of this emphasis are provided by S. Aliev, "Islam i politika," *Aziia i afrika segodnia* 12 (1981):5-9; T. Saidbaev, *Islam i obshchestvo* (Moscow: Nauka, 1978); and A. Vasil'ev, "Islam v sovremennom mire," *Mezhdunarodnaia zhizn'* 10 (1981):56-64. There is another edge to Soviet discussions of Islam, however, more critical and attuned to the atheistic foundation of the official ideology. See R.P. Mavliutov, *Islam* (Moscow: Politizdat, 1974).

35. For a good example of the cultural-ambassador function see the account of the visit by a Soviet Uzbek delegation to Libya in *Foreign Broadcast Information Service Daily Reports, Soviet Union*, 13 February 1981, p. I15. Further examples of this use of Soviet Islam are provided by Jeremy Azrael, "The 'Nationality Problem' in the USSR: Domestic Pressures and

Foreign Policy Constraints," in Seweryn Bialer, ed., *The Domestic Context of Soviet Foreign Policy* (Boulder: Westview Press, 1981), pp. 139-154; and Alexandre Bennigsen, "Soviet Muslims and the World of Islam," *Problems of Communism* (March/April 1980):42-46. Azrael notes the "disproportionate" number of Turkic personnel assigned to Soviet aid offices, embassies, and military missions in the Middle East. The Soviet Union has also sponsored a large number of international conferences in Soviet Central Asia, though since the failure of the fall 1980 Tashkent conference this seems to be being downplayed.

36. See V.P. Sherstobitov, ed., *Natsional'nye otnosheniia v SSSR na sovremennom etape (na materialakh respublik Srednii Azii i Kazakhstana)* (Moscow: 1979).

37. John C. Griffiths, *Afghanistan: Key to a Continent* (Boulder: Westview Press, 1981), p. 89.

38. For an argument to this effect see Robert S. Wistrich, ed., *The Left against Zion* (London: Vallentine, Mitchell, and Co., 1979).

39. See, *inter alia*, V.I. Kiselev, G.S. Nikitina, and A.F. Fedchenko, eds., *Mezhdunarodnyi sionizm: istoriia i politika* (Moscow: Nauka, 1977); and L. Rubinskii, *Sionizm: reaktsionnye tseli i prestupnye sredstva* (Odessa: Maiak, 1980).

40. Arnold Krammer, *The Forgotten Friendship: Israel and the Soviet Bloc 1947-53* (Urbana: University of Illinois Press, 1974).

41. Primakov, *Anatomiia blizhnevostochnogo konflikta*, pp. 130-158.

42. Soviet concerns are expressed in B.A. Semenink, *Sionizm v politicheskoi strategii imperializma* (Minsk: Belarus', 1981); and Ia. Shraiber, "Izrail': Ochag reaktsii i voiny," *Mezhdunarodnaia zhizn'* 5 (1978):53-60. Echoing Soviet fears, one prestigious U.S. analyst has gone so far as to suggest Israel's association with NATO in combination with a U.S.-sponsored regional settlement. Alvin Z. Rubinstein, "Israel in NATO: Basis for a Middle East Settlement," *Orbis* (Spring 1978):89-100.

43. Osipova and Rogov, "SShA i blizhnevostochnyi uzel," pp. 20-22, list Jewish opinion second after oil monopolies as domestic sources of U.S. Middle Eastern policies. V. Rustov in *Krasnaia zvezda*, 24 March 1982, p. 2, calls the influence of "zionist circles" in Washington "predominant" in forming U.S. policy.

44. A.A. Kokoshin, *SShA: za fasadom global'noi politiki (vnutrennie faktory formirovaniia vneshnei politiki amerikanskogo imperializma na poroge 80-x godov* (Moscow: Politizdat, 1981), pp. 271-279.

45. I. Zviagel'skaia, "Armiia Izrailia v obshchestvenno-politicheskoi i ekonomicheskoi strukture," *Aziia i afrika segodnia* 3 (1978):16-20; and Amnon Kapeliouk, "Israël: un pays possédé par son armée," *Le Monde diplomatique* (April 1982):22.

46. *Prospects for Soviet Oil Production* ER-1977 10270 (Washington, D.C.: Central Intelligence Agency, 1977).

47. For balanced views of the problem see *Energy in Soviet Policy* (Joint Economic Committee, U.S. Congress) (Washington, D.C.: U.S. Government Printing Office, 1981); and Leslie Dienes, "An Energy Crunch Ahead in the Soviet Union?," in Morris Bornstein, ed., *The Soviet Economy: Continuity and Change* (Boulder: Westview Press, 1981), pp. 313-349.

48. For an argument to this effect see Dennis Ross, "Considering Soviet Threats to the Persian Gulf," *International Security* (Fall 1981):169.

49. R.N. Andreasian, "OPEK: razvitie, problemy, perspektivy," *Aziia i afrika segodnia* 10 (1978):10.

50. R.N. Andreasian and A.D. Kazinkov, *OPEK v mire nefti* (Moscow: Nauka, 1978) provides a definitive Soviet evaluation.

51. E.V. Bugrov, *SShA: neftianye kontserny i gosudarstvo* (Moscow: 1978); R. Boronov, "Amerikanskie monopolii i blizhnevostochnaia neft'," *Aziia i afrika segodnia* 4 (1978):7-8; R. Andreasian, "Neftianye monopolii— orudie neokolonializma," *Mezhdunarodnaia zhizn'* 10 (1982):50-58; and Kokoshin, *SShA: za fasadom global'noi politiki,* pp. 92-104.

52. Dina R. Spechler and Martin C. Spechler, "The Soviet Union and the Oil Weapon: Benefits and Dilemmas," in Yaacov Ro'i, ed., *The Limits to Power: Soviet Policy in the Middle East* (New York: St. Martin's Press, 1979), pp. 96-123.

53. D. Zverskii, "Neftedollary i AVAKS," *Novoe vremia*, 4 September 1981, pp. 24-26; and R. Andreasian, "'Neftianoe protsvetanie' i kapital-isticheskaia transformatsiia arabiiskikh monarkhii," *Aziia i afrika segodnia* 1 (1979):10-14. See also the account of the May 1982 summit, R. Andreasian, "OPEK: ekzamen vyderzhan," *Novoe vremia*, 28 May 1982, p. 15. The author clearly acknowledges OPEC's dilemmas despite an attempt to maintain an optimistic tone.

54. The emphasis is confirmed on the basis of the decisions of the Twenty-sixth Party Congress in N. Orlov, "Problemy razvitiia vneshnei torgovli v svete reshenii XXVIs"ezda KPSS," *Vneshniaia torgovlia* 9 (1981): 8. For a more general discussion see V.A. Mal'kevich, *Vostok-Zapad: Ekonomicheskoe sotrudnichestvo. Tekhnologicheskii obmen* (Moscow: Obshchestvennye nauki i sovremenost', 1981). For attempts to describe the structural causes of the Soviet search for integration see Timothy W. Luke and Carl Boggs, "Soviet Subimperialism and the Crisis of Bureaucratic Centralism," *Studies in Comparative Communism* (Spring/Summer 1982): 95-124; and Ursula Schmiederer, *Die Aussenpolitik der Sowjet-Union* (Stuttgart: W. Kohlhammer, 1980).

55. See Andrew J. Pierre, *The Global Politics of Arms Sales* (Princeton: Princeton University Press, 1982) passim, and especially pp. 73-78, on the importance to Moscow of hard currency derived from arms transfers.

56. See Adrienne Armstrong, "The Political Consequences of Economic Dependence," *The Journal of Conflict Resolution* (September 1981):422.

57. The excellent study by Elizabeth Kridl Valkenier, "Development Issues in Recent Soviet Scholarship," *World Politics* (July 1980):485-508, is especially to be recommended on this point.

58. "Soviet Trade Dependence Cited in the New U.S. Study," *Wireless Bulletin from Washington* no. 130, 13 July 1982, pp. 13-14.

59. Lawrence J. Brainard, "Foreign Economic Constraints on Soviet Economic Policy in the 1980s," in Bornstein, ed., *The Soviet Economy*, p. 227, defines a "basic thrust of Soviet economic development towards the east."

60. Arthur Jay Klinghoffer, *Soviet Oil Politics in the Middle East and Soviet-American Relations* (Tel Aviv: Russian and East European Research Center, 1976), pp. 23-26.

61. Chris Kutschera, "L'étoile rouge pâlit-elle à Aden?," *Le Monde diplomatique* (October 1982):22-23.

62. Robert M. Cutler, "The Formation of Soviet Foreign Policy: Organizational and Cognitive Perspectives," *World Politics* (April 1982): 418-436, enthusiastically summarizes work in this area.

63. Richard Ned Lebow, *Between Peace and War: The Nature of International Crisis* (Baltimore: Johns Hopkins University Press, 1981) is particularly good on the role of crisis in international politics. See also Hannes Adomeit, *Soviet Risk-Taking and Crisis Behavior: A Theoretical and Empirical Analysis* (London: Allen and Unwin, 1982).

64. Karen Dawisha, "Soviet Decision-Making in the Middle East: The 1973 October War and the 1980 Gulf War," *International Affairs* (Winter 1980-1981):43-59, attempts to examine the anatomy of Soviet crisis diplomacy in the Middle East.

65. The best example of work of this type is Ilana Kass, *Soviet Involvement in the Middle East: Policy Formulation, 1966-1973* (Boulder: Westview Press, 1978). For an even more rigorous (though not necessarily more satisfying) attempt to interpret systematically Soviet press commentary see William Zimmerman and Robert Axelrod, "The 'Lessons' of Vietnam and Soviet Foreign Policy," *World Politics* (October 1981):1-24.

66. Ilana Dimant-Kass, "The Soviet Military and Soviet Policy in the Middle East 1970-73," *Soviet Studies* 4 (1974):502-521. Some remarkably candid commentary has also appeared in the Soviet military press concerning the difficulties encountered by Soviet occupation forces in Afghanistan. See "My—internatsionalisty," *Krasnaia zvezda*, 23 February 1981; and *Krasnaia zvezda*, 8 November 1982.

67. O. Fomin, "Edinstvo Arabov i blizhnevostochnoe uregulirovanie," *Mezhdunarodnaia zhizn'* 5 (1981):30-39.

68. For elaboration of the *socialist-orientation* concept see A.V. Kirov, *Strany sotsialisticheskoi orientatsii. Osnovnye tendentsii razvitiia* (Moscow: Nauka, 1978); and E. Primakov, "Strany sotsialisticheskoi orientatsii:

trudnyi no real'nyi perekhod k sotsializmu," *Mirovaia ekonomika i mezhdunarodnye otnosheniia* 7 (1981):3-16.

69. Soviet descriptions of the Iranian revolution have been broadly supportive. See the somewhat contrasting accounts by P. Demchenko in *Izvestiia*, 11 February 1982, and *Pravda*, 9 March 1982. See also P. Demchenko, "Iran: stanovlenie respubliki," *Kommunist* 9 (June 1979):110-116.

70. For examples of Soviet initiatives toward the Saudis see Igor Beliaev, "Saudovskaia Araviia: shto zhe dal'she?," *Literaturnaia gazeta*, 31 January 1979, p. 14; and A. Vasil'ev, "Saudovskaia Araviia mezhdu arkhaizmom i sovremennost'iu," *Aziia i afrika segodnia* (8 and 9/1980): 19-26, and 17-21.

71. See L. Andreev, "Blizhnevostochnaia politika Kitaia," *Mezhdunarodnaia zhizn'* 9 (1980):49-58; and L. Dadiani, "Blizhnevostochnaia politika Pekina," *Mezhdunarodnaia zhizn'* 4 (1978):53-63. For accounts of China's initiatives in the region see Hashim S.H. Behbehani, *China's Foreign Policy in the Arab World, 1955-1975: Three Case Studies* (London: Kegan Paul, 1981); Yitzhak Shichor, *The Middle East in China's Foreign Policy 1949-1977* (Cambridge: Cambridge University Press, 1979); and Bettie M. Smolansky and Oles M. Smolansky, "The Sino-Soviet Interaction in the Middle East," in Herbert J. Ellison, ed., *The Sino-Soviet Conflict: A Global Perspective* (Seattle: University Press, 1982), pp. 240-267.

72. Yaacov Vertzberger, "Afghanistan in China's Policy," *Problems of Communism* (May/June 1982):1-23.

73. Serge Schmemann, "Brezhnev Spells Out a Six-Point Proposal for Peace in the Mideast," *International Herald Tribune*, 16 September 1982, p. 2.

74. "Bonn's Soviet Gas Deal: A Pipeline or Pipedream?," *Business Week*, 13 July 1981, p. 42.

75. Robert W. Tucker, "Lebanon: The Case for the War," *Commentary* (October 1982):19-30, poses this argument lucidly.

76. An evaluation of the impact of the October War upon Soviet involvement in the Middle East that presents this interpretation is Ro'i, ed., *Limits to Power*. The perception of Soviet policy as frustrated and powerless during the war in Lebanon has been widespread and bipartisan. The daily organ of the Italian Communist Party reflected a consensus by editorializing "never has their [the Soviets'] presence in the region appeared so tenuous." Giuseppe Boffa, "Quel che Israele cerca a Beirut," *L'Unità*, 14 August 1982, p. 1.

77. For statements reflecting Soviet priorities by Nur al-Din Kiyanuri, the leader of the Tudeh Party, see Nureddin Kiianuri, "Narodnaia revoliutsiia v Irane," *Kommunist* 5 (March 1980):79-89; and Nureddin Kiianuri, "Iranskaia revoliutsiia: ee druz'ia i vragi," *Problemy mira i sotsializma* 11 (1981):32-36.

78. Francis Fukuyama, "New Directions for Soviet Middle East Policy in the 1980s: Implications for the Atlantic Alliance," in Steven L. Spiegel, ed., *The Middle East and the Western Alliance* (London: Allen and Unwin, 1982), pp. 129-144. Zbigniew Brzezinski has also used the term *Finlandization* to describe Soviet goals in the region. *Business Week*, 4 February 1980, p. 46.

79. Shahram Chubin, "Gains for Soviet Policy in the Middle East," *International Security* (Spring 1982):122-152 develops ideas similar to those outlined above.

80. The concept is favored by Robert Freedman. See Robert O. Freedman, *Soviet Policy Toward the Middle East Since 1970* 3rd ed. (New York: Praeger, 1982), and his article in this book.

81. Halliday, *Soviet Policy in the Arc of Crisis*, convincingly demonstrates the regional sources of many of the problems the Soviet Union has been accused of abetting.

82. Fouad Ajami, *The Arab Predicament: Arab Political Thought and Practice since 1967* (Cambridge: Cambridge University Press, 1981), p. 21.

83. Malcolm Toon, "Deal Moscow in on the Middle East?," *International Herald Tribune* 2 August 1982, p. 4; and W.W. Rostow, "Clipping Mideast Fuses," *International Herald Tribune*, 4 October 1982, p. 6.

84. "Peace and Security in the Middle East," *U.S. Department of State Current Policy Bulletin* no. 395 (Washington, D.C.: Bureau of Public Affairs, 26 May 1982).

4

The Soviet Reaction to the Reagan Middle East Policy: From the Inauguration to the Arab Summit at Fez

Robert O. Freedman

When the Reagan administration came to power, the most salient aspect of its foreign-policy approach was a very strong anti-Sovietism, and nowhere was this foreign-policy orientation more apparent than in the Middle East. Indeed, during virtually all of 1981, the primary goal of U.S. Middle Eastern policy appeared to be the construction of an anti-Soviet bloc of Middle Eastern states. As might be expected, Moscow strongly opposed Reagan's policies. But, to better understand the nature of the Soviet reaction to the new U.S. administration's Middle Eastern strategy, it is first necessary to deal with the problem of defining Soviet goals in the region and analyzing the strategy and tactics Moscow uses in quest of its goals. Observers of Soviet policy in this oil-rich and strategically located region are generally divided into two schools of thought on the question of Soviet goals in the Middle East.[1] While both agree that the Soviet Union wants to be considered a major factor in Middle Eastern affairs, if only because of the USSR's propinquity to the region, they differ on the ultimate Soviet goal in the Middle East. One school of thought sees Soviet Middle Eastern policy as being primarily defensive in nature; that is, as directed toward preventing the region from being used as a base for military attack or political subversion against the USSR. The other school of thought sees Soviet policy as primarily offensive in nature, as aimed at the limitation and ultimate exclusion of Western influence from the region and its replacement by Soviet influence. It is my opinion that Soviet goals in the Middle East, at least since the mid-1960s, have been primarily offensive in nature; and in the Arab segment of the Middle East, the Soviet Union appears to have been engaged in a zero-sum game competition for influence with the United States.[2] A brief discussion of the tactics and overall strategy employed by Moscow in its quest for Middle Eastern influence will serve as a background for the subsequent analysis of Soviet policy since the Reagan administration took office.

In its efforts to weaken and ultimately eliminate Western influence from the Middle East, and particularly from the Arab world, while promoting Soviet influence, the Soviet leadership has employed a number of tactics.

First and foremost has been the supply of military aid to its regional clients.[3] Next in importance comes economic aid; the Aswan Dam in Egypt and the Euphrates Dam in Syria are prominent examples of Soviet economic assistance, although each project has had serious problems. In recent years Moscow has also sought to solidify its influence through the conclusion of long-term Friendship and Cooperation treaties such as the ones concluded with Egypt (1971), Iraq (1972), Somalia (1974), Ethiopia (1978), Afghanistan (1978), the People's Democratic Republic of Yemen (South Yemen) (1979), and Syria (1980)—although the repudiation of the treaties by Egypt (1976) and Somalia (1977) indicate that this tactic has not always been successful. Moscow also has attempted to exploit both the lingering memories of Western colonialism and also Western threats against Arab oil producers.[4] In addition, the USSR has offered the Arabs diplomatic support at such international forums as the United Nations and the Geneva conference on an Arab-Israeli peace settlement. Moscow has also given aid to such countries as Ethiopia and South Yemen in establishing governmental and secret-police organizations. Finally, the Soviet Union has offered the Arabs aid of both a military and diplomatic nature against Israel, although that aid has been limited in scope because Moscow continues to support Israel's right to exist—both for fear of unduly alienating the United States with whom the Russians desire additional SALT agreements and improved trade relations and because Israel serves as a convenient rallying point for potentially anti-Western forces in the Arab world.[5]

While the USSR has used all these tactics, to a greater or lesser degree of success over the last two decades, it has also run into serious problems in its quest for influence in the Middle East. The numerous inter-Arab and regional conflicts (Syria-Iraq; North Yemen-South Yemen; Ethiopia-Somalia; Algeria-Morocco; Iran-Iraq, and so forth) often have meant that when the USSR has favored one party, it has alienated the other, occasionally driving it over to the West. Secondly, the existence of Arab Communist parties has proven to be a handicap for the Russians, as Communist activities have, on occasion, caused a sharp deterioration in relations between the USSR and the country in which the Arab Communist party has operated.[6] The Communist-supported coup d'etat in the Sudan in 1971, and Communist efforts to organize cells in the Iraqi army in the mid- and late-1970s are recent examples of this problem. Third, the wealth that flowed to the Arab world (or at least to its major oil producers) since the quadrupling of oil prices in late 1973 has enabled the Arabs to buy quality technology from the West and Japan, and this has helped weaken the economic bond between the USSR and a number of Arab states such as Iraq and Syria. Fourth, since 1967 and particularly since the 1973 Arab-Israeli war, Islam has been resurgent throughout the Arab world, and the USSR, identified in the Arab world with atheism, has been hampered as a result.[7]

Finally, the United States—and to a lesser extent France and China—has actively opposed Soviet efforts to achieve predominant influence in the region and this has frequently enabled Middle Eastern states to play the extraregional powers off against each other.

Given the problems that the USSR has faced, Moscow has adopted one overall strategy to seek to maximize its influence while weakening that of the West. The strategy has been to try to unite the Arab states (irrespective of their mutual conflicts) together with Arab political organizations, such as the Arab Communist parties and the Palestine Liberation Organization (PLO), into a large "anti-imperialist" Arab front directed against what the USSR has termed the linchpin of Western imperialism—Israel—and its Western supporters. Given the heterogeneous composition of the anti-imperialist front it has sought to create, the USSR has only had mixed results in pursuing this strategy. On the one hand, it appeared to bear fruit during the 1973 Arab-Israeli war when virtually the entire Arab world united against Israel and placed an oil embargo against the United States, while also reducing oil shipments to the Western European allies of the United States, an action that caused considerable disarray in NATO. On the other hand, however, in the aftermath of the war, the astute diplomacy of Henry Kissinger and policy changes by Egyptian President Anwar al-Sadat led to a splintering of this anti-imperialist Arab unity. The U.S.-sponsored Camp David accords and the subsequent Egyptian-Israeli peace treaty of March 1979 seemed to once again hold out the possibility of the creation of this anti-imperialist front of Arab states (albeit without Egypt) as virtually the entire Arab world joined to condemn Egypt. Unfortunately for Moscow, however, this period of anti-Egyptian (and anti-Israeli) Arab unity was to be a brief one as a renewal of the conflict between Iraq and Syria in July 1979; the Soviet invasion of Afghanistan in December 1979; and the Iran-Iraq war that began in September 1980 all served to seriously divide the Arabs.[8] Indeed, by January 1981, the Arab world was very badly split and this was to be only one of the problems facing Moscow in its quest for Middle East influence at the time when the Reagan administration took office.

The Soviet Position in the Middle East in January 1981

In surveying their Middle Eastern position at the time that the Reagan administration took office, the Soviet leaders may well have felt that their position was a mixed one. In the first place, despite the division in the Arab world, Sadat remained isolated because of Camp David—which no other Arab state had endorsed. In addition, Moscow had close relations with the so-called Front of Steadfastness and Confrontation (Syria, Libya, Algeria, South Yemen, and the PLO) who were the most vocal of the anti-Sadat nations in the Arab world and who dutifully echoed the Soviet policy line on such issues as Afghanistan in return for Soviet military aid and diplomatic support (Algeria was a partial exception to this pattern). In addition, Moscow had good relations with non-Arab and non-Muslim Ethiopia, a key African, as well as Middle Eastern state, although at the cost of alienating Somalia, which had gone over to the United States and had granted the United States port facilities as well as a base for the U.S. Rapid Deployment Force. While benefiting from its increasingly close ties to Ethiopia and the Steadfastness Front, Moscow also faced a number of problems. In the first place, while the Steadfastness Front Arab states and Ethiopia were willing to overlook the Soviet invasion of Afghanistan, both Iran and the centrist, or so-called moderate Arab states (Saudi Arabia, Kuwait, Jordan, the United Arab Emirates, North Yemen, Somalia, Bahrain, Qatar, the Sudan, Morocco, and Tunisia) denounced the Soviet action. And, Soviet efforts to demonstrate its fidelity to the Moslem cause by championing Iran in its conflict with the United States over the hostages and by diverting Moslem attention from the situation in Afghanistan to the Arab-Israeli conflict were not notably successful.[9]

An even more serious problem for Moscow lay in the Iran-Iraq war, which put the Soviet Union in a very difficult position since a good argument could have been made in the Kremlin for favoring either side. On the one hand, Moscow was linked to Baghdad by a Treaty of Friendship and Cooperation and had long been Iraq's main supplier of military weaponry. In addition, Iraq had been a leading foe of the U.S.-sponsored Camp David agreements and, as a nation with pretentions to leadership in the Arab world, could one day become the focus of the anti-imperialist Arab unity that Moscow had sought for so long. Indeed, by its leadership at the two anti-Camp David Baghdad Conferences, Iraq demonstrated a potential for just such a role,[10] and the growing relationship between Iraq and Saudi Arabia that was in evidence before the Iran-Iraq war erupted may have been seen by Moscow as a development that would further move the Saudis out of the U.S. camp. Yet another argument that could have been made in the Kremlin for aiding Iraq was the fact that such aid would be a demonstration to the Arab world that Moscow was indeed a reliable ally (some Arab states had questioned this, despite Soviet aid to the Arab cause in the 1973 war). From the point of view of the Soviet economy, aid to Iraq would help assure the continued flow of Iraqi oil to the USSR and its East European allies.

Soviet opponents of aid to Iraq could point to the continued persecution of Iraqi Communists[11] and Iraq's clear move away from the USSR since the treaty was signed in 1972, as typified by its condemnation of Moscow because of its invasion of Afghanistan; its February 1980 Pan-Arab Charter that called for the elimination of both superpowers from the Arab world,[12] and the growth of its economic and even military ties with France and other West European nations.[13] On balance, however, since the Russians see Iraq as objectively a major anti-Western force, a very good argument could have been made to aid the Iraqis in the war. On the other hand, however, a very good case could also have been made for aiding Iran. First and foremost, the Khumayni revolution detached Iran from its close alignment with the United States, thereby striking a major blow to the U.S. position in both the Persian Gulf and the Middle East as a whole. In addition, by holding on to the American hostages, the Khumayni regime carried on a daily humiliation of the United States, a factor that lowered U.S. prestige in the region. Consequently, any major Soviet aid effort to Iraq contained the possibility of ending the hostage impasse and even moving Iran back toward the U.S. camp because of Iran's dependence on U.S. military equipment. Given Iran's large population (three times that of Iraq) and its strategic position along the Persian Gulf and at the Strait of Hormuz, such a development clearly would not be in Moscow's interest. Another strategic factor that the Soviet leadership had to take into consideration was that Iran, unlike Iraq, had a common border with the USSR, as well as with Soviet-occupied Afghanistan. While Iranian efforts on behalf of the Afghan rebels had so far been limited, one could not rule out a major increase in Iranian aid to the Afghan rebels should Moscow side with Iraq, as well as a more pronounced effort on the part of Khumayni to infect the USSR's own Moslems with his brand of Islamic fundamentalism.[14] Finally, as in the case of Iraq, there was an important economic argument. While Iran had cut off gas exports to the USSR, the signing of a major transit agreement between the two countries just before the war erupted[15] may well have seemed to Moscow as the first step toward the resumption of natural-gas exports. Given Iran's large available reserves of this fuel, Moscow may have wished to encourage the supply relationship, as Iranian natural gas was helpful in maintaining the Soviet Union's energy balance, particularly in Transcaucasia.

Soviet opponents of aid to Iran could have pointed to the Islamic fundamentalists' treatment of the Communist Tudeh party, although it was not as brutal as Iraq's treatment of its Communists, as well as its treatment of Iranian minorities with whom the USSR hoped to cultivate a good relationship. Here again, however, Iran's treatment of its Kurds seemed no worse than Iraq's. Finally, opponents of aid to Iran could have pointed to Iran's leading anti-Soviet role in Islamic conferences, although again there may not have been too much to choose between Iran's and Iraq's anti-Sovietism. The main factor in the Soviet evaluation of both countries was that they seemed far more anti-American than anti-Soviet, and both contributed to the weakening of the U.S. position in the Middle East. For this reason, Moscow needed a good relationship with both and could not afford to alienate either.

Given this situation, it is not surprising that Moscow remained neutral while urging a speedy settlement of the war "lest the imperialist benefit." Indeed, the outbreak and prolongation of the war brought with it a number of rather serious problems for Moscow. In the first place, there was a major split in the anti-Sadat forces in the Arab world, as Libya and Syria came out for Iran while Jordan openly backed Iraq. In addition to Iraq breaking diplomatic relations with Syria and Libya, Saudi Arabia broke diplomatic relations with Libya, although the Saudis did not associate themselves with Iraq formally. The end result of the war therefore was a further disruption of the "anti-imperialist" Arab unity that Moscow had wanted for so long, a split that was underscored when the Steadfastness Front Arab states led by Syria boycotted the Arab summit in Jordan at the end of November 1980. Indeed, as *New Times* commentator Aleksandr Usvatov lamented:

> Fought between two non-aligned countries pursuing anti-imperialist policies, the war is bound to weaken them in the face of intensified imperialist scheming, and sows divisions and disarray in the world's anti-imperialist front, creating a serious threat to peace and international security.[16]

Compounding this problem still further was the Syrian military build-up along the Jordanian border at the end of November 1980, an event that caused King Husayn to postpone further his long-planned trip to the USSR. Indeed, given Husayn's statement that the USSR was behind Syria's military pressure against Jordan, Moscow may well have feared that the Syrian action might push Jordan back to the United States and that the Hashemite Kingdom might embrace Camp David as a result.[17]

In addition to the split in the anti-Sadat front, Moscow feared another major U.S. gain in the conflict. The emplacement of U.S. AWACS aircraft and ground-radar personnel in Saudi Arabia, which resulted from Iranian threats against the Saudis, seemed to demonstrate U.S. willingness to help defend Saudi Arabia and other Arab states in time of need—a development that made the U.S. military build-up in the Indian Ocean more acceptable diplomatically, therefore refuting Moscow's charge that the U.S. build-up was a threat to the Arab world. Indeed, the AWACS move appeared to reverse the decline in Saudi-U.S. relations and held out the possibility of a further improvement in relations, and Moscow became concerned that Saudi Arabia might also be enticed to support the Camp David process.[18]

A related problem for the USSR was the formation of the Gulf Cooperation Council, an organization composed of Saudi Arabia, the United Arab Emirates, Oman, Bahrain, Qatar, and Kuwait. Precipitated both by the Soviet invasion of Afghanistan and the Iran-Iraq war, the organization was composed of conservative and basically pro-Western monarchies, three of whose members (Oman, Saudi Arabia, and Bahrain) had military ties to the United States while only one, Kuwait, had diplomatic relations with the

Soviet Union. As the organization took shape,[19] Moscow feared that it would provide both a military and political backdrop for increased U.S. activity in the Persian Gulf, especially since Oman had already agreed to provide a base for the U.S. Rapid Deployment Force (RDF).

Yet another problem for the USSR resulting from the Iran-Iraq war lay in the fact that as Iraq and Iran continued to bomb each other's oil installations, Moscow became worried that, once the war was over, both countries might turn to the United States and Western Europe for aid in reconstruction.[20]

As the war continued, Moscow appeared to be able to do little but urge its immediate end, proclaim Soviet neutrality, and warn both Iran and Iraq, along with other countries of the Middle East, that the United States was exploiting the war for its own benefit. The Soviet media also highlighted U.S. efforts to create an international armada to patrol the Persian Gulf and emphasized the threat to the region posed by the visit of General David Jones, chairman of the U.S. Joint Chiefs of Staff, to Oman, Egypt, Saudi Arabia, and Israel.[21] In addition to denouncing U.S. efforts to exploit the war, Moscow seemed to try to maintain some ties with both belligerents by allowing a limited amount of Soviet weaponry to be transhipped to both Iran and Iraq, although the USSR publicly denied any such shipments.[22]

Nonetheless, the outbreak and continuation of the war seemed to cause a mounting frustration in Moscow that not only was unable to effect an end to the conflict but also saw a major strengthening of the Middle Eastern position of the United States—and a concomitant weakening of the Soviet position—in the zero-sum game view of the Middle East held by Moscow.

Indeed, just as Reagan's inauguration was taking place, the American hostages were being released from Iranian custody, thanks in part to the aid of Steadfastness Front member Algeria, which played an important mediating role—despite a major Soviet propaganda effort that tried to convince the Iranians that the United States was using the hostage negotiations as a cover for a military attack on Iran.[23] Thus, as Reagan took office, Moscow had to be concerned about a number of negative trends in the Middle East including a possible reconciliation between Iran and the United States, the increasing diplomatic acceptability of the US military forces in the Persian Gulf, a very severe split in the anti-Sadat grouping of Arab states, and the possibility that centrist Arab states like Jordan and Saudi Arabia might yet be drawn into the U.S.-sponsored Camp David peace process.

Moscow Reacts

By the time the CPSU convened its Twenty-sixth Congress on 23 February 1981, the outline of the Reagan administration's Middle East policy was already clear. The United States was seeking to build an anti-Soviet alliance of Middle East states, irrespective of their mutual conflicts, thereby pursuing a policy that was the mirror image of Soviet efforts to build an anti-imperialist bloc in the region. In his speech to the CPSU Congress, Brezhnev outlined the thrust of the Soviet response to the Reagan policy and to the negative trends in the Middle East that had hampered Moscow in its quest for influence in the region.[24] In the first place, to counterbalance the growing military power of the United States in the Persian Gulf and Indian Ocean region, and the growing diplomatic acceptability of that presence because of both the Soviet invasion of Afghanistan and the Iran-Iraq war, the Soviet leader reiterated his call, first made in India in mid-December 1980,[25] for an international agreement to neutralize the Persian Gulf. The Soviet leader also offered—for the first time—to combine discussions of the Afghanistan situation with that of the Persian Gulf, although he made it clear that Afghanistan's internal situation (that is, its Communist government) was not a matter for discussion and that the USSR would not withdraw its forces from Afghanistan until the "infiltration of counter-revolutionary bands" was completely stopped and treaties were signed between Afghanistan and its neighbors to ensure that no further infiltration would take place.

As far as the Iran-Iraq war was concerned, the Soviet leader once again called for its immediate termination and stated that the Soviet Union was taking so-called practical steps to achieve that goal. In discussing the Arab-Israeli conflict Brezhnev denounced the Camp David peace process and again enumerated the tripartite Soviet solution for the conflict: (1) Israeli withdrawal from all territories captured in 1967; (2) the right of the Palestinians to create their own state; and (3) the ensuring of the security of all states in the region, including Israel. Brezhnev also repeated the Soviet call for an international conference on the Arab-Israeli conflict, with the participation of the Arabs, including the PLO, and Israel, along with the United States and some European states. All in all, the Soviet proposals on Afghanistan, the Persian Gulf, and the Arab-Israeli conflict, together with the announced efforts to end the Iraq-Iran war, seemed aimed at placing Moscow at the center stage of Middle Eastern diplomacy, a diplomatic position not enjoyed by the Soviet Union since the 1973 Arab-Israeli war.

Interestingly enough, the Soviet leader also made note in his speech of two related Middle Eastern phenomena to which the USSR was having difficulty in adjusting its policies: the Khumayni revolution in Iran and the rise of fundamentalist Islam. As far as Iran was concerned, Brezhnev noted that "despite its complex and contradictory nature, it is basically an anti-imperialist revolution, although domestic and foreign reaction is seeking to alter this character." Brezhnev also offered Soviet cooperation with Iran (no mention was made of Soviet-Iraqi relations in his speech), but only on the grounds of "reciprocity," perhaps a reference to continuing anti-Soviet speeches and activities in Iran including the seizure of the Soviet embassy in Tehran (on the anniversary of the Afghan invasion), an action that was both tolerated and justified by the Iranian leadership.[26] In discussing Islam, Brezhnev acknowledged that "the liberation struggle could develop under the banner of Islam," but also noted that "experience also indicates that reaction uses Islamic slogans to start counterrevolutionary insurrections."

In the aftermath of the Twenty-sixth Party Congress, Moscow pursued two diplomatic policies. In the first place it sought to strengthen its ties with two of its Steadfastness Front allies—Libya and Algeria—with whom there had been some recent difficulties. Secondly, Moscow sought to cultivate two centrist Arab states, Kuwait and Jordan, to prevent them from moving toward the United States.

Libyan leader Mu'ammar al-Qadhdhafi arrived in Moscow on April 27 at a time when he was isolated in the Arab world (the alliance with Syria, signed in September 1970 was inoperative)[27] and was also in difficulty with many of his African neighbors because of the Libyan intervention in Chad. Moscow appeared rather ambivalent about Libya's efforts at unity with Chad, in part because of its negative effects on other African states (especially the Sudan and Nigeria) while Qadhdhafi's ideological pretensions also continued to bother the Soviet leadership. Nonetheless, Qadhdhafi's vehement anti-Americanism was, on balance, an asset for Soviet diplomacy, while his political isolation and increasing conflict with the United States (the United States was to close Libya's diplomatic mission in Washington a week after Qadhdhafi's visit to Moscow, in part because of Libya's role in supporting international terrorism) made Libya increasingly dependent on the USSR.[28] For his part, Qadhdhafi, who made no secret of his desire to destroy Israel, continually requested more Soviet aid than Moscow was willing to offer; and his request for more aid against Israel was made again during this visit to Moscow, his first since 1976.[29] Nonetheless, while the final communique—which referred to the talks as having taken place in "an atmosphere of broad mutual understanding" (code words for disagreement over several issues)—only praised the Steadfastness Front and, while in his welcoming speech, Brezhnev pointedly noted the differences—including ideological differences—between the USSR and Libya, the USSR did go a long way toward legitimizing the Libyan role in Chad, as the final communique noted the "positive role that has been played by Libya's aid to Chad."[30] Moscow also denounced U.S. efforts to brand Libya as a terrorist state and supported the Libyan position in the dispute over the former Spanish Sahara, by endorsing the call for the right of self-determination for the Western Saharan people. While Moscow got Libya's support for the Soviet call to make the Persian Gulf and Indian Ocean areas what were termed zones of peace, Moscow evidently was unable to get Qadhdhafi's agreement for an international conference on the Arab-Israeli conflict, as there was no mention of the conference—long a major Soviet goal—in the final communique.

The second Steadfastness state leader to come to Moscow for talks with the Soviet leadership in 1981 was Algerian President Chadli Benjedid who came to the Kremlin on June 8. While the USSR and Algeria had maintained close ties since Algerian independence in 1962, the death of Houari Boumedienne in 1979 had raised questions about the future course of Algerian foreign policy. In addition, despite U.S. military aid to Morocco, the United States and Algeria had developed close economic ties (interestingly enough, despite Soviet military aid to Algeria, Morocco and the USSR had also developed close economic ties). Finally, Algeria's role in the freeing of the U.S. hostages in Iran could not have been to Moscow's liking, although the Algerians were to deem it a "debt of honor" in repayment of John F. Kennedy's support of their drive for independence.[31] Nonetheless, the onset of the Reagan administration was to cause a chilling of U.S.-Algerian ties. In the first place the United States began to step up its military aid to Morocco and stated that it would no longer link arms sales to Morocco with Moroccan progress in achieving a negotiated settlement of the Spanish Sahara conflict.[32] Secondly, the long negotiations between Algeria and El Paso Natural Gas on a major U.S.-Algerian natural-gas agreement fell through, leaving Algeria with an infrastructure expense of $2.5 billion for natural-gas wells, pipelines, and liquification plans.[33] Finally Reagan's general tough line toward the Third World on such issues as the Law of the Sea served to alienate the Algerians. Thus when Benjedid came to Moscow, Algerian-U.S. relations had cooled considerably and Moscow may have looked forward to a further consolidation of Soviet-Algerian relations.

Nonetheless, all was not complete harmony during Benjedid's visit, as evidenced by the joint communique's assertion that the talks had taken place in an atmosphere of "frankness," and, as in the case of Libya, there was no mention of Algerian support for Brezhnev's call for an international conference on the Middle East.[34] For its part, however, Moscow endorsed Algeria's position on the Sahara conflict as the communique noted that both sides agreed that the people of the Western Sahara had the right to self-determination, and both Algeria and the USSR condemned foreign bases in the Persian Gulf.[35] Moscow also used the Algerian leader's visit to call for the transformation of the Mediterranean into a zone of peace, a maneuver that, if successful, would have meant the ejection of the U.S. Sixth Fleet from the Mediterranean.[36]

In sum, it would appear that in the case of the visits of both Algerian President Chadli Benjedid and Libyan leader Mu'ammar al-Qadhdhafi, Moscow gave somewhat more in diplomatic support than it got in return. Nonetheless, at a time when the Middle East was in a great state of flux with many trends moving in a negative direction as far as the USSR was concerned, the Soviet leadership seemed willing to pay the diplomatic price to reinforce ties with both states. Interestingly enough, however, Moscow was to meet with greater diplomatic success during the visits of representatives of the centrist wing in Arab politics, Kuwait and Jordan.

Even before Shaykh Sabah al-Ahmad Al Sabah of Kuwait and King Husayn of Jordan visited Moscow, a number of the centrist Arabs seemed to be pulling back from the close tie with the United States that had been precipitated by the Iran-Iraq war.[37] Thus when the new U.S. Secretary of State Alexander Haig toured the Middle East in early April in an effort to rally support for the U.S. plan to create an anti-soviet alignment while putting the Arab-Israeli dispute on the diplomatic back burner, he met with little success as two of the Arab states he visited, Jordan and Saudi Arabia, indicated that they were more concerned with what they perceived as the threat from Israel (Saudi Arabia said this explicitly) than the threat from the Soviet Union.[38] In addition, fighting had once again escalated in Lebanon and Haig took the opportunity to strongly condemn Syria for its "brutal" actions in that country, a move not calculated to drive a wedge between Damascus and Moscow. The lack of success of the Haig visit arrested the momentum of U.S. policy in the region and set the stage for some diplomatic successes by the Soviet Union during the visits of Shaykh Sabah and King Husayn.

Kuwait, whose Deputy Premier Shaykh Sabah visited Moscow on April 23, was a key target of Soviet diplomacy. As the only state in the Gulf Cooperation Council (GCC) with diplomatic relations with Moscow, it was also the most nonaligned and the Soviet leaders evidently hoped to use Kuwait's influence within the GCC (it is the second most important country after Saudi Arabia) to prevent that organization from committing itself too closely to the side of the United States. For its part Kuwait had been carefully cultivating a relationship with the USSR since 1975, the last time Shaykh Sabah had journeyed to Moscow. Then, as in April 1981, Kuwait's regional problems made it seek protection.[39] In 1975 Kuwait was confronted with territorial demands by Iraq; in 1981, while relations had improved with Iraq, a far more serious problem lay on its border with Iran whose war planes were occasionally bombing and strafing Kuwaiti territory because of Kuwaiti aid to the Iraqi war effort. Under these circumstances (and also under pressure from the powerful Palestinian community in Kuwait), the Kuwaitis evidently felt they needed support not only from the United States, whose ability to aid Kuwait was increasingly in doubt since the fall of the shah, but from the Soviet Union as well. And, the Kuwaiti deputy premier, who was also his country's foreign minister, went a long way toward meeting his hosts' diplomatic needs during his visit to Moscow.[40] Thus, not only did he denounce Camp David but he also came out in favor of an international conference on the Middle East, thereby supporting a cardinal Soviet goal, something neither Libya nor Algeria was willing to do. In addition he also announced Kuwait's opposition to the creation of foreign military bases in the Persian Gulf, thus supporting yet another central Soviet foreign-policy goal. Finally, he joined Moscow in calling for an international conference on the Indian Ocean aimed at turning it into a "zone of peace," thereby supporting another Soviet diplomatic ploy to eliminate the U.S. military presence from the region.[41]

To be sure, there were areas of disagreement during the talks in which *Pravda* reported a "detailed exchange of views on the situation in the Persian Gulf."[42] Probably the most important issue of disagreement was Afghanistan (Kuwait continued to oppose the Soviet presence in Afghanistan) of which no mention was made in the final communique. Nonetheless, on balance it was a most successful visit as far as Moscow was concerned since it was able to obtain Kuwaiti support for a number of major Soviet Middle East policies.

The visit of Jordan's King Husayn in late May could also be considered a diplomatic success for Moscow. The USSR had been seriously concerned that because of Syrian military pressure, Husayn might be pushed back into the U.S. camp and into support of Camp David (Jordan had distanced itself from the United States in 1978 because of Camp David). Perhaps heightening Soviet concern was the so-called Jordanian option that was being promoted by Israeli Labor party leader Shimon Peres. Until May, Peres's Labor party was leading all the Israeli public-opinion polls for the election scheduled for June 30 and Moscow may have seen a Peres victory as yet another enticement for Jordan to become involved in Camp David. For its part, however, since the 1978 Baghdad Conference, Jordan was very much a centrist Arab state and saw far more benefit in maintaining close ties with Iraq and Saudi Arabia (which subsidized a considerable portion of the Jordanian economy) than in joining Israel and Egypt in the highly ambiguous autonomy negotiations.[43] By 1981, the once-isolated Jordanian monarch was now part of the general Arab concensus against Camp David, although Jordan's bitter dispute with Syria continued to simmer. Indeed, the Syrian-Jordanian conflict was undoubtedly one of the topics of discussion between Brezhnev and Husayn, and *Pravda*'s reference to the talks having taken place in a "business-like atmosphere" may very well have referred to disagreements over Syria.[44] It is quite possible that Husayn may have asked the USSR to use its influence with Syria to ease its pressure against Jordan, in return for Jordanian willingness to endorse Moscow's views on a number of key Middle Eastern issues. First and foremost was the convening of an international conference on the Middle East. Both in his speech at the welcoming banquet[45] and in the final communique Husayn supported this Soviet goal, thereby also demonstrating his opposition to the Camp David process. In addition Husayn also joined Moscow in opposing foreign bases in the Persian Gulf, thus supporting another key Soviet goal. Given the fact that the Jordanian defense minister accompanied Husayn, the groundwork may have also been laid during this visit for the subsequent Soviet-Jordanian SAM arms deal, as the joint communique noted that the two sides had agreed to work on further increasing trade, economic, cultural, and other (that is, military-related) matters. All in all, Moscow was quite pleased by Husayn's visit.[46]

While Moscow had gained considerable diplomatic mileage from the visits of Jordan's King Husayn and Kuwait's Shaykh Sabah, the diplomatic shift by Sudanese President Ja'far al-Numayri ran counter to the Soviet goal of keeping Egypt isolated in the Arab world. Under pressure from Libyan forces in Chad (again, Moscow must have wondered if the Libyan move into Chad was of benefit to the USSR), Numayri decided to come out in support of Sadat's Camp David policy by restoring full diplomatic relations with Egypt at the end of March and urging the other Arabs to do so as well. Further angering Moscow was the Sudanese offer of military bases to the United States—if the United States would upgrade them first.[47]

Despite the Sudanese shift back toward Egypt, on balance Moscow's Middle Eastern diplomatic position had clearly improved by the spring of 1981, and the USSR was to try and exploit a series of Middle Eastern crises in the spring and summer to improve its position still further.

Moscow and the Middle East Crisis of 1981

The Syrian Missile Crisis

The first major crisis the USSR sought to exploit, albeit very carefully, was the crisis over the emplacement of Syrian antiaircraft missiles in Lebanon, a crisis that was also of considerable benefit to Syria.

At the outbreak of the April fighting in Lebanon, in which Syria attacked Phalangist positions in Beirut and near Zahlah, a Christian Lebanese city that lay astride a major Syrian communication route into Lebanon (the Phalange was seeking to consolidate a communications link between Zahlah and the Christian positions in northern Lebanon), Syria remained in a state of isolation in the Arab world, primarily because of its support for Iran in the Iran-Iraq war. In addition, because Saudi Arabia and Kuwait had cut off funds for the Syrian forces in Lebanon, Syria's economic position had weakened, a development exacerbated by the continuing domestic unrest in Syria. When Syrian attacks against the Christians near Zahlah escalated, Israel responded by shooting down two Syrian helicopters involved in the operation. Syria responded by moving surface-to-air missiles across the border into Lebanon opposite Zahlah, thus breaking the tacit agreement with Israel made in 1976 whereby Israel did not interfere with the Syrian invasion of Lebanon so long as no SAM missiles were moved into Lebanon and no Syrian forces were sent to south Lebanon. Israeli Prime Minister Menahem Begin responded by saying that if the missiles were not moved back into Syria, Israel would destroy them. The crisis was on.

While the exact nature of the Soviet role in the missile crisis is not yet known, several things do appear clear. In the first place, Syrian leader Hafiz al-Asad's decision to move the missiles seems to have caught the USSR by surprise (as in the November 1980 crisis with Jordan, Asad apparently took action without consulting Moscow—despite the Soviet-Syrian treaty)[48] and it was not until more than a week after the crisis began that Moscow made any public comment about it. Indeed, Moscow did not make any public comments about the crisis until after it became clear that other Arab countries, particularly such centrist states as Saudi Arabia and Kuwait, were rallying to Syria's side.[49] Such a development benefited the USSR by moving its clients out of isolation in the Arab world and held out the possibility of rebuilding the anti-imperialist Arab unity that Moscow continued to hope for. An additional benefit flowing to the Soviet Union from the missile crisis was that it served to further weaken the U.S. effort to build an anti-Soviet bloc of Arab states and further complicated relations between Saudi Arabia, which promised to aid Syria, and the United States, Israel's main supporter, at a time when relations had already become strained over Congressional opposition to the Airborne Warning and Control Systems (AWACS) sale to Saudi Arabia. Yet another benefit of the crisis for Soviet diplomacy, albeit a fleeting one, lay in the fact that in the initial stages of the conflict the United States sought Soviet assistance in defusing it,[50] thereby once again demonstrating the importance of the Soviet Union to Middle East peacemaking. Although the United States was not pleased by the subsequent lack of Soviet assistance during the crisis, Brezhnev was also to exploit it, and the visit of King Husayn to Moscow, to repeat Moscow's call for an international conference to solve the crisis.

While Moscow sought to exploit the missile crisis for its own benefit, once that crisis was underway, Moscow faced a number of dangers as well. First and foremost was the possibility that a full-scale war between Syria and Israel might erupt, into which Moscow could be drawn. For Moscow, this was not an opportune time for such a war. With Reagan now willing to allow grain sales to the USSR and considering the resumption of the stalled SALT talks (a key Soviet priority), any major Middle Eastern war in which Moscow got involved might well reinforce the basically anti-Soviet tendency of the Reagan administration, doom the SALT talks, and possibly reverse Reagan's decision on grain sales. While Moscow, as well as Damascus, would profit from the extension of the radar-SAM network to Lebanon

(Soviet radar on Lebanese mountain peaks would aid Moscow's air deployments in the eastern Mediterranean), it would be far better for Moscow if this could be done without war. So long as war threatened, but did not break out, the Arabs would rally around Syria, and attention would be focused on the Arab-Israeli conflict—and away from the continuing Soviet occupation of Afghanistan. In addition, Moscow may have feared that a Syrian-Israeli war would bring the collapse of the Syrian regime, one of Moscow's closest allies in the Arab world.[51]

A second problem facing Moscow lay in the fact that President Reagan had sent an experienced troubleshooter, Philip C. Habib, to the Middle East in early May to try to prevent war. While Moscow and Damascus utilized the respite granted by the Habib mission to strengthen the missile position in Lebanon (Israel was unlikely to strike a blow at the missiles with Habib in the Middle East lest U.S.-Israeli relations be severely damaged), the Soviet leadership had to be concerned that Habib, in his shuttle diplomacy, might succeed in drawing Damascus away from Moscow, much as Kissinger had done in 1974. For this reason Moscow bitterly attacked the Habib mission, claiming it was a device to impose Israel's will on Syria and the other Arabs.[52]

In the face of these dangers, Moscow adopted the dual policy of discrediting U.S. mediation efforts while also playing down the possibility of war. This strategy became evident in mid-May as the Soviet ambassador to Lebanon, Aleksandr Soldatov, on May 16, stated that the developments in Lebanon "are unrelated to the Soviet-Syrian treaty."[53] Soldatov's comments may well have been a response to the article that appeared several days earlier in the Syrian journal *al-Ba'th*, which stated that if Israel attacked the SAM batteries it would risk confronting not only Syria and its Arab supporters, but also "the strategic world of Syrian-Soviet Friendship and Cooperation."[54] Then *Pravda*, in a commentary by Soviet Middle East specialist Pavel Demchenko, on May 17, praised Syria as the main bastion of Arab forces opposed to Camp David and denounced Israel's demand for the removal of the Syrian missiles, which were there for "defensive" purposes, as a maneuver worked out by the United States and Israel. Brezhnev himself entered the Middle East commentary with a speech in Tbilisi on May 22 in which he warned of the dangerous situation in the region, blaming Israel and the United States, and also called for international talks to solve the crisis in a peaceful manner.[55] This was also the theme of his speech at a dinner honoring the visit of King Husayn on May 27 in which he noted that the USSR wanted good relations with Israel.[56] Significantly, in neither speech did he mention the Soviet-Syrian treaty.

As the crisis continued, Syria obtained increasing support for its position from the other Arabs, as an Arab foreign-ministers conference, called on the initiative of Algeria and the PLO in late May, pledged financial support to

Syria (Saudi Arabia and Kuwait, which had cut off funds for the Syrian forces in Lebanon, resumed their contributions), and the Arab states pledged "total" military assistance to Syria in case of an Israeli attack on Syrian forces in Lebanon or Syria.[57] Much to Moscow's satisfaction the Arab states also warned the United States that continuation of its "unconditional" support to Israel "would lead to a serious confrontation between the Arab nation and the U.S."[58] Soon after this meeting, however, both Jordan and Iraq qualified their support to Syria, while for its part Syria did not even send a delegation to the Baghdad meeting of Islamic foreign ministers called to deal with the Lebanese crisis at the start of June.

The Destruction of the Iraqi Nuclear Reactor

On June 9, however, the missile crisis seemed to pale in importance as another Middle Eastern crisis replaced it in the headlines.[59] On that date Israeli aircraft destroyed an Iraqi nuclear reactor, which the vast majority of Israelis feared was being constructed to develop a nuclear weapon for use against Israel. The Israeli action inflamed the Arab world far more than did the Syrian-Israeli confrontation over the Syrian missiles in Lebanon as many Arabs felt humiliated by the fact that the Israeli aircraft, which flew over Jordanian and Saudi airspace on the way to and from Iraq, were able to come and go unscathed while eliminating the most advanced nuclear installation of any Arab country. As might be expected Moscow moved quickly to try to exploit this situation, not only condemning the Israeli raid but also pointing to the fact that the Israeli action was carried out with U.S.-supplied aircraft and that it took place despite—or indeed because of—the U.S. AWACS radar planes operating in Saudi Arabia.[60] Reagan's decision to postpone shipment of additional F-16 fighter bombers to Israel because of the action was deprecated by Moscow, which sought to exploit the Israeli action by utilizing it to focus Arab attention on the *Israeli threat* to the Arab world (rather than the *Soviet threat*) and to undermine the U.S. position in the region as Israel's chief supporter, while at the same time improving Soviet-Iraqi relations. In addition, Moscow evidently hoped that the Israeli attack would help to rebuild the anti-imperialist Arab unity that had been so badly dissipated by the Iran-Iraq war. As a commentary by *Pravda* commentator Iurii Glukhov noted on June 16: "[The Israeli raid] has again demonstrated the extent of the imperialist and Zionist threat hanging over the Arab countries, forcing them to set aside their differences, which have become more pronounced of late."[61]

Moscow may have also seen the Israeli raid as undercutting Egyptian efforts to reenter the Arab mainstream, since it took place only four days after a Begin-Sadat summit. In addition to reestablishing full diplomatic relations with the Sudan, Egypt had sold Iraq thousands of tons of Soviet ammunition and spare parts to aid it in its war with Iran[62]—something noted with displeasure in Moscow, which was concerned about Sadat's lessening isolation.[63] Fortunately for Moscow, the Israeli raid did serve to abort any Iraqi-Egyptian rapprochement, despite Sadat's denunciation of the Israeli action.

Moscow, however, was to be less successful in its goal of exploiting the Israeli raid to undermine the U.S. position in the Arab world, and in particular to improve Soviet ties with Iraq. While there had been calls in the Arab world to embargo oil to the United States because of the raid, the Reagan administration's decision to join with Iraq in a UN Security Council vote condemning Israel seemed to deflate any such Arab pressures.[64] Indeed, the Iraqi-U.S. cooperation at the United Nations seemed to set the stage for improved Iraqi-U.S. relations, as Iraqi President Saddam Husayn, on the American Broadcasting Corporation (ABC) television program "Issues and Answers" stated his interest in expanding diplomatic contacts with the United States and announced that he would treat the head of the U.S. interests section in the Belgian Embassy in Baghdad as the head of a diplomatic mission.[65]

In taking this posture, the Iraqi leader appeared to be trying to drive a wedge between the United States and Israel, which was very unhappy with the U.S. vote in the United Nations. On the other hand, Moscow may have seen that the United States was seeking to drive a diplomatic wedge between the USSR and Iraq. In any case, Soviet-Iraqi relations had been declining for a number of years and they were not helped by Moscow's position of neutrality in the Iran-Iraq war. A further deterioration in Soviet-Iraqi relations came in February 1981 at the Twenty-sixth CPSU Congress (which the Iraqi Ba'thists had not attended) when the head of the Iraqi Communist party (ICP) Aziz Muhammad denounced the Iraqi government for its acts of repression against the ICP and the Iraqi Kurds. He also condemned the Iran-Iraqi war and demanded the immediate withdrawal of Iraqi troops from Iran.[66] As Soviet-Iraqi relations were deteriorating, the United States moved to improve relations with the regime in Baghdad. Secretary of State Haig noted the possibility of improved Iraqi-U.S. relations in testimony to the Senate Foreign Relations Committee in mid-March (Iraq was seen as concerned by "the behavior of Soviet imperialism in the Middle Eastern area")[67] and followed this up by sending Deputy Assistant Secretary of State Morris Draper to Iraq in early April.[68] To improve the climate for the visit, the United States approved the sale to Iraq of five Boeing jetliners.[69] While nothing specific came out of Draper's talks, Washington continued to hope that because of Iraq's close ties with Jordan and Saudi Arabia, the regime in Baghdad might abandon its quasi Steadfastness Front position and move toward a more centrist position in the Arab world on the issue of making peace with Israel. (Because of its conflict with Syria, Iraq refused to formally join the Steadfastness Front in 1977 when it was formed, but nonetheless had maintained a rejectionist policy toward peace with Israel.) Indeed, Saddam Husayn himself, in his ABC interview, gave some hints about just such a move. Nonetheless, the future direction of Iraqi policy remained to be determined, especially since as the Iran-Iraq war dragged on, the possibility existed that Iraq might have to turn back to Moscow to get sufficient arms to score a major victory. Indeed, a large shipment of Soviet tanks to Iraq in the late fall seemed to signal a Soviet desire to improve relations.[70]

The Bombing of Beirut

While the furor of the Israeli attack on the Iraqi reactor slowly died, Middle East tensions were kept alive by a number of other events during the summer, which Moscow sought to exploit. In the first place, following the reelection of Menahem Begin's Likud party, Israel launched a series of attacks against Palestinian positions in Lebanon. The fighting quickly escalated with the PLO shelling towns in northern Israel and the Israelis bombing PLO headquarters in Beirut, causing a number of civilian casualties in the process. While the United States condemned the bombing of Beirut and again delayed the shipment of F-16s to Israel—while at the same time sending Habib back to the Middle East to work out a ceasefire (something he accomplished in late July)—Moscow seized the opportunity to once again link the Israeli actions to the United States and called for sanctions against Israel.[71] The bombing of Beirut also served to further inflame Arab tempers both against Israel and against the United States (there were once again calls for an oil boycott of the United States and heavy criticism of U.S. support of Israel not only from the Steadfastness Front but also from such centrist states as Jordan and Kuwait.) All this activity, of course, served to further divert Arab attention from the continued Soviet occupation of Afghanistan while underlining the Soviet claim that it was U.S.-supported Israel, not the Soviet Union, that was the main threat to the Arab world.

The Libyan-U.S. Clash over the Gulf of Sidra

The fourth in the series of Middle East crises took place in mid-August, and for the first time it was the United States, not Israel, that was directly involved. A number of questions remain about this incident, which involved the shooting down of two Libyan interceptor aircraft (SU-22) that had initially

fired upon two U.S. aircraft protecting U.S. maneuvers in the Gulf of
Sidra, a region Qadhdhafi claimed as Libyan territorial waters but that the
United States (and most of the international community, including the
USSR) claimed was international waters.[72] In the first place, was the matter
merely an accident in which an overeager Libyan pilot decided to fire his
missiles (Libya had been challenging U.S. maneuvers in the Gulf of Sidra
for several years and there had already been a number of incidents) or was it
deliberately staged by Qadhdhafi? Secondly, was Moscow involved in the
planning of the event, or was it caught by surprise? As far as Libya's planning of the incident is concerned, there are two factors to consider. On the
one hand, Qadhdhafi was out of the country negotiating a treaty in South
Yemen at the time of the incident. On the other hand, however, there were a
number of coincidences that, when taken together, lead one to believe there
is a good possibility that Libya may indeed have planned the incident. In the
first place, Libya was striving to emerge from its position of isolation in the
Arab world and had restored diplomatic relations with Morocco, while also
seeking to mend fences with Iraq and Saudi Arabia. Qadhdhafi may well
have noted how Syria moved out of its position of isolation vis-à-vis the
mainstream Arabs by means of its confrontation with Israel over the
missiles in Lebanon. And since Israel did not border Libya, Qadhdhafi may
have wished to utilize a military confrontation with the United States—
whose reputation among centrist Arabs had suffered as a result of the
Israeli bombing of Beirut and the Iraqi reactor—for a similar purpose.
Secondly, since he was in the process of negotiating a tripartite alliance with
Ethiopia and South Yemen, he may have wished to use the incident to
demonstrate that the alliance was needed against "U.S. imperialism" and
was not directed at such Arab states as Saudi Arabia or North Yemen,
which otherwise might have been concerned about it. Third, an OPEC
meeting was beginning in Geneva, and Qadhdhafi may have wished to use
the incident as a backdrop for his demand for higher oil prices. Finally, with
a Soviet foreign-office delegation led by Aleksei Shvedov visiting the country, and under increasing pressure from the United States, Qadhdhafi may
have wished to utilize the incident as a justification for turning to Moscow
for a treaty of friendship and cooperation while ensuring that the United
States would not escalate its retaliation against Libya. (It remained to be
seen, of course, if Moscow would want to sign a treaty with such a mer-
curial Arab leader, yet if the USSR were to get base rights in return, the
possibility could not be excluded.)

Whether or not Libya actually planned the incident, it did not take long
for Moscow to try to exploit the battle over the Gulf of Sidra for its own
benefit. Based on the initial Soviet reaction to the Gulf battle, it appears as
if Moscow was caught by surprise. Nonetheless, after a day of reporting the
events without commentary, once Moscow appeared certain that there would

be no escalation, it began to try to show the Arabs that the incident demonstrated how dangerous it was for them to have a U.S. fleet operating off their shores. Thus in a political-commentary broadcast by TASS international service, Sergei Kulik set a tone for later Soviet treatment of the event:

> In commenting on the reports of the attacks by U.S. fighter planes on Libyan aircraft, many foreign observers agree that this dangerous incident has once again demonstrated the great threat which is created by the constant presence of American naval and air forces on the territories and waters belonging to other states thousands of kilometers away from the U.S. . . . off Africa's eastern coastline, in the Indian Ocean and the Persian Gulf, a whole armada of American vessels continues to parade while keeping the oil producing countries of the Near East in their sights.[73]

A French language broadcast to North Africa on August 26 made this point even more explicit:

> Until now, when Washington concentrated an armada of warships in the Mediterranean and the Persian Gulf, when it created a network of military bases in the vicinity of Arab countries, everybody understood it was a dangerous thing but not everybody, far from it, realized to what extent this was dangerous.
>
> The U.S. provocation in the Gulf of Sidra has made a great many people look at the American military presence in quite a different light.[74]

In addition to using the Gulf of Sidra incident to try to lessen the diplomatic acceptability of the U.S. military presence in the Persian Gulf, and also noting the highly negative Arab response to the role of the United States in the incident, Moscow also cited it as justification for the signing of the Tripartite Treaty by Ethiopia, Libya, and South Yemen. The USSR also praised the treaty as "an important stage in strengthening the national liberation movement's solidarity and in stepping up their struggle against imperialism and reaction and for peace and progress."[75]

Moscow also maintained, however (in an apparent effort to reassure Saudi Arabia and North Yemen) that the treaty was "not directed against any other country or people."[76] Nonetheless, the text of the Tripartite Treaty, which noted that one of its goals was the struggle against "reaction"—a commonly used term for the conservative Arab states of the Persian Gulf along with Egypt and the Sudan—may, in the long run, prove counterproductive to Soviet efforts to improve relations with the conservative Gulf states, given the close tie between the Tripartite Treaty nations and Moscow.[77]

The Upheavals in Iran

While Moscow was seeking to exploit the Libyan-U.S. clash in the Gulf of Sidra to weaken the U.S. position in the Middle East, it was trying to follow the same policy during the upheavals in Iran, which witnessed the ouster and escape to Europe of Iranian president Abulhasan Bani Sadr; the assassination of his successor Muhammad Ali Raja'i along with a number of key Iranian Islamic Republican Party leaders such as Ayatallah Muhammad Bahashti; and a series of additional bombings and other attacks directed against the fundamentalist Khumayni government by the opposition *Mujahhidin i-Khalq.*

The central Soviet concern in its policy toward Iran was a fear that after the hostage release, the United States and Iran might move toward a rapprochement, particularly because of Iranian military requirements due to the Iran-Iraq war. Fortunately for Moscow, anti-Americanism remained the central foreign-policy theme of the Khumayni regime during 1981 as it had been the previous year, and the regime's enemies were usually branded U.S. or Zionist agents. Given Moscow's previous displeasure with Bani Sadr, his departure was no loss. But the Soviet leadership was quite unhappy with the assassination of Bahashti, whom *Pravda* characterized on July 3 as being "one of the most consistent proponents of an anti-imperialist, anti-American policy."[78] The bombings at the end of June and at the end of August, while eliminating a number of top Iranian leaders, gave Moscow the opportunity to reinforce Tehran's suspicions that the CIA was behind the incidents. Thus, in a Persian-language broadcast immediately after the August bombings, Moscow radio commentator Igor Sheftunov stated:

> It is impossible to deny Washington's role in the terrorist activities against the Islamic Republic of Iran and its leaders. Since the fall of the monarchy and the installation of the Islamic Republic, U.S. imperialists have been doing their utmost to topple the republican regime and replace it with the old one. . . . Washington has shown its sympathy toward Baktiar, the last Prime Minister of the Shah, and Bani-Sadr the former President of Iran who is now a refugee. Both of these men are engaged in extensive terrorist activities against the Islamic Republic of Iran and its leaders.[79]

Moscow also sought to link aid to the Afghan rebels (early in 1981 Reagan had announced publicly that the United States was aiding the Afghani resistance) with U.S. aid to the opposition in Iran, in an effort both to discredit the Afghan resistance in Iran and also to drive a further wedge between Tehran and Washington.

Yet while Iranian-U.S. relations remained highly strained, it did not appear as if Moscow was making a great deal of headway in improving its own position in Iran. Iranian leaders continued to be suspicious of Moscow both for its centuries-long record of hostility toward Iran and because of suspected ties between Moscow and Iranian ethnic minorities fighting for independence, such as the Kurds. Indeed, Moscow may well have been placed in a difficult position when in late October the Kurdish Democratic party of Iran, led by Abd al-Rahman Qasimlu, joined the opposition front headed by Bani Sadr and Mujahhidin leader Mas'ud Rajavi.[80] Moscow and Qasimlu had long maintained friendly ties and the formation of the opposition front once again posed a difficult problem of choice for the USSR.

Yet another irritant in the Soviet-Iranian relationship has been Tehran's unhappiness that Moscow has taken only a neutral position on the Iran-Iraq war in the face of "flagrant Iraqi aggression," as the late Iranian prime minister Ali Raja'i told Soviet Ambassador Vladimir Vinogradov on February 15,[81] a message repeated in October by the Iranian ambassador during an Iranian delegation's visit to Moscow in October.[82] A third area of conflict has been Iranian unhappiness with the Soviet intervention in Afghanistan, despite Soviet efforts to tie the CIA to the resistance movements in both Iran and Afghanistan. Finally, while the Islamic fundamentalist regime has so far tolerated the Communist (Tudeh) party and its ally, the majority faction of the *Fida'iyin* guerrillas, it clearly remains suspicious of them as shown by Iranian prime minister Mir Husayn Musavi's declaration that members of the Tudeh and majority Fida'iyin would be executed if, upon joining the revolutionary guards or other fundamentalist organizations, they failed to state their party affiliation.[83]

For its part Moscow was clearly not happy with a number of Iranian policies, including frequent anti-Soviet comments by Iranian leaders,[84] the continued war with Iraq, and Iran's continuing controversy with Saudi Arabia (Iranian pilgrims had been arrested for demonstrating in Mecca) which helped reinforce the tie between Saudi Arabia and the United States. While Iran's growing international isolation (in 1981 Iran quarreled with France over a hijacked gunboat and French asylum for Bani Sadr, while Japan decided to end its three-billion-dollar investment in a huge Iranian petrochemical plant) may appear to Moscow as the factor that will ultimately push Iran over to the Soviet camp, by the end of 1981 no such movement had taken place.

The U.S.-Israel Strategic Cooperation Agreement

If Moscow sought to exploit the domestic upheavals in Iran to reinforce anti-U.S. feelings there, it was to also move to exploit the Israeli-U.S. agreement in principle on strategic cooperation reached during Israeli prime minister Begin's visit to Washington in early September. Moscow had already deplored the reelection of Begin and the appointment of so-called superhawk Ariel Sharon as Israel's defense minister—and sought also to exploit Reagan's decision in mid-August to finally allow the F-16s to go to Israel. Indeed, several Soviet commentators actually linked the release of the F-16s to the U.S.-Libyan air clash that took place several days later.[85]

It was the strategic cooperation agreement (later to be formally signed when Sharon visited the United States in early December), however, that came in for the most criticism.[86] Moscow, which tends to have a military view of world events, may well have felt that the combination of the Israeli air force and army with the U.S. Sixth Fleet would militarily dominate the Middle East, while the U.S. use of Israeli air bases in the Negev and the stockpiling of equipment in Israel for the U.S. Rapid Deployment Force would greatly enhance the ability of the United States to deploy its ground forces in the Middle East.

While Moscow sought to show that the Israeli-U.S. agreement, coming after the Israeli bombing of Beirut and the Iraqi reactor and the Libyan-U.S. clash over the Gulf of Sidra, was a policy aimed at threatening the entire Arab world, the Soviet leaders themselves may have felt some need to make a gesture toward Israel before that country came totally into the U.S. camp. Thus, during Gromyko's visit to the United Nations in late September, he agreed to meet Israeli foreign minister Yitzhak Shamir (the meeting was at Shamir's initiative). It appears as if Moscow's willingness to meet with the Israeli foreign minister, the first such official meeting in six years, was a Soviet effort, as in the past at a time of flux in Middle Eastern politics, both to maintain some contact with the Israelis and also to seek Israeli support for Moscow's idea of an international conference on the Arab-Israeli conflict.[87] While no Israeli support was to emerge from the conference, it appears that the meeting was seen as useful by both sides.[88] In any case, the Soviet-Israeli meeting was soon superceded in the thrust of Middle Eastern events by the assassination of Anwar al-Sadat, a development that once again put the region in an upheaval.

The Assassination of Sadat and Its Aftermath

Relations between Sadat and the USSR had been worsening steadily since the 1973 war, but in 1981 the deterioration accelerated. Not only was Sadat openly proclaiming himself to be the leading anti-Soviet force in the Middle East, but he had also announced that Egypt was sending aid to the Afghan rebels and he had agreed both to the stationing of U.S. troops in the Sinai (as part of the multinational force to separate Egypt and Israel after the April 1982 Israeli withdrawal) and also to use and development by the United States of the Egyptian base at Ras Banas for its Rapid Deployment

Force.[89] In sum, Egypt under Sadat had become a centerpiece of the anti-Soviet Middle Eastern bloc the United States was seeking to create and Soviet-Egyptian relations plummeted to a new low as a result.

Three weeks before Sadat's assassination, the Egyptian leader had expelled seven Soviet diplomats, including the Soviet ambassador and about one thousand Soviet advisers, on grounds that they were fomenting sedition in Egypt.[90] In addition, he dissolved the Egyptian-Soviet Friendship Society and arrested its president as part of a major crackdown on Egyptians opposed to his policies from both the Egyptian left and from the fundamentalist Moslem right.[91]

The assassination of Sadat by Muslim fundamentalists was greeted with considerable relief in Moscow, although there was a difference of opinion on the part of Soviet commentators on the future policies of the new regime. *Pravda* on October 14 cited the statement of the National Progressive Party, which opposed the referendum for the election of Hosni Mubarak to Egypt's presidency on the grounds that he intended to pursue Sadat's policies, "in particular to continue the Camp David policy and strengthen the alliance with the U.S." On the other hand *Izvestiia* commentator Aleksandr Bovin, a senior Soviet analyst on the Middle East, said that he thought Egypt's policies might change after Israel withdrew from the Sinai in April 1982.[92] In any case, while Moscow saw the possibility of an improvement in relations with Egypt—and both before and after the assassination was giving propaganda support to General Shazli, the exiled leader of the Egyptian Patriotic Front based in Libya, (Shazli was urging Egypt to return to the Arab fold and improve ties with Moscow)—[93] it expressed considerable irritation with the U.S. response to Sadat's assassination. Perhaps hoping for a repeat of the uncertain U.S. reaction to the collapse of the shah's regime in Iran, Moscow seemed particularly upset by Reagan's strong response to Sadat's assassination, which included the alerting of U.S. forces in the Mediterranean along with elements of the Rapid Deployment Force in the United States; the movement of ships of the Sixth Fleet toward Egypt; and the dispatch of former U.S. presidents Carter, Ford, and Nixon to Egypt for Sadat's funeral.[94] On October 12 Moscow issued a warning to the United States against what it termed a "gross interference" in the internal affairs of Egypt, stating that "what is going on around Egypt cannot help but affect the security interests of the Soviet Union," which will "keep a close watch on the development of events."[95]

Unlike the situation in Iran in 1978-1979, however, the United States did not appear deterred by the Kremlin warning. Indeed, in addition to pledging support to Mubarak, it dispatched several AWACS radar planes to patrol the border between Egypt and Libya, while also announcing that it would expand the planned U.S.-Middle East military exercise "Bright Star" scheduled for November 1981. In addition, the United States promised to step up arms shipments to both Egypt and the Sudan, both of whom were seen as being threatened by Libya.[96.]

In the face of both the U.S. pledge of support for Mubarak and the new Egyptian president's initial consolidation of power (he overwhelmingly won the referendum on October 13 and was sworn in on October 14), Moscow appeared to change course somewhat on October 15 as Brezhnev sent Mubarak a congratulatory telegram on his election, pledging that Moscow would reciprocate any Egyptian readiness to improve Soviet-Egyptian relations.[97] In making this move, Moscow may have realized that there would be no immediate change in Egyptian foreign policy despite Sadat's assassination and the most that could be hoped for was a "change in the direction of the wind," as Bovin had stated[98] after the Israeli withdrawal in April. Nonetheless, the announcement on October 20 that the United States would replace cracked Soviet-made turbines for the Soviet-built Aswan Dam—the major symbol of Soviet-Egyptian cooperation—seemed to underline the fact that U.S. influence was to remain predominant in Egypt, at least in the short term.[99]

The assassination of Sadat, as a major turning point in the Middle East, also gave Moscow the opportunity to again call for an international conference to settle the Arab-Israeli conflict. This was one of the themes of the visit by PLO leader Yasir Arafat to Moscow two weeks after the Sadat assassination, as the PLO leader gave strong support to Moscow's call for the conference.[100] For its part Moscow granted the PLO mission in Moscow full diplomatic status, thus conferring increased diplomatic legitimacy on the Palestinian organization. While the Soviet move was the culmination of an increasingly close Soviet-PLO relationship, and the USSR may have wished to consolidate the relationship further in the period of uncertainty following the death of Sadat, Moscow nevertheless may also have wished to counter the possibility of the development of a formal relationship between Washington and the PLO. During his mediation of the fighting in Lebanon in July, U.S. special representative Philip Habib had, de facto, negotiated with the PLO (albeit via intermediaries) and in August both Sadat and former U.S. national security adviser Zbigniew Brzezinski had advocated a U.S. dialogue with the PLO.[101] Then, following Sadat's funeral former presidents Carter and Ford stated that at some point the United States would have to begin to talk to members of the PLO, if not to Arafat himself.[102]

Less than a week after Arafat's visit came a trip to Moscow by North Yemeni president Ali Abdallah Salih. Like Jordan and Kuwait, North Yemen was a key centrist Arab state that Moscow wished to keep from going over to the U.S. camp, something Moscow feared might happen after a South Yemen invasion of North Yemen in February 1979 led to a major U.S. military-supply effort.[103] Nonetheless, a lack of coordination between the United States, which was supplying the equipment, and Saudi Arabia, which was paying for it and which was concerned that North Yemen might become too strong if it obtained the weapons too quickly, led the North Yemeni president to turn to Moscow for arms later that year. Complicating the North Yemeni political situation still further was the South Yemeni-supported National Democratic Front that posed both a political and military challenge to the regime in Sana'a. The end result was that the North Yemen government had to walk a delicate tightrope between Saudi Arabia (which financed and influenced a number of North Yemeni tribes), and South Yemen (which supported the National Democratic Front and alternately invaded and advocated union with North Yemen) as well as between the United States, Saudi Arabia's main supporter, and the Soviet Union, the primary backer of South Yemen. President Salih's primary aim in the talks in Moscow, therefore, appeared to be the acquisition of additional weaponry to deal with his internal and external problems. He was successful in his quest as the final communique issued at the close of his visit stated that the two countries expressed the desire to continue "broadening and perfecting their advantageous cooperation" in the military field.[104] In return, Salih thanked the USSR for its aid in strengthening North Yemen's "national independence and sovereignty," supported Moscow's call for an international conference on the Middle East, and condemned the establishment of foreign military bases in the Persian Gulf while also supporting Moscow's peace plan for the Persian Gulf and Indian Ocean. In sum, like the visits by the leaders of Kuwait and Jordan, the trip of North Yemeni president Salih can be considered a clear plus for Moscow, although Salih immediately was to visit Saudi Arabia following his visit to Moscow in an effort to secure his position with that country.

Although the North Yemeni leader's visit to Moscow was greeted with satisfaction by Moscow—as was the election of the anti-NATO Andreas Papandreou to the premiership of Greece in late October and the failure of President Reagan to either convince Jordan's King Husayn to join Camp David or get the king to reject a major surface-to-air missile deal with Moscow in favor of a U.S. system during Husayn's visit to Washington in early November[105]—a number of other Middle Eastern developments took place during the fall of 1981 that were not to Moscow's satisfaction. In the first place, after a long and bitter debate the U.S. Senate agreed to the sale of the AWACS aircraft to Saudi Arabia in late October, a development that appeared to cement U.S.-Saudi ties. Second, in a major policy change a number of European states agreed to provide troops for the Sinai multinational force, thereby at least tacitly supporting Camp David. Third, the United States successfully mounted a major military exercise in the Middle East (Bright Star), thus demonstrating that it was developing the capability of a quick intervention there to aid its friends.

The debate over the AWACS highlighted the ambivalent Soviet position toward Saudi Arabia. On the one hand, as the leading centrist Arab state opposed to Camp David and as a major financial and political backer of the PLO, Saudi Arabia pursued two key Middle Eastern policies that Moscow also strongly supported. On the other hand, however, as a leading opponent of Soviet policy in Afghanistan and as a nation with increasingly close military ties to the United States, as evidenced by the emplacement of U.S.-controlled AWACS in Saudi Arabia soon after the start of the Iran-Iraq war, and as a nation that had sought to use its financial power to pry several Arab states out of the Soviet camp, Saudi Arabia was also a leading anti-Soviet force in the Arab world. Moscow's ambivalent position toward Saudi Arabia was especially apparent in 1981. In April Moscow warmly welcomed both Saudi Arabia's rebuttal of U.S. Secretary of State Haig's call for an anti-Soviet alliance, made during Haig's visit to the Middle East, and Saudi foreign minister Sa'ud al-Faysal's statement that Israel, not Moscow, was the main threat to the Arabs.[106] One month later, a key article in *Literaturnaia gazeta*, written by Soviet commentator Igor Beliaev, noted in discussing the failure of Haig's visit:

> Arab politicians, even the conservative ones, have never refused Soviet assistance in the struggle against their real enemy—the Israeli expansionists. The Arabs will hardly become accomplices in an anti-Soviet crusade under the aegis of the US.[107]

On the other hand, in late August, Moscow's chief oil analyst, Reuben Andreasian, bitterly noted Saudi Arabia's unwillingness to act against U.S. interest during an OPEC meeting to set oil prices, as he complained that despite the Israeli raid on the Iraqi nuclear reactor and the recent attack by U.S. air force planes on Libyan aircraft—on the very day the OPEC meeting opened—there was no agreement on prices.[108]

Moscow's central fear in the AWACS debate was that congressional approval for AWACS would cement the Saudi-U.S. relationship to the point that Saudi Arabia might be persuaded both to support the Camp David agreements and also provide facilities for the U.S. Rapid Deployment Force "in direct proximity to the extremely rich Persian Gulf oil fields,"[109] a fear that was even more openly expressed after the Senate approved (by failing to vote down) the AWACS agreement. Moscow Radio Peace and Progress on October 30 asserted that the AWACS deal was "aimed at transforming the Wahhabi Kingdom into a source of threat to the entire Islamic world."[110]

While the AWACS approval was a blow to the Soviet Middle East position since it strengthened Saudi-U.S. ties, so too was the decision of several key European states to provide troops for the multinational force the United States was organizing for the Sinai. The rapid evolution of the multinational force during the course of 1981 was of clear concern to Moscow, which saw it as a cover for the U.S. RDF.[111] Ironically, it was because of Moscow's July 1979 veto of the UN force to patrol the Sinai (which, most likely, would have remained composed primarily of Third World states and thus not a possible military threat against Soviet positions in the region) that the United States worked to create the multinational force.

The commitment of U.S. troops for the force, a goal long pursued by Israel, which saw the United States as a far more reliable barrier to a future Egyptian attack than the United Nations, was not approved by the U.S. Congress or Sadat until well into 1981, and, for most of the year, Western Europe held aloof from participation in the multinational force. The election of François Mitterrand to the presidency of France, however, together with the assassination of Sadat, galvanized the Europeans to take a more active role and by the end of November the participation of France, England, Holland, and Italy in the Sinai force, despite some initial objections by Israel on the terms of their participation, was set. As might be expected, Moscow strongly opposed both U.S. and especially Western European participation in the multinational force. In the case of Western Europe, Moscow had long seen the Middle East as an area where, because of a much greater European oil dependency, a wedge could be driven between the United States and its NATO allies.[112] Consequently, Moscow condemned what it saw as a Western European ''knuckling under'' to Washington's ''diktat'' on the multinational force.[113] Secondly, because the multinational force was tied to Camp David agreements, Moscow saw European participation in the Sinai force as a de facto legitimization of Camp David, a development that ended U.S. isolation as the sole Western state supporting the agreement.[114]

The Bright Star military exercise, which also involved some British and French participation, may be considered another gain for Washington— and concomitantly a loss for Moscow. The exercises took place in Egypt (with the participation of units of the Egyptian army and airforce), the Sudan, Somalia, and Oman. While Moscow denounced Bright Star as a rehearsal for the invasion of both Libya and the Middle East oil fields (the Bright Star exercise was commanded by the head of the RDF); as a device for intimidating ''progressive'' governments in the Middle East such as Libya, Ethiopia, and South Yemen; and as a technique for strengthening pro-U.S. regimes in the region,[115] it had to be concerned about the rather impressive showing of the U.S. military, including a bombing run by B-52 bombers on a direct flight from the United States. This stood in sharp contrast to the difficulties encountered by the United States in its abortive hostage-rescue mission in Iran in April 1980. Indeed, Moscow may well have been concerned that the successful U.S. Rapid Deployment Force exercise might have a positive influence on such Arab countries as Kuwait, which had turned to Moscow, in part, because it could not be sure that the United States either had the capability or will to help it in case of a conflict with an unfriendly neighbor like Iran, which had again bombed Kuwaiti territory in early October. The conclusion of a major U.S.-Pakistani military agreement, which held out the possibility of U.S. use of the Pakistani naval base at Gwandar and air base at Peshewar, seemed to further enhance U.S. capabilities for military intervention in the Persian Gulf.[116] Finally, the Egyptian component of Bright Star in which four thousand U.S. and Egyptian troops participated also served to improve relations between the U.S. and Egyptian military and between the Mubarak and Reagan governments, and the Egyptian defense minister stated that the exercises were "a rehearsal for a possible joint operation" to protect the oilfields of the Persian Gulf.[117]

As Bright Star was concluding its Egyptian phase on November 24, the Arab states, except for Egypt, were preparing for a major Arab summit conference in Fez, Morocco, one that was closely watched by Moscow. The central issue at the conference was the so-called Fahd Plan, a Saudi peace initiative first put forth in August that held out, albeit somewhat vaguely, the possibility of Arab recognition and peace with Israel in return for a total Israeli withdrawal from all territories captured in 1967, including east Jerusalem, and the establishment of a Palestinian state. The assassination of Sadat, which seemed to make possible a rapprochement between Egypt and Saudi Arabia,[118] along with the U.S. Senate approval of AWACS gave a new momentum to the Fahd Plan, which received little attention when it was first broached in August.

The Soviet reaction to the Fahd Plan was an interesting one. On August 12, Moscow Radio praised the plan, noting that it conformed in many ways to the Soviet Middle East peace plan (that is, total Israeli withdrawal; the establishment of a Palestinian state; and the right to exist of all states in the region).[119] Five days later, however, Moscow Radio Peace and Progress in Arabic attacked the plan because of its tie to U.S. policy,[120] and *Izvestiia* further criticized the plan on August 23 as an effort to undermine the PLO and decide the Palestinian people's fate "behind their backs." Moscow's criticism of Saudi Arabia and the Fahd Plan grew even harsher at the time when the AWACS deal was approved by the U.S. Senate as it was portrayed as a device to split the Arabs and spread Camp David,[121] but Moscow shifted its position again when Prince Faysal of Saudi Arabia called for Soviet participation in the search for peace in the Middle East and sought to get Soviet support for the Saudi peace plan.[122] From Moscow's point of view, cooperation on the Fahd Plan, particularly when the Reagan administration was at best lukewarm about it, could be a means of driving a wedge between Saudi Arabia and Washington, despite the AWACS deal. From the Saudi perspective, Soviet support for the Fahd Plan may have been seen as necessary for rallying the Steadfastness Front Arab states to the support of the Fahd Plan at the Fez Summit. Indeed, Riyadh made a further gesture to Moscow—possibly for the same purpose—at a meeting of the Gulf Cooperation Council in mid-November when it supported the Kuwaiti view in the final communique, which "confirmed the need to keep the region as a whole away from international conflicts, especially the presence of military fleets and foreign bases."[123] If this was indeed Riyadh's purpose in giving strong support to the principles of nonalignment at the GCC meeting (Riyadh may also have been embarrassed by a 1 November 1981 article in the *Washington Post* describing U.S. plans to make Saudi Arabia a major military and air-command base for the U.S. RDF,[124] and by Reagan's press-conference statement on October 1 that the United States would not let Saudi Arabia be an Iran),[125] it did not work since the Steadfastness Front states, and particularly Syria and Libya, were to strongly oppose the Fahd Plan at the Fez Summit. Indeed, the Steadfastness Front had its own agenda at Fez—one endorsed by Moscow—which called for sanctions against Arab states making available military facilities to the United States and against European states providing troops for the Sinai force; the use of all Arab resources, including oil and petrodollars, to "resist the U.S.-Israeli strategic alliance"; and strengthening of relations with the USSR.[126] Neither the Fahd Plan nor the Steadfastness Front agenda, however, were to receive support at the Fez Summit, which was to collapse less than six hours after it had begun because of the Steadfastness Front's hostility to the Fahd Plan, leaving the Arab world in a major state of disarray. In an attempt to put a positive light on the events at Fez, a Moscow Radio Arabic-language broadcast rather plaintively urged the Arabs to rebuild their unity on an anti-imperialist basis,[127] something that even the most optimistic observers in Moscow must have realized was a very distant goal.

In any case, the Soviet call for the reestablishment of anti-imperialist Arab unity in the aftermath of the collapse of the Arab summit at Fez provides a useful point of departure for drawing some conclusions about the Soviet reaction to Reagan's Middle East policies.

Conclusions

In examining the course of Soviet policy toward the Middle East in the first year of the Reagan administration it is possible to draw several conclusions. In the first place Moscow's position in the region in December 1981 appeared to be somewhat stronger than it was in January. This was due primarily to the fact that the centrist Arab states were basically unwilling to join the anti-Soviet bloc that the Reagan administration was seeking to create—in part because of the fact that as the Iran-Iraq war stalemated, the centrist states, and particularly the Gulf Cooperation Council, felt less danger and, in part, because as the Arab-Israeli conflict escalated during 1981 with the missile crisis in Lebanon, Israel's raid against the Iraqi nuclear reactor, and the Israeli bombing of Beirut, the centrist states felt a need to distance themselves somewhat from the United States, which was Israel's main supporter. To be sure there were nuances in the centrist Arab policy, with Saudi Arabia—because of the AWACS deal—and Oman— because of the threat from South Yemen—maintaining close ties to Washington, while Kuwait—for both domestic and foreign-policy reasons— enhanced its ties to Moscow. Nonetheless, what is of interest to note is the fact that Moscow took very little in the way of positive action during this period to improve its position, other than inviting Kuwait's Shaykh Sabah, Jordan's King Husayn, and North Yemen's President Salih to Moscow. Moscow's primary gains (in the form of U.S. losses) came from an exploitation of the numerous Middle East crises during 1981, crises that Moscow neither planned nor seemed able to control.

It should also be pointed out, however, that there were a number of crises that Moscow did not prove too successful in exploiting. Thus the crises caused by Israel's destruction of the Iraqi nuclear reactor seemed, at least initially, to lead to closer Iraqi-U.S. relations, rather than enhanced ties between Moscow and Baghdad. Similarly, despite the continuing upheavals in Iran, Moscow did not appear to be able to improve its position to any great degree in that country. Finally, the assassination of Sadat, the linchpin of U.S. strategy in the Arab world, did not appear to bring any immediate benefit to Moscow as his successor, Hosni Mubarak, pledged to continue cooperation both with the United States and with Israel.

A second conclusion that may be drawn is that in 1981 Moscow remained far from achieving some of its central Middle Eastern goals. Its call for an international conference on the Middle East, while getting support from Kuwait and Jordan, was far from gaining general acceptance, with even such Steadfastness Front states as Libya and Algeria failing to endorse it. Indeed, the peacemaking that was accomplished in 1981 was done by the United States, as U.S. special representative Philip Habib kept the peace between Israel and Syria during the missile crisis while also negotiating a ceasefire between Israel and the PLO during the fighting in Lebanon. These events may well have reinforced the view in the minds of most Arabs that the keys to the settlement of the Arab-Israeli conflict lay in Washington, not Moscow.

A second goal Moscow appeared very far from achieving in 1981 was the establishment of Arab unity on an "anti-imperialist" basis. Despite the escalation of the Arab-Israeli conflict in 1981, the Iraqi-Syrian, Syrian-Jordanian, Libyan-Sudanese, South Yemen-Oman, and Algerian-

Moroccan conflicts continued, and the prolongation of the Iran-Iraq war (despite professed Soviet efforts to terminate it) was also a contributing factor to the disunity in the Arab world. In addition, the consolidation of Mubarak's regime in Egypt, together with the Saudi proposal of the Fahd Plan (despite its rejection by a number of Arab states at the Fez Summit) seemed to hold out the possibility of a reconciliation between Egypt and some key centrist Arab states, a development long desired by the United States. The conclusion of the tripartite Libyan-Ethiopian-South Yemeni alliance may also serve to push some centrist Arab states back toward Egypt (and toward the United States) much as Libyan activity in Chad and pressure against the Sudan were the key factors in prompting Sudanese president Numayri to reestablish full diplomatic relations with Egypt and offer the United States military bases in his country.

Finally, it should also be pointed out that by obtaining European support for the multinational force in the Sinai and thereby, in effect, broadening the base of Camp David, and by mounting the successful Bright Star military exercise in the Middle East, thereby demonstrating to some skeptical Arab leaders that the United States did have the capability to help them in case of an emergency, the United States, despite the general Arab rejection of Reagan's proposal to form an anti-Soviet alliance, had made some significant moves to strengthen its own position in the region.

In sum, therefore, while Moscow had improved its position in the Middle East during the first year of the Reagan administration, the improvement was not a major one and the USSR, still very much at the mercy of Middle Eastern events that it neither caused nor seemed able to control, remained very far from achieving its basic objectives in the region.

Notes

1. For recent studies of Soviet policy in the Middle East, see Robert O. Freedman, *Soviet Policy toward the Middle East Since 1970* 3rd ed. (New York: Praeger, 1982); Jon D. Glassman, *Arms for the Arabs: The Soviet Union and War in the Middle East* (Baltimore: Johns Hopkins University Press, 1975); Galia Golan, *Yom Kippur and After: The Soviet Union and the Middle East Crisis* (Cambridge: Cambridge University Press, 1977); Yaacov Ro'i, *From Encroachment to Involvement: A Documentary Study of Soviet Policy in the Middle East* (Jerusalem: Israel Universities Press, 1974); and Yaacov Ro'i, ed., *The Limits to Power: Soviet Policy in the Middle East* (London: Croom Helm, 1979).

2. Political-science models dealing with the exertion of influence in Soviet foreign policy in general and Soviet foreign policy toward the Middle East in particular are still relatively rare. For a general study of influence,

the interested reader is advised to consult J. David Singer's article "Inter-Nation Influence: A Formal Model," in James N. Rosenau, ed., *International Politics and Foreign Policy* (New York: Macmillan, 1969). Singer makes the useful distinction between influence leading to behavior modification in a target state and influence leading to behavior reinforcement. Another useful study, which examines the phenomenon of influence from the perspective of the target state, is Marshall R. Singer, *Weak States in a World of Powers* (New York: Free Press, 1972), esp. chapters 6, 7, and 8. See also Richard W. Cottam, *Competitive Interference and Twentieth Century Diplomacy* (Pittsburgh: University of Pittsburgh Press, 1967).

3. For studies of Soviet military aid, see Glassman, *Arms for the Arabs;* George Lenczowski, *Soviet Advances in the Middle East* (Washington, D.C.: American Enterprise Institute, 1972); and Amnon Sella, "Changes in Soviet Political-Military Policy in the Middle East After 1973," in Ro'i, ed., *The Limits to Power*, pp. 32-64.

4. Moscow also uses *disinformation*, as in 1979 when Soviet agents spread the rumor that the United States was responsible for the seizure of the Grand Mosque in Mecca. See *Soviet "Active Measures": Forgery, Disinformation, Political Operations* (Washington, D.C.: U.S. Department of State, Special Report no. 88, October 1981).

5. For a view of the role of Israel in Soviet Middle East strategy, see Freedman, *Soviet Policy toward the Middle East*, chapter 8.

6. For a study of Soviet policy toward the Communist parties of the Arab world, see Robert O. Freedman, "The Soviet Union and the Communist Parties of the Arab World: An Uncertain Relationship," in Roger E. Kanet and Donna Bahry, eds., *Soviet Economic and Political Relations with the Developing World* (New York: Praeger, 1975), pp. 100-134; and John K. Cooley, "The Shifting Sands of Arab Communism," *Problems of Communism* (March/April 1975):22-42.

7. Moscow has tried to use its own Moslems, such as the *mufti* of Tashkent, to influence Arabs and other Moslems, but without notable success. For an analysis of the Islamic revival, see Daniel Pipes, "This World is Political! The Islamic Revival of the Seventies," *Orbis* (Spring 1980):9-41.

8. For background on these events see Robert O. Freedman, "Soviet Policy in the Middle East: From the Sinai II Accord to the Egyptian-Israeli Peace Agreement," in W. Raymond Duncan, ed., *Soviet Policy in the Third World* (New York: Pergamon, 1980); and Robert O. Freedman, "Soviet Policy toward the Middle East Since the Invasion of Afghanistan," *Journal of International Affairs* (Fall/Winter 1980-1981):283-310.

9. Freedman, "Soviet Policy toward the Middle East Since the Invasion of Afghanistan." Iraq, which shared the Steadfastness states' goal of destroying Israel but was not a member of the Steadfastness Front because of its enmity toward Syria, also denounced the invasion while opposing

Camp David. The centrist Arab states seemed willing to entertain the idea of peace with Israel, the Steadfastness Front members did not.

10. Freedman, "Soviet Policy in the Middle East: From the Sinai II Accord to the Egyptian-Israeli Peace Agreement."

11. See Zakhar Kuznetsov, "In Unison with Imperialism," *New Times* 52 (1979):21-22.

12. The text of the Pan-Arab Charter may be found in *The Middle East*, April 1980, p. 20.

13. See Robert O. Freedman, "Soviet Policy Toward Ba'athist Iraq," in Robert Donaldson, ed., *The Soviet Union in the Third World* (Boulder: Westview Press, 1981), pp. 161-191.

14. See Alexandre Bennigsen, "Soviet Muslims and the World of Islam," *Problems of Communism* (March/April 1980):38-51.

15. See TASS report, 16 September 1980.

16. Alexander Usvatov, "Put Out the Fire," *New Times*, 40 (1980):12.

17. For a discussion of these events, see Robert O. Freedman, "Soviet Policy toward Syria Since Camp David," *Middle East Review* (Fall/Winter 1981-1982).

18. See *Izvestiia*, 3 October 1980.

19. For an analysis of the Gulf Cooperation Council, see Judith Perea, "Caution: Building in Progress," *The Middle East*, April 1981, pp. 8-12.

20. See remark in *Foreign Broadcast Information Service Daily Report, Soviet Union (hereafter FBIS: USSR)*, 14 October 1980, p. H3.

21. See TASS report in English, 3 October 1980 (*FBIS: USSR*, 6 October 1980, p. H4).

22. See report by David K. Willis, *Christian Science Monitor*, 14 October 1980; and *Middle East Intelligence Survey*, 1-15 October 1980. See also TASS report in English, 10 October 1980; and Radio Moscow in Persian, 10 October 1980 (*FBIS: USSR*, 14 October 1980, p. H1).

23. See *Pravda*, 17 January 1981; and Moscow Radio in Persian, 17 January 1981 (*FBIS: USSR*, 19 January 1981, pp. A2-A3). Former Secretary of State Henry Kissinger's trip to the Middle East in early January was linked by Moscow to the invasion plan.

24. For the text of Brezhnev's speech to the Twenty-sixth Party Congress, see *Pravda*, 24 February 1981, (translated in *Current Digest of the Soviet Press*—hereafter CDSP—vol. 38, no. 8, pp. 7-13.

25. For a description of this plan see Freedman, "Soviet Policy toward the Middle East Since the Invasion of Afghanistan," pp. 304-305.

26. See ibid., p. 305.

27. For an analysis of the development of inter-Arab politics to early 1981, see Bruce Maddy-Weitzman, "The Fragmentation of Arab Politics: Inter-Arab Affairs since the Afghanistan Invasion," *Orbis* (Summer 1981): 389-407.

28. For a recent analysis of Libyan policy, see Ronald Bruce St. John, "Libya's Foreign and Domestic Policies," *Current History* (December 1981):426-429.

29. See *Pravda*, 28 April 1981, for Qadhdhafi's banquet speech in which he portrayed himself as the representative of the Steadfastness Front. See *Al-Watan* (Kuwait), 29 April 1981, for his frank interview about areas of agreement and disagreement with Moscow (*FBIS: Middle East and Africa*, 4 May 1981, pp. Q4-Q5.

30. See *Pravda*, 28 April 1981; and *Pravda*, 30 April 1981. A Libyan Arabic broadcast made a major point of this (See Radio Tripoli "Voice of the Arab Homeland," 29 April 1981) in *FBIS: Middle East and Africa*, 4 May 1981, pp. Q4-Q5.

31. For a recent analysis of Algerian policy under Chadli Benjedid, see Robert Mortimer, "Algeria's New Sultan," *Current History* (December 1981):418-421, 433-434.

32. Statement by Morris Draper, deputy assistant secretary of state for Near Eastern and South Asian Affairs, as cited in the report by Bernard Gwertzman, *New York Times*, 26 March 1981.

33. For an analysis of the natural-gas situation and other problems of U.S.-Algerian relations, see the report by Jonathan C. Randal, *Washington Post*, 25 March 1981.

34. *Pravda*, 11 June 1981.

35. Soon after Benjedid's visit to Moscow Morocco was to agree to a ceasefire and a referendum to determine the future of the former Spanish Sahara (See report by Jay Ross, *Washington Post*, 27 June 1981), but the modalities of the proposed referendum led a number of observers to believe that this was just a Moroccan ploy. For an analysis of the Saharan problem, see William H. Lewis, "Western Sahara: Compromise or Conflict?," *Current History* (December 1981):410-413, 431.

36. For a description of Moscow's Mediterranean plan, see A. Usvatov, "USSR-Algeria: Common Approach," *New Times* 25 (1981):7.

37. At the Islamic summit in Taif, Saudi Arabia, in late January for example, the emphasis was on Islamic opposition to Israel and the so-called "Soviet threat" was played down, as was the Soviet invasion of Afghanistan. (See Claudia Wright, "Islamic Summit," *The Middle East*, March 1981, pp. 6-10). The absence of Iran, which had played a militantly anti-Soviet role in the previous Islamic conference in May 1980, however, may have been a factor along with Saudi Arabian efforts to achieve an Islamic consensus.

38. UPI report in *Jerusalem Post*, 9 April 1981. As a gesture to the United States, however, Saudi Arabia broke diplomatic relations with Afghanistan on the eve of the Haig visit (See Reuters report, *New York Times*, 8 April 1981).

39. For an analysis of the 1975 visit, see Freedman, *Soviet Policy toward the Middle East Since 1970*, pp. 216-217.

40. For an interview with Shaykh Sabah, see *The Middle East*, March 1981, p. 18. For an analysis of the domestic situation in Kuwait at the time of Shaykh Sabah's visit to the USSR, see Helena Cobban, "Kuwait's Elections," *The Middle East*, April 1981, pp. 14-15. Kuwait's foreign-policy problems and strategy are discussed in Claudia Wright, "India and Pakistan Join in Gulf Game," *The Middle East*, June 1981, pp. 31-32. According to Wright, Shaykh Sabah also went to Moscow to get a nonaggression treaty negotiated between the PDRY and Oman so as to lessen Omani dependence on the United States. On this point see also *Al-Hadaf* (Kuwait), 7 May 1981 (translated in *FBIS: Middle East and Africa*, 13 May 1981, p. C5).

41. *Pravda*, 26 April 1981.

42. Ibid.

43. For an analysis of the changing alliances of King Husayn, see Adam M. Garfinkle, "Negotiating by Proxy: Jordanian Foreign Policy and U.S. Options in the Middle East," *Orbis* (Winter 1981):847-880.

44. The joint communique was printed in *Pravda*, 30 May 1981.

45. *Pravda*, 27 May 1981.

46. See Alexander Usvatov, "King Hussein's Visit," *New Times* 23 (1981):10. One issue on which Jordan and the USSR obviously did not agree, however, was the Iran-Iraq war.

47. See report by Jonathan Randal, *Washington Post*, 13 April 1981. For an expression of Moscow's displeasure see the *Izvestiia* commentary of 14 April 1981, translated in CDSP, vol. 33, no. 15, p. 18.

48. See Freedman, "Soviet Policy toward Syria Since Camp David."

49. By the end of the first week in May, Arab army chiefs, meeting in Tunis, had pledged to aid Syria as had Kuwait and Saudi Arabia (See report by Pranay Gupte, *New York Times*, 8 May 1981; and AP report, *Baltimore Sun*, 3 May 1981). TASS on May 8 and *Pravda* and Moscow Radio (Arabic-language broadcast) on May 9 carried stories about the missiles, referring to them as a defensive measure. The stories coincided with the end of a visit to Damascus by Soviet First Deputy Foreign Minister Georgii Kornienko.

50. See report by Don Oberdorfer, *Washington Post*, 30 April 1981.

51. To at least one Soviet commentator, the situation was somewhat reminiscent of June 1967. See Dmitry Volsky, "May 1981 is not June 1967," *New Times* 21 (1981):5-6.

52. See Moscow Radio in Arabic, 13 May 1981 (*FBIS: USSR*, 14 May 1981, p. H1).

53. Cited in Robert Rand, "The USSR and the Crisis over Syrian Missiles in Lebanon: An Analysis and Chronological Survey," *Radio Liberty Report* no. 227/81, 3 June 1981, p. 6. Rand's study is an excellent analysis of the missile crisis from 28 April 1981 to 29 May 1981. (TASS on May 5

denied that Soldatov had said the USSR regarded the Biqa' valley (where Zahlah is located) as a sector of substantial importance to the security of Syria.)

54. Cited in report in *New York Times*, 13 May 1981.

55. *Pravda*, 23 May 1981.

56. *Pravda*, 27 May 1981.

57. Cited in *Jerusalem Post*, 24 May 1981.

58. Cited in *Pravda*, 26 May 1981.

59. Moscow, however, had not forgotten the missile crisis and in early July carried out a joint military exercise with Syria including, for the first time, naval landings. For a report on the exercise, which could be seen as a Soviet show of support for Syria after Begin's reelection, see the UPI report in the *New York Times*, 10 July 1981.

60. See *Pravda*, 10, 11, and 16 June 1981.

61. Translated in CDSP, vol. 33, no. 24, p. 17.

62. See report by Nathaniel Harrison, *Christian Science Monitor*, 1 April 1981.

63. See Andrei Stepanov, "Taking Up a Point (Soviet Neutrality in the Iran-Iraq War)," *New Times* 17 (1981):31.

64. See report by Michael J. Berlin, *Washington Post*, 19 June 1981.

65. Cited in report by Edward Cody, *Washington Post*, 29 June 1981.

66. Aziz Muhammad's speech was also printed in *Pravda*, 3 March 1981.

67. Cited in report by Bernard Gwertzman, *New York Times*, 20 March 1981.

68. See report by Don Oberdorfer, *Washington Post*, 11 April 1981.

69. Ibid. Permission for the sale of the planes had been previously refused.

70. In early November, the *London Daily Telegraph* reported the shipment of 650 tanks from Poland (*Baltimore Sun*, 12 November 1981).

71. See TASS statement in *Pravda*, 22 July 1981.

72. For an analysis of the background to this incident, see the report by Bernard Gwertzman, *New York Times*, 21 August 1981. For an examination of Qadhdhafi's attempt to improve his diplomatic position, see Claudia Wright, "Libya Comes in From the Cold," *The Middle East*, August 1981, pp. 18-25.

73. TASS International Service, in Russian, 20 August 1981 (translated in *FBIS: USSR*, 20 August 1981, p. H2). Reprinted with permission.

74. Translated in *FBIS: USSR*, 28 August 1981, p. H6. Reprinted with permission.

75. *Pravda*, 23 August 1981. Criticism of U.S. action came from such centrist Arab states as Jordan, Kuwait, Bahrain, and the United Arab Emirates, and from the secretary of the Gulf Cooperation Council and the Organization of African Unity (See *FBIS: Middle East and Africa*, 20 and 21 August 1981).

76. See Moscow Radio in Turkish to Turkey, 20 August 1981 (*FBIS: USSR*, 21 August 1981, p. H2).

77. Oman denounced the treaty in very strong terms (See Muscat Domestic Service, 26 August 1981; and Salalah Domestic Service, 27 August 1981, in *FBIS: Middle East and Africa*, 27 August 1981, pp. C1-C2) and strongly criticized the decision by the secretary of the Gulf Cooperation Council to denounce the U.S. attack on the Libyan aircraft without consulting the membership (See *FBIS: Middle East and Africa*, 31 August 1981, p. C3). For an interview with the GCC's secretary general, Abdallah Ya'qub Bishara, who is trying to push the organization toward nonalignment, see *The Middle East*, September 1981, pp. 35-36. At its August ministerial meeting, however, several days after the Tripartite Treaty, the GCC decided "to strengthen political and security coordination between the member states" (see Nadia Hijab, "Gulf Council Shifts Into Second Gear," *The Middle East*, October 1981, pp. 25-26).

78. For Soviet attitudes toward the Iranian leadership, see Freedman, "Soviet Policy toward the Middle East Since the Invasion of Afghanistan," pp. 290-291, 295-297.

79. Translated in *FBIS: USSR*, 3 September 1981, p. H1. Reprinted with permission.

80. Cited in AP report, *New York Times*, 7 November 1981.

81. Cited in report in *Washington Post*, 16 February 1981.

82. Tehran Domestic Service, 20 October 1981 (*FBIS: USSR*, 22 October 1981, p. H7).

83. Cited in Reuters report, *New York Times*, 23 November 1981.

84. See A. Ulansky, "Presidential Election in a Tense Atmosphere," *New Times* 40 (1981):10.

85. See Radio Moscow in English, 29 August 1981 (*FBIS: USSR*, 31 August 1981, p. H4).

86. See *Pravda*, 8, 12, 14, 25 September 1981.

87. See TASS International Service in Russian, 25 September 1981 (*FBIS: USSR*, 25 September 1981, p. CC3); and Radio Moscow in English to North America, 5 October 1981 (*FBIS: USSR*, 6 October 1981, p. H4).

88. See report by William Clayborn, *Washington Post*, 26 September 1981.

89. For articles summarizing Moscow's displeasure with Sadat at the time of the Egyptian president's visit to Washington in early August, see *Izvestiia*, 9 and 28 August 1981.

90. *Pravda*, 18 September 1981.

91. Moscow Radio announced, however, on 1 October 1981 that the Soviet branch of the Friendship Society would continue to operate (*FBIS: USSR*, 2 October 1981, p. H1).

92. Bovin's comments came on Moscow television on October 25 (*FBIS: USSR*, 26 October 1981, p. H1).

93. See Moscow Radio Peace and Progress in Arabic, 7 September 1981 (*FBIS: USSR*, 10 September 1981, p. H1); TASS in English, 8 October 1981 (*FBIS: USSR*, 9 October 1981, p. H1); and Moscow Radio in Arabic, 26 October 1981 (*FBIS: USSR*, 27 October 1981, p. H6).

94. For an analysis of Soviet and U.S. policy during the fall of the shah, see Freedman, "Soviet Policy in the Middle East: From the Sinai II Accord to the Egyptian-Israeli Peace Agreement," pp. 173-175.

95. *Pravda*, 12 October 1981. Reprinted with permission.

96. See report by Don Oberdorfer, *Washington Post*, 15 October 1981.

97. *Pravda*, 16 October 1981.

98. See note 92.

99. Cited in report by Don Oberdorfer, *Washington Post*, 21 October 1981. For a good analysis of Moscow's initial approaches to Mubarak and his attitude toward the USSR, see Robert Rand, "Mubarak on the USSR," *Radio Liberty Report* no. 462/81, 17 November 1981.

100. Moscow Radio Domestic Service, 20 October 1981 (*FBIS: USSR*, 21 October 1981, p. H1). Arafat was quoted as saying at a press conference, "We fully endorse the Soviet proposals advanced at the Twenty-sixth CPSU Congress and we view them as the basis for a just settlement of the Palestinian problem." *Pravda*, on 21 October 1981, reported the joint Soviet-PLO support for the international conference and the granting of official diplomatic status to the PLO mission in Moscow.

101. Cited in report by Bernard Gwertzman, *New York Times*, 13 August 1981.

102. The text of the former president's comments is in the *New York Times*, 12 October 1981.

103. For an analysis of this event, see Freedman, "Soviet Policy toward the Middle East: From the Sinai II Accord to the Egyptian-Israeli Peace Agreement," pp. 175-176.

104. *Pravda*, 29 October 1981.

105. See reports by Bernard Gwertzman, *New York Times*, 3 November 1981; Don Oberdorfer, *Washington Post*, 6 November 1981; and Reuters, *Washington Post*, 9 November 1981.

106. *Pravda*, 12 April 1981.

107. *Literaturnaia gazeta*, 27 May 1981. (Translated in CDSP, vol. 33, no. 21, p. 11).

108. Ruben Andreasyan, "Disagreement in OPEC," *New Times* 35 (1981):13.

109. *Pravda*, 26 August 1981.

110. *FBIS: USSR*, 2 November 1981, p. H2.

111. *Pravda*, 29 March 1981.

112. This, of course, had happened during the 1973 Arab-Israeli war. See *Izvestiia*, 8 January 1981.

113. TASS, 1 November 1981 (*FBIS: USSR*, 2 November 1981, p. H3).

114. See *Izvestiia*, 31 October 1981.

115. See Moscow Radio in Arabic, 8 November 1981 (*FBIS: USSR*, 9 November 1981, pp. H1-H2).

116. As might be expected, Moscow was highly critical of Pakistan's increasingly close military tie to the United States (See *Pravda*, 27 September 1981).

117. Cited in AP report, *Baltimore Sun*, 24 November 1981.

118. Unlike Sadat who by 1981 was on very poor personal terms with the Saudi ruling family, Mubarak had kept up good personal relationships.

119. Radio Moscow in Arabic, 12 August 1981 (*FBIS: USSR*, 13 August 1981, p. H1).

120. See *FBIS: USSR*, 20 August 1981, p. A3.

121. *Izvestiia*, 5 November 1981.

122. See Moscow Radio in Arabic, 5 and 6 November 1981 (*FBIS: USSR*, 6 November 1981, pp. H1, H4).

123. The text of the communique is found in *FBIS: Middle East and Africa*, 12 November 1981, p. C4. Moscow, however, at least as reflected in a Moscow Radio Peace and Progress Arabic broadcast on 12 November 1981 was critical of the GCC meeting (*FBIS: USSR*, 13 November 1981, p. H4). One of the key issues not settled in the GCC meeting was Oman's proposal regarding Gulf security. If adopted the proposal would move the GCC closer to the United States.

124. See article by Scott Armstrong, *Washington Post*, 1 November 1981.

125. See *New York Times*, 2 October 1981.

126. See *Pravda*, 20 September 1981; and Moscow Radio Peace and Progress in Arabic, 20 October 1981 (*FBIS: USSR*, 21 October 1981, p. H7).

127. Moscow Radio in Arabic, 27 November 1981 (*FBIS: USSR*, 1 December 1981, pp. H5-H6).

5 Socialism, Communism, and Islam: Soviet Ideological Appeal in the Middle East

Udo Steinbach

The question of the ideological appeal of socialism in the Middle East has been a popular topic since the end of the Second World War. The 1950s and 1960s witnessed a proliferation of studies on the relationship between socialism, communism, and Islam in both the Middle East and the West.[1] At that time the guiding interest focused on varying perspectives of the future role of the Soviet Union in the area.[2] The fact that the Arab nationalist regimes that came to power in those years adopted socialism as a model for political, economic, and social transformation in their own countries seemed to bring them closer to the orbit of the Soviet Union and to open the door to an increase in Soviet influence. Given the resurgence of Islam as a political factor during the 1970s, there is speculation that this so-called re-Islamization, although creating turbulence in the relations between the West and some Islamic countries, might also constitute a natural barrier to the expansion of Communist Russia into the Middle East in particular and the Islamic world in general. This question, therefore, had a political connotation right from the beginning. It was assumed that in answering it, certain political conclusions with regard to the future of the relations between the Islamic world and the Soviet Union could be drawn. These, in turn, could be related to the East-West constellation, particularly with respect to the situation around the Persian Gulf.

Before trying to define more precisely the scope of problems we are going to deal with, it must be admitted that even a brief overview of the history of Soviet policy in relation to the Islamic states (from the 1950s up to Soviet relations with the revolutionary Islamic Republic of Iran and Soviet attitude toward the Iraq-Iranian conflict) shows an assessment of the ideological component to be extremely complex. The ambiguity in relations of the Arab nationalists (many of whom have remained practicing Muslims) with the local Communist parties and the Soviet Union in the 1950s and 1960s suggests that the answer to our question is not an easy one. Similarly, there are the cases of the staunchly anticommunist policy of the conservative Saudi regime, the volte-face of Libya's Qadhdhafi (who shows considerable Islamic fervor despite moving in 1974 from an anticommunist and anti-Soviet line to become a political ally of Moscow), the ambiguous attitude of the Islamic regime in Tehran toward both the Moscow-oriented Tudeh party and the Soviet Union, the resistance of the Islamic groups against the Soviet occupation of Afghanistan and, finally, the conservative Islamic garment adopted by the military dictatorship in Pakistan. These are only a few contradictory and confusing observations that indicate that the relations between Islam and the Soviet Union as well as Islam and communism are far from being one-dimensional.

It is therefore important to define more precisely what one really wants to discuss. For, as has been said by Bernard Lewis in 1953 in an article on Islam and communism,[3] there is no doubt that "the devout and pious Muslim theologian who has studied and understands the implications of dialectical materialism will reject that creed, but such a combination of circumstances is not common occurrence, nor likely to be of far-reaching significance."[4] So the real questions are two-fold. First, one has to consider what qualities and tendencies exist in Islam and in Islamic civilization and society that might either facilitate or impede the advance of communism. Secondly, one has to go beyond the generalizations that are necessarily the result of this approach and to analyze the specific political, social, economic, and cultural elements in the attitude adopted by Islamic regimes and groups toward the leading Communist state. This requires dealing with the question on a more or less political level.

Socialism, Islam, and Anticolonialism

It has been repeatedly stated—rightly one may say—that Islam and communism are two ideological systems of a totalitarian nature.[5] Islam dominates every act and every thought of the faithful. In principle, all actions are regulated by the ideological system, the foundations of which are the *Qur'an* and the *Sharia* tradition, which took the shape of Islamic law. This applies to the basic structure of the social and political system as well as to every other aspect of public life. Much of the same is true for Marxism, although it must be said that the doctrine never took over all the areas of life affected under Islamic totalitarianism. The Islamic ideological system (being derived from a religious revelation) and the Marxist ideology (being based on a materialist interpretation of history) would appear to be mutually exclusive. In terms of doctrine one cannot be a Marxist and a Muslim at the same time.

On the other hand, historical evidence proves that relations between the Islamic world and the Soviet Union (as well as between foreign ideologies adopted by the Islamic world in the course of the last hundred years and communism) have had a dynamic character. First of all, it was the anti-

Western theme on which both sides increasingly used to play. Right from the beginning, Soviet communism was anti-Western in two senses: it was both against the Western political and social systems and the Western states and governments and also against the West's way of life with its perceived immorality and emphasis on consumption. Islam, since its massive confrontation with the West in the nineteenth century, was, it is true, not anti-Western in itself. The Islamic elites to a great extent welcomed economic and social modernization along Western principles, and even some cultural patterns were accepted. Political liberalism and nationalism were regarded as a way out of backwardness and despotism. Even Islamic reformist movements in India or in Egypt (such as the one led by Muhammad Abduh, who died in 1905) aspired to bring about a synthesis of the basic tenets of Islam and the determining elements of the West, which were perceived as being superior from an economic and political point of view.

By the end of the First World War, however, this attitude was reversed. The Western states not only betrayed their own political principles, but where they had implemented them in the Middle East, they were exploited by the colonial powers to their own advantage. The new leading forces, which increased in strength before and during World War II and gradually seized power after the war, adopted an anticolonialist and—what became more and more synonymous—anti-Western attitude. Arab nationalism and Arab socialism, derived from Western ideologies, at first tried to define themselves against the background of corresponding Western ideologies but finally came into confrontation with the West. Islamic reformism after the First World War turned more and more into Islamic fundamentalism; the fact that in 1928 the Muslim Brotherhood was established, which directed its propaganda at the same time against the corrupt regimes as well as against negative Western influences, was indicative of the mood that prevailed. The masses, though different from the elites, always have been opposed to adopting the elements of Western culture and civilization, which they felt would destroy their own tradition, values, and the way of life that was deeply rooted in Islam.

Since that time, therefore, Communist propaganda against the West could always count on a ready response, especially when striking the anti-imperialist or anticolonialist drum. Since the second half of the 1950s when Nasir consolidated his power (as a kind of prototype of the new leadership that took over in many parts of the Arab world) anti-imperialism became one of the most important elements—in fact very often the only one—that constituted an alliance between Arab nationalists and the Soviet Union. This was in spite of the many differences that separated Nasir, for example, from the Soviet Union and from Marxist ideology.

A second element of a more general nature that lent Marxism a certain attraction was the level of social and economic backwardness in the Middle

East between the two world wars. The colonial powers had not shown any real interest in encouraging the independent economic development of the colonized countries but considered them as sources of raw materials for their own economy and as a market for their own industrial products. The colonialist powers cooperated with the local landlords and parts of the upper classes who made their profit from this cooperation. Thus, economic and social tensions increased.

Socialism in the Arab world came as a response mainly to this situation; its purpose was to abolish colonialism as an impediment to economic development, to cease feudalism and exploitation (particularly in agriculture), and to raise the standard of living of the entire population. Socialism, thus, was complementary to the struggle for national independence and, in fact, was part of it.

There were a number of questions related to the introduction and—from the end of the 1950s onward—implementation of Arab socialism: What kind of socialism was to be applied? Would it be molded according to the model of Western European social democracy or Marxism, or would it have a specific content in accordance with the traditions of the area? Would it be reconciled with Islamic principles of economic and social development, or would it be looked at by the *ulama* as a kind of apostasy?

There is no need to summarize the numerous volumes published on Arab socialism.[6] In principle, no fundamental contradiction was seen between Arab socialism and Islam. In his Charter of 1962, Nasir uses, it is true, a terminology that stems from Marxism: that the revolution is the only way toward progress and change; that the socialist solution is a historical necessity in order to abolish economic and social disparities; that class struggle is unavoidable; that the revolution should seize on the means of production, and so forth. But at the same time he confesses his belief in God and stresses that the revolution is guided by the principles of Islam. And the principles of change obviously are inspired by the basic principles of Islam: to a certain degree the right to private property was acknowledged, and the Marxist dictatorship of the proletariat as the final stage of revolutionary class struggle was rejected. In the ideal society, which according to Islamic principles should be characterized by perfect equality of all believers of the Islamic community (*umma*), there was no room for domination of one class over another, even domination by the proletariat. In a number of religious judgments, however, the highest authority of *al-Azhar* confirmed that there is not only no basic contradiction between Islam and socialism but also that socialism has been embodied in Islam right from the outset.[7]

Ba'th socialism, although of a more secular nature, claims (as a minimal concession to Islam) that the historical and cultural heritage of Islam is an inspiration for all Arabs as far as their common political destination is concerned.[8] In the Algerian constitution socialism is said to be the goal of social transformation, while at the same time Islam is regarded as the religion of the state.[9]

It is logical, therefore, that the relations between Arab socialists and the Soviet Union have been characterized by ambiguity. On one hand, the Islamic element in Arab socialism, as well as the fact that the socialists considered themselves part and parcel of the Islamic and Arab tradition, made them continuously emphasize the independence of their ideological approach as well as of their political line. Moreover, they reproached the Soviet Union for the materialistic and atheistic character of its ideology. On the other hand, it was not only the anticolonialist line that brought them closer to each other. There were striking similarities as far as the approach of the Arab socialists to economic and social politics was concerned: the terminology itself, of which some examples have been quoted in the preceding paragraphs; the role of the state in the economic system; some of the measures being implemented such as nationalizations, land reform, and the establishment of either unity parties or other parties, which (like the Ba'th party) claim to have a quasi-monopoly of power and consider themselves as vanguards of social and political change. All these elements amounted to a certain similarity of political, social, and economic structures between the Communist and Islamic socialist systems. Consequently, although insisting on a Third Way (which was more systematically elaborated in 1973 by the Libyan leader Qadhdhafi in his Third International Theory[10]) and independence from both the capitalist and the socialist blocs, the Arab socialists were during the late 1950s, the 1960s, and—as far as they have survived—also in the 1970s, closer to the Soviet Union than to the West.

It was the Soviet Union itself that had some ideological difficulties in giving the new ideology its place within Moscow's rigid Marxist coordinates of real economic and social progress. The ideology of Arab or Islamic socialism and its protagonists in the Arab world stemmed, in most cases, from petty bourgeois or rural origins. They were looked at with mistrust, and Soviet propaganda (even after Stalin's death in 1953) still categorically insisted that socialism would only be brought about by a Communist party. It was not until the second half of the 1950s that an ideological thaw permitted Soviet ideologues to admit that the so-called national democratic forces in the Third World had a role to play in the process of the transformation of backward traditional societies into progressive ones. Nevertheless, it was maintained that the final stage of transformation—the real socialist society—could only be achieved under the leadership of Communist forces. On the way toward a more realistic and flexible attitude, the Twentieth Congress of the Communist Party (1956) can be considered a turning point.[11]

Incompatibilities

As a whole, socialism has remained a vague notion in the Islamic world. According to a definition by Gebran Majdalani, a leading member of the Ba'th party in the 1950s, a party is called socialist "whose programme includes the abolition of social classes, the vesting of the principal resources of the country in the community, and the struggle against capitalism—first international and then national capitalism."[12] The important point is that there was nothing in this understanding of socialism that could not be made compatible with Islam; Islam even could be interpreted to have embodied socialism right from its outset. This explains why, for a while, socialism had a considerable impact on many Muslims, particularly in the Arab world, who were aspiring toward the modernization of their countries and toward social justice. The opposition and animosity against socialism shown by a number of traditionalist and Islamic regimes, particularly on the Arabian peninsula, had its roots not so much in the fact that they had considered socialism irreconcilable with Islamic traditions or that coexistence was impossible. It had more to do with the aggressive political propaganda directed against the conservative regimes by some Arab socialists. An antisocialist attitude became more of a precautionary measure for the political survival of the conservative regimes than it was a matter of ideological and/or religious principles.[13]

On the other hand, communism and Arab socialism have been two competing ideologies in the Islamic world. The rise of communism as a political force dates back to the 1920s when Communist parties were founded in some parts of the Middle East.[14] For a variety of reasons, the role these parties have been playing in the past and the appeal of communism in general have remained very limited. For one, the mutual exclusiveness of the two most stringent ideological systems, which already has been mentioned, is to be cited as one of the most relevant factors. The materialist approach of Marxism is rejected by a Muslim, and it must be emphasized once more that on purely doctrinal grounds it is impossible to reconcile Islam and communism. The central theme of Islam, and indeed its raison d'être, is God and belief in God as the sovereign ruler of the universe. As a system, Islam measures all things in terms of its all-inclusive divine code, even the institution of private property and the regulation of its possession, disposal, and inheritance.

The second reason is the absence—at least until recently—of the economic and social conditions out of which communism grows. There was practically no working class and no real proletariat that would constitute a socially and politically active factor. Hence, there were only small circles that accepted the Communist parties as their political spearhead. The arguments of Communist propaganda remained rather intellectual and therefore appealed mainly to intellectuals.[15]

Finally, the complete dependence of the Communist parties on the Soviet Union remained a handicap. Even if sympathizing with one or another element of Communist propaganda or even of Soviet politics (for instance anticolonialism), the nationalist elites as well as the majority of the politically conscious parts of the masses were not ready to undergo a new dependence on Moscow while trying or having succeeded in shaking off the yoke of European colonialism.

As a modernizing ideology Arab socialism after the Second World War has won the day over communism—ideologically and politically. Although many Arab Communists tried to exploit Islam to their purposes and to insert references in their propaganda to the Qur'an, the number of their followers always remained rather limited. Arab socialism seemed to be more adequate in view of the manifold problems the Arab world was facing: it could more easily be reconciled with the religious and historical traditions and—last but not least—it was more in accordance with the nationalist aspirations of the new leaders who strove for independence and the national grandeur of their own state or for the Arab nation as a whole.

Islam in the 1970s and 1980s

Obviously, the situation has undergone significant changes during the last decade. The most striking feature has been the revival of Islam not only from a religious point of view but even more conspicuously as an element of social and political development.[16] Even by the middle of the 1970s many observers and analysts would not have predicted that revolutionary Islam could become such a dynamic force and constitute a threat, not only to the secular states but also to the conservative Islamic regimes. This was despite taking notice of the re-Islamization coming—partly as a consequence of the increase in self-assertiveness of the Muslims, in general, and the growing influence, in particular, of conservative Islam in the wake of the explosion of oil income for the conservative Arab oil states.

Walter Laqueur, who in the mid-1950s was one of the first to turn his attention toward the relationship between the Soviet Union and Islam in the Middle East, even went further: "If anything, the Arab countries are no more likely than most others in the world to provide a favorable breeding-ground for communism. The problem of the affinity between Islam and communism is . . . of secondary importance at the present time. What is decisive is that Islam has gradually ceased to be a serious competitor of communism in the struggle for the soul of the present potential elites in the countries of the Middle East."[17] Developments since then have proved that Laqueur was wrong in a double sense: not only has Islam become a political and social element more vigorous than ever, but the question of affinity between Islam and communism has regained a certain relevancy. A brief glance at the genesis of the phenomenon is necessary.

It has been stated correctly that the year 1967 (that is, the year of the defeat of Nasir and various other regimes in the Middle East at the hands of the Israelis) can be considered a kind of watershed for the ideological and political developments in the Middle East. With the defeat it became dramatically obvious that the ideologies that had provided the guiding orientations since the end of the Second World War had failed. Nationalism, it is true, had led to independence of most parts of the Middle East but had at the same time brought to the fore the deep fragmentation of the entire area along political, ideological, social, and economic lines. The great unity that some had dreamed of ever since the First World War, and for which the Arab League should have been a symbol, had not been achieved. The defeat showed at one stroke how hollow the propaganda of Arab nationalism had been. At the same time the crisis of nationalism meant a crisis of the principles and ideologies that had guided economic and social developments in many parts of the region. Arab socialism had failed to lay the foundations for sound economic and social development in individual states as well as throughout the Middle East and to bring a higher degree of social justice as the precondition to real national cohesiveness between the various groups, layers, and classes of the population.

The revival of Islam is a complex process. What many Muslims felt to be necessary was to look for other principles that might be more adequate to overcome the apparent political, economic, and social stagnation. From the outset, communism played no role in this search for alternatives. There was no Communist party from which serious inspirations could be expected, not the least reason being that they had been weakened by the ruling Arab regimes throughout the 1960s. Moscow lacked credibility not only because it had failed to lend support to the Communist parties, which had come under pressure, but because for a long time it had been a close ally of those establishment forces that had been defeated in 1967. Furthermore, some attempts to gain greater influence by leftist forces were frustrated in the beginning of the 1970s in countries such as Egypt or Sudan.

In this situation many Muslims turned toward Islam as a new hope that would bring about tangible political, economic, and social change. At the same time, the desire was to remain fully in accordance with the basic tenets of the Islamic religion, maintaining a Muslim identity and avoiding alienation, which inevitably had been a consequence of the decision to develop the Islamic world according to Western principles, goals, and values.

Although many external factors have had an impact, the rise of the fundamentalists (who soon turned out to dominate the Islamic scene) must be seen first and foremost as a reaction to the failure of the ideologies aforementioned. Now the approach was completely different. While socialism was a Western notion, one that had taken pains to prove that it could be reconciled with Islam, now a political, social, economic, and cultural system was to be established that rested upon Islamic foundations and represented a fundamental alternative to the existing order that was determined and still partly dominated by the West.

The ideological and theological tools of the fundamentalist movement had been mainly forged in the nineteenth and early twentieth century by a modernizing movement within Islam called *Salafiyya* (derived from Arabic *as'salaf as salih*, "the sound ancestors"), with the Wahhabi movement in the eighteenth century being a forerunner to Salafiyya. It was constituted by a number of prominent theologians who responded to the challenge from the West. The starting point was the question of how one could overcome European superiority without giving up the Islamic foundations of private and public life. The decisive step taken by the Salafiyya reformists consisted in referring to an ideal of early Islam, which made it possible to accept new ideas as being Islamic or to reject them as not being consistent with Islam. They were inspired by the wish to modernize Islam and to show that there was no contradiction between Islam and modernity. It was not a reactionary approach to reality but an attempt at establishing an order, which on the one hand would use the criteria of modernity taken from the West and at the same time would be totally determined by the principles of Islam as laid down in the Qur'an and as practiced in the first decades of Islamic history.[18]

Different Strands of Islam

Saudi Arabia

Islamic fundamentalism as a political force is by no means a homogeneous and monolithic movement. With regard to the problem dealt with in this chapter, one has to distinguish between two types of Islamic fundamentalism. One can be said to be represented by Saudi Arabia. The alliance between the Wahhabi movement and the family of Saud, which dates back over more than two centuries, is still the backbone of the regime. Wahhabism has long since lost its revolutionary fervor and Islam has to lend legitimacy to a regime that for a number of reasons comes under internal and external pressure. There is an increasing number of critics of the regime who question if the Saudi regime is still really Islamic (this was the case, for example, with the group that occupied the Grand Mosque of Mecca in November 1979). Therefore, Saudi Islam is totally status quo oriented; it is staunchly antirevolutionary whether these revolutionary forces be of a Marxist or militant Islamic nature. Given the status quo orientation of the regime within an Arab world full of anti-status quo forces that partly have adopted Communist ideology or at least are politically backed by Moscow, the Saudis cannot help being anticommunist. They are staunchly anti-Marxist even as they react against militant Islamic fundamentalism, especially as propagated by the Islamic Republic of Iran. It is mainly this perception of a threat to the regime, emanating from Marxism and from other militant anti-status quo forces in and outside the country, that makes the Saudis pro-Western. There is no inherent affection on the part of conservative Islamic fundamentalism for the West. Furthermore, with anti-Western forces in the Middle East on the rise, mainly fomented by militant Islamic fundamentalism, it has become more difficult to follow a pro-Western orientation.

Iran

At this point the question has to be raised as to why changes in the area since the outbreak of the Iranian revolution have led to an estrangement in the relations between the West and the Middle East, but why this cannot be said with regard to Soviet-Middle Eastern relations? To answer this question one has to refer to the second strand of Islamic fundamentalism. It consists of the numerous religious and political forces that advocate a complete turnover of nearly all the existing regimes into an Islamic Order. So far, it is true, Khumayni is the most "successful" of them. But as developments in Egypt and Syria have shown, the Muslim Brotherhood and their even-more militant offshoots like *Takfir wa Hijrah* ("Penance and Retreat")[19] are other forces that have gained considerable political momentum. The very complex relationship between the Islamic regime in Tehran and the Soviet Union on one hand and between the ruling Islamic Republican party and the Marxist (Moscow-oriented) Tudeh party on the other, gives the question of the relations between revolutionary Islam and Marxism its actuality.

First of all it seems that anti-Westernism now has a new dimension. To an increasing number of Muslims the West appears to be a danger in that its attractions are nearly irresistible to a Muslim whose world has lapsed into backwardness compared to the West. The revival of Islam first and foremost seeks to restore spiritual independence. This is manifested in external independence if not in polemics and open hostility against the West. In general its intensity is most vehement where Western influence has been strongest. While the West is perceived to be a spiritual threat, Marxism remains "only" an external threat, represented by the Soviet Union and its military power. For the Muslim, real attraction emanates neither from Marxism nor from the Soviet Union. The latter, it is true, should not be underestimated, but after all it is a calculable element, the expansion of which can be controlled and—if necessary—resisted. As a consequence of this, although in principle Marxism and Islam exclude each other, the West remains a more dangerous threat than Marxism to the Muslim and the Islamic set of values as understood by Islamic militants. So developments during the last years have reached a point at which the United States is identified with all the negative effects of the economic and social-development process. With the attempt made by Islamists at preserving or achieving true independence as they understand it, the threat from Marxism grows pale compared to the West in general and the United States in particular.

Islam and Communism: Points of Convergence

Another argument that comes up at this point is a negative one. In the eyes of an average Westerner who believes in liberalism and democracy, the authoritarian and totalitarian character of Marxist regimes has a repugnant effect. This applies even to those who might sympathize with one or another element of Communist doctrine. This is not the case with a Muslim. The Islamic historical experience is characterized by living under totalitarian rule. Although there are many Muslims who try to prove that Islam is democratic in principle, there are only several moments in the history of the Middle Eastern and Islamic world in which attempts at establishing democratic rules have been made. The earthly state is an integral part of the Islamic religion. It is not only the instrument to expand Islam and the divine realm all over the world, but it also guarantees the Muslim that he can live an Islamic life in accordance with the divine law, the sharia. It is the ruler who has to take care that the sharia is observed by the subjects. In the early centuries of Islamic history, as long as power rested with the Caliphs who were regarded as successors to the Prophet, the religious and political ideal was in harmony with the way power was exerted. Later on, however, power was more and more usurped by force without a credible religious legitimation. It was at this stage of Islamic history that many theologians took pains to elaborate that every order—even an unjust one—was better than anarchy. The argument of Ibn Jama'a, the Chief Qadi of Cairo (died 1333), is not untypical: "Whoever has effective power, has the right to obedience, for a government, even the worst one, is better than anarchy, and of the two evils one chooses the lesser."[20]

There is no need to prove the totalitarian character of present-day Islamic governments. If one looks at expressly Islamic regimes such as Saudi Arabia, Libya, or Pakistan, and if we bear in mind what has happened since the beginning of the Islamic Republic of Iran, it is self-evident. Even if there are Islamic groups or parties with programs that contain some elements that sound democratic—such as the Muslim Brotherhood or the *Jamaati-i Islami* in Pakistan[21]—the formulations remain vague enough so that one is justified doubting how serious they are. Therefore, given this historical experience as well as the political circumstances under which most of the Muslims live, the totalitarian and repressive character of Communist political systems would not in itself represent an argument against Communist ideology. Moreover, political liberalism, individual freedom, and a multiparty system are considered by many members of the modernizing elites to be a luxury the Islamic world cannot afford, given the problems of underdevelopment. In addition to this, the policy of the colonial powers, which propagated Western liberalism on the one hand and kept large parts of the Islamic world under colonial rule on the other, has discredited liberal political values in the eyes of many Muslims.

Beyond the lack of political and physical freedom in both systems, there is also a lack of freedom in a humanistic sense. Islam and communism subordinate the right of the individual to the fulfillment of the collective interest. The Muslim is not only subject to the will of God; in fact, he very often sees his fate predestined by it. In the same way, the interests of the state as the manifestation of God on earth are given priority over the aspirations of the individual. To a high degree the welfare of the state (or of Islam) is identified with the prosperity of the individual. Man has no rights in himself; this is the reason why human rights as autonomous values inalienably linked to the individual is a concept so difficult to understand for a Muslim. The Marxist on his part also tends to see the value of the individual subordinated to collective categories, whether social class, the party, or, finally, the state itself.

Both Islam and communism are to a high degree utopian as they believe that all social injustices and ills afflicting this world will be rectified and a sort of utopia will prevail once the external factors that throw society out of balance are done away with and balance is restored. For the Muslim, perfect society can be hoped for by the establishment of the external order within which, apart from human inward change, it can be actualized.[22]

The Communists, too, believe that the proletarian utopia is attainable once a set of external factors replaces another set; that is, once communism replaces capitalism. Society would ultimately become so perfect that the restraining hand of government becomes superfluous. The only difference between Islam and communism in this respect is the means by which their respective utopias are to be brought about.

At this point there is an opening for communism to intrude into Islam. Islam does not draw a clear line between the two realms—the spiritual and temporal. That is why the common man in Islam is exposed to the danger of obliterating the spiritual when the temporal is overemphasized. Herein lies the danger in terms of a possible intrusion of communism into Islam, and it is precisely what has been happening. One finds a race between modern Muslim writers and Communists aimed at showing which system offers more of the fruits of this temporal world and which can better bring about social justice, security, and solidarity. By placing most of their emphasis on the temporal, modern Muslim writers have in effect reduced Islam to a social program. The result of this transformation, irrespective of all good intentions, is twofold. First, it undermines the raison d'être of Islam itself: belief in God as the sovereign ruler of the universe. Once this is done in total or in part, the second result becomes inevitable. Muslims will find their social program in a more attractive form, and buttressed with an apparently perfect and comprehensive philosophy, in communism. They can find in communism all the temporal blessings of Islam improved, refined, and embellished by technology and free from all metaphysical difficulties.

These reflections might enable us to understand to a certain extent what happened recently in Iran and what is likely to happen in the future. One example of the remarkable alliances between Islam and communism is the case of the Iranian *mujahhidin i-khalq*, in which Islam is blended with a pure Marxist program.[23] Here we can see how the utopian desire for a just and perfect society, which grew out of the ugly circumstances prevailing under the shah and was cherished by young Muslims, became adapted to Marxist terminologies and strategies. The mujahhidin understand themselves as Muslims and insist in steering a leftist course independent from Moscow.

Even the doctrine and propaganda of the more fundamentalist forces show various features that remind one of Communist elements. There is, for example, the case of economic policy. Although the majority of the theorists of an Islamic economy state that Islam allows private property, there are a number of fundamentalists who tend to restrict the legitimacy of private property. Bani Sadr, for example, argues that "the Islamic notion of property means exclusively man's continuous right to his own labour, and this in turn means a classless society." The objective of the Qur'an, he holds, is to "abolish man's domination over man and build a unitary society."[24] *Iqtisad-j touhidi* ("unitary economics") is popular not just with the Khumaynists but also with the Tudeh, the *fida'iyin*,[25] and the mujahhidin. In substance, much of the government's economic program—the extension of state control, nationalization, and ensuring the worker's rights to the fruits of his own labor—is virtually identical to what the fida'iyin and mujahhidin called for in their programs of February 1979.

Similarly, in many points the rhetoric of the leaders of the Islamic Republic of Iran resembles Communist propaganda. This applies not only to the anti-Western rhetoric or the fact that they strongly advocate the Palestinian cause. Equally important is the leaders' support for the *mostaz'afin* ("disinherited masses"). At the same time, Khumayni and his followers encourage opposition to capitalism and imperialism, seek a classless society in which wealth is redistributed, advocate state nationalization of industries, and pursue a foreign policy of militant nonalignment.[26]

This similarity between the extreme right and the extreme left at times makes them virtually indistinguishable. It is precisely this interdependence between radical right and left that accounts for the erosion of the center and the leftward drive of the Iranian revolution in the name of Islam.

These similarities provided the ground on which the Marxist Tudeh party was able to coexist with the Islamic Republican party as long as the latter's totalitarian claim on power permitted another independent political party to exist. Only in the course of 1982 was the Tudeh forced to go underground and to follow the precedent of all the other parties and groups that had emerged after the establishment of the Islamic Republic. From an ideological point of view, the Tudeh followed the pattern introduced by the Soviet Union in the beginning of 1979 in explaining the developments in Iran. Social and political elements of the Iranian revolution were hailed as were some of the economic measures implemented by the new leadership, while at the same time ignoring or at least playing down the religious element. For the Islamic regime in Tehran, on the other hand, Tudeh remained the only political group that backed many of the basic political, economic, and social orientations and measures of the Islamic regime and was ready to acquiesce in the repression of the various other political groups. In the end, it makes no great difference whether one sees the opposition as relics and representatives of a foreign—namely Western—*Weltanschauung* or as capitalist and imperialist stooges; they are reactionaries anyhow and have to be eliminated.

Conclusions

The question of whether there is Soviet ideological appeal in the Middle East can be answered as such in the negative if it is posed merely on the level of ideology. If there is a danger that communism, and this would mean Soviet influence, will spread into the Islamic world, it stems from the fact that in Islam and communism as ideologies there are so many similarities in terms of political system and economic as well as social policy and strategy. It is not inconceivable that communism might be regarded by Muslims simply as another strategy to achieve the Islamic vision of an earthly utopia. Or, as Elie Kedourie has stated, Islamic doctrines, although they embody a backward-looking vision of a society in which Qur'anic prescriptions would be supreme, also merge with the most powerful current of revolutionary doctrine in the world today, that of Marxism.[27]

There are two other points that should be taken into consideration—one of a more general, the other one of a more specific nature. The rise of Islamic fundamentalism in the last decade has made Islam—more than it ever has been the case—an ideology to determine the fate and the structures of the Islamic world in all its aspects. The fundamentalists, who claim that the sound state of Islamic society cannot be separated from the right belief of the Muslim, have stressed the Islamic appearance and structures of state and society even more than they have cared for the spiritual salvation of the believer. This orientation toward the worldly aspects of Islam makes them think and act primarily in terms of political interests. To materialize these interests, the majority of the religious regimes as well as parties and groups follow a highly unscrupulous and sometimes even immoral policy. Their interests vary from case to case. Their scope ranges from the necessity to defend a regime against internal opposition (such as Iran or Saudi Arabia) to an active struggle against external interference as is the case with the Afghan resistance groups. The decision of which side the various fundamentalist regimes or groups ally themselves rests with a complex set of factors.

The minor point that makes one suspect that the fundamentalist movement could fall prey to communism is the fatalism that, at least in Iran, is gaining ground due to the political and economic failure of the Islamic regime. Given the continuous Islamic interference in daily life, given the bottlenecks in the supply of many goods (especially food), and given the insecurity of life in general, an increasing number of people could come to believe that communism—in spite of all its well-known shortcomings—might be better than nothing. It could be seen as an alternative to a situation in which people have no employment, where they are suffering from soaring prices, in which music is forbidden and traveling restricted. The frustration, therefore, could diminish the resistance against communism of those politically conscious groups that under more normal conditions in Iran had resisted an overt or covert Communist takeover.

Finally, one must see, that as the more fundamentalist Islam is striving to create the paradise on earth, it comes close to communism, which not only promised it again and again but can show considerable achievements as far as the standard of living of the Muslims in the Soviet Union is concerned. Soviet Central Asia might be far from being a paradise, but in any case it has become more developed than most parts of the Islamic Middle East. That some Muslims in the Soviet Union are aware of this fact can be seen in a quotation from a *khutba* ("Friday sermon") by Kazy Kamal Bashirov in the Ufa mosque in April 1970: "Our government prizes man most of all. That is why it gives all riches of the earth to the service of man. . . . Our state strives to create for you and us, for all Soviet people, a paradise on earth."[28] The quotation sheds light on the fact that a Muslim who places the earthly utopia over spiritual perfection could be seduced by the promises and achievements of communism. At least he ceases to see a fundamental contradiction between Islam and communism and comes to terms with the latter. Such a mood, however, could pave the way for those who are determined to use any opportunity to introduce communism as a solution to the tremendous political, social, and economic problems most of the Middle Eastern states are experiencing.

Once the Muslims—disillusioned with Western economic models and convinced that Western liberalism is not feasible as a political model—turn to Islamic fundamentalism, and once fundamentalism proves that it is not able to live up to the expectations of the Muslim masses and to create a political, economic, and social order worthwhile to live in (not to speak of a paradise), communism might be at hand to provide the blueprint for the establishment of the ideal order of which so many Muslims dream.[29]

Notes

1. For bibliographical references, see *Encyclopedia of Islam*, New Edition, vol. 4, s.v. ishtirakiyya (Leiden: Brill, 1978), p. 186; and Wolfgang Ule, *Bibliographie zu Fragen des arabischen Sozialismus, des Nationalismus und des Kommunismus unter dem Gesichtspunkt des Islams* (Hamburg: Deutsches Orient-Institut, Dokumentations-Leitstelle Moderner Orient, 1967).

2. See Walter Z. Laqueur, *Communism and Nationalism in the Middle East* (London: Routledge and Kegan Paul, 1956); and Laqueur, *The Soviet Union and the Middle East* (London: Routledge and Kegan Paul, 1959).

3. Bernard Lewis, "Communism and Islam," in Walter Z. Laqueur, *The Middle East in Transition* (New York: Praeger, 1958), pp. 311-324.

4. Ibid., p. 311.

5. Maxime Rodinson, "Relationships Between Islam and Communism," in his *Marxism and the Muslim World* (London: Zed Press, 1972), pp. 34-59.

6. For bibliographical references see note 1. For a presentation of the main currents of Arab socialism as well as of the arguments of its adversaries, see Wolfgang Ule, *Der arabische Sozialismus und der zeitgenössische Islam* (Opladen: C.W. Leske Verlag, 1969).

7. Ibid., pp. 89-102. Examples of this attitude are given in Kemal Karpat, ed., *Political and Social Thought in the Contemporary Middle East* (London: Pall Mall Press, 1968). See pp. 122-125 (Mustafa al-Siba'i); pp. 126-132 (Mahmud Shaltut); and pp. 153-156 (Ramadan Lawand).

8. For an extensive bibliography, see John F. Devlin, *The Ba'th Party: A History From Its Origins to 1966* (Stanford: Hoover Institution Press, 1976); and Werner Schmucker, "Studium zur Baath-Ideologie," *Die Welt des Islams* 14 (1973):47-80. See also vol. 15 (1974):146-182.

9. For the full text of the new constitution, see *Orient* 17, no. 4 (1976): 152-174.

10. Muammar Al-Kadhafi, *The Green Book* (Tripoli, Libya: Distributed by the Public Establishment for Publishing, Advertising, and Distribution).

11. An overview of the development of Soviet attitudes toward Arab socialism from an ideological point of view is given by Jaan Pennar, *The USSR and the Arabs: The Ideological Dimension* (London: Hurst, 1973);

Pennar, "The Arabs, Marxism and Moscow," *The Middle East Journal* 22, no. 4 (1968):433-447; and Hans Bräker, *Marxismus-Leninismus und Islam zur ideologischen Einordung des Islams in der Sowjetunion*, Berichte des Bundesinstituts für ostwissenschaftliche und internationale Studien, vol. 36, 1968.

12. Gebran Majdalani, "The Arab Socialist Movement," in Walter Z. Laqueur, *The Middle East in Transition* (New York: Praeger, 1958), pp. 337-350.

13. This has to be seen in the context of King Faysal's efforts initiated in the mid-1960s to rally conservative forces against Nasir under the banner of an Islamic conference. One of the strongest arguments used by those against Arab socialism was to equate it with communism and thus to discredit it in the eyes of the Muslim world.

14. For the role of communism in the Arab world, see M.S. Agwani, *Communism in the Arab East* (London-Bombay: Asia Publishing House, 1969). A brief survey has been given recently by Arnold Hottinger, "Arab Communism at Low Ebb," *Problems of Communism* 30 (July-August 1981):17-32.

15. Hottinger, ibid., pp. 17-22; Dankwart A. Rustow, "The Appeal of Communism to Islamic Peoples," in J. Harris Proctor, ed., *Islam and International Relations* (New York: Praeger, 1965), pp. 40-60; Wolfgang Ule, "Kommunismus und Ba'th-Sozialismus in Syrien im Wettstreit um die Macht," in *Vierteljahresberichte des Forschungs-instituts der Friedrich-Ebert-Stiftung* 27, 1967, pp. 15-36; and Robin Buss, *Wary Partners: The Soviet Union and Arab Socialism* (London: The Institute for Strategic Studies, 1970).

16. There is a vast literature on this subject. See, for example, D. Khalid, *Die politische Rolle des Islam im Vorderen Orient: Einführung und Dokumentation* (Hamburg: Deutsches Orient-Institut/Dokumentations-Leitstelle Moderner Orient, 1979); Bassam Tibi, *Die Krise des modernen Islams: Eine vorindustrielle Kultur im wissenschaftlich-technischen Zeitalter* (München: Beck Verlag, 1981); R.H. Dekmejian, "The Anatomy of Islamic Legitimacy Crisis," *Middle East Journal,* 34, no. 1 (1980):1-12; and Daniel Pipes, "'This World is Political!' The Islamic Revival of the Seventies," *Orbis* 24, no. 1 (1980):9-41.

17. Laqueur, *Communism and Nationalism*, p. 6.

18. Wilfred Cantwell Smith, *Islam in Modern History* (Princeton: Princeton University Press, 1963); Malcolm H. Kerr, *Islamic Reform: The Political and Legal Theories of Muhammad Abduh and Rashid Rida* (Berkeley: University of California Press, 1966); C.C. Adams, *Islam and Modernism in Egypt: A Study of the Modern Reform Movement Inaugurated by Muhammad Abduh* (New York: Russell and Russell, 1968); and N. Keddie, *An Islamic Response to Imperialism: Political and Religious*

Writings of Sayyid Jamal al-Din 'Al-Afghani' (Berkeley: University of California Press, 1968).

19. M.W. Wenner, "Modern Islamic Reform Movements: The Muslim Brotherhood in Contemporary Egypt," *Middle East Journal* 36, no. 3 (1982):336-361; and S.D. Ibrahim, "Anatomy of Egypt's Militant Islamic Groups: Methodological Note and Preliminary Findings," *International Journal of Middle East Studies* 12, no. 4 (1980):423-453.

20. H.A.R. Gibb, "Constitutional Organization," in M. Khadduri and H.J. Liebesny, *Law in the Middle East* 1 (Washington, D.C.: 1955), p. 23; Badr ud-Din ibn Dschama'a, "Tahrir al-ahkam fi tadbir ahl al-Islam," translated by Hans Kohler, in *Islamica* 4 (Leipzig: 1934); and G.E. v. Grunebaum, *Der Islam im Mittelalter* (Zurich: 1963), pp. 169-204.

21. K. Bahadur, *The Jama'at-i Islami of Pakistan: Political Thought and Political Action* (New Delhi: Chetana Publications, 1977), and D. Khalid, "The Final Replacement of Parliamentary Democracy by the 'Islamic System' in Pakistan," *Orient* 20, no. 4 (1979):16-38. On Moudoodi (founder of Jamaat'i Islami), see S.R. Ahmad, *Maulana Maududi and the Islamic State* (Lahore: People's Publishing House, 1976).

22. K. Cragg, "The Impact of Communism Upon Contemporary Islam," *Middle East Journal* 8 (1954):127-138.

23. For details on the origins and evolution of the mujahhidin (and other groups), see Ervand Abrahamian, *The Guerilla Movement in Iran, 1963-1977*, MERIP Reports (Washington, D.C.), no. 86, March-April 1980.

24. *Iqtisad-i touhidi* is the title of Bani Sadr's most important work on Islamic economics. More easily accessible for the Western reader who does not know the Persian language are his French writings. The most comprehensive is *Quelle révolution pour l'Iran?* Preface de Paul Vieille (Paris: Fayolle, 1980). For a summary of his thinking, see Wolfgang S. Freund, *Welche Zukunft für den Iran? Die entwicklungs-politischen Grundideen des Abolhassan Banisadr* (Wien: Wilhelm Braumüller, 1981).

25. On this extreme leftist group, see Abrahamian, *The Guerilla Movement in Iran*.

26. Shahram Chubin, "Leftist Forces in Iran," *Problems of Communism* 29, no. 4 (1980):1-25, particularly pp. 23-24.

27. Elie Kedourie, *Islamic Revolution*, Salisbury Papers no. 6 (London: The Salisbury Group), p. 4.

28. Sergei A. Shuiskii, "Muslims in the Soviet State: Islam, a Privileged Religion? (1955-1980)," *Oriente Moderno* 60, 7-12 (1980):400.

29. Réné Jammes, "Communisme et Islam: Inconciliables?" *L'Afrique et l'Asie* 55, no. 3 (1961):3-16.

6 Western Strategic Options in the Middle East

Kenneth Hunt

The Strategic Setting

No region has seen in the last decade so many events of strategic importance as has the Middle East. The first oil crisis, coming on top of the October 1973 war, dramatically brought home to the West its dependence on oil, and particularly Persian Gulf oil. It should be said at once that the West should have no more reason to expect to have control over these oil supplies than the oil producers should expect to have control over advanced Western technology.[1] But the West does need security of oil supplies if its economies are to be stable. Countries may hope to achieve this by normal trading in normal times, but the problem is that conditions in the Middle East are too often abnormal.

Just as nations, for example, had slowly and uncomfortably learned to live with the first oil-price increases, the revolution in Iran in February 1979 produced a second oil crisis and a doubling of prices within a year. But that was not all. The fall of the shah was also the collapse of the Western strategic position in the Gulf, and the continuing hostility of the new regime to the United States made matters worse. Then in December 1979 came the invasion of Afghanistan and the installation of strong Soviet forces within striking distance of the Gulf. Though this action united the Muslim world in protest, the invasion of Iran by Iraq in September 1980 divided it again.

Unhampered access to Gulf oil is clearly a vital interest for the West (and should be for the producers, too), and at least a degree of stability in the region may be needed to preserve this. Stability, however, is also important in its own right. In the Middle East there are the seeds of conflict that, once started, could well spread beyond it, and also tensions that can be exploited by the Soviet Union to undermine the Western strategic position. The political scene in the Middle East traditionally has been extremely confusing and remains so today.[2] Although there are some common threads (oil, militant Islam, the Arab-Israeli dispute), regional rivalries tangle the web: Syria and Iraq, Iran and Iraq, India and Pakistan, Somalia and Ethiopia, the two Yemens, Oman and South Yemen. Not surprisingly, the Soviets have attempted to gain advantages from these disputes, and have conducted an assertive foreign policy backed by a capability and willingness to use force and to supply weapons to others willing to use it. Soviet activity has, therefore, extended from the Horn of Africa to Afghanistan, and its influence is felt across the Middle East and Africa to India and beyond.

The Threats

In the Gulf, a dispiriting list can be made of the things that can go wrong in the future. Iranian military successes against Iraq now threaten the conservative Gulf regimes. Regardless of the war's outcome, there will still remain a legacy of bitterness and mistrust, probably ensuring continuing border confrontation and clashes. This may offer scope for outside manipulation through arms supplies and aid. Kurdish rebellion in either country could prosper. In Iran the West has lost its strategic foothold and its political influence. This discomfiture no doubt brought Soviet satisfaction but has not immediately been translated into Soviet influence: Godless Moscow may be hardly more acceptable than satanic Washington.[3] But Iran could still virtually disintegrate, with Azerbaidzhan, Kurdistan, and Khuzistan challenging whatever authority the central regime claims. Oil production could fall even lower than now. Worse still, factions friendly to the Soviet Union might attain power in Tehran and call for Soviet military support to protect them on the pattern of Afghanistan.

Other Gulf states will face internal unrest as they attempt to deal with the rapid transition from desert shaykhdoms to relatively modernized societies. It can be expected that their populations may demand a greater role in the management of affairs. Militant Islam, resisting imported cultures and change, could be a disruptive influence. Shi'i-Sunni antagonisms have already made themselves widely felt.[4] Other causes of instability could be Palestinian-inspired unrest or even terrorism among expatriate workers; Communist, Iranian, or Palestinian-aided subversion and insurgency; and the spill-over of Arab-Israeli clashes. Soviet exploitation would be inherently likely. Moscow will see good reason to seize any opportunity to help overturn regimes that are pro-Western, precisely as has been done in Africa. Such political action does not carry the risks that Soviet military intervention would. It is more difficult to counter because of its gradual nature and because it can fasten on local discontents. In due course, invitations may be extended to the Soviets, leading to an increased physical presence in the Middle East.

Not all the Gulf regimes seem likely to survive the coming decade in their present form. This may not affect the flow of oil for long, since a rough continuity of relationships with consumers might remain. But then it might not. The flow could be diverted into directions favorable to the Soviet Union through commercial deals and military aid. Indeed, the mere entry of the Soviet Union into the oil market once it is no longer slack could itself pose a threat, but for the near term this is unlikely.

Threats to the political future and direction of Gulf regimes, notably the major producers such as Saudi Arabia, are matters of great consequence to the West, as of course would be any physical threat to their security. The West can hardly be against change that seems likely to come anyway, but it has every interest to see that if this happens, it occurs within an orderly framework. Hopefully, there will be a moving equilibrium. To help bring this about will require great political skill with a willingness in some circumstances to back this with military power, not least if the Soviet Union or any of its proxies show signs of military adventurism.

The potential threats are thus many and varied, internal and external. Some may be only short term in nature, others could dramatically reshape oil flows away from the West. How to deal with them, or to attempt to, will be a major concern of the remainder of this chapter. But included in any Western strategy must also be a concern for the Middle East problems outside the Gulf, since these could significantly affect Western interests as well. They have not been set out here as direct threats to oil supply but will be discussed below as part of the political problems that have to be faced.

Strategic Options

The West has to find a strategy to counter many threats. Will it be possible to agree on this? Is it necessary to do so? Strategy is, of course, nor merely a military matter. Political and economic measures form part of it as well. It is, for example, obvious that adequate oil stocks can give valuable flexibility when dealing with some contingencies. Their maintenance is thus an essential ingredient in any strategy. Diplomacy also has a key role as Soviet expansionism is more likely to be political than military, since this runs lower risks and may be harder to contain.[5]

There have been well-publicized differences of view between European governments and the present U.S. administration about Middle East policy (there may be differences between the United States and her Pacific allies, too, but these states have been less directly involved). Europe has tended to see the dangers in the Middle East as likely to arise from regional tensions and disputes, which should therefore have priority for attention if only because the Soviet Union is able to exploit them. The U.S. government has stressed the Soviet military threat to the region and concentrated on military measures needed to counter this, seeming to treat regional problems as secondary.[6]

The views of the regional states are generally nearer to those of Europe. For them the primary threat is not the Soviet Union. Some spend much energy and emotion on disputes with their neighbors, as with Iran and Iraq, or India and Pakistan, or on the many complex frictions between Arab states. Islamic tensions concern a lot of them, since these can and do lead to internal unrest or external subversion. Then there is Israel, always uncompromising and for most Arab states the main and immediate enemy. For Israel herself the threat is within the region from Arab states and the Palestinians. Her hostility to the Soviet Union is largely a function of Moscow's support of Palestinian claims.[7]

Political Strategy

There is a certain problem, therefore, in trying to fashion a common strategy when virtually all the states that might play a part in it, from within the region and without, disagree to some extent with the views held by the United States. While it is taken for granted that hostility to the Soviet Union and strong pro-Israeli sympathies will have a great deal to do with the direction of U.S. Middle Eastern policy, other elements in it are not always so clear such as U.S. attitudes toward Arab states. Nor can it be relied on for consistency or subtlety, in particular where military actions are concerned. These political differences between allies or with friendly countries, which perhaps attract much more attention than the areas of agreement, do not rule out some harmony of policy if long-term and short-term aims are separated.

Consider, for example, the Arab-Israeli problem. The general European view is that over time some form of Palestinian autonomy or state will have to be established, and failure to work toward this will bring continuing tensions, strengthening the Soviet position and weakening that of the West. The United States does not share this view and is unwilling to press Israel to accept it (even if it could), which is very doubtful. Europe sees little left for the Camp David formula, but Washington is tied to it.

But these differences are about the longer term. Views about the problems more immediately ahead are much more compatible. Both the Americans and the Europeans want to prevent fighting breaking out because the effects would be likely to spread beyond the immediate participants. Neither wants to see relations between Egypt and Israel become cool, or Egypt return to the Arab military ranks or once more draw closer to the Soviet Union.

A common strategy for the short term is therefore possible and there are indeed signs of one emerging. To help Cairo follow its present policy, European states have contributed to the Sinai Peacekeeping Force, which in 1982 was principally concerned with seeing that the Sinai was safely handed over to the Egyptians as well as contributing to stability in the area. Egypt is being given economic aid (with Japan taking part) and is also receiving help in modernizing its armed forces. The United States is, of course, providing a great deal of aid and forging some military links—but unfortunately with more fanfare than is politic. To the north, the Lebanon powder keg exploded in June of 1982 with the Israeli invasion. It remains to be seen what role the West can play in restoring some degree of stability to this divided country, but here again European forces participated alongside a U.S. contingent in supervising the PLO withdrawal from west Beirut and in subsequent efforts to restore a degree of stability to the tortured city.

In the short term, therefore, the West should concert its efforts to deal with the immediate dangers, using any suitable mechanisms from bilateral diplomacy to the United Nations. For the longer term there should be a real attempt among allies not only to downplay differences of view but also to construct an evenhanded policy. Europe should use such influence as it may have on individual Arab states and on the Palestinian leadership. The United States will have the main part to play with Israel. The coordination of arms supplies is important, and national and commercial consideration should be subordinated to the need to keep a stable military balance in the region.

It is easy to say that a Western strategy should attempt to move matters safely forward, but the difficult question is toward which particular end? A solution to the Arab-Israeli dispute is obviously not just around the corner, notwithstanding the Israeli actions in Lebanon. The differences are too deep seated for that to occur. But to avert conflict is not just an immediate task but also a continuing one and should be an essential basis of Western policy. Another full-scale war would not only set back any eventual solution, it would have effects that would spread across the Middle East as a whole.

The Gulf States

As for the Gulf states (as distinct from a Soviet threat to the Gulf, which will be dealt with later), a Western strategy may pose less of a problem. This is partly because there is no time bomb with a fuse as short as was in the case of Lebanon and partly because the very diversity of the Western allies can be a source of strength. It may, for example, be easier for some European states or for Japan to maintain relations with Iran, however tenuous, than for Washington to do this. Many allies have special links with particular parts of the Gulf, such as Britain with Oman. It is wise, therefore, to try to keep a multiplicity of ties with Gulf rulers to offset any loss of U.S. influence arising from support of Israel.

Obviously, policy should be concerted where possible, as it has been over the arrangements for oil sharing. As noted, arms transfers should certainly be coordinated when necessary, though diversity can be a help to fend off Soviet intrusion into this field.

An obvious difficulty is that of restoring relations with Iran in order not to leave the way entirely free for Moscow. The strategic importance of the country is self-evident as is the problem of exercising any influence over a regime of the present sort. Contacts have to be attempted (but discreetly) through whatever links individual Western states can forge with the present leaders or alternative factions. The fact that the United States can do little directly, or that the ayatallahs may have unattractive features, should not prevent the West from trying to reestablish its position before the Soviet Union does.

The essential challenge for the West in the Gulf as a whole will lie in keeping in touch with—or ahead of—political change. It is not easy to avoid a simple adherence to the status quo because of the current political and commercial ties with existing regimes, but it must be done lest the Soviet Union be left as the only supporter of change in a region where change seems inevitable. The different historical backgrounds and perspectives of the allies allow for a variety of links, but it will require skilled diplomacy to maintain a prudent political distance from the internal problems that rulers may face while also helping to provide such stability as can be done from outside. Where military activity is needed, this should be low key and away from the glare of publicity (as in the case of Britain in Oman throughout the 1970s). Regional or domestic politics may not easily bear the weight of obvious links with the West, least of all any that involve Israel strategically and perhaps even Egypt. The position of a ruler may be weakened—and with it Western interests—by prevailing upon him to do too much overtly.

South Asia

In South Asia, Pakistan has now been caught up in the affairs of the Middle East as a result of the Soviet invasion of Afghanistan. Actions in relation to Pakistan, however, have to take account of India; the two states cannot be divorced given their recent history and their myopic view of each other. The United States and India long have had an awkward relationship, which has to carry the load of U.S. ties with China and Pakistan and also Indian links with the Soviet Union (which were initially encouraged by the unwillingness of the United States and Britain to supply India with arms that were likely to be used against Pakistan). Other strains have arisen because of the U.S. government's intention to provide Pakistan with F-16 aircraft to strengthen the country militarily against a possible Soviet threat and to facilitate support of the Afghan people.

The West should (by one means or another) try to continue this support, though the less said about it may be the better. The main need, however, is to keep Pakistan stable, which is not easy in the face of internal unrest prompted by the prolonged suspension of democratic government. There is the possibility of renewed Baluchi separatist agitation, which the Soviet Union will no doubt try to foster. Pakistan occupies a strategic position that is extremely important to the West—but even more important is to deny it to the Soviet Union. While there will be no disagreement in the West about the need to do this, the precise policies to be followed toward Pakistan may not be so easy to agree upon. But once again it is best not to approach the problem in a monolithic fashion. A number of countries can help dissuade India from forging closer links with the Soviet Union in reaction to U.S. support of Pakistan and China. It is not in India's interests to become too reliant on Moscow (or on any one source) and it should therefore be possible to maintain Western influence in New Delhi. Arms supplies, trade, and aid can play their parts. Political skill will be needed in face of the efforts that Moscow seems likely to make in this part of the world.

Preventing Soviet political expansion into the Middle East in general certainly demands coordinated Western policies. Obviously there must be attempts to find solutions to regional problems that the Soviet Union can exploit, but more direct action will be needed as well. The difficulty of achieving this has been shown by the divergent Western views on economic sanctions and arms-control negotiations after the invasion of Afghanistan. More harm than good may come from trying to press all these views into the same mold; there are domestic imperatives in all countries as the U.S. grain and European gas deals make clear. But simply to adopt the lowest common denominator as a strategy will not do. More than this is required, even if it hurts.

For the European and Pacific allies, a prerequisite is that they should give political support—at the very least—for the military role being undertaken by the United States. The U.S. government may be the self-appointed guardian of the Gulf, but that is because there is no other available. The U.S. public must not be left with the feeling that the oil, on which the allies depend heavily, is being defended only by Americans; that way spells political disaster for the alliance. The allies, therefore, will have to be willing to be associated politically with a deterrent policy and to assume some share of the burden, directly or indirectly. Some will have to do what they can to facilitate the movement of U.S. forces to the region. In their own direct interest allied countries must be prepared to make efforts to replace U.S. forces that have to be withdrawn or diverted from Europe or the Pacific. Some may be able to provide military forces for the Gulf, which however small would have major political significance. It is to the military problem that this chapter now turns.

Military Strategy

A direct military threat to the Gulf may be the least likely contingency, but it would be the most serious and difficult problem for the West to face. As has been said, there has been allied criticism of the emphasis that Washington has placed on the Soviet military threat rather than on regional sources of tension. There has been skepticism, too, about the ability to meet a military threat if it came.

There is some force in this argument, but the determination of the United States to do what can be done to deter Soviet military incursion is warranted. After all, few European governments think that a Soviet armed attack against West Europe is very likely, but they guard against it nevertheless because their whole security is at stake. The probability of attack may not be high, but the penalty of not preparing for it could be enormous. Hence, a concern for deterrence in Europe. The case of the Gulf is not dissimilar. The odds against Soviet military intervention may be high but the stakes are huge—nothing less than a stranglehold on Western economies. So there is a very strong case for military deterrence.[8] (See table 6-1.)

Can this be provided? On land the Soviet Union enjoys great advantages, as it could get troops into the Gulf far faster and in greater numbers than could the United States. Instead of getting there first with the most, U.S. forces could get there last with the least, not normally an attractive situation militarily. But, as will be shown in a moment, it is neither as bad nor as simple as that. Elements of the U.S. Rapid Deployment Force could be positioned to get there fast enough to "lay an American across the road." This form of deterrence is practiced in Europe but is also applicable in the Gulf, even if it may not be quite clear at the moment just where that road might be. The presence of quite small U.S. forces would face Moscow with costs and with potential risks, which include that of major war. This is a very salutary consideration and it is in this light that the function of the RDF must be mainly seen and supported. The Western position as a whole is protected by the U.S. readiness to deter.[9]

This may look like the West defending its own interests, but they are the interests of the local states as well. Soviet military expansion into the Gulf would menace Western oil supplies but it would also menace many local regimes and freedoms. While some of the rhetoric surrounding the RDF has attracted regional criticism of U.S. military preparations, Afghanistan has shown the Soviet willingness to use force if the circumstances are thought to require it. Local rulers no more want to see Soviet soldiers there than the West does, though understandably their preference is to see none from anywhere. At the moment, the military confrontation between East and West in the region is a maritime one, though it is on land that any decisive outcome would have to be sought.

Table 6-1
Forces Available for Persian Gulf Contingencies

United States	USSR
Naval forces:	Naval forces:
Two carrier battle groups on station in the Indian Ocean (16 surface combatants) with some 110 fighter and attack aircraft.	Indian Ocean flotilla (eight surface combatants).
Air-force units:	Air-force units:
AWACS early-warning and air-defense-control aircraft on station in Saudi Arabia.	Two tactical air armies (combined total of over 600 combat aircraft). These aircraft could not conduct operations from Soviet bases against targets in southern Iran or much of Iraq.
One tactical air wing stationed in Europe (about seventy combat aircraft) with support equipment available in twenty-four hours.	Backfire and Badger medium-range bombers that could attack a wide range of Persian Gulf land targets and naval forces in the Indian Ocean.
B-52 bomber strikes from bases in Spain or Guam within a few days.	Ground forces:
Four U.S.-based tactical air wings and support equipment available in about ten days.	Two airborne divisions (about 7,000 men each); six other airborne divisions could be available on short notice from other military districts in the Soviet Union. These are Category I units with a high state of readiness and have 75 to 100 percent of their authorized personnel.
Ground forces:	Twenty-one motorized rifle divisions (authorized strength 14,000 each). These are Category II and III units that have a lower state of readiness, are manned at 10 to 50 percent of their troop authorization, and have older equipment than the Category I divisions generally found deployed against NATO and China.
Two light-infantry battalions (one army-airborne battalion from Italy and one marine amphibious battalion in Indian Ocean) in twenty-four hours.	One tank division (about 11,000 men) of Category II or III status.
One marine amphibious brigade (about 12,000 men and forty attack aircraft) in seven days using prepositioned equipment stored on commercial ships at Diego Garcia.	KGB border guards of several-thousand men equipped with armored vehicles. These units would secure the rear of an attacking force.
One airborne brigade (about 5,000 men) within seven days and the entire division (16,500 men) in about fourteen days.	
One Pacific-based marine amphibious brigade (about 12,000 men and forty attack aircraft) in twenty-one days with amphibious ships.	
One airmobile division (about 18,000 men) in four weeks.	
One mechanized infantry division (about 18,500 men) by ship in about six weeks.	

Sources: Carnegie Panel on U.S. Security and the Future of Arms Control, *Challenges for U.S. National Security—Assessing the Balance: Defense Spending and Conventional Forces* (Washington, D.C.: Carnegie Endowment for International Peace, 1981); and *The Military Balance 1980—1981* (London: International Institute for Strategic Studies, 1980), as appeared in Thomas R. Wheelcock, "U.S. Conventional Forces," in *America's Security in the 1980s, Part I,* Adelphi Papers no. 17 (London: International Institute for Strategic Studies, Spring 1982):43. Reprinted with permission.
Note: Except where noted, ground and air forces come from the southern military districts of the Soviet Union: North Caucasus, Trans-Caucasus, and Turkestan.

Naval Forces

U.S. naval forces in the Arabian Sea have been increased in strength substantially since the Iranian revolution. Two carrier task forces have been detached from the Mediterranean and Pacific Fleets and an amphibious unit (MAU) of some eighteen-hundred marines (also from the Pacific) has been kept afloat there. Ships carrying stores and equipment for a marine brigade have been prepositioned at Diego Garcia, as have logistic vessels, and the runway has been made suitable for use by B-52 bombers.

In response to this U.S. build-up, Soviet naval forces (which have been on station in the Indian Ocean since the mid-1960s) have been augmented with ships less powerful than their U.S. counterparts. They generally number twenty to twenty-two ships with eight being combatants, including guided-missile cruisers and destroyers. They lack, however, the offensive and defensive air power that the U.S. carriers provide; the Soviet task force is heavily dependent on land-based air support from Aden or from Soviet airfields a considerable distance away. Soviet naval reinforcements would have to come from other fleets, notably from the Far East, where the use of Cam Ranh Bay in Vietnam has now afforded a useful staging post halfway along the very long route from Vladivostok or Petropavlovsk. The Suez Canal lies between the Indian Ocean and the Soviet Mediterranean and Black Sea fleets and might be closed in a crisis, so that reinforcements would then have to sail the length of the Mediterranean and around Africa.[10]

The United States enjoys naval superiority in the Arabian Sea area and can continue to do so, even taking into account the Soviet ability to operate antishipping aircraft, like the Backfire bomber, from Soviet airfields. While both fleets are a long way from their home ports, the U.S. Navy has large forward-operating bases and airfields in the South Pacific whereas Cam Ranh Bay offers only certain facilities, as would any ports that the Soviet forces might be able to use in the Red Sea. The United States has been negotiating naval and air facilities, too, in a number of regional countries (so as not to be too dependent on one): Berbera in Somalia, Kenya, Oman, Egypt—and, of course, has the use of Diego Garcia as well (the latter, however, is 2,500 miles from the Straits of Hormuz). Not to be overlooked is the French naval base at Djibouti and the bases in Singapore and Australia that are available for Western use. For both the United States and the Soviet Union, maintaining naval forces in the huge Indian Ocean is a very expensive business, but the U.S. Navy does have strategic advantages and maritime nations as allies. One price of any Soviet action on land could be the loss of its naval forces in the region.

Western Strategic Problems

Western navies have the traditional task of keeping oil routes open. Patrolling the Straits of Hormuz is part of this, and such activity fulfills at the same time the subsidiary aim of dissuading any regional power such as Iran from offensive action in the area. The U.S. Navy, however, is also in the Arabian Sea to project force on land through air strikes and the support of marine or other landings. In any land battle the strategic advantage at once moves to the Soviet Union, geographically much nearer the Gulf (1,100 miles). With airfields in Afghanistan, they are now near enough to give fighter cover to operations on the eastern side of the Gulf. In the Soviet Union itself there are eight airborne divisions of 56,000 troops (two located in the southern military districts) very well equipped with light armor and the air transport to enable them to mount operations in the Gulf in a much shorter time than forces sent from the United States, which is 7,000 air miles and 12,000 sea miles away. In addition, the Soviets have twenty-one divisions in the Caucasas, Transcaucasas, and Turkmenistan military districts. The U.S. Rapid Deployment Force is to consist of five army divisions, two Marine Corps divisions and their air wings, ten air-force tactical-fighter wings, and assorted naval forces.[11]

The United States is slowly building up the RDF and its means of movement. Tactical air squadrons could be moved quickly (from Europe if need be), but the problem of getting land forces rapidly and in sufficient numbers to the Gulf is an immensely difficult one. To be timely, initial movement must be by air, apart from those forces kept locally. This means that ground troops can take with them only light, airportable weapons and equipment. Anything heavier would have to follow by sea. Even weapons prepositioned are likely to be a considerable distance from a forward-operating area, and much time would still be taken in moving troops forward from the points at which they collect their stores. This movement might have to be by sea, or perhaps overland where suitable, due to lack of airlift capability for heavy weapons such as tanks.

The long-distance air movement from the United States would have to be via the Atlantic, Mediterranean, and Middle East (though some forces in all probability would come from the Pacific). This entails air refueling and transit arrangements in such countries as Egypt, Somalia, Kenya, and Oman, with only the last affording a tactical jumping-off point for operations in the Gulf itself. Lacking at the moment are any forward-operating airfields or facilities further north, yet it must be clear that U.S. forces could only operate there if the local states agreed to this. If a Soviet military threat became more visible, facilities might be made available. U.S. Air Force units currently operate in Saudi Arabia with fighter and AWACS aircraft, and there is compatibility with much of the Saudi equipment. While these forces are there at Saudi invitation, the Gulf regimes in general are not ready to forge overt military links with the United States, largely because of Washington's links with Israel.[12] It should be noted, however, that there are well-developed airfields in eastern Turkey that are very near to the head of the Gulf. The U.S. Air Force can operate from them in a NATO role, but a Gulf contingency would have political implications for Turkey whose willingness to see them used could depend very much on the attitude of the Gulf states.

The United States is very good at solving strategic mobility problems, not the least by throwing dollars at them. It will nevertheless be many years before forces could be deployed in timely fashion and in numbers that could begin to match those of the Soviet Union, even on the assumption that the various procurement programs involved are carried through.

Soviet Strategic Problems

If the United States faces these obvious difficulties, those of the Soviet Union (while not of the same kind) are not so simple either. Without doubt, Soviet forces could move into Azerbaidzhan in northern Iran and little could be done to impede this. Geography is too much on the Soviet side, though crossing the Elbruz, Qareh Dagh, or Golul Pagh mountains would not be an easy task. Further south the problems are of a greater magnitude. To operate in southern Iran on the strategically very important eastern side of the Gulf would have its political attractions for Moscow, but the distances over which Soviet troops would have to travel are great (over five hundred miles even from Afghanistan to the Strait of Hormuz), and the mountainous and desert terrain is extremely difficult to traverse. It would not be too hard to get airborne forces to the coast quickly, though their transport aircraft would be very vulnerable. But making the necessary link-up later with the heavier formations and giving them logistic support would be time consuming and could be very costly. Both the forward bridgeheads and the troop columns that would have to travel very slowly overland would be open to air attack mounted from U.S. Navy carriers and by long-range land-based fighters. Soviet tactical air support for ground forces would be restricted due to range limitations and lack of air refueling capability.[13] Quite light U.S. ground forces or marines could disrupt the bridgeheads themselves if they could get there early enough. The climate can be most inhospitable (in the dry season temperatures go over 120 degrees Fahrenheit in the desert regions) and the local forces could be equally inhospitable. In the meantime, the Soviet naval vessels in the area would be hard put to survive the attacks that would be made on them from the outset. Though the U.S. land forces might be relatively much weaker, U.S. air interdiction could be powerful and prompt. The whole operation could be made singularly unattractive to the Soviet leaders.

On the western side of the Gulf—the vital one for the West—the distances from the Soviet Union to critical areas are considerable and the terrain and climate again unforgiving. An important factor here would be the attitude of Iraq, which could be a conduit or a barrier to Soviet forces depending on the relations between the two states following the Iran-Iraq war. As with southern Iran, to get Soviet airborne formations on the ground is one thing. But to link-up with them and give air cover to their operations is quite another. U.S. air action from airfields in the area (which would almost certainly be made available under these circumstances) would make the conduct of such a campaign very costly to the Soviet Union, militarily and politically. And that is quite apart from what is really the most important consideration: the risks of a wider war. Such risks are implicit in any major Soviet action against the oilfields of the Gulf.[14]

It is in this light that the purpose of the RDF should be seen. The U.S. determination to resist militarily any Soviet military expansion into the area helps to deter it by presenting potential costs and risks to Moscow, not excluding that of a major war. While an extension of conflict from the Gulf to other areas may not include the threat of the use of nuclear weapons (which both sides would seem to have an interest in avoiding), it is hard to see how conventional fighting could be neatly contained within the region.

If this is the case, it follows that priority should be given to the capability to mount strong air attacks throughout the Gulf area, and to the maintenance of a sufficient force of marines, or other mobile units in the region, that are able to operate very quickly against any Soviet bridgeheads. The faster they can operate, the fewer will be needed on the spot. The navy will, of course, be there to help project power on land and to carry out its naval tasks. Clearly, there will have to be reinforcements from outside, principally from the continental United States.[15] But careful thought has to be given to the size of such forces. The Gulf is not an area in which the West wants to commit itself to a full-scale war; if that eventuality seemed to be in danger of arising, the battle might have to be carried on elsewhere.

The Western position as a whole is protected by a deterrent posture in this part of the Middle East. The main burden would fall on the United States but the allies should certainly bear part of it. France and Britain, long accustomed to this part of the world, could provide some military help and experience, valuable in itself for not being American. Other allies could take some of the weight off Washington by, for example, financial aid to countries such as Egypt, Pakistan, or Turkey.

Attention should, of course, be given to helping regional states with their own defense. Only large countries such as India and Pakistan could defend themselves against threats of any size. But in the Gulf there is a new awareness of the needs of security, as well there might be given the political uncertainties and the way that military force is regularly used in the Middle East to achieve political aims. Weapons are being bought by many states with close contacts with Western countries. If, however, a real threat is present, external help will be needed. Oman has recognized this in the past and made successful use of it. If the shadow of Soviet military action were seen to hang over the Gulf, the counterweight of the United States would most likely become more acceptable to Gulf states.

Conclusions

The West has both political and military strategic options open to it in the Middle East. The two must go hand in hand; an undue emphasis on the military aspects may prejudice the political position. Both must be approached with sensitivity. Too strong an insistence on purely East-West considerations may contribute to instability by forcing local regimes to bear more political weight than they can stand. While military capabilities must be maintained and developed, this should be generally carried out in a low-key manner and with a sense of what is practicable and achievable.

A strong level of deterrence can be achieved. Indeed, it is currently partly in place. The West as a whole must be prepared to subscribe to this. European and Pacific allies of the United States may contribute relatively little to the military component of the strategy, but their political and economic efforts can be helpful. Western agreement on a harmonized political strategy would be ideal but some diversity of perspectives and links is not without its uses. It need not be the hindrance that it may sometimes appear to be to Washington.

The United States may be the self-appointed guardian of the Gulf, but there is no substitute available. The Western position as a whole is protected by this determination to resist any Soviet military expansion, and the allies should be prepared to give support accordingly.

Notes

1. The term *Western* refers not to the Western trading community as a whole but to the United States and her European and Pacific allies because it is their strategic options that will be discussed.

2. The Soviet Union has friendship treaties with both Iraq and Syria, who are bitterly opposed to each other. Iran sought military supplies from unlikely sources such as Israel in order to fight the war with Iraq. Only Israel, with its bombing of the nuclear plant in Iraq and the invasion of Lebanon, produces some measure of unity in the Arab world, though the death of Sadat was an occasion for showing the divisions that still persist. See Oles M. Smolansky, *The Soviet Union and Iraq, 1968-1979* (New York: Praeger, 1982); and Itamar Rabinovich, *The Soviet Union and Syria in the 1970s* (New York: Praeger, 1982).

3. For an account of Soviet-Iranian relations during the first years of the revolution, see Alvin Z. Rubinstein, "The Soviet Union and Iran Under Khomeini," *International Affairs* 57, no. 4 (Autumn 1981):599-617.

4. G.H. Jansen, *Militant Islam* (New York: Harper and Row, 1979): and Ali E. Hillal Dessouki, ed., *Islamic Resurgence in the Arab World* (New York: Praeger, 1982).

5. Stephen S. Kaplan, et. al., *Diplomacy of Power: Soviet Armed Forces as a Political Instrument* (Washington, D.C.: The Brookings Institution, 1981).

6. For discussions of the national and regional sources of conflict, see Shahram Chubin, ed., *Security in the Persian Gulf I: Domestic Political Factors* (Montclair, N.J.: Allanheld, Osmun Co., 1981); Christopher Van Hollen, "Don't Engulf the Gulf," *Foreign Affairs* 59, no. 5 (Summer 1981):1064-1078; and Udo Steinbach, "Sources of Third-World Conflict," *Third-World Conflict and International Security, Part I,* Adelphi Paper no. 166 (London: International Institute for Strategic Studies, 1981):21-41. On differing alliance perspectives on the Middle East, see Adam M. Garfinkle, "America and Europe in the Middle East: A New Coordination?" *Orbis* 25, no. 3 (Fall 1981):631-648.

7. See Galia Golan, *The Soviet Union and the Palestine Liberation Organization: An Uneasy Alliance* (New York: Praeger, 1980).

8. Approximately 61 percent of Western Europe's imported oil comes from the Persian Gulf, 72 percent of Japan's, and 34 percent of the United States's. For discussions of possible Soviet intervention in the Gulf, see: Dennis Ross, "Considering Soviet Threats to the Persian Gulf," *International Security* 6, no. 2 (Fall 1981):159-180; Karen Dawisha, "Moscow's Moves in the Direction of the Gulf—So Near and Yet So Far," *Journal of International Affairs* 34, no. 2 (Fall/Winter 1980/81):219-233; Francis Fukuyama, "Nuclear Shadowboxing: Soviet Intervention Threats in the Middle East," *Orbis* 25, no. 3 (Fall 1981):579-605; Shahram Chubin, "Soviet Policy toward Iran and the Gulf," Adelphi Paper no. 157 (London: International Institute for Strategic Studies, 1980); Albert Wohlstetter, et al., *Interests and Power in the Persian Gulf* (Marina del Ray, Calif.: Pan Heuristics, 1981); A. Yodfat and M. Abir, *In the Direction of the Gulf* (London: Frank Cass, 1977); James H. Noyes, *The Clouded Lens: Persian Gulf Security and United States Policy* (Stanford: Hoover Institution Press, 1979); Hossein Amirsadeghi, ed., *The Security of the Persian Gulf* (London: Croom Helm, 1981); George R. Berdes and Donald R. Fortier, *U.S. Security Interests in the Persian Gulf,* Report to the Committee on Foreign Affairs, U.S. House of Representatives (Washington, D.C.: U.S. Government Printing Office, 1981); and Thomas L. McNaugher, *Persian Gulf Security: The Military Dimension* (Washington, D.C.: Brookings Institution, forthcoming).

9. For somewhat critical views of the RDF, see: Robert Tucker, "American Power and the Persian Gulf," *Commentary* (November 1980):25-41; Jeffrey Record, *The Rapid Deployment Force and U.S. Military Intervention in the Persian Gulf* (Cambridge, Mass.: Institute for Foreign Policy Analysis, 1981); Jeffrey Record, "The RDF: Is the Pentagon Kidding?" *The Washington Quarterly* 4, no. 3 (Summer 1981):45-51; James Wooten, *Rapid Deployment Forces,* Issue Brief no. IB80027 (Washington, D.C.: The U.S. Library of Congress, Congressional Research Service, 3 November 1980); Sir John Hackett, "Protecting Oil Supplies: The Military Requirements," in *Third-World Conflict and International Security, Part I,* Adelphi Papers no. 166 (London: International Institute for Strategic Studies, 1981):41-51; Albert Wohlstetter, "Meeting the Threat in the Persian Gulf," *Survey* 25, no. 2 (Spring 1980):128-188; and Edgar O'Ballance, *The US Rapid Deployment Force* (Foreign Affairs Research Institute, October 1981). For a more confident analysis, see Kenneth N. Waltz, "A Strategy for the Rapid Deployment Force," *International Security* 5, no. 4 (Spring 1981):49-73. See also Shahram Chubin, "U.S. Security Interests in the Persian Gulf in the 1980s," *Daedalus* 109, no. 4 (Fall 1980):31-65.

10. "Soviet Naval Presence Doubles in Indian Ocean, Lacks Support," *Aviation Week and Space Technology* (6 April 1981):60; Geoffrey Jukes, *The Indian Ocean in Soviet Naval Policy,* Adelphi Papers no. 87 (London: International Institute for Strategic Studies, 1972). For an alarming view of possible Soviet naval action in the area, see Patrick Wall, ed., *The Southern Oceans and the Security of the Free World: New Studies in Global Strategy* (London: Stacey International, 1977). For an overview of the development of Soviet naval policy, see Michael MccGwire, "The Evolution of Soviet Naval Policy: 1960-1974," in Michael MccGwire, Kenneth Booth, and John McDonnell, eds., *Soviet Naval Policy: Objectives and Constraints* (New York: Praeger, 1975); and John Erickson, *Soviet Military Power* (London: United Services Institute, 1971).

11. "Special U.S. Force for Persian Gulf Is Growing Swiftly," *New York Times,* 25 October 1982, p. 1. The twenty-one Soviet divisions are of a Category II or III status, meaning they are manned at or below 50 percent of authorization level. Thomas R. Wheelcock, "US Conventional Forces," in *America's Security in the 1980s, Part I,* Adelphi Papers no. 173 (London: International Institute for Strategic Studies, Spring 1982):43. As always, it is extremely difficult to determine the manning levels and state of readiness of Soviet forces. See, for example, John M. Collins, *US-Soviet Military Balance: Concepts and Capabilities, 1960-1980* (New York: McGraw Hill, 1980):213.

12. An exception would be Oman. Saudi airfields, however, are built to U.S. military specifications. More than four thousand Americans in Saudi Arabia are associated with various military programs such as the U.S.

Military Training Mission that trains the army, air force, and navy. The AWACS and ground-control systems were purchased from the United States at a cost of $8.5 billion. "A Survey of Saudi Arabia," *Economist* (London), 13 February 1982, p. 12. For a discussion of Saudi perspectives on a number of related issues, see William B. Quandt, *Saudi Arabia in the 1980s: Foreign Policy, Security, and Oil* (Washington, D.C.: The Brookings Institution, 1981); and Adeed Dawisha, *Saudi Arabia's Search for Security,* Adelphi Papers no. 158 (London: International Institute for Strategic Studies, Spring 1980). Concern over Iranian military successes versus Iraq spurred greater military cooperation among members of the Gulf Cooperation Council. "Saudi's Urging Gulf Countries to Coordinate Air Defense," *International Herald Tribune,* 13 April 1982, p. 1.

13. For a detailed listing, see Keith A. Dunn, "Constraints on the USSR in Southwest Asia: A Military Analysis," *Orbis* 25, no. 3 (Fall 1981):615.

14. For discussions of the military problems the Soviets would face in invading Iran, see Dunn, ibid.; and Joshua M. Epstein, "Soviet Vulnerabilities in Iran and the RDF Deterrent," *International Security* 6, no. 2 (Fall 1981):126-158.

15. Based on the experiences in Czechoslovakia and Afghanistan, it would take the Soviets three months to build-up their forces. This should be ample warning time. The key, of course, is the ability of Western intelligence analysts to interpret correctly such activity and for Western political leaders to make the necessary decisions. On the invasions of Czechoslovakia and Afghanistan, see Jiri Valenta, "From Prague to Kabul: The Soviet Style of Invasion," *International Security* 5, no. 2 (Fall 1980):114-141. On intelligence problems, see Richard K. Betts, "Analysis, War, and Decision: Why Intelligence Failures Are Inevitable," *World Politics* 31, no. 1 (October 1978):61-89.

7

Perspectives on Arabian Gulf Security

Mamoun Kurdi

The strategic importance of the Arabian Gulf area goes much beyond its obvious economic value. The area is the very heart and center of Muslim culture and civilization; it is a link between the three continents of the Old World; and it constitutes a political buffer between the Communist and capitalist worlds. Thus, to view the area simply as a huge well of oil—regardless of the values of its people, its culture, its civilization, and its actual and potential role in the international system—is simplistic and a grave misconception.

This chapter aims to stimulate discussion on perspectives of Arabian Gulf security and to eliminate any misconception thereof. It adopts the following framework:

1. It examines the strategic value of the Arabian Gulf area taking into account the people and their cultural heritage in the prevailing political, economic, and social environment;
2. It identifies the potential internal, regional, and international threats to the area's security and considers their possible remedies; and
3. It assesses the various alternative arrangements to preserve the area's security as perceived by the regional states (individually and/or collectively) and by nonregional powers (particularly the superpowers), and examines whether they are feasible, practicable, and adequate to meet the challenges posed by the potential threats.

The Strategic Value of the Arabian Gulf Area

The strategic importance of the Arabian Gulf area is determined by its geopolitical situation and its human and natural resources in the prevailing political, economic, and social environment. The Arabian Gulf region comprises an area of approximately 4.76 million square kilometers (2.9 million square miles) situated between the Soviet Union, Afghanistan, Pakistan, the Arabian Sea, the People's Democratic Republic of Yemen, the Arab Republic of Yemen, the Red Sea, Jordan, Syria, and Turkey. Thus, the

The views expressed are those of the author and do not reflect the official attitudes or opinions of the government of Saudi Arabia or any of its affiliated agencies.

Arabian Gulf area lies in a prime strategic location between the east Mediterranean region and the Indian Ocean, bordering the Soviet Union in the north, and provides a link between Africa, Asia, and Europe.

The area is known for its richness in mineral resources: it holds one of the largest proven oil reserves—estimated at 330 trillion barrels—and currently exports over 15 million barrels per day (b/d), representing approximately 40 percent of the free world's oil imports.[1] Furthermore, the area is also rich in many other minerals so far unexploited.

The population of the area is estimated at seventy-six million inhabitants dispersed among eight developing states: Bahrain, Kuwait, Iraq, Iran, Oman, Qatar, Saudi Arabia, and the United Arab Emirates. The population is predominantly Muslim, evenly divided between Arabs and non-Arabs, Sunni and Shi'a Muslims. Iran is the only non-Arab state in the region and is predominantly inhabited by Shi'a Muslims. The Arabs are predominantly Sunni Muslims except for Iraq where the population is evenly divided between Sunni and Shi'a Muslims.

The prevailing political, economic, and social environment is influenced by the following factors: (1) the population is predominantly Muslim; (2) the majority of the states in the area are Arab states; and (3) all the nations of the area are developing nations. An understanding of the impact of these factors on the prevailing political, economic, and social environment is a prerequisite to the understanding of the strategic value of the area. Therefore, a brief consideration of these three factors is required.

The Islamic Factor

The Arabian Gulf area is the very heart of the Muslim world. It is the site of the holiest Muslim shrines and the direction to which millions of Muslims turn in their five daily prayers. The people of the area are very closely attached to Islam and share a profound sense of solidarity and fraternity with the rest of the Muslim population all over the world. Thus it is important to note that: (a) politics in the Gulf area are subjected to and governed by the principles of Islamic law and tradition; (b) social and economic change is only tolerated and accepted if it is compatible with Islamic law and tradition; and (c) Islam dictates the direction of the area's conduct in international relations as the people of the area are sensitive to and affected by the conditions of their fellow Muslims in the world at large—whether they reside in the Philippines, in India, in Afghanistan, in the Soviet Union, in Eastern Europe, or in Africa. Hence, the security of the Arabian Gulf area cannot be totally isolated from the security of the Muslim world as a whole.

The Arab Factor

The Arab states of the Arabian Gulf are integral parts of the Arab world. Their population shares with the rest of the Arab nations the same language, religion, culture, civilization, traditions, aspirations, and a profound sense of solidarity and fraternity. Therefore, it is useful to make the following observations: (a) despite the population's staunch observance of Islam, and despite the universal approach of the message of Islam, nationalism is present and alive in the Arabian Gulf region; (b) political, social, and economic activities are influenced by Arab nationalist aspirations and expectations; and (c) the region's international relations are therefore influenced by the perceived interests of the Arab world. Hence, the Arab-Israeli conflict is paramount in the minds of both the governments and people of the Arab Gulf area.

It follows that the security of the Arabian Gulf area cannot conceivably be isolated from the security of the Arab world as a whole. The Palestinian problem is a case in point for it is a problem for the Arabian Gulf states as much as it is a problem for Jordan, Lebanon, Syria, and the Palestinians themselves.

The Development Factor

The economies of the Arabian Gulf area are heavily dependent on a single commodity: oil. This creates a vulnerability similar to that encountered by the majority of developing countries whose economies depend heavily on the export of a single, or few primary, commodities. However, the Arabian Gulf countries export a commodity of vital importance to the economies of developed, as well as developing nations. Oil-demand forecasts for the remainder of the century suggest that the developing countries possess the greatest potential for substantial growth in oil demand. Developing nations are already highly dependent on oil imports to meet their energy requirements and to sustain their economic and social development; all forecasts point toward greater dependence in the foreseeable future.[2] Therefore, it is worthwhile to observe that: (a) the Arabian Gulf states naturally tend toward a greater identification with the demands and aspirations of the developing countries for the establishment of a new international economic order to provide for a fair and equitable relationship between the developed and developing countries; (b) continued and uninterrupted supplies of oil to the developed countries are likely to be linked to continued and improved access of the Arabian Gulf area to the technology and markets of the developed countries; and (c) the importance of the Arabian Gulf area to the continued prosperity and, indeed, stability of the developing countries should not be underestimated. It follows, therefore, that the security of the Arabian Gulf area is crucial to the security of both developed and developing countries.

The foregoing statements highlight the strategic value of the Arabian Gulf area in the international context, which includes, by extension, East-West relations as well since both blocs are geopolitical rivals in this important region.

The Islamic factor is of great, but scarcely understood, significance to the East-West relationship. It is often suggested that the strengthening of Islamic institutions in the area may seriously threaten Western security, as it may lead to a polarization of the society into fundamentalists and secular elements that will ultimately work to the benefit of the Communists, who are traditionally well organized to take advantage of social division. This is a serious misconception, for communism is essentially incompatible with Islam, and Muslim countries on the southern border of the USSR should be viewed as a potentially strong safety belt containing the spread of communism. Islam as a powerful social and spiritual force is crucial to the strengthening of this safety belt because Islam is a great unifier that can prevent the creation of the social divisions that are the breeding ground of communism.

A thorough examination of the compatibility of communism with Islam falls beyond the scope of this chapter. However, one basic conceptual divergence that makes Islam and communism irreconcilable is the relationship between the mosque and the state. Communism implies not only a full separation between the mosque and the state but a virtual denouncement of all religious institutions. In Islam, spiritual and materialistic lives are inseparable. This is, of course, in contrast to Christianity, where a reconciliation between religion and communism is thought to be possible as a result of the separation between church and state. The involvement of the church in supporting Communist elements in Latin America and in Africa illustrates this point. Even in Poland, where the Solidarity movement attracted the attention of the world at large and enjoyed the full support of the Catholic Church, communism was never denounced. The very best that the West could have expected as a result of the emergence of Solidarity in Poland was the emergence of another Rumania, but not another Yugoslavia.

Islam is a much more cohesive socioreligious force than the mass media depicts. The so-called rift between Sunni and Shi'a Muslims has been represented as a confrontation of the magnitude of the Catholic-Protestant sectarian confrontation in Ireland. This notion, it seems, has sprung from the Iranian revolution and the Iran-Iraq war. While it is true that some minor differences do exist between the two sects, it is equally true that both sects have coexisted in peace and harmony for centuries. The relationship between them has been and continues to be a fraternal one. The fact that

Iraq, the Arab country with the highest proportion of Shi'ites among its population, went to war against Iran, a predominantly Shi'a country, suggests that the nature of the conflict is essentially geopolitical and nationalistic, not sectarian. It might be argued that sectarianism was present in the Iran-Iraq conflict. It is alleged that some leading Shi'a figures in Iraq were persecuted by the Iraqi government prior to and during the hostilities between the two countries. The answer to this argument is very simple indeed. It suffices to mention that when the Shi'a leadership in Iran was persecuted by the regime of the late shah, it was the present regime of Iraq that granted them not only asylum but also the grounds and means to pursue their antishah activities. No sectarian question was raised then despite the Sunni color of the Iraqi leadership. This is sufficient to refute the argument that the conflict between the two countries is sectarian in nature. It is basically nationalistic. These events once again reinforce the essentially political nature of the conflict.

Bahrain has never manifested any sectarian opposition to the revolutionary regime of Iran, yet the Iranian regime is pursuing subversive activities against Bahrain.[3] Given the well-known Iranian claims to sovereignty over Bahrain, even under the nonsectarian regime of the late shah, it is safe to suggest that the revolutionary regime of Iran is pursuing objectives of a nationalist rather than a sectarian nature there as well as in Iraq.

The development factor is likely to have a significant impact in both East-West and North-South contexts. Obviously oil, being the single predominant resource in the world-energy mix, is the key influencing factor. The Gulf area possesses a substantial proportion of world-proven oil reserves and accounts for a significant proportion of the free-world oil imports. The structure of the economies in the area suggests that this shall be the case for a very long time to come. Many countries currently produce oil, but the ability of most of the major non-Arab oil-producing countries to maintain oil exports—and even to preserve self-sufficiency beyond the end of the century—is doubtful. The Soviet Union barely will be able to meet the oil requirements of its East European allies by then, though gas exports may continue beyond the turn of the century. Views on Soviet energy prospects are not unanimous. However, most analysts now believe that oil production in the Soviet Union is very near its peak.[4] The United States is currently a net importer of oil and whether she will achieve self-sufficiency in oil in the future is quite uncertain. The Western allies of the United States are not in a comfortable position either. Their dependence on oil imports is much higher than the United States and self-sufficiency in energy is far from achievable. In an East-West context, this situation is very unsatisfactory not only for the Western alliance but also for the free world as a whole, as competition for access to oil resources is likely to become more intense. In this regard, the plight of the developing countries is of great concern.

The Gulf area, through its oil-supply potential, is likely to hold the key to the balance between East and West, North and South, in the short, medium, and long term. Communist inroads into the Third World are dependent on the deterioration of the economic performance of developing countries and the continued imbalance in the relationships between developed and developing countries inherent in the current international economic order, since Communists claim to offer an alternative economic model. Given the dependence of most developing countries on oil imports to sustain their social and economic development, the importance of the Gulf area to their future security and stability easily follows.

The success of the oil-exporting countries in raising their oil revenues in the 1970s, coupled with the implementation of ambitious development programs in the Gulf area, has provided ample trading opportunities between the area and the rest of the world, particularly the developed countries. As the area is sparsely populated and labor supply is short, the development programs countenance the need to attract foreign labor from the rest of the world, particularly the developing countries.

Furthermore, most of the Gulf countries still hold substantial surplus funds, the investment of which is of crucial importance to the world economy in its present state of recession. As developing countries are increasingly encountering difficulties of access to the world capital markets, the contribution of the Gulf states to alleviate these difficulties cannot be underestimated.

The Arab factor is also significant in terms of the East-West context. For despite the past subjugation of all the Gulf countries—except Saudi Arabia—to some form of colonialism, the West is still highly regarded by the people of the area. Unlike other developing countries, where the struggle for decolonization was frequently associated with anti-West sentiments leading to a closer identification with the socialist bloc, the West still enjoys substantial goodwill in the region. However, the Soviet Union has managed successfully to gain inroads in many hitherto pro-Western countries in many parts of the world. The Arab world is no exception to this. The strategy of the Soviet Union in making these inroads was based on a false identification with the aspirations of the masses in an attempt to exploit them against the Western powers. Illustrations of such incidents are abundant, particularly in Latin America, Africa, and Asia. Banking on the Arab-Israeli conflict and the Arab aspirations for the realization of Palestinian national rights, the Soviet Union has made significant progress in identifying itself with the legitimate and inalienable rights of the Palestinian people. This has enabled it to enhance its position and influence in the area.

Potential Threats to the Arabian Gulf's Security

The potential threats to the security of the region can be classified in three categories: internal, regional, and/or international threats. Internal threats include riots, turmoil, rebellions, and revolts. Regional threats cover, *inter alia*, interference with the internal affairs of neighboring states, the potential use of violence to settle disputes, and potential spillover of bilateral conflicts. International threats cover outside interference in regional affairs, involvement in superpower contests, export of ideologies alien to the cultural and social fabric of the region, membership in military alliances with a superpower, and/or permission for a superpower to use the facilities of a state or states of the region for its military purposes.

Internal Threats

The sources of internal threats to the security of the state have been thoroughly investigated by many prominent social scientists. Their findings are well known and well documented. The roots of social unrest are to be found in the inability of state institutions to respond to changing circumstances and to cater to the realization of people's aspirations and expectations.[5]

The generally prescribed remedy for internal threats to state security is to provide for greater popular participation in the running of the state's affairs. However, participation alone cannot provide the decisive answer to these threats. Equitable distribution of income, fair administration of justice, equal opportunities, and wide and adequate sharing of services are considered to be essential complements to such participation.

It is most unfortunate that the nature of state institutions in the Arabian Gulf area is widely misunderstood. There are two major reasons. First, the focus on the Middle East, particularly in the Western media, has often been influenced by the Arab-Israeli conflict. Within this context, Western sympathies for the Jews as a result of their sufferings in Europe at the hands of the Nazis has greatly tilted the balance in favor of the Israelis. This in turn has subjected the Western focus on the Middle East to simplistic stereotyped notions. The general public of the West is often offered a scenario whereby a democratic, civilized, and peace-loving country—Israel—is rejected by neighboring Arab states governed by undemocratic and despotic rulers; a scenario of a good guy molested by bad guys. Secondly, many writers specializing in the area have fallen victims to the strict application of theories developed in totally different environments and circumstances than the Gulf. Substance has often been sacrificed for a narrow adherence to form. The misuse of such labels as parliamentary democracy, absolute monarchy, totalitarian regimes, and such are often the source of misconception about the area.

Parliamentary democracy is, in essence, a form of government developed in the West, which allows popular participation in the running of state affairs. It is simply a means and definitely not an end in itself. The absence of parliaments in many countries of the Arabian Gulf has been wrongly construed as an absence of popular participation. Such impressions reveal ignorance of the nature of Islamic institutions.

The principle of popular participation is firmly established in Islam. It is enshrined in the Holy *Qur'an—Waamruhum Shoura Baynahum*—Muslims consult among themselves in the process of decision making. The concept of consultation in Islam is wider conceptually than the literal meaning of the word. It does not necessarily imply nonbinding views, for Islam prescribes the constant search for consensus—*Yadu Allah Maa Aljamaah*—God's blessings are with the consensus views of the community.[6]

The form of exercising *Shoura* in the Arabian Gulf area might be seen by outsiders as primitive and inappropriate. However, it is simple, objective, and effective. In Saudi Arabia, for instance, Shoura is exercised through the daily sitting *Majalis*, or councils, held by the king, as well as by the governors of the provinces, where state affairs are discussed and every interested citizen has the opportunity to make his voice heard and his views known. Serious complex issues are referred to panels of experts and prominent specialists to study and report back. Conscious of the fact that state affairs are growing in complexity and magnitude, and firmly committed to preserve and improve the Shoura institution, serious consideration is currently taking place in Saudi Arabia to find ways and means of reconciling the needs of both.

No form of popular participation in decision making relieves those exercising power from the responsibilities for the decision taken. This applies to Saudi Arabia no less than it applies to the United States or the United Kingdom. The responsibility for the final decision of the executive is that of the king of Saudi Arabia in the same way as it is the responsibility of the president of the United States or the prime minister in the United Kingdom. Hence, the contention that government in Saudi Arabia is a personal affair of the king is groundless.

Absolute monarchy is another label frequently used to describe the form of government in many countries in the Arabian Gulf area. The term has Western medieval connotations and implies that the will of the sovereign is the will of God; it cannot be contested or criticized. In Islam rulers are proclaimed through the process of *Bayaah* to implement and observe the provisions of the Holy Qur'an and Sharia, which constitute the Divine Constitution of Islam. The ruler is, therefore, the servant of the Divine Constitution and definitely not its master. The ruler is expected to adhere strictly to the Divine Constitution, for obedience is only due to him if he does so. Nonconformity of the ruler to the Divine Constitution entails impeachment and eventual removal from office.[7] Thus, the application of theoretical frameworks alien to the environment and culture of the Arabian Gulf region leads to serious misconceptions. Stability in the Arabian Gulf region is remarkable compared with other developing countries. Domestic politics in the region are dominated by economic issues. The improvement of the living conditions of the total population of the area is the real concern of each and every citizen. In our world of today, this means greater industrialization and utilization of technology. Given the ambitious development programs that are being implemented in the area, transfer of technology and import of manpower are badly needed.

It is frequently suggested that economic development may entail a change in the existing social values, as modernization is only possible if the society is prepared to accept and adopt as its own the ways of life prevalent at the source of the imported technology. This is, indeed, another serious misconception. The technology transferred has to be adapted to suit the existing social values and not vice versa. Otherwise, the economic and social objectives of the process of development can never be achieved and the process would result in transplanting industrial enclaves in totally alien environments.

The flow of migrant workers from different parts of the world is bound to have an impact on the society of the host country. Increased social contacts between migrant and native workers should in principle help to improve the social climate of the host country. However, just as technology must be adapted to fit the needs of the country to which it has been transferred, migrant workers have to adapt to the social conditions of the host country and not vice versa.

The foreign policies of the Gulf states are basically orientated toward nonalignment and noninvolvement in superpower contests, though the West enjoys a great deal of goodwill and sympathy. However, this should not suggest that the relationship between the Gulf states and the West is trouble-free. As indicated earlier, the Soviet Union has successfully managed to identify itself with the aspirations of the Palestinian people while the West, particularly the United States, has increasingly tilted toward Israeli policies, thereby enabling the Soviet Union to increase its influence in the area. The end result of this position is increased Arab resentment toward the Middle Eastern policies of the West. Given the degree of interdependence between the Gulf area and the West in terms of oil, capital goods, and technology, the current situation is totally unsatisfactory.

Regional Threats

The source of regional threats to the security of the state are to be found in the disharmony of national interests, the absence of machinery for the peaceful resolution of disputes, and the lack of coordination and consultation among regional states. The harmonization of national interests calls for the avoidance of zero-sum approaches to conflict.[8] Cooperation is the means to achieve a positive-sum approach to conflict. It is conducive to the peaceful resolution of disputes and to the promotion of constant coordination and consultations.

Fortunately, the majority of the states in the Arabian Gulf region have recognized the value of cooperation. A Gulf Cooperation Council has recently been established. It was clearly stated at the outset that the council is not an exclusive club, it is not aimed against any other state, and it welcomes the cooperation of all the states of the Gulf for the good of all of them. The Gulf Cooperation Council aims toward greater economic and social integration, is making a constructive attempt to harmonize the national interests of its members, provides the institutional framework for the peaceful resolution of disputes, and creates opportunities for coordination and consultations.

The Iran-Iraq conflict, however, is a very dangerous and explosive threat to the security of the Arabian Gulf area. It is a major source of anxiety for the members of the Gulf Cooperation Council and indeed to the international community as a whole. As indicated earlier, the roots of the conflict between Iraq and Iran are of a nationalistic nature. The European experience with nationalism in the early part of this century clearly demonstrates how nationalism helped contribute to fascism leading to a world war.[9] The prominence of nationalism in the Iran-Iraq conflict and the Iranian zero-sum approach to it constitute a serious threat to the security of the Arabian Gulf area, much in the same manner that Europe has experienced in the past. A zero-sum approach to the resolution of the conflict can only result in a constant attrition of the human and material resources of both parties. The losses of one party can never be considered the gains of the other party but are, rather, common losses. Further, the war threatens the security of the region as a whole, as it invites nonregional powers to interfere in support of one party or the other. Thus, it is imperative to see a transformation of the conflict from a zero-sum one to a positive-sum one.

The Gulf Cooperation Council's members have so far managed successfully to contain the conflict and avoid any spillover effects. Unfortunately, the revolutionary regime of Iran views the conflict as a zero-sum one. Their insistence on the removal of President Saddam Husayn from office illustrates this dangerous approach. The absence of a government in Iran capable of assuming its historical responsibilities toward its people by accepting negotiations as a means to resolve the conflict is aggravating the situation. The question is whether the Iran-Iraq dispute can be decided by force. The experience of the last two years suggests clearly that it cannot. Iraq has already reached this conclusion and has consequently withdrawn from the territories it occupied at the outset of the armed conflict. It remains to be seen whether Iran will come to the same realization. This is only possible if the Iranian approach to the conflict is transformed from a zero-sum to a positive-sum approach. This calls for a greater focus on common values and common interests. Neighboring states are better off if they focus on what brings them together and helps them to coexist peacefully rather than focusing on what separates them.

The universality of the message of Islam, in its true sense, holds the key to the transformation of the Iran-Iraq conflict from a zero-sum to a positive-sum one. Islam does not allow nationalism to guide the conduct of international relations between Muslim states. The spiritual principle upon which mankind can be grouped, according to Islam, takes the form of devotion to the ideal of justice and not to color, race, or privilege.[10] Thus, the notion that Islam is the cause of the Iran-Iraq conflict is a grave misconception. It is, rather, the only hope to bring a lasting resolution to the conflict. The good offices of the Islamic Conference to promote a peaceful resolution of the conflict enjoy the full support of the Gulf Cooperation Council and merit the support of the world at large.

International Threats

The Arabian Gulf area is of high strategic value for the world as a whole. Due to its oil-supply potential, the area is likely to hold the major hope for the preservation of the balance between East and West for the short, medium, and long term. Thus, it is in the interest of the international community to proclaim the area as a zone of peace and to invite the superpowers to exclude it from their contests. The interference of one superpower calls for the intervention of the other, and a superpower contest in the area carries with it the danger of exposing the whole world to a devastating war. Though the security of the area is of prime interest to the entire international community, the preservation of the area's security is primarily the responsibility of the constituent states of the region.

While the intentions and interests of the West are well known, those of the Soviet Union are a source of anxiety. The Communist bloc has been active recently in making inroads in Afghanistan, the Horn of Africa, and southern Arabia. The strategy followed by the Soviet Union is based on a false identification with the aspirations of the masses in an attempt to exploit any eventual opportunity against the Western powers. The key to their influence in the Arabian Gulf area is closely linked to the Arab-Israeli conflict, where the Soviet Union is increasingly attaining the status of the principal friend of the Arab cause thereby driving the United States to the position of close identification with Israeli policies and adventures in the Middle East. The continued identification of the United States with Zionist policies, giving virtually a blind endorsement to the Israeli policies in the occupied Arab territories, contributes significantly to the growth of Soviet influence in the area.

The Arabian Gulf states are aware of the true nature of the Soviet Union. They firmly believe that communism is as dangerous to their security as Zionism. The Soviet Union is equally aware of the perception of the Arabian Gulf states and considers them a target for its future expansionist designs.

Such an expansion of influence might conceivably be achieved through three possible scenarios that are not mutually exclusive. The first scenario is for the Soviet Union to instigate a revolt in one or several states of the Arabian Gulf region. The advent of industrialization and the growth of migrant-labor power might provide the grounds for such intervention as new social strains become an eventual danger. The second scenario is an intervention by proxy whereby the Soviet Union may choose a client state to act on its behalf. The third scenario is an outright direct Soviet intervention—Afghanistan style. The international threats to the security of the Arabian Gulf region are discussed within the framework of these scenarios in the following section.

Security Arrangements in the Arabian Gulf

Arrangements for the security of the Arabian Gulf are contemplated at the individual-state level, regional level, and international level. On the individual-state level, the question of security is very high on the priority list of the decision makers. Individual states of the region have significantly stepped up their defense expenditures to enable their armed forces to acquire the best available defense equipment and training. Given the vast area of land, the long coasts, and the low population densities, the focus of the defense planners is concentrated on technology-intensive defense equipment. The West is the principal supplier of defense equipment and the arms trade represents a lucrative source of income for the West.

On the regional level, members of the Gulf Cooperation Council have recently concluded a series of bilateral defense agreements providing for coordination of mutual defense arrangements. Conscious of the dangerous nature of the Iran-Iraq conflict, they have actively pursued the objective of containing it and preventing any spillover effects. They have equally endeavored to promote the cause of peace and fully endorsed and supported the efforts of international organizations to mediate in the conflict, particularly the Islamic Conference.

On the international level, the United States has developed its response to the Soviet threat to Arabian Gulf security in the form of a Rapid Deployment Force. Other Western powers are divided on this response; some have openly endorsed it and others are still skeptical about it. One must indeed carefully consider whether these arrangements are feasible, practicable, and adequate to meet the challenges posed by potential internal, regional, and international threats.

Stability in the Arabian Gulf area depends heavily on the preservation of the indigenous social values and the successful implementation of development programs to provide for improved opportunities for the realization of popular aspirations and expectations. The commitment of the Arabian Gulf countries to preserve their cultural and social values and to adhere strictly to the Islamic Sharia, coupled with the serious efforts being made to implement ambitious programs to develop their economies and to improve the standard of living of their citizens, has already produced a climate for the eventual realization of their people's hopes. The success of the Arabian Gulf countries in fulfilling their Islamic commitments and in achieving the objectives of their development programs is the best insurance against the internal threats to their security.

Despite the vital importance of the region to the strategy of the West and the extensive trade opportunities it generates, the Arab-Israeli conflict still constrains defense supplies to the region. The Israeli lobby is making cooperation in this field extremely complex, confused, and difficult. Western policies, and particularly those of the United States, are not helpful. The attempt of the West to maintain a so-called balance between the Arabs and Israel is undermining the efforts of the Gulf states in the field of defense. These policies are tantamount to a virtual sacrifice of real interests in the Gulf to illusionary security concerns over Israel. Historical evidence clearly demonstrates that it is Israel that poses a real threat to the security of the Arab states, including the Gulf states, and not vice versa. The destruction of the nuclear-power plant on the outskirts of Baghdad and the recent invasion of Lebanon demonstrate the nature of the Israeli threat.

The international threats to the security of the region are basically the result of the superpower contest. The recent inroads of the Soviet Union in Afghanistan, the Horn of Africa, and southern Arabia, coupled with the Soviet attempt to exploit the Arab-Israeli conflict to its advantage represent a major threat to the area's security. The U.S. response, the Rapid Deployment Force, is best discussed in terms of the three suggested scenarios for potential Soviet aggression in the region. Briefly, these scenarios, which are not mutually exclusive, deal with a Soviet instigation of revolt in one or several Gulf states, an invasion by proxy through a Soviet client-state, and/or a direct Soviet invasion—Afghanistan style.

As for the first scenario, it goes without saying that no superpower or other external actor has ever been able to bring about a lasting solution to an internal problem by force. The direct involvement of the United States in any internal conflict in the Gulf area will aggravate such a conflict and possibly help to internationalize it. As for the second scenario, the intervention of the United States is equally unlikely to be helpful. It is virtually an open invitation for the other superpower to match its interference and this will almost certainly lead to an intensification of the conflict. On the third scenario, one might say that only a superpower can deter another superpower. But even here the regional powers have an important role to play; that is, to make it impossible for the Soviet Union to achieve its objectives by conventional means. The point is that a massive and protracted Soviet invasion, which might be required as a result of enhanced Gulf capabilities, increases the risk of escalation into nuclear confrontation between the superpowers. Thus, the U.S. message of deterrence for the Soviet Union should not be "if you interfere in the Gulf we shall also interfere to prevent you," but rather "if you do so, you run the risk of the mass destruction of your own homeland."

Conclusions

The foregoing arguments do not suggest that the international community has no role to play in enhancing and ensuring Arabian Gulf security. It is true that the responsibility for Gulf security is primarily that of the regional states. However, the international community, and the Western powers in particular, can in many ways help in this regard. Such help can be directed, *inter alia*, in the following directions.

1. A sincere and constructive effort to resolve the Arab-Israeli conflict is imperative. The permanent and lasting resolution of the conflict is only possible if it is based on justice and equity and recognizes fully the legitimate and inalienable rights of the Palestinian people to live in peace and security in a sovereign Palestinian state. It is encouraging to note that the Arab League summit conference at Fez has finally adopted a comprehensive framework for the peaceful settlement of the conflict based on the initiative of His Majesty King Fahd of Saudi Arabia. It is also encouraging to note that the U.S. administration finally has decided to take the initiative in the peace-making process in the Middle East. The Reagan initiative, though it falls far short of the full recognition of the right of self-determination for the Palestinians, as the United Nations has repeatedly recommended, represents a step forward in creating momentum for peace despite its outright rejection by Israel. The international community must seize these opportunities to build an irreversible approach to peace.

2. The Arabian Gulf states should be given adequate means to defend themselves. In this regard, the supply of AWACS and similar technology-intensive defense material is to be welcomed and commended. Western policies should be freed from the constraints posed by the Israeli lobby to maintain an illusionary and dangerous balance between the Arabs and Israel. The veritable security of Israel can never be served by such policies. Rather, they encourage Israel to frustrate the quest for peace and continue with its arrogant and aggressive policies in the region.

3. The approach of the Iranian government to the Iran-Iraq conflict is a most dangerous threat to the security of the Arabian Gulf. The international community must make it clear to Iran that such an approach is unacceptable. Extraregional powers should refrain from interference in the conflict directly or indirectly and join the Gulf Cooperation Council's efforts to promote the cause of peace.

4. The security of the Gulf area is greatly enhanced by the positive response of the industrial world to the aspirations of developing countries. It is no coincidence that Soviet inroads in many areas of the world, particularly in Afghanistan, the Horn of Africa, and southern Arabia, have taken place in least-developed countries. The deterioration in the economic performance of the developing countries and the imbalanced relationships between developed and developing countries inherent in the current international economic order provide the Soviet Union with the ideal opportunity to expand its influence in the developing countries' area. Therefore, an early and successful launching of the global round of North-South negotiations should be considered as a means of reducing the potential for social unrest in developing countries and thereby as a means to mitigate the spread of Soviet influence in the Third World.

Notes

1. Proven oil reserves are derived from the *BP Statistical Review of World Reserves of Oil and Gas* at the end of 1981. Figures for production and exports of oil are derived from various Organization of Petroleum Exporting Countries (OPEC) bulletins.

2. Most forecasts of petroleum demand for the remainder of the century point to a slight growth in the Organization for Economic Cooperation and Development (OECD) area and significant growth in the rest of the free world. See, for example, "Free World Energy Outlook Forecast Tables," Texaco's Finance and Economic Department, July 1981.

3. For reports describing the discovery of an attempt to overthrow the government of Bahrain see the *Guardian* and the *Financial Times*, 17 December 1981. The late shah of Iran officially renounced any interest in Bahrain in 1971. However, after the Iranian revolution a revival of the Iranian claim to Bahrain was attempted, although the Khumayni government quickly dissociated itself from the claim. See the *Times* (London), 6 February 1980.

4. *Petroleum Economist* reports in its June 1980 issue that the USSR planned a standstill in annual deliveries from 1981 onward, in spite of the fact that the Soviets must be interested, for their own sake, in the economic well being of their allies and satellites, most of whom are in a highly precarious situation with regard to energy supplies. The report concludes by confirming that the Soviet bloc's oil and energy prospects are viewed locally with unease.

5. Many writers have examined in depth the causes of conflict. Readers are referred to Ted Robert Gurr, *Why Men Rebel* (Princeton: Princeton University Press, 1970) for an illuminating analysis of the causes of conflict.

6. For an in-depth analysis of the institutions of the Islamic state, see ABU Alala Mawdudi, "Political Theory of Islam," in Khurshid Ahmad, ed., *Islam, Its Meaning and Message* (Leicester: The Islamic Foundation, n.d.).

7. See Ibid. In Mawdudi's words, "The executive under this [Islamic] system of government is constituted by the general will of the Muslims who have the right to depose it."

8. The zero-sum approach to conflict is a well-known aspect of game theory. For an illustration of the concepts of zero-sum and positive-sum approaches to conflict, see J.W. Burton, *Conflict and Communication* (London: Macmillan, 1969).

9. The relationship between fascism and nationalism within the context of the Second World War is alluded to by many thinkers and writers. The recurrence of similar circumstances in Europe might be considered remote and irrelevant. However, in the developing countries and in particular in the Gulf area, the danger is real. For a discussion of fascism as a political and social phenomenon see Martin Kitchen, *Fascism* (London: Macmillan, 1976).

10. Allah Bukhsh K. Brohi, "The Quran and Its Impact on Human History," in Ahmad, ed., *Islam, Its Meaning and Message*, p. 96.

8

The Soviet Union and Egypt after Sadat: Premises, Prospects, and Problems

Mohammed Anis Salem

The assassination of President Anwar al-Sadat on 6 October 1981 had all the ingredients of the cliff-hanging political drama of our time. A figure known to the man in the street in many parts of the world, Sadat came to be admired in the West although this admiration was taxed by the political arrests he ordered a month earlier. In addition, the circumstances that surrounded the assassination gave reason for apprehension; the killers were led by an officer who chose a military setting for his deed, and it soon became obvious that the assassins were part of a radical Islamic movement that aspired to a takeover of power. The Iranian parallels came to mind immediately, particularly because of U.S. deliberations about "losing" Iran. With the Reagan administration without a coherent Middle Eastern policy but with an anti-Soviet posture, the loss of Sadat was perceived as a major blow.

The problems related to the smooth succession of Hosni Mubarak to office did not immediately remove these worries. The new president adopted a different style than that of his predecessor. Modest, disinterested in cultivating the world media, he attempted to operate within the confines of the Egyptian consensus. The difficulty of this was that Mubarak inherited problems that many Egyptians expected him to redress. Internally, the country's democratic experience introduced by Sadat had suffered a severe setback, while a wave of Islamic fundamentalism and sectarian confrontation threatened the fabric of society. The peace agreement with Israel alienated sections of the Egyptian intelligensia, who saw their country isolated from the Arab world at a time when Israel seemed intent on devouring more Arab territories. As inter-Arab schisms multiplied, Egyptians felt that they were constrained in playing their traditional central role in the region.[1] This was also reflected in a feeling that Cairo had lost its leading position within the nonaligned movement at a time when this grouping was losing direction. Finally, a close Egyptian-U.S. connection[2] was coupled with a severe deterioration in relations with Moscow.[3] All of these factors heightened expectations about Mubarak's intentions to change tack.

Once the immediate security threat was over, it was realized that Mubarak would require a period of grace to consolidate his position. This, and the fact that Egypt was due to receive the rest of Sinai from Israel in April 1982, caused a sense of skepticism toward vows of continuity by the new Egyptian president. Furthermore, as Mubarak moved toward reconciliation with various opposition groups, avoided attacking other Arab leaders, asserted his country's nonalignment, and requested the return of some expelled Soviet technicians, worries were expressed about the future orientation of Cairo's new ruler. Former secretary of state Alexander Haig voiced these concerns during a State Department meeting, the minutes of which have since been leaked to the press.[4]

The superpower competition was superimposed on these developments. Immediately after the assassination, the U.S. administration issued a warning to outside powers not to interfere, dispatched two AWACS early warning aircraft to Egypt to patrol its eastern front, and took other military moves.[5] The Soviet response came in the form of a declaration that referred to gross U.S. pressure on Egypt "incompatible with generally accepted norms of relations between states." The declaration went on to condemn U.S. interference and asserted that events in Egypt affected the security interests of the Soviet Union and that Moscow would attentively follow their development.[6]

Moscow sent a terse message of condolence to Cairo that referred to the Egyptian president as "A. Sadat" and sent a low-level representative to the funeral.[7] The message of congratulations to Mubarak sounded a more positive note, stating that Cairo's willingness to improve relations between Egypt and the Soviet Union and establish a just peace in the region "will always encounter understanding and support from the Soviet side."[8] This suggested some prior communication or signal from Cairo, but soon a shadow was cast on this brief lull. The joint Egyptian-U.S. maneuvers, code named Bright Star-82, took place in Egypt during November. Moscow and several Arab leaders condemned this exercise, but soon the thaw began again. Mubarak was given a better press in the USSR and thereafter by Eastern European newspapers, who may have taken their cue from Moscow. The new Egyptian president indicated that a return of ambassadors was inevitable eventually and accepted that the Soviet Union had a role to play in an Arab-Israeli settlement, but not at that stage.[9] In addition, Cairo asked for the return of about sixty Soviet technicians to complete and service Russian-built industrial plants.

A second setback to this process of diffusing Egyptian-Soviet tensions occurred in April 1982 at the time of the Sinai handover. The Russian media derided the event, spoke of Egypt's limited sovereignty over the returned territories, and focused on U.S. and NATO participation in the Multinational Force and Observers (MFO), accusing it of being a part of the Rapid Deployment Force and an extension of Western military bases.[10] Cairo responded by reminders that the MFO was established to overcome the threat of a Soviet veto to a UN force.

Premises of Soviet-Egyptian Relations

The events alluded to here make the questioning of the future of Egyptian-Soviet relations a legitimate matter, but there remains a need to clarify the *premises* that underline this questioning. What are the factors that bear on Cairo's relation with Moscow? How can we predict their future course? And what, if any, operational response by the West may influence this future?

Analysis

There have been tendencies to interpret Soviet behavior in the Arab world as a mixture of design and opportunities. Several years ago, CIA estimates of future Soviet oil requirements encouraged the view that Moscow was engineering a pincer movement toward Arab oil. National Security Adviser Dr. Brzezinski spoke of "the arc of crisis"; the curve from Angola, through the Horn of Africa, South Yemen, Iran, and Afghanistan where the USSR had opportunities. Now that Sadat had disappeared, it was thought, yet another opportunity had been opened to the Soviet Union. In the wake of Sadat's assassination, a mood of self-criticism came into the U.S. media about U.S. support of Sadat. The late president was likened to the shah, implying that the United States had experienced another setback in Egypt; there was criticism of the high diplomatic profile maintained by the United States in Cairo and a feeling that "we make the same mistakes everywhere."[11] These views carried some truth, but they remained oblivious to broader factors that influence the Arab environment: the central position of the Arab-Israeli question, the contrast of affluence and poverty between and within states, the revival of Islam as an ideology of political change, and the growing popularity of nonalignment as a foreign-policy posture, particularly for states that aspire toward leading regional roles. Added to these factors is the substance of the internal political consensus in a country like Egypt, a consensus that Sadat sought to shock, reshape, and lead with mixed results. It is these structural factors, as opposed to those related to sporadic upheavals or mismanagement of U.S. diplomatic style, that are more relevant to the analysis of future opportunities and constraints on the development of Egyptian-Soviet relations.

Prediction

The expectation of radical changes following the demise of Third World leaders certainly seems plausible. In such countries, power is personalized and centralized in the hands of the man at the top, particularly in the areas of foreign and defense policies. The pharaonic heritage of centralized government in Egypt make such an expectation all the more relevant. The fact that Sadat himself had administered a series of dramatic decisions (what came to be known as *shock diplomacy*) reinforced this forecast. Had he not expelled Soviet advisers, embraced Henry Kissinger, and flown to Israel? So, the logic goes, why not his successor?

And yet, such assertions ignore both the more profound reasons for Sadat's change of direction and the characteristics of the situation that faces Mubarak. In short, while not dismissing the personality traits of Third World leaders as an important factor in their foreign-policy orientation, this chapter bases its expectations on the structural prospects and problems that face the future course of the Cairo-Moscow relation.

Operational Response

There is a school of thought, particularly reflected by the Reagan administration, that believes that the West should adopt a tougher military posture in the Middle East. This prescription, based on the primacy of the Russian threat, ignores the experience of the 1950s where U.S. pressures to build a regional security organization resulted in a confrontation between U.S. policies and Arab nationalist aspirations, thus providing more opportunities for the USSR.

Another attitude, particularly exhibited when dealing with the Arab-Israeli question, emphasizes that conflict management can see the United States through without any need for difficult decisions. This, it is argued, could be maintained through clever footwork, tactical decisions, and dividing roles. But the deadlocked negotiations on Palestinian autonomy, the preferential military treatment received by Tel Aviv,[12] and the U.S. vetoes on UN draft resolutions condemning Israeli behavior (particularly its invasion of Lebanon in June 1982), all add up to the sense of frustration felt in Cairo toward the Reagan administration. Needless to say, such equivocation opens more opportunities for the USSR in the Arab world and further isolates Arab governments that maintain close relations with the United States. Thus, it is important to remember that the development of Egyptian-Soviet relations cannot be analyzed in a vacuum but must be seen in the context of Washington's future policy decisions toward Cairo and the Arab world.[13]

Historical Considerations

Before tackling the subject of future Egyptian-Soviet relations, however, it is useful to look at the history of Egyptian foreign policy to understand its parameters and characteristics. Three key factors may be identified as influencing Egyptian history and foreign policy since at least the early nineteenth century. First, there is the contradiction between the country's *location* and its *capabilities*. The former dictates a dynamic role commensurate with its location at the intersection of three continents, Egypt's large population base, and its historical and cultural preeminence. But in many instances the means for fulfilling this role have been absent, thus inviting foreign intervention or demanding foreign protection or assistance. The alternative, increasing indigenous capabilities by modernization, has been met by European obstructions, or at least manipulation. This applies, for example, to the conditions imposed on Muhammad Ali by the European powers in 1841, those imposed on Khedive Ismail following the construction of the Suez Canal, and those encountered by Egypt when it attempted to build a modern army in the 1930s.[14] The second element of interest in contemporary Egyptian history is the strength of the nationalist movement from the time of Orabi's insurrection in 1882, to the 1919 and 1952 revolutions. This has left a sensitivity toward foreign domination or interference whatever form it may take. Finally, there are Egypt's aspirations toward playing a regional role; a disposition that is fired by images of history, cultural affinity with other Arab countries, and reasons of self-interest.

This background is essential in understanding President Abd al-Nasir's experience of 1952-1970. He had come to personify the breaking of colonial bonds, the quest for economic and social development, and the assertion of his country's leadership role in the Arab, African, and Third World at large. During his rule, the foundations of Egyptian-Soviet relations were set, based on Russian support for the effort of building a modern Egyptian army, industrializing the economy, and furthering Cairo's Arab and African influence.

Two qualifications need to be made for a better understanding of the nature of Egyptian-Soviet relations. The first has to do with the dynamic that motivated this relationship, the second with the problems that faced it.

History and Dynamics of Egyptian-Soviet Relations

The Egyptian nationalist movement had focused on the British presence in Egypt since the 1880s. This shaped its ideas, its vision of the world, and its program. It also shaped Egyptian attitudes toward the Allied cause during the Second World War—hence the general feeling that Egypt did not have any interest in active participation on their side. While there was disappointment with the ineffectiveness of Wilsonian ideas, there remained a glimmer of hope because of the image of the United States as a noncolonial power and because of the aspirations centered on the United Nations. Parallel to that, Egypt's relations with the Soviet Union had remained ambiguous. The Egyptian legation to Moscow, opened in 1943, had been established at British prodding, notwithstanding King Faruq's deep suspicion of so-called Bolshevism. The UN decision to partition Palestine and the establishment of Israel both received Soviet backing because of Moscow's perception of Zionist labor as a progressive force in the Middle East, an analysis Moscow would revise later in the 1950s. Combined with the Russian interest in becoming a trustee over Libya, this did not serve to enhance the image of the Soviet Union in Egypt, notwithstanding the verbal support for the Egyptian nationalist movement. The muddled course of the few Egyptian Communists since 1924 had not served Russian purposes well either. As foreigners or minority members, they were often unsure about their position vis-à-vis the Zionist movement in Palestine and changed their views on cooperation with the nationalist forces according to Moscow's directions. Egyptian Communists never managed to attract much more than the attention of the political police.[15]

But meanwhile, and paradoxically, the dynamic that fired Egyptian-Soviet relations was being laid in the context of Egypt's experience with the West. The Egyptians felt that London was vacillating on the issue of evacuation, that it continued to drive toward separating the Sudan from Egypt, that Britain's policy in Palestine had been unfair to the Arabs, and that Western security schemes were a cover for continuing a quasi-colonial relationship. *Herein lies a basic problem in Egypt's relations with the West, forever to return in more bitter forms.* The Western powers viewed the area in terms of its position in the geostrategic map bordering the USSR, its mineral wealth, and its weak politicoeconomic and social infrastucture (indeed, the area was to be considered a vacuum by Eisenhower in 1957). The old colonial powers, often joined by the United States, added to this their suspicions about the emerging revolutionary experience in Egypt. Committed as they were to Israel's security, the maintenance of their positions in the Arab world (France in Algeria, Britain in Iraq, Jordan, the Gulf, and Aden, the United States in Saudi Arabia and Iran), and keen on combating Egyptian opposition to the introduction of Western pacts, the West was soon to see in Nasir the villain of the peace.

The Egyptian revolution, idealistic and keen on banishing the old order, aspired toward a more active regional role. Nasir's instinct was to turn first to the United States for arms supplies, but he was frustrated in his quest.[16] Meanwhile, the Israeli raid on Gaza in 1955 humiliated the new leaders in Cairo, who refused to enter a Western-sponsored Middle East pact and felt wary of Western moves to include Iraq, and possibly Syria, in such a scheme.[17] The dramatic response was the now-famous arms deal with the USSR.

The scene was set for a cycle that was to repeat itself in the years to come. Egypt had presented a demand to the West, was rebuffed, and responded in its own way. The next move came from the West in the form of sanctions—refusing to grant aid for the High Dam. Thus, the Cold War became linked not only to the question of arms supplies to Cairo but also to that of development. Nasir completed the circle by striking back at the main remaining colonial link and nationalizing the Suez Canal. The tripartite attack on Egypt improved Egypt's relations with Washington, but soon these were taken over by new tensions. Cairo opposed the concept of the Eisenhower Doctrine, and Washington was worried because of the nationalistic tide Nasir rode; Egypt had united with Syria in 1958 and the royal regime of Iraq was removed in a bloody coup. U.S. troops landed in Lebanon and British forces landed in Jordan to maintain the pro-Western regimes there.

No sooner had these problems subsided when Syria seceded from the union with Egypt and a Saudi-Egyptian contest ensued. The revolution in Yemen brought this to a head with Egyptian forces attacking the Saudis who called on U.S. support.[18] By this time, Egypt was receiving important backing from the USSR; indeed a Soviet-piloted airbridge had ferried Egyptian troops to Yemen. Nasir was on a collision course with Washington. U.S. wheat aid was severed and Cairo attacked Saudi Arabian moves to form a Pan-Islamic organization, which was suspected of being a new forum for creating pro-Western structures. The 1967 war saw relations with the United States take a further turn for the worse and increased Egypt's dependency on the USSR. Moscow took on rearming Egypt and Syria, representing them in negotiations with Washington on the Arab-Israeli question,[19] and providing a Russian-manned air-defense system to protect the Egyptian hinterland from in-depth Israeli raids.

Problems in Egyptian-Soviet Relations

But throughout this period (1954-1970), Nasir's relations with Moscow were far from harmonious. The Russians did not approve of the Egyptian union with Syria, and Nasir quarrelled bitterly with Khrushchev after the new regime in Iraq took a Communist direction. Moscow disapproved of Egypt's treatment of local Communists and Nasir's continuing relations with the West, while Cairo looked askance at Soviet suggestions for arms limitations in the Middle East. The 1967 war saw bitter feelings on both sides, and in 1970 the Russians were unhappy because Nasir had reestablished contacts with Washington and accepted the peace plan presented by Secretary of State Rogers.

U.S. peace efforts came to nought, and Nasir's successor, Sadat, became more convinced of the need to consolidate his relations with Moscow, particularly since he realized that the Russians were worried because of a purge he had conducted against the clique that ruled the country for his predecessor. Thus on 27 May 1971, a Soviet-Egyptian Treaty of Friendship and Cooperation was signed in Cairo. Sources of suspicion, however, continued in the relationship between the countries. When Sadat realized that he was not receiving the amount of military aid he required to give him a military option, he expelled the Soviet military personnel from Egypt in July 1972.

Later, relations improved between the two parties, and the USSR resumed arms shipments to Egypt. By this time, secret contacts with the United States had established the futility of hoping for a change in the U.S. position,[20] and in October 1973, Egypt and Syria attempted to liberate part of their occupied territories by force. The diplomatic momentum generated by the war resulted in a peace conference with both superpowers attending, but soon the real work was left to Dr. Kissinger's shuttle diplomacy that produced two disengagement agreements between Egypt and Israel (1974, 1975) and one between Syria and Israel (1974).

After the 1973 war, the divergencies continued between the Soviet role and self-perception as a superpower with global and Middle Eastern interests and the Egyptian perception of what constituted an arms transfer suitable for Cairo's own needs. The Soviets felt excluded from the peace process and could not see themselves as arms merchants only. Also, they could not see Egypt treating them and the United States as equals, let alone promoting what they saw as a Pax-Americana.

The Egyptian leadership viewed the Soviets as being too wary of detente, unreliable when it came to honoring commitments, following the czarist search for access to the Middle East, and interested in promoting a certain political and economic structure in Egypt that did not correspond with Egyptian needs. Sadat had visited Moscow several times and, after Nixon's visit to Cairo, Brezhnev was invited. The Soviets delayed this visit. Egyptian Foreign Minister Fahmy and Chief of Staff Gamassy went to Moscow in October 1974, then again in December, just after the death of Field Marshall Ismail (Gamassy was to become minister of defense).[21]

Some improvement occurred because in March 1975 Sadat confirmed that Egypt had taken delivery of MiG-23s and that Egyptian pilots were training in the Soviet Union. This was, however, in fulfillment of a pre-1973 contract. Meanwhile, Egypt was aware of Soviet armaments supplied to Syria and Libya. The Egyptian concept of *replacements* of lost equipment in 1973 was repeatedly used in negotiations with the Russians, but to no avail. At the time, reports spoke of reduction in the standard flying schedule of Egyptian pilots from twenty to fifteen hours per month because of the lack of spare parts and services,[22] and the Egyptian air-defense commander stated that he had not received a single missile replacement from the Soviet Union since the end of the October War.[23]

Sinai II was signed in September 1975, and Egyptian-Soviet relations took a further turn for the worse. Egypt, perhaps despairing of an improvement, became actively engaged in widening its army connections with Western Europe.[24] Then in March 1976, Egypt canceled its Treaty of Friendship with the Soviet Union and the last naval facilities available to the Soviets. Contacts with India to circumvent the Soviet refusal to service MiG aircraft failed because of Soviet pressure. Now reports spoke of Egyptian pilots flying only ten hours per month.[25]

In mid-1977 the Egyptian minister of foreign affairs went to Moscow. Six relevant points were made clear to him according to President Sadat:

1. Brezhnev stated that he would not allow the Soviet Union to be ignored in any Middle East settlement.
2. The Soviets requested a return of the Friendship Treaty;
3. Cancellation of previous armament agreements; and
4. Refusal of the concept of replacing military losses.
5. Payments for spare parts should be made in hard currency and in advance of delivery.
6. Nothing could be delivered before the end of 1977.

In 1977, the USSR returned fifty out of one-hundred and seventy-five MiG-21 engines that were sent there for servicing. In August all remaining Egyptian military personnel training in the Soviet Union were withdrawn.

The Egyptian-Libyan military clash in the summer of 1977 further worsened Cairo's relations with Moscow. By this time Egypt's relations with the United States had improved dramatically and Sadat had introduced a new economic policy (the *open door*) that gave more opportunities to foreign and private capital, something that was severely criticized in the Soviet press. Meanwhile, problems had emerged because Egypt demanded a rescheduling of its debts to Moscow (estimated at eleven billion dollars) most of which was a result of arms supplies. In October 1977, Sadat suspended debt repayments to the USSR.

Soviet-U.S. efforts during 1977 to reconvene the Geneva Conference on the Middle East did not result in much progress, and in November Sadat made his initiative to go to Israel. The Soviet Union stayed away from the subsequent Cairo conference and backed the Arab rejectionists in their attack on the Camp David Agreements (1978) and the Peace Treaty between Egypt and Israel (1979). By this time the Egyptian president had formulated what could be called the Sadat Doctrine. According to this theory, the Soviet Union is engaged in building a belt of influence from Angola to Ethiopia and South Yemen, and at the same time performing strategic pincer movements toward the oil resources of the Gulf as well as to isolate

Egypt (thus Libya's efforts to undermine Numayri's regime in Sudan and interfere in Chad were presented as part of Moscow's global design). The doctrine went on to define Egypt's response to these moves, emphasizing its interest in the sources of the Nile, the entrance of the Red Sea, and the security of the Gulf. The ensuing military obligations related to these interests would be performed by Egypt, and the United States should be ready to underwrite this effort. In case of a Russian threat to the Gulf, indeed to "any Moslem country up till Indonesia," the United States would be able to use "facilities" in Egypt.

The rhetoric from Cairo was more anti-Soviet than that of Washington. In his last interview before the assassination, President Sadat spoke of how Marxism doubled the number of social problems and added that the Soviet citizen is sacrificed for the state. He went on to accuse the Russians of placing obstacles in the way of the peace process in the Middle East ("simple sabotage," he called it) and asserted that peace is possible without the Soviet Union, but not without the United States.[26]

Summary

This brief overview of Egyptian-Soviet relations in the last thirty to forty years needs to be interpreted carefully. The complexity of action-reaction cycles, the direction of the flow of influence, and the impact of regional and international factors on the Cairo-Moscow relationship are some of the many considerations that need to be taken into account when explaining the history of our subject. Four broad examples could be given to demonstrate this point.

First, one should not overlook the fact that Egypt has derived substantial gains from its relations with the Soviet Union. It is obvious that the USSR also benefited, that Moscow's motivations were not entirely benevolent, and that Egypt paid substantial costs for the rewards it reaped. But, in the end, the building of the High Dam, the industrialization of Egypt, and the equipping of the Egyptian army must be considered a plus to Egypt. Professor Alvin Rubinstein gives a table of eleven *key events* or issue areas in Egyptian-Soviet relations in the period 1967-1975, nine of which resulted from Egyptian influence on the USSR and benefited Egypt, one that favored Moscow, and one of which was of shared advantage.[27]

Second, despite the intensified interaction between both parties, this was not related to an increase in Russia's influence over Egypt. Thus, Egyptian exports to the USSR after 1967 rose to fifty percent and more of its total exports in 1970-1973 while the country was indebted to Russia for an equal percentage of its medium- and long-term loans, but Egyptians remained

independent in a number of their major and minor decisions. Examples of
the former were the launching of the war of attrition and the October War
against Israel. An interesting example of less spectacular decisions concerned the purchase of civil aircraft. The USSR was interested in selling
Cairo such planes since 1968. Finally, this was agreed to in 1972 but was
revoked in 1975 following an air crash, and the planes were returned.[28]

Third, the Soviet Union was often acting in response to Egyptian
demands when it upgraded its military presence in the eastern Mediterranean and Egypt. Thus, in the wake of the 1967 war, Nasir saw that a
stronger Soviet presence in the Mediterranean and in Egypt would redress
the imbalance between Egypt and Israel. Soviet naval vessels in Egyptian
ports were seen as a way of restraining Israeli attacks. Later, when Israel in
1969 smuggled some naval vessels from France, the Egyptian navy reported
that the U.S. Sixth Fleet was protecting the ships on the way to Israel; a factor that further convinced Nasir of the need to balance the U.S. naval
presence in the Mediterranean by a stronger Soviet presence. When Israel
resorted to in-depth raids on Egyptian civilian targets in response to attempts to activate the military status quo on the Suez Canal, Nasir requested direct Russian involvement in the protection of Egypt. Missile
crews and pilots were dispatched from the USSR, but published minutes
show that the Russians insisted on a withdrawal of these units before in-
itiating hostilities. It is interesting to remember that the principal Russian
action, taken when they realized that Egypt was about to launch the 1973
war, was to withdraw all advisers and experts in the country, much to the
annoyance of President Sadat. The most dramatic illustration of this point
is the immediate compliance of Moscow to Sadat's request in 1972 that all
Soviet military personnel leave the country.[29]

Fourth, notwithstanding the general proviso that Egyptian-Soviet relations should be understood in a wider context, it should be emphasized that
Egyptian actions have shown a great degree of independence. The operational lesson here is that Cairo's actions are not a result of overt or covert
Western designs as much as the result of Egyptian perceptions of self-
interest, available options, and Soviet responses to demands made on
them.[30]

The Egyptian-Soviet rift demonstrated that Egyptian calculations, for
Egyptian reasons, produced dissatisfaction with the Soviet Union. Kissinger
has testified his surprise at Sadat's decision to expel the Soviet advisers
without prior agreement on dividends from Washington.[31] Later, Egyptian-
Soviet relations were to improve, then deteriorate again, despite Egyptian
attempts to maintain the military relationship with Moscow. These attempts
met with some success, but in the end it became obvious that unless Moscow
were to be included in the Arab-Israeli peace process, there was not much
prospect for arms supplies.[32]

Prospects of Soviet-Egyptian Relations

With the aforementioned in mind, we can now turn to the future prospects of Egyptian-Soviet relations. Since the relations had reached an all-time low in September 1981 and there wasn't much room for further deterioration, one could argue that the options available would be either a continuation of that condition or an improvement of relations through gradual and uneven steps. At the time of writing (late summer 1982) it is this second possibility that seems to prevail. Eight principal arguments or reasons could be identified as contributing toward this outcome:

1. *The Rebound Theory.* It could be argued that the Sadat assassination, and the internal reactions to it, demonstrated a sense of dissatisfaction with the Egyptian president's Western connection.[33] Recoiling from the West, particularly the United States, some change in Egypt's foreign-policy stance would thus be expected toward a more nonaligned posture. This would be particularly expected since it is not uncommon for successor regimes or governments, more so in the Third World, to repudiate much of the political heritage of their predecessors. Also, it could be predicted that the superpower closest to the preceding ruler would receive some, or most, of the flack directed against him during the ensuing political postmortem. It could be said that such a possibility was made even more probable by what appeared to be the cold shoulder given to Sadat by the Reagan administration, especially during his visit to Washington in August 1981. To some, this seemed to indicate that the U.S. administration had written off Sadat as being of no further use to it and had concentrated on Israel as the true strategic ally in the area.[34] This coincided with a series of U.S. decisions, ranging from abandoning the shah to what was seen as a hypocritical reaction to the invasion of Afghanistan,[35] that seemed to reinforce the idea that "it doesn't pay to become allied to the Americans."

2. *Rebuilding the Egyptian Consensus.* Islamic radicalism had made a dramatic point by the assassination. In various forms, this movement has haunted Egypt's political life since the 1930s but has never managed to capture power. It was thought that Egypt—secular, multireligious, moderate, with a millenial tradition of centralized power—would never become another Iran. Now, suddenly, all bets were off. This leads to the second argument for an improvement in Egyptian-Soviet relations. If the Islamic radical groups are to be identified as the main threat to whomever is in power in Cairo, and if the security-state solution to this threat is to be dismissed as inadequate at best and ultimately self-defeating, then the support of the various secular power groups would be required, including that of the opposition parties. But this support, in turn, would not be forthcoming unless domestic and foreign policy were to be reshaped to accommodate a new consensus.[36] One of the most relevant points in this consensus, particularly to

nationalist and leftist groups in the country, is the normalization of relations with Moscow and a more discriminating attitude toward Washington.

3. *Arab Leadership Prerequisites*. Some Egyptians see that the absence of their country from Arab councils since 1977 had brought a litany of sins to the region. The impasse on the Palestinian issue, the Lebanese situation, and the Iraq-Iran war, among many other things, are perceived as results of this situation. Three decades earlier Nasir had written that a leadership role was wandering through the region, searching for an actor to play it. Egypt, he argued, accepted the burden as no other Arab state was able to do so.[37] Now once again, in the eyes of some people, this role needs to be filled.

There are, however, prerequisites for the role. In further theatrical language, the qualities of the actor are important, not just those of the make-up, lighting, and sound effects. An image of balanced international relations or nonalignment is required. This is particularly important, it is argued, for a country like Egypt that sees itself as a trend setter, a leader in its own right, irrespective of the wishes of outside powers. The lesson of history has shown, the argument continues, that too strong a relation with one or another superpower curtails the leadership qualities of a country. Evidence of this is shown, for example, in the case of Saudi Arabia.

A more balanced foreign-policy posture would open to Cairo the possibilities of mediating in several regional conflicts, moving to avoid the polarization of relations in the Arab world and Africa between the two superpowers, and thus reducing tensions and the possibilities of explosions. Furthermore, regional solutions would be available to conflicts such as those of the two Yemens, the Horn of Africa, Chad, and the Western Sahara, which would further strengthen the Arab League, the Organization of African Unity, and the nonaligned group. It is further argued that this approach would be beneficial even from the point of view of the United States, since by distancing Cairo from unpopular U.S. policies it gives Egypt the capability of backing more moderate regimes without appearing to be doing so at the behest of Washington.

4. *The Arab-Israeli Dimension*. While the Israelis occupy Arab lands, the Arab countries will continue to agitate for a global settlement of the Arab-Israeli question; a solution that encompasses the problem in its entirety and produces a lasting peace settlement. This would be imperative to secure the Egyptian-Israeli peace agreement, stem the radicalization of the Arab world, avoid an Arab confrontation with the United States (Israel's main protector), and reduce the possibilities for further superpower confrontation in the area.

Two subarguments flow from these generalities. The first emphasizes the benefits of Russian participation in a solution. Thus, if it is admitted that the USSR has the ability to obstruct, undermine, or limit the possibilities for an Arab-Israeli settlement, then it would be beneficial to bring it somehow into such a settlement to forestall its wrath. The United States has contemplated, and exercised, this policy at various times, notably in the Soviet-U.S. joint declaration on the Middle East of October 1977. Western Europeans are known to be sympathetic to this view. Egypt invited the USSR to attend the Mena House conference in Cairo in December 1977, which President Sadat convened following his trip to Israel. Israel, for her part, has had contacts with Moscow that culminated in a meeting between the foreign ministers of both countries in New York in September 1981. Syria, Jordan, and the Palestine Liberation Organization have come out in favor of Russian participation in an Arab-Israeli settlement and have viewed with suspicion U.S.-sponsored efforts in this field. If these tendencies were to be taken to their logical conclusion, they point in the direction of an Arab-Israeli peace based on a detente between the two superpowers, as opposed to one that reflects the cold war between them. In such a case an improvement of Egyptian-Soviet relations would be both a prerequisite and a result of a global solution of the Arab-Israeli question.

The second argument sees the United States as inextricably linked to Israel. Accordingly, the only interest of the United States in the Camp David Agreements was to isolate Egypt from the Arab world, deny the Arabs the military option, separate the issue of oil supplies from that of Palestine, and stem the possibilities of Russian influence in the area by devising a Pax-Americana. The Reagan administration upgraded these worries as it concluded a strategic agreement with Tel Aviv, spoke of an anti-Soviet strategic consensus in the area, appeared disinterested in the Arab-Israeli conflict, and seemed to condone the Israeli invasion of Lebanon in June 1982. These U.S. signals produced a backlash in the Arab press with some of the most virulent attacks on a U.S. administration since the 1973 war.[38]

At a time when the Soviet Union appears as the champion of the Arab cause, albeit subject to severe restraints, Egypt would find it difficult to resist for long the temptation of responding to U.S. support for Israel by improving relations with the USSR, even if that were a mere maneuver to nudge the United States toward reassessing its policies. But this could be seen as more than that; an effort to diversify the options available to Egypt and avoid sitting passively at the receiving end of objectionable U.S. policies. As one prominent Egyptian journalist has stated, lack of contact with the Soviet Union places Egypt and Israel in a situation comparable to that faced by Turkey and Greece: both are members of a strategic alliance dominated by Washington and hence their options are restricted in dealing with each other.[39]

5. *Nonaligned-Role Requirements.* In the 1960s Egypt played a dynamic role in the emergence of the nonaligned movement, something that is perceived with some nostalgia within the country. The move toward peace

with Israel, the Egyptian-Soviet rift, and the close relationship with the United States (particularly joint military maneuvers between both countries and the offer of Egyptian facilities to U.S. forces) have combined to make Egypt an attractive target for attack from antagonistic Arab and Third World countries. A drive to expel Egypt from the movement was narrowly averted.

The assassination of President Sadat, the conciliatory movements and statements of the Mubarak government, and the Iranian victories over Iraq have combined to dampen the criticism Egypt was facing from other nonaligned countries. Iraq, for example, invited Egypt to attend the scheduled nonaligned summit in Baghdad in September 1982. But the reactivation of Cairo's nonaligned role would require a less anti-Soviet posture, and a downgrading of overt strategic cooperation with the West. Egypt's minister of state for foreign affairs, Dr. Boutrus Ghali, noted that Egypt was seeking to improve relations with the USSR because of its membership in the nonaligned movement, which is based on the principle of good relations with the two superpowers and of remaining at a balanced point from both blocs.[40]

6. *Machiavellian Diplomacy*. A further argument for the need to improve relations with Moscow could be provided by cynical self-interest. It is often said that Third World countries benefited from the Cold-War situation of the 1950s and 1960s because both blocs were keen on offering various forms of support to outbid their rivals. It could also be argued that superpower competition ensured a degree of security for Third World countries that otherwise would have been under irresistable pressure to join one or the other of the two camps. In addition, this opened the opportunity for more powerful Third World countries to pursue their own foreign-policy objectives that may differ or contradict those of one or both superpowers.

At a time of a more diversified distribution of power in the international system, with the return of some of the symptoms of a new Cold War, and to maximize the freedom of maneuver and the possible gains that would result from it, a good argument could be made for an Egyptian return to a more balanced posture between the Big Two. Even if Cairo wanted to continue with its close cooperation with Washington, it could be argued that normal relations with Moscow would be to Egypt's ultimate benefit, since it would jolt the U.S. administration into looking at Egyptian requirements more seriously and avoid being taken for granted by the White House.

7. *Economic Conditions*. As mentioned earlier, a substantial part of Egypt's industries are equipped with Soviet machinery that requires spare parts and servicing. This applies to major plants such as iron, steel, and aluminum; it also applies to the High Dam. Meeting these requirements is not costly in economic terms and has ancillary benefits to the Egyptian economy. Since payment for Russian imports is often made by bartering

them with Egyptian exports, this not only means that there are no negative balance of trade results because of economic relations with Moscow but also that such relations actually result in encouraging productive sectors in Egypt. Socially, there is the advantage that such an exchange spreads its benefits throughout the Egyptian economy with small-scale private industries (which tend to be labor intensive) producing many of the exports to the USSR (furniture, knitwear, leather goods, and such).[41] The fact that Egyptian exports, whether those resulting from the drive to industrialize or those produced by other sectors, are exportable to Eastern-bloc markets goes some way toward solving a problem faced by many newly industrialized countries that find that the quality and price of their goods make them difficult to sell abroad, particularly in the face of the protective barriers of the West. A corollary could be drawn by the Yugoslav experience where there exists an acute need to export to the West to earn hard currency, to meet the repayment of loans, and to ensure political balance. However, Belgrade found that notwithstanding its efforts, its trade with OECD countries decreased by 18 percent in the first five months of 1981 while its trade with the Council for Mutual Economic Assistance (CMEA or COMECON) countries increased by 55 percent in the same period.[42] It is possible that this type of foreign economic relationship would be useful in offsetting some of the negative results of the open-door policy Egypt has moved toward since the late 1960s.

8. *Military Considerations.* Egypt depended almost exclusively on the USSR for the development of its armed forces between 1955 and 1975. This has left the country with large quantities of inherited Russian equipment, a Russian-trained officer class, and familiarity with the military doctrine of the USSR. While it is true that Egypt has managed to find a number of alternative sources to acquire spare parts and manufactures many of these locally, it would be advantageous to have a direct source of such material from Russia. Some pieces of equipment have had to be serviced and refurbished in Western European countries at such a high cost that in some cases it has exceeded the price of the equipment itself.

Egypt's experience with Western sources of armaments has given evidence of their inadequacy and unreliability. U.S. supplies would be subject to the scrutiny and opposition of the pro-Israeli lobby in Washington as well as to U.S. fears that such supplies would limit Israel's military superiority over its Arab neighbors. Financial difficulties complicate the purchase of arms from Western Europe, something that could be overcome by petro-Arab aid but that in turn remains subject to Egypt's relations with other Arab countries. In any case, experience has shown that Western sources are subject to cut-offs or embargoes under certain circumstances (witness Argentina in the Falkland war, for example). All of this adds to another argument for reestablishing a degree of military cooperation with the USSR.

Problems of Soviet-Egyptian Relations

The preceding list of reasons, arguments, and structural factors that delineate the brighter prospects for Egyptian-Soviet relations needs to be qualified by a number of countervailing forces and influences, some of which are unknown at the moment. For example, how will the advantages and disadvantages of improving relations with the USSR be perceived by the decision-making elites in Cairo and Moscow? What pace or rate of improvement, if any, will ensue? What are the constraints on such an improvement, and will there be any setbacks for the process caused by unforeseen developments?

Whatever the answers to these questions, it must be expected that Egyptian-Soviet relations have a number of obstacles that shall constrain the positive impact of the eight factors mentioned in the previous section. To understand the parameters of the future development of Egyptian-Soviet relations, those eight points need to be read in conjunction with the following overview of the problems and limitations these two countries shall face; both are part and parcel of the same process and cannot be viewed in isolation.

The Sadat Legacy

In many ways Sadat represented powerful sections of the Egyptian society. His assassination, in the end, was not an Iranian-type revolution but rather a breakdown in the Egyptian political system. The power of the state remained paramount, and a strong accent was placed on continuity by his successor, albeit while signaling that some changes were necessary. The components of the Egyptian consensus Sadat left behind range from an agreement on the need for a multiparty system, an open-door economic policy, peace with Israel, and friendly relations with the West. Some of these factors, it is felt, would require modification, such as furthering the internal democratic experiment. Other factors need to be introduced, such as close relations with the Arab world or a thaw in relations with the Eastern bloc. Others still remain debatable; what "type" of peace should exist with Israel and at what price to Egypt's other obligations? Taken in this context, the question becomes how to engineer an evolutionary process that would include all of these components rather than introduce fundamental changes of direction.

The Regional Environment

The deep changes in the regional environment in the Arab world, the "new Arab order,"[43] need to be taken into consideration when attempting to

predict the extent of the aforementioned evolutionary process. Decolonization is passé for all intents and purposes as an issue in the contemporary
Arab world, with the major exception of Palestine. This limits the possibilities for future clashes with the West in comparison to the 1950s and
1960s and thus reduces the need to resort to Russian support. Arab oil
wealth brought with it a new set of problems concerning varying degrees of
wealth, relations between aid donors and aid recipients, and questions
about the pace and direction of change. But it also glossed over many old
issues in the Arab world, such as the dichotomy between progressive and
reactionary regimes, the messianic calls for Arab unity, and the theorizing
about socialism. No single country has the capabilities to assume the leadership of the Arab world, and, increasingly, pragmatism governs relations
between different Arab states, particularly those between the have and the
have nots. This qualifies what was mentioned earlier about Egypt's aspirations for again playing leading roles in the Arab, African, and nonaligned
worlds. Because Cairo is concerned with solving its internal problems, and
since it has an interest in developing relations with the more conservative
oil-rich countries of the area, it will be sensitive toward any fears they may
have of radical movements or excessive Soviet influence in the Arab world
and Africa.

Regional U.S. Influence

In the minds of most Arabs, the United States remains the primary power
responsible for Israeli actions. While this nourishes anti-U.S. feelings, it
also makes Washington the chief depository for complaints of Israeli
behavior; it is thought that in the final resort it is the White House that has
the power to influence Israel. In contrast, the USSR or the West Europeans,
who may issue declarations of condemnation or support, hold little effective influence over Israeli behavior. Herein lies a source of frustration for
the Soviet Union, which feels that the Arabs turn to Moscow at the time of
war but to Washington in search of peace. On the other hand, Egypt has its
own reasons for complaining of Russian behavior. Moscow is often
suspected of a willingness to sacrifice its position on the Arab-Israeli conflict in exchange for gains elsewhere, particularly in its relationship with the
United States. One example of this was Egypt's adverse reaction to the
Nixon-Brezhnev agreement on military relaxation in the Middle East in
1972. This was seen as a model of superpower detente, or condominium,
that involved deep-freezing Third World problems rather than solving
them. Similarly, Moscow's agreement to allow Jewish emigration from
the USSR to placate Washington irritated the Arabs who suspected that
many of these immigrants would end up living on occupied Palestinian

land. Moscow's restraint in supplying arms to Egypt and the Palestinians[44] was the ultimate confirmation of Arab doubts about Moscow's intentions of fostering a no peace-no war situation without pushing toward a resolution one way or the other. The fact that Cairo perceives various Russian moves as mere attempts at obstructing a peace settlement adds to these suspicions.

Soviet Activities

To further augment these doubts, Cairo has looked askance at the regional intentions of the USSR. Moscow's support of Libya, South Yemen, and Ethiopia, its hostility toward the Numayri regime in Sudan, and the continued occupation of Afghanistan will continue to raise concern in Cairo no matter who is in power. These countries are in areas of traditional Egyptian security interests whether because of their impact on a vital source of water (the Nile), a major source of revenue (the Suez Canal), or because of possible threats to the Arab states of the Gulf.

Egypt's response to these perceived threats has been mainly in a bipolar balance of power framework; "if the threat comes from one power, seek support from the other." Because of the weaknesses of Arab military capabilities and regimes, inter-Arab rivalries, and the Arab-Israeli problem, Cairo doubts that the Arab world would be able to mobilize a credible response to possible Soviet threats or to regional powers like Iran. Accordingly, until a viable regional security system is devised, there shall be a school of thought in the Arab world that insists on the need for a credible deterrence to counter super- or regional-power threats. At the moment, several Gulf states and Egypt expect the United States to play this role, an expectation that has had operational implications ranging from the development of facilities, joint military maneuvers, U.S. arms supplies, and close economic and political relations with Washington. Herein lies another constraint on the development of relations with the USSR.

A critical examination of the remaining reasons for improving Egyptian-Soviet relations reveals further limitations on their forcefulness. The concept of nonalignment should not be viewed as an iron-cast mold; the movement includes countries as different as Cuba and Saudi Arabia. Historically, and at present, the countries of the movement have rejected equidistance from the two superpowers; instead they have insisted that their relationships toward the superpowers should be shaped by a combination of principles (anticolonialism, for example) and self-interest. The Havana nonaligned conference rejected the notion of the Soviet Union being a natural ally to the nonaligned.[45] Furthermore, so-called special relationships with one superpower or the other have been presented as not being contradictory to nonalignment. This argument was employed in the past to explain Egypt's Treaty of Friendship and Cooperation with the Soviet Union.[46] President Mubarak has repeated this point in relation to Egypt's links with the United States, adding that India's special relationship with the USSR does not mean that the former was not nonaligned.[47]

Economically, Egypt has forged important links with the United States, Europe, and Japan. Particularly in the area of its relations with the United States, Egypt has been allocated large amounts of U.S. aid amounting to $7.5 billion in the period 1975-1982. It is probable that Egypt would like to consolidate this relationship and, parallel to that, attract as much Western and Arab investments as possible. Under these circumstances, it is possible that Cairo would feel no great pressure to upgrade dramatically its economic relations with the USSR.

Militarily, Egypt has managed to deal with numerous spare-parts problems, thus prolonging the life expectancy of its Russian equipment. As an example, over one-thousand different spares for armored equipment are produced locally—as is most of the army's ammunition. Here Egypt has also forged close relations with the United States, particularly since 1977. Egypt has received important aircraft (C-130, F-4, and F-16), armored personnel carriers, tanks, and antitank weapon systems and has formulated a five-year development plan for its armed forces based on U.S. assistance.[48] In addition, Cairo has attempted to diversify its military sources by signing agreements to purchase the French *Mirage*-2000, and other British, Italian, Canadian, and Chinese arms. The political aim is to avoid being trapped into heavy dependency on one single source of hardware. Under these circumstances, new Russian equipment, though possibly useful, would lose its previous relevance to Egyptian purposes.

Psychologically and practically, the shadow of the past Egyptian-Soviet relations must disturb the efforts of both sides to improve them. For Moscow, Egypt represented a historical breakthrough into the Arab and African worlds. Billions of rubles were invested in its effort to build, consolidate, and expand this relationship. Despite setbacks, the two countries would return to new and higher forms of cooperation; the Treaty of Friendship in 1971 was one example, the first such treaty between the USSR and a Third World country (with the exception of the treaty with Afghanistan in the 1930s). Then, suddenly, the curve reversed and plunged.

Russian negotiators have often complained in the past that they could not allow Egypt to treat them the way Sadat did after 1972 and 1973-1974. A superpower depended too much on its prestige, they said, and the precedent Cairo was setting would be damaging to Moscow's relations with other countries around the world.[49] Added to that was the Egyptian decision to suspend the payment of its debts to Moscow (nonmilitary debts of about four billion dollars and military debts of about seven billion dollars).[50] It is probable that Cairo will demand that part of these debts be written off, something that would add to the difficulties of normalizing relations. But the USSR could possibly reverse this situation by making a gesture to the Egyptian people by unilaterally canceling part, or all, of these debts; a step that would be of practically no real cost but of tremendous psychological impact.

Conclusion: Soviet Constraints and Dilemmas

So far this chapter has focused primarily on Egyptian factors under the assumption that is where change may occur in the aftermath of the assassination of President Sadat. But to form a more complete picture it is necessary to turn briefly to the USSR's side of the coin.

The Soviet Union has built-in advantages in its quest to return to the core of the Arab world and to extricate itself from being trapped with awkward regimes on the periphery. The continuing Arab-Israeli conflict, the blunders of U.S. policy, intraregional competition, and internal upheavals offer numerous entry points. But at the same time there are barriers and unknowns. Arab nationalism, Islamic revival, and the middle-class consumerism of the area's elites are some of these.

In addition, Russia is constrained by the contradiction between its position as a superpower on the one hand and revolutionary headquarters on the other. What degree of support should be offered to nationalist regimes? How should the Kremlin react to countries that persecute Moscow-oriented Communists or forge close relations with the West? What degree of military aid should be extended to the Palestinians? What degree of confrontation with Washington is acceptable on account of the Arab-Israeli conflict? These are some of the continuous soul-searching questions the Soviets have to ask.

At this moment in history, the USSR faces a host of demanding issues: internal economic needs, Eastern Europe, the Iran-Iraq war, Afghanistan, and China. Parallel to that there is the interest in placating Washington and achieving some progress on strategic arms negotiations. And all of this is happening at a time when the issue of political succession is on the minds of those in the Kremlin.

Under these circumstances, much depends on Russia's ability to perceive opportunities in the Arab world and its cost-benefit assessment of following them through. The main factor, however, will remain the will of the indigenous forces in the area.[51] Egypt is back at the center of these forces, and its own calculations will take into consideration its immediate material interests plus its view of U.S. policies, Israeli attitudes, the outcome of the Iran-Iraq war, and the process of inter-Arab reconciliation.

The accent in Cairo will probably be on pragmatism, gradual evolution, and delicate balances among the aforementioned international, regional, and internal factors.

Notes

1. Mohammed Anis Salem, "Arab Schisms in the 1980s: New Order or Old Story?" *The World Today* (May 1982):175-184.

2. In the period 1974-1982, $7.3 billion had been allocated to Egypt by the United States, although more than $2 billion had been unspent because of red tape at both ends. *International Institute for Strategic Studies, The Strategic Survey, 1981-1982* (London: 1982), p. 75.

3. In September 1981 the Soviet ambassador was expelled from Cairo with the accusation of interfering in the internal affairs of Egypt. About one thousand technicians were also asked to leave at the same time.

4. Bob Woodward, "Meeting Notes Show the Unvarnished Haig," *Washington Post*, 19 February 1982, p. 1.

5. See Secretary of State Haig's press conference in the *New York Times*, 8 October 1981; *Los Angeles Times*, 7 October 1981 (for alert of U.S. forces following the assassination); and the *Washington Post*, 15 October 1981 (dispatch of AWACS).

6. *Pravda*, 12 October 1981, p. 1.

7. This was in contrast to the United States, which sent the secretary of health, education, and welfare to Nasir's funeral in 1980 despite the absence of diplomatic relations between Cairo and Washington.

8. *Pravda*, 15 October 1981, p. 1.

9. Fuad Mattar, "Cairo and Moscow . . . the Other Normalization," (in Arabic), *Al-Mustaqbal*, 6 February 1981, no. 259, pp. 32-33.

10. For a translation of the statement by TASS describing the return of Sinai as a "farce," see *Summary of World Broadcasts* (SWB), SU/7012/A4/9, 27 April 1982. Moscow's Arabic service hammered on these themes, see *SWB*, SU/7013/A4/4-5, 28 April 1982; and SU/7015/A4/1-3, 30 April 1982. TASS carried a report of George Habash, leader of the PFLP, in the same vein. Dr. Habash was in Moscow at the time.

11. Christopher Walker, "Diplomats Express Concern at Scale of US Commitment to Egypt," *Times* (London), 20 October 1981, p. 1. See also *New York Times*, 19 October 1981.

12. Egyptian officials argue that the Carter administration promised them equal military aid to that received by Israel. However, in 1982 the U.S. Congress agreed to give Israel $1.7 billion of military aid, $850 million of which took the form of nonrefundable grants. Meanwhile, Egypt was allocated $1.3 billion, $400 million of which was a grant. Probably the

symbolic message carried in these allocations is more important than the actual figures, although there is also the question of the validity of U.S. promises. See the interview with Egypt's minister of defense, Abu-Ghazala, in *Al-Musawar,* 4 June 1982, pp. 18-21, 78-79 (in Arabic).

13. This does not mean that the question of style should be ignored. Cairo has been irritated by U.S. demands to utilize bases in the Sinai, its terms for military facilities in Egypt, leaks to the press, covert dealings with Libya, and the arrival of the U.S. contingent of the MFO on the Israeli airline El-Al.

14. The Foreign Office papers reveal London's attitude toward Egypt's demands. One interesting comment by a Foreign Office official reads "the more confidence the Egyptians can place in their army the less strong will be the ultimate foundation of our own influence in the country." See FO371/ 23307-J4142/1/16, Kelly's minute dated 17 October 1939, on dispatch from Lampson to Halifax.

15. Mohamed Heikal, *Sphinx and Commissar: The Rise and Fall of Soviet Influence in the Arab World* (London: Collins, 1978), pp. 35-52; and M.S. Agwani, *Communism in the Arab East* (Bombay: Asia Publishing House, 1969), passim.

16. Numerous memoirs and interviews by previous Egyptian leaders and their assistants have described this period. One of the most significant is that by al-Baghdadi, Abd al-Latif, *Muthaqirat (Memoires)* Al-maqtab al-masri al-hadith (Cairo: 1977), pp. 195-213.

17. Patrick Seale, *The Struggle for Syria: A Study in Post-War Arab Politics, 1945-58* (London: Oxford University Press, 1965), passim.

18. Ahmed Yussuf Ahmed, *al-Dawr al-musri fi al-Yemen (The Egyptian Role in Yemen)* (Cairo: al-hayaa el-masria el-ama ll-qtab, 1981).

19. Nasir argued that Egypt was too weak militarily to negotiate directly with the United States. He thus delegated the USSR to do so on his behalf since there would be more of a balance between the two superpowers. He also saw that when the USSR realized how inflexible the U.S.-Israeli position was, it would be more sympathetic toward his requests for arms. What is not obvious is whether Nasir realized that the Arab-Israeli problem would thus be frozen in the context of the East-West contest. For an account of these negotiations, see the memoirs of the Egyptian foreign minister at that time, Mahmoud Riad, *The Struggle for Peace in the Middle East* (London: Quartet Books, 1981).

20. See Henry Kissinger, *Years of Upheaval* (Boston: Little, Brown and Co., 1982), passim.

21. For an account of these events, see Karen Dawisha, *Soviet Foreign Policy toward Egypt* (London: Macmillan and Co., 1979).

22. *Aviation Week*, 30 June 1975.

23. Ibid., 7 July 1975.

24. Sadat said later that Boumedienne, the Algerian president, told him of a visit by Grechko, the Soviet minister of defense, to Algiers in 1976. Grechko spent three of his four days' visit, according to Boumedienne, complaining of Sadat's attitude toward Soviet armaments. Boumedienne told Sadat that it was Egypt's decision to diversify its armament sources that hurt the Soviets—not expelling the experts, starting the 1973 war without consultation, or canceling the Friendship Treaty. *Al-Ahram*, 5 March 1978, p. 6.

25. *International Herald Tribune*, 20 March 1976.

26. *Encounter* 58, no. 1 (January 1982):75-81 (this was an interview with *Der Spiegel* that *Encounter* published in full).

27. Alvin Z. Rubinstein, *Red Star on the Nile: The Soviet-Egyptian Influence Relationship since the June War* (Princeton: Princeton University Press, 1977), appendix 1, pp. 348-351.

28. Ibid., pp. 334-335.

29. See Heikal, *Sphinx and Commissar*; and Heikal, *The Road to Ramadan* (London: Collins, 1975). Anwar Sadat, *In Search of Identity: An Autobiography* (London: Collins, 1978). Abd El-Magid Farid, *Min mahadir igtimaat Abd al-Nasser al-arabia wa el-dawlia, 1967-70* (from the minutes of Nasser's Arab and international meeting) (Beirut: Muassassat al-Abhath al-Arabiya, 1979).

30. Tahseen Basheer, *A Conversation with Ambassador Tahseen Basheer: Reflections on the Middle East Peace Process* (Washington, D.C.: American Enterprise Institute for Public Policy Research, 1981), p. 21.

31. Henry Kissinger, *The White House Years* (London: Weidenfield and Nicolson and Michael Joseph, 1979), pp. 12-95.

32. See Gromyko's response to the Egyptian minister of foreign affairs in March 1975, Heikal, *Sphinx and Commissar*, p. 273.

33. For example, David Wood, "Sadat's Growing Ties to West Seen as Main Reason for Assassination," *International Herald Tribune*, 8 October 1981. Also Karen Elliot House, "Sadat's Assassination Creates Crisis of Confidence in U.S. Mideast Role," *Wall Street Journal*, 8 October 1981. Henry Fairlie, "How American Kindness Can Be Dangerous," *Times*, (London), 14 October 1981, p. 16.

34. Claudia Wright, "The Dance of Death," *New Statesman*, 9 October 1981, pp. 8-10.

35. For an example of the type of criticism directed against Washington on this score, see the statement by Saudi Arabia's minister for foreign affairs, Prince Saud al-Faysal, in M. Anis Salem, "Gulf States Seek Cooperation in an Area of Conflict," *South* (June 1981):28.

36. One Egyptian analyst applied a Hegelian model to this process. In the first moment during Nasir's rule, Egypt went for social justice, industrialization, and close relations with the USSR, but suffered from a lack

of internal freedom. Sadat represented the second moment, with the open-door policy encouraging consumption, allowing the emergence of inequalities, a pro-Western foreign policy, and a democratic multiparty experience that stalled. The challenge for Mubarak, the writer concludes, would be how to synthesize these two experiences, implying a new balance between both extremes. Sayed Yassin, "Tahadiyat al-marhala al-thalitha min al-tagriba al-masria al-haditha," (Challenges of the Third Stage of the Contemporary Egyptian Experience), *Al-Ahram*, 11 December 1981, p. 15.

37. See Nasir's "Philosophy of the Revolution," in *Nasser Speaks: Basic Documents*, translated by E.S. Farag (London: Morsett Press, 1972), p. 45.

38. In Egypt, the prominent novelist Yussuf Idris wrote that there is a Catholic marriage between Israel and the United States. Both share the same aims, interests, and enemy (the Arabs). Yussuf Idris, "Al-idwan bilnawaya" (Aggression by Intention), *Al-Ahram*, 14 June 1982, p. 13.

39. Interview with M.H. Heikal, in *Al-Watan Al-Arabi*, 11-17 June 1982, no. 278, p. 41.

40. *Al-Sharq Al-Awsat*, 6 June 1982, p. 2.

41. Saad Eddin Ibrahim, "Superpowers in the Arab World," *Washington Quarterly* (Summer 1981):86.

42. See the special survey published in the *Financial Times*, 17 July 1981, pp. 13-17, particularly the article by Anthony Robinson, "Kosovo Brings Risk to Unity."

43. See the special section in the Egyptian quarterly *Alsiyasah Aldawliyyah* (International Politics), October 1980, entitled "A Futuristic View of the New Arab Order."

44. Galia Golan, *The Soviet Union and the PLO*, Adelphi Paper no. 131 (London: International Institute for Strategic Studies, 1976).

45. For a recent analysis of these developments, see Milos Minic, "Twenty Years the Belgrade Conference of Non-Aligned Countries," *Socialist Thought and Practice* (Yugoslavia, September 1981), no. 9, pp. 3-21; and Minic, "The Forceful Presence of Non-Alignment in the World," *Review of International Affairs* 31, no. 737 (20 December 1980):1-5.

46. Boutros Boutros-Ghali, "The Foreign Policy of Egypt," in Olajide Aluko, ed., *The Foreign Policies of African States* (London: Hodder and Stoughton, 1977), pp. 41-45.

47. *Al-Ahram*, 24 March 1982, p. 6.

48. For a detailed picture of this program, see the Report by the Comptroller General of the United States, *Forging a New Defense Relationship with Egypt*, C-ID-82-1, U.S. General Accounting Office, Washington, D.C., 5 February 1982.

49. Heikal, *Sphinx and Commissar*, p. 273.

50. Dawisha, *Soviet Foreign Policy Toward Egypt*, p. 76.

51. For a similar conclusion, see Karen Dawisha, "The Soviet Union in the Middle East: Great Power in Search of a Leading Role," in E.J. Feuchtwanger and Peter Nailor, eds., *The Soviet Union and the Third World* (London: Macmillan and Co., 1981), pp. 117-136. On the same day of announcing that forty-seven people would be put on trial for forming a Communist party in Egypt, an agreement was signed with East Germany for extending electricity to forty-seven towns in the Delta. *Al-Ahram*, 6 April 1982, pp. 8 and 10. The first conference of Egypt's opposition labor party referred to U.S. support of Israel's invasion of Lebanon and called for a scrupulous policy of Egyptian nonalignment and exchanging ambassadors with the USSR. *Alshaab*, 15 June 1982, p. 10.

9

The Soviet Union and the Palestine Liberation Organization

Galia Golan

The Soviet Union generally supports national liberation movements on a tactical basis; that is, viewing them instrumentally as a tactical option in Moscow's pursuit of its more strategic long-range objectives. Indeed, the commencement of Soviet support often represents no more than a Soviet decision to cultivate an additional option or potential channel for the pursuit of Soviet interests in a particular country or region. This general approach has certainly been the case with regard to the Soviet attitude toward the Palestine Liberation Organization. The relationship is a tactical one, determined by the broader Soviet-Arab and, especially, the Soviet-U.S. relationships.

Development and Nature of the Relationship

The Soviet Union apparently did not see even any tactical value in the PLO during the latter's first few years of existence (1964-1968), for it rejected efforts by the new organization to make contact and gain Soviet support. Typical of the Soviets' almost indiscriminate investing for the future, Moscow did permit contacts with Palestinian youth and labor groups, bringing a small number of students to the Soviet Union for university studies. Moscow continued, however, to view the Arab-Israeli conflict as a conflict between *states* and saw the Palestinian problem only in terms of a refugee problem (as stated in UN Security Council Resolution 242) and made no effort to compete with the Chinese support offered the PLO. This negative attitude began to change only late in 1968 and early 1969 following Yasir Arafat's inclusion in an Egyptian delegation, led by Nasir to Moscow in the summer of 1968. At this time the Soviets began to refer to the Palestinians as a "people" calling the PLO (in 1969) a "national liberation movement." They began providing propaganda support and by 1970, following another trip by Arafat to Moscow, gave permission for indirect supply of arms and equipment to the PLO.[1] The major reasons for this change were:

1. The fact that the Arab states, particularly Moscow's major Arab client, Egypt, had begun actively to champion the Palestinian cause, having decided to make it a focal point in the Arab-Israeli conflict; and

2. The achievement by the PLO of significant publicity in the world as a result of terrorist activities.

The Soviets still had serious reservations about fully supporting the PLO. This was evidenced by the reprimand delivered the Syrian Communist party in 1971 for placing too much emphasis on the Palestinians, a reprimand that contained criticism of almost every one of the PLO's positions and policies. Nonetheless, in 1972 Soviet support for the PLO was raised, following another trip by Arafat, when Moscow agreed to the direct supply of arms and military equipment to the PLO. This elevation of support was the direct result of the deterioration in Soviet-Egyptian relations; that is, an effort by Moscow to compensate for its losses in Egypt by deepening its relations with its other clients in the Arab world, including Syria and Iraq. In the fall of 1974, the Soviets came out officially in favor of a Palestinian state. This was a reversal of its earlier position and a significant increase in its support for the PLO. This step was taken for a combination of reasons, coming as it did just prior to the Rabat conference of Arab heads of state. It would appear that the Soviets were aware of the decision taken by the Arab leaders to pass a resolution in favor of a Palestinian state (on the West Bank and Gaza) as had finally been agreed in principle earlier that year by the Palestine National Council. The decision, however, was controversial. George Habash, head of the Popular Front for the Liberation of Palestine, one of the constituent parts of the PLO, disapproved of the idea of declaring for a state at that time. Because of his opposition to a ministate on the West Bank and Gaza, he refused to participate in Rabat, just as he refused to go to Moscow in the summer of 1974 because of his differences with the Soviets on this and other issues.

By supporting the idea of a Palestinian state, the Soviets most likely hoped to counter both the pro-U.S. stance Egypt would be advocating at the conference and the very real possibility of continued U.S. progress in the region given the two disengagement agreements negotiated by Washington and also U.S. efforts to open talks for a second Egyptian-Israeli agreement and of a Jordanian-Israeli disengagement agreement.

Probably with the same objectives in mind, the Soviets had agreed a few months earlier to the opening of a PLO office in Moscow. The decision finally was implemented only two years later on the eve of an official visit by King Husayn to Moscow. It is possible that the decision regarding the PLO office was also dictated by bilateral PLO-Soviet considerations in addition to the broader regional and global calculations: in 1974, the Soviets may have sought to strengthen Arafat in his battle with George Habash over various issues, including the issue of limited demands for statehood; and in 1976 the Soviets had been trying to mitigate Arafat's dissatisfaction over Moscow's position of restraint with regard to the PLO in the Lebanese conflict (Arafat did not visit Moscow in 1976, reportedly because of this displeasure). In 1977 a temporary increase in Soviet support occurred when the Soviets, for a few months, placed the return of the Palestinian refugees in their official slogan on a settlement. This elevation was in direct response to a PLO request, but Soviet acquiescence probably came to counter (in a manner of oneupsmanship) what appeared to be a U.S. approach to the PLO when President Carter spoke of the need for a "homeland" for the Palestinians. More significant and direct was the official Soviet recognition of the PLO as the sole legitimate representative of the Palestinian people, immediately after Camp David in November 1978. Finally, in October 1981, there was the granting of diplomatic status to the PLO office in Moscow. This may have been prompted by Moscow's renewed concern over possible U.S.-PLO contacts (encouraged at about this time by various U.S. figures). As in the other cases connected with the PLO offices, this step-up may also have been an effort to reassure the Palestinians, in view of Moscow's improved relations with Jordan, and to placate Arafat over the Soviet failure to supply all arms requested by the PLO in South Lebanon (the issue reportedly was Sam-6s; Arafat apparently did not visit Moscow in 1980 because of his differences with Moscow on this and other issues).

From this brief history of Soviet-PLO relations, it emerges that the Soviets have used their stances on the Palestinian issue to enhance Moscow's position in the Arab world and increasingly to counter U.S. in-roads, successes, or potential successes in the Middle East. This use of sup-port of the PLO is part of Soviet tactics since the October 1973 war of sup-porting the more radical Arab demands to prove Moscow's usefulness in the eyes of the Arabs, and essentiality in the eyes of the United States and Israel, with regard to the negotiating process in the Middle East. Thus, the Soviets can claim to be the only superpower interested in a comprehensive settlement rather than the partial agreements offered by the United States. At the same time they can claim to the latter that only Moscow could con-trol the war option and moderate the radicals—or even bring them to the negotiating table and/or gain recognition of Israel.

Increased support for the PLO has been part of this tactic, assuming ever-increasing importance as the Palestinian issue itself assumed the dimensions of an issue of superpower competition. Yet the tactical nature of the relationship remained. The Soviets have never let their support for the PLO overshadow or interfere in the pursuit of Soviet interests (such as the reentry of the Soviet Union into the negotiating process) or change their basic positions on the nature of an Arab-Israeli settlement or other regional or global issues. A revealing example of this occurred in the spring of 1977. Rather than let the problem of PLO participation prevent the planned reconvening of the Geneva conference, Moscow agreed to the formulation of PLO participation only at some, as yet undetermined, second stage of the forthcoming conference. Although the Soviets sought some formula for Palestinian participation (such as using the Soviet-U.S. joint communique of October 1977 as a possible substitute for Resolution 242), Moscow was nonetheless willing to ignore its formally proclaimed commitment on PLO participation "from the beginning and on an equal footing" so as to obtain its own return to the negotiating process. In examining a number of divisive factors in the Soviet-PLO relationship, we shall see other positions that the Soviets have refused to alter or compromise, despite opposition by the PLO to what is viewed as an undermining of PLO interests.[2]

Divisive Factors

Those factors that provide for potential or actual conflicts between the Soviet Union and the PLO (or at the very least create problems in their ongoing relationship) can be divided into two categories: factors connected with the nature of the PLO and factors connected with the policies and methods of the PLO.

Nature of the PLO. Within the first category, the fact that the PLO is an umbrella organization encompassing several varied, indeed diverse, groupings often at loggerheads with each other, poses a number of problems for Moscow. The Soviets prefer that all the national liberation forces be organizationally under one roof. Such a situation eliminates the necessity of supporting one group to the exclusion of all others, which would limit Soviet options and increase the risks and future vulnerability of having banked on the wrong group. Moreover, such a situation theoretically rules out costly (in terms of energy and resources) rivalries while providing a clear address for the channeling of Soviet aid and advice to a responsible decision-making unit. Unfortunately for the Soviet Union, the PLO only partially fulfills these requirements. The organization is torn by internal disagreements and rivalries, complicated by the involvement of various Arab states that support, or even direct, one faction or another. Thus the interference of Saudi Arabia, Iraq, Syria, or Libya can affect PLO decision making or behavior, while the inherent instability of the leadership groups (specifically of Arafat) places in jeopardy what gains or concessions the Soviets have often had to struggle hard to achieve with regard to PLO decisions and policies.[3]

Within the internal kaleidescope of the PLO, the Soviets have no choice but to support Arafat and his Fatah organization, for it is by far the largest and most dominant group. Yet the Fatah is basically bourgeois in class background and composition, permeated with religious Muslim elements (who, like Arafat himself, sympathize to some degree with the revival of fundamental Islam in Iran). It lacks any ideology, save what the Soviets view as bourgeois nationalism. All of these negative characteristics are clearly noted by the Soviet media, indicating the persistence of these factors that operate against Soviet control or influence over Fatah in the long as well as the short run. Yet it is Fatah that gives the tone and major content to the PLO. The two Marxist organizatons—Nayif Hawatimah's Popular Democratic Front for the Liberation of Palestine (PDFLP) and George Habash's Popular Front for the Liberation of Palestine (PFLP) are, at least ideologically, more acceptable to the Soviet Union. But even combined they represent only a very small proportion of the PLO membership and stand no chance of taking control. Moreover, while Hawatimah's extremely small PDFLP is very close to Moscow and may even be counted upon, to a large degree, to do Moscow's bidding, the somewhat stronger Habash is a much more radical and independent breed of Marxist. His positions on policies and tactics are, more often than not, diametrically opposed to those of Moscow.[4] Indeed, between 1974 and 1978 there was an open, polemical split between Moscow and the PFLP. Relations improved and eventually deepened only after Camp David and with Habash's support of the Soviet invasion of Afghanistan. The other smaller organizations such as al-Sa'iqah, the Popular Struggle Front, the Palestine Liberation Front, and the Arab Liberation Front are of little interest to Moscow, directly controlled as they are by various Arab states.

There have been various attempts by the Soviets to gain greater influence in the PLO via a more dependable channel; that is, a Communist channel, but the PLO has consistently resisted such encroachments. Al-Ansar, created by the Arab Communist parties, was disbanded in 1972, having been criticized within the PLO for its position in favor of the continued existence of Israel and its opposition to the use of terror. Its successor, the Palestine National Front, organized primarily for use on the West Bank, was somewhat more successful. It achieved two places in the PLO Executive Committee, but its chances for gaining any influence in the PLO were severely hampered by the disintegration of the organization on the West Bank due to deportations on the part of the Israeli authorities. Its place on the West Bank was taken by the more radical National Guidance Committee, established after Camp David, but the Communists were unsuccessful in their efforts to take over this group.

Moreover, the direct bid to place more Communists in the PLO Executive at the most recent Palestine National Council (1981) failed altogether. Moscow probably hopes that with the creation of an independent Palestine Communist party on the West Bank, the Communists will have a firmer basis for demanding direct representation in the PLO. In 1974 the West Bank branch of the Jordanian Communist Party was declared the Palestine Communist Organization. Sometime late in 1981 this organization became a full-fledged, independent Communist party. The creation of such a party probably had less to do with the gaining of influence in the PLO than it did with the goal of securing a more dominant position on the West Bank in anticipation of autonomy and the political jockeying connected with the possibility of the creation of a Palestinian state. The Soviet tactic is not to attempt to substitute the Communists for the PLO or compete with it; tactically the old idea of a common front with noncommunists has priority. But the overall purposes are, on the one hand, to strengthen the Communists by giving them an open, publicly recognized role and, on the other hand, to establish a basis for Soviet control and thereby ensuring Moscow's interests and line.

Issues, Methods, and Tactics. In addition to the nature of the PLO and its contingent parts, other divisive factors in the Soviet-PLO relationship stem from differences of opinion on certain substantive issues, tactics, and methods.

The substantive issues include the existence of the state of Israel, the locale of a Palestinian state (alongside or instead of Israel, either within its 1947 partition-plan borders or its 4 June 1967 border); the return of the refugees; and possibly the issue of Jerusalem; southern Lebanon; and Afghanistan. The Soviets consistently have argued with the Palestinians that it is unrealistic, and therefore undesirable, to seek the destruction of Israel either militarily or politically (by creating a secular Palestinian state in all of Palestine) or even to try drastically to reduce it to the 1947 partition-plan lines. According to the Soviets, the only objective worthy of pursuit (that is, one that stands a chance of success and, most important for the Soviets, does not carry with it the certainty of war and superpower military confrontation), is the creation of a Palestinian state alongside the Israel of the 4 June 1967 borders—in other words, a Palestinian state on the West Bank and Gaza.[5] This is the position implicitly accepted by Fatah and even the Palestine National Council insofar as the latter's 1974 resolutions called for the setting up of a Palestinian *authority* on any territory liberated. The PLO, Fatah, and even Arafat refuse to go beyond this explicitly because of the strong opposition within the PLO, and even within Fatah, to accepting the existence of Israel. Only Hawatimah (and the Communists) explicitly and openly accept the Soviet position, although Hawatimah occasionally claims that this is only the first step, presumably leading to the 1947 borders or all of Palestine (the Soviets delete such comments from their own accounts of Hawatimah's statements). This issue has had a most divisive effect on the Soviet-PLO alliance. The Soviets were not willing to support the demand for a Palestinian state until there was at least implicit PLO agreement to the Soviet position, but agreement will probably remain so long as Arafat retains his power.

The refugee issue is much less important or pressing from the Soviet point of view, though the differences in Soviet-PLO attitudes could cause some difficulties in the future. Probably realizing that the PLO position favoring the return of all the Palestinian refugees, their descendents, and families to their former homes in Israel could be viewed by Israel as tantamount to an attempt to destroy the Jewish state, the Soviet position (though rarely expressed) calls for "return" of the refugees to the new Palestinian state when created or "to their homes in accordance with the UN resolution"; that is, UN Resolution 194 of 1948, which calls for the return of those willing to live in peace with their neighbors.[6] Similarly, Jerusalem is not a bone of contention between the Soviet Union and the PLO at present. But a difference in positions (the Soviets being much less committed than the PLO to all of Jerusalem being the capital of the Palestinian state) could cause difficulties in the future.

The Palestinian struggle in southern Lebanon, first against the Syrians and then against the Israelis, has been a serious source of incompatibility. The PLO, particularly Fatah, had long pressed the Soviets to take a more direct military role, or at the very least, provide more advanced weapons. The Soviets, for their part, had been relatively restrained out of concern that massive Israeli retaliation could lead to a new Arab-Israeli war. Arafat reportedly refrained from visiting Moscow in 1976 and again in 1980 because of this issue. His second-in-command, Abu Iyad, has explicitly criticized the Soviet Union for its reticence. There are other points of dissent on the Palestinians' part regarding issues not directly connected with the Arab-Israeli conflict. The change in the Soviet position on the Fatah-backed Eritrean liberation struggle was undoubtedly one of them. More important, however, was (and possibly still is) the Soviet invasion of Afghanistan. The PLO has officially, if unenthusiastically, supported the Soviets on this issue. But Arafat, unlike Hawatimah and Habash, has been much more sympathetic to the Muslim cause than Moscow would like. Although willing to mediate between the Afghanistan regime and Pakistan and even Iran, Arafat has not endorsed the invasion or given Moscow his full backing on the matter.

Numerous issues of methods and tactics are also the source of controversy between the Soviet Union and the PLO. The most fundamental and important of these is the complex of issues connected with negotiations; that is, recognition of Israel, acceptance of Resolution 242, Geneva versus armed struggle, and terrorism. While the Soviets have over the years tried to persuade the PLO to agree to the idea of Israeli-PLO mutual recognition, they have invested much more energy and time in trying to get the PLO to accept Resolution 242 with its implicit recognition of Israel. They hoped this would pave the way for Palestinian participation in negotiations such as Geneva. After some initial hesitation, the PLO did accept unofficially the

Soviet-U.S. statement of October 1977 as a substitute for Resolution 242, and there are signs that in view of the general Arab rejection of this resolution (such as the decision of the Arab summit in Amman in 1981), Moscow has abandoned its direct pressure for 242 in favor of some other formula. Thus Moscow no longer advocates the reconvening of the Geneva conference, based as it was on 242, but rather some other form of international or multilateral conference.

Yet there are many forces in the PLO, even in Fatah, that oppose negotiations and advocate only armed struggle. These forces came to the fore most recently on the issue of the European initiative, the acceptance of which some would view as Palestinian capitulation. Arafat just barely won out on this matter (pronegotiations) in the Palestine National Council (PNC) of 1981, but his foes were joined by Moscow and its supporters. While not essentially opposed to PLO contacts with Europe, the Soviets see in the European initiative hints of the most serious source of a Soviet-PLO rift—the possibility that the PLO under Arafat might eventually opt for Western, and behind it U.S., sponsorship. This has been and will probably remain the most serious dilemma for the Soviets. By attempting to persuade the PLO to accept the idea of negotiations and seeking to bolster the moderates within the organization, Moscow is strengthening the very elements that render a shift toward the West more feasible. It is in this context that Soviet opposition, or at least discomfort, over such matters as the Jordanian-PLO rapprochement or PLO support for the Saudi Arabian peace plan must be seen. The Soviet Union has no fundamental objection to these options; it opposed them because of the pro-Muslim, pro-Saudi, and therefore pro-U.S. and possibly anti-Soviet, nature of the consequences. Even as Moscow improves its own relations with Jordan and seeks such an improvement with Riyadh, it has to combat these same tendencies within the PLO that are personified by Arafat.

Even though the Soviets find themselves in temporary agreement with the more radical elements against Arafat on some matters, the basic Soviet support for the idea of a negotiated settlement has placed Moscow at loggerheads with most elements of the PLO at one time or another on the issue of armed struggle. While agreement exists with individuals such as Arafat, at least on the simultaneous use of political as well as military methods, the issue of terrorism has been a source of strain. While the Soviets train Palestinians in the use of arms and armed struggle, they prefer that this method be subordinated to political means and limited to sabotage or resistance in the occupied territories. Moscow's attitude toward operations inside Israel is somewhat more ambivalent, even condemnatory. But when the operation is carried out by Fatah, the Soviets generally try to characterize it as an action against military targets so as to legitimize it as resistance. International terror, however, is not advocated or supported, ostensibly because Moscow considers it counterproductive. In reality, however, this is probably because the Soviets themselves are vulnerable to acts of terrorism such as hijackings. Thus for all that the KGB is involved with extremist groups around the world and does, in fact, provide training, one of the issues on which Moscow and the PLO have argued is the issue of terrorism.[7] Along with the idea of a ministate, the issue of terrorism was the point over which Moscow and Habash broke forces in 1974. The Soviets would appear to have been less adamant after Camp David, but PLO use of international terrorism also declined after 1978.

Cohesive Factors

There are two types of factors that operate (or are hoped by the Soviets to operate) in the direction of cohesiveness in the Soviet-PLO relationship: the dependency of the PLO upon the Soviet Union and the mutuality of interests between the two. In fact, however, as stated from the outset, the real degree of cohesiveness is determined primarily by factors *outside* the bilateral relationship itself; that is, by the state of Soviet-Arab relations (and the position of the Arab states vis-à-vis the PLO) and the state of Soviet-U.S. relations (and the position of the United States vis-à-vis the Palestinians).

Dependency of the PLO. The PLO is dependent upon the Soviet Union for the provision of *political support*. This consists of support for the Palestinians' demands and for the PLO as an organization on the international scene (for example, in the UN and its affiliates); in bilateral talks between the Soviet Union and representatives of other countries, including Western countries (mainly to have the Palestinian issue and/or the PLO at least mentioned); in conferences and meetings organized by the Soviets, or in Soviet fronts such as the World Peace Council. One form of this support has been in the matter of opening PLO offices and providing official recognition of the PLO as the sole legitimate representative of the Palestinians, all of which enhances the status of the PLO as the only group designated to negotiate for the Palestinians and assume power in a Palestinian state. Soviet political support also comes in the form of assistance in the PLO's propaganda effort and includes direct Soviet media propaganda on the PLO's behalf and on the Palestinian issue. In all areas of political support Moscow's allies, including Cuba but excluding Rumania, follow the Soviet lead. At times they provide the Soviet Union with a proxy for those occasions when the Soviets do not want to act directly; for example, stating a more extreme position than Moscow is yet ready to advocate formally, launching trial balloons. Rumania, in keeping with its generally independent foreign-policy stance, has its own position on the PLO and provides political support in other ways independent of Moscow.

A second means employed by the Soviets to create PLO dependency is *military support*, which consists of the provision of training and arms and equipment. PLO members are trained in camps located in the Soviet Union, Eastern Europe, Cuba, and North Korea (the last is not necessarily part of the Soviet effort inasmuch as the North Koreans tend to be independent of Moscow and lean toward China, which, in any case, also aids the PLO). While this training is military (use of explosives, conventional warfare, sabotage, and such), political indoctrination is also provided while training in political intelligence and agitation-propaganda work is presumably also offered to certain trainees. There is no evidence that Soviet or Soviet-bloc advisors have been sent to instruct PLO forces in the Middle East aside from unconfirmed rumors in 1978 that twenty to thirty Soviet instructors were present in Lebanon along with some East Germans, and later, Cubans.

On the other hand, Soviet and East-bloc so-called diplomatic personnel in Lebanon are in regular contact with the PLO, some of them presumably operating as at least security/intelligence advisors, if not more. The presence of Libyan advisors in Lebanon does not appear to be connected directly with the Soviet Union. Arms and military equipment have been provided since 1970, both directly and indirectly, through Syria, Libya, and Iraq (and possibly South Yemen). The Soviet bloc is by far the major source of armaments for the PLO with Saudi Arabia, and to a lesser extent other Arab states, paying the bills. China also provides some equipment. Western equipment (including U.S., French, and West German) has been found among the Palestinians' arms, presumably having been obtained through international arms merchants and/or provided through third parties. Other types of Soviet support include medical, educational, and economic aid, but none of these categories is particularly large or significant. According to Palestinian sources, the Soviet Union does not provide any direct financial aid; Saudi Arabia is the PLO's main financial backer.

Dependency may also be sought by Soviet involvement in internal power plays and politics, such as the effort to inject Communists into the PLO's ruling bodies, the attempt to increase Communist influence among the Palestinians in the occupied territories, and the attention given the PLO-Marxists, particularly the pro-Soviet Marxists around Hawatimah. Whether the Soviets have supported any of the efforts to replace Arafat is not at all certain, however, inasmuch as the contenders such as Abu Iyad or non-Fatah people have all tended to be more extremist in their views. They are sometimes critical of Soviet moderation, and, in some cases, directly connected with various Arab governments (therefore offering little prospect for Soviet control). Furthermore, the inner alliances shift so often and are so stormy, often accompanied by violence, that the Soviets probably prefer not to join the fray.

All of the aforementioned types of dependency-creating tactics, insofar as they are successful, may also be used by the Soviets as instruments of control and channels for influence. At least theoretically, political support can be withheld as a lever for bringing about changes in PLO policies, tactics, and personnel. The Soviets withheld support for a Palestinian state until the PLO agreed to the ministate idea, and Moscow for quite a long time withheld official recognition of the PLO as the sole legitimate representative of the Palestinian people. However, neither of these Soviet concessions, nor any others, came about as a direct result of some change in the PLO but rather as a result of other Soviet considerations (growing U.S. influence and the coming Rabat decisions, Camp David, and so forth). For all that Soviet historians try to depict Soviet support as a function of the change in the PLO to a progressive mass organization bent on negotiations and reason, other Soviet writers have been sanguine enough to admit that these attributes are far from having been attained and imply that Moscow has not succeeded in converting the PLO to a Marxist-oriented ideology or to the Soviets' various substantive and tactical positions. As far as can be determined, Moscow has continuously pressed its views without tying compliance to any threat of loss of Soviet political support. Indeed, the picture that has emerged is one more of the Soviet Union, rather than the PLO, as the supplicant—and one that depicts Moscow as being acutely aware of the potential for a shift in PLO orientation.

In the area of military aid, the Soviets have achieved somewhat more dependency, insofar as the nature of the aid supplied can directly affect certain end results. Thus, the Soviets generally have succeeded in controlling the combat options open to the Palestinians in southern Lebanon, though it is not certain that they have had similar success in influencing the PLO's decisions as to when, where, and how to use the weapons that the PLO already possesses. While it is possible that the Soviets have used arms supplies as a lever for influencing PLO decisions (much the way they tried to do in the past with Egypt, 1971-1973, and Syria, 1976), there is no evidence that such arms blackmail has, in fact, succeeded any more than it did with Egypt and Syria in the past. The facts that the PLO can (and does) obtain much of its Soviet equipment indirectly from various Arab states and can purchase weapons with Saudi money limit the effectiveness of arms supplies as a lever for control. No other channel of potential control (medical, education, economic support, or involvement in internal PLO politiking) has achieved sufficient dimensions or importance to be of any use to the Soviets at present.

From the Soviet point of view, the last of these (involvement in internal PLO politiking), carries the greatest potential for future control or influence. The recruitment of pro-Soviet PLO people, their elevation to positions of power, assistance to one group against another in internal political fights, penetration among the masses as well as inside the organizations and ruling bodies—these are the means the Soviets traditionally have used for achieving dependency and control. But whatever efforts are being expended in this direction at present, the results are nowhere near sufficient to be considered the achievement of an effective channel of control or influence. The major conveyer of Soviet wishes remained (up until the PLO evacuation of Beirut) the Soviet ambassador in Beirut and other Soviet officials who met with PLO leaders. The Palestinian Communists are still fighting an uphill battle for acceptance by the PLO leadership, and the pro-Soviet PLO-Marxists or Soviet agents within the PLO do not yet have sufficient power to dictate Soviet wishes to the PLO executive.[8]

Mutuality of Interests. The second type of factor for cohesiveness of the Soviet-PLO relationship is the mutuality of interests between the two. This is, basically, mutual instrumentality or exploitation. The fundamental mutual interest is opposition to the ascendency of U.S. influence in the Middle East: on the PLO side, so long as this ascendency is used for the benefit of Israel; on the Soviet side, so long as this ascendency means exclusive U.S. influence at the expense of Moscow. The battle against Israel is of primary importance to the PLO so long as Israel is the obstacle to Palestinian aspirations for self-determination and national existence. For the Soviet Union, opposition to Israel will continue as long as it serves Soviet efforts to gain certain strategic, political, and economic benefits in the Middle East. If the PLO can offer the Soviet Union another client in the Middle East (specifically in the Arab-Israeli arena at a time when such clients are few), the Soviet Union can offer the PLO another champion in the international arena, and a most powerful champion at that. Secondarily, the PLO can offer the Soviets certain services, such as mediation—as in the past between Iran and Afghanistan, Pakistan and Afghanistan, Eritrea and Ethiopia, Somalia and Ethiopia—as well as channels for contacts with various movements such as the Sandinistas, the Italian Red Brigades, the Japanese Red Army, and others who have trained in PLO camps. The Soviets, for their part, can offer the PLO the various types of support discussed above (political, military, economic, medical, educational). The relationship, from the view of mutuality of interests, is not entirely balanced, and we have already examined the divisive factors that render the mutuality of interests somewhat vulnerable. Yet, although the PLO appears to be the greater beneficiary and the dependency necessary for control is sorely lacking in reality, so that the PLO is still not the organization the Soviets would have it be, Moscow obviously considers the PLO a sufficient asset to warrant effort to strengthen the cohesive factors in the relationship.

The Future: Moscow and a Palestinian State

It is impossible to predict what Brezhnev's successor or successors will think of the issue of Soviet-PLO relations. One might speculate that the only gradual development of Soviet support of the PLO was the result of differences of opinion in the Kremlin on the matter, although there is no direct evidence of this. Brezhnev himself was said to be disdainful of Arafat, agreeing to receive him officially for the first time not until the spring of 1977. The so-called detentists in the Politburo, on the whole, seem less interested in the Palestinian issue, perhaps because they view it as an obstacle to achieving Soviet-U.S. cooperation toward a Middle East settlement. The so-called ideologues, on the other hand, have expressed support, though they are the ones most often to raise the issue of Fatah's nonideological stance. The head of the CPSU Central Committee's International Department and candidate Politburo member, Boris Ponomarev, appears to be a supporter of PLO interests, probably ex officio, as the party secretary responsible for relations with nonruling Communist parties and national liberation movements. If one can judge from the army daily *Krasnaia Zvezda,* the Soviet military has become increasingly enthusiastic over the years regarding the PLO, but the nationalists' organ, *Sovetskaia Rossiia,* tends to prefer anti-Semitic attacks on Zionism and Israel rather than positive support of the Palestinians' cause. On the whole, however, the relationship with the PLO does not appear to be a central bone of contention. Rather, it is a component of the broader opinions—of which there are several in the Politburo—regarding the Arab-Israeli conflict itself and the need for a settlement.

The question of a Palestinian state may offer some indication of the Soviet's own estimate of future trends, at least with regard to the relative weights of the divisive versus the cohesive factors in the relationships.[9] On the *benefits* side of the ledger, Soviet support for the creation of a Palestinian state serves not only to please and, therefore, strengthen Moscow's position with the radical Arab states. It also improves Moscow's chances of obtaining an additional option in the negotiating process—as the PLO's protector—even to the point of being able to pressure the United States and Israel to include Moscow in this process due to its influence on the level of PLO militancy or moderation. Such support presumably will provide the Soviets a future foothold in the region in the event of an Arab-Israeli settlement, with or without the creation of such a state. A Palestinian state would give the Soviet Union another client-state in the area, and one whose continued grievance against Israel might provide a factor for keeping the conflict alive should the Soviets be so interested. The same "troublemaker" function would also be present in the event of a settlement that left the Palestinians' aspirations for a state unfulfilled.

Conversely, if the Soviet objective is, in fact, a settlement of the Arab-Israeli conflict with a role for Moscow as coguarantor, the Soviets may well believe that a lasting settlement cannot in fact be achieved without the creation of a Palestinian state. In any case, their own position with such a state would be stronger if they could claim even partial credit for its creation. It is even conceivable that the Soviets believe that the Palestinian leadership would be more stable, rational, even controllable, if faced with the responsibilities of statehood, especially as they would be dependent upon outside (presumably Soviet) assistance of all types.

On the *liability* side of the ledger, however, one might list the following. In the present situation prior to a settlement and Palestinian statehood, the list of problems raised by supporting the Palestinians' demand for statehood is a long one. Not only does the lack of unity within the organization make it difficult for the Soviets to control the movement, or even influence its policies, but the internal struggles tend to sway the organization toward rejectionist positions. Such positions not only contradict substantive and even tactical positions of the Soviet Union but, in fact, threaten to impede the negotiations for which Moscow has been striving. The fact that the rejectionist groups inside the organization are linked with various Arab regimes only complicates the matter for Moscow, as do the fluctuating alliances of moderate as well as rejectionist PLO groups with various states and the PLO's financial dependence on Saudi Arabia. And, if ultimately the PLO is dependent upon the Arab states, so, too, is Soviet policy. For it is still the Arab states that can provide—or deny—the Soviets their basic strategic interests in the area. Thus, the PLO would clearly be a liability should the Arab states decide to abandon the Palestinian issue in an effort to gain a settlement with Israel. Assuming that they should do this as continued clients of the Soviet Union, Moscow might well be expected to recognize the purely secondary nature of its relationship with the PLO, subordinate to its interests in the Arab states. It is unlikely that the Soviets would *prefer* to remain outside a settlement with only the Palestinians as their clients. And, indeed, under such circumstances, there would hardly be any guarantee that the PLO itself would not find a *modus vivendi* with the United States. In any case, such a threat generally exists regarding the PLO's orientation, just as it has with the Arab states themselves. Nor would all of these problems vanish in a postsettlement situation with or without a Palestinian state.

In the case of a settlement without the creation of a Palestinian state, it is not certain that the Arab states would be willing to jeopardize their agreements with Israel, or risk renewed conflict and war, by supporting PLO actions. Presumably the Soviets would opt for the Arab states, assuming that Moscow had not been totally excluded from the settlement and thus left *only* with the PLO option. Yet, given PLO dependence—not only financial—upon the Arab states, there would, in fact, be little the Soviets might do on the PLO's behalf short of sponsoring local civil wars with all their negative implications (both with regard to preventing PLO defeats and avoiding U.S. intervention).

In the event of the somewhat more likely case of an Arab-Israeli settlement *with* the creation of a Palestinian state, the Soviets would still be faced with numerous problems. There is no guarantee that such a state would be any more certain or stable a Soviet ally than the PLO as a national liberation movement is today. Neither the domestic nor the foreign-policy orientation of such a state is entirely clear, given the presence of various, even conflicting, ideologies or tendencies within the Palestinian movement: bourgeois, Muslim conservative, radical, Marxist, pro-Chinese, pro-Egyptian, pro- (or at least not anti-) Jordanian, and even pro-U.S.

Even assuming that the new state would opt for what the Soviets call a noncapitalist path of development, oriented toward the Soviet-led socialist camp, the problem of control would still remain. The Soviets would have the burden of making the state viable economically, and they would have to provide for its defense. These missions are both costly and risky and, as proven by past Soviet relations with Third World states, do not guarantee control. As in other cases of Soviet patron-client relationships, the U.S. option for economic assistance would be a persistent threat. Nor could the Soviets count on benefiting financially from the supply of arms if the Arab states were unwilling to pay the Palestinians' bills. Moreover, the risk of war with Israel would create a problem for the Soviet Union, much the way it has in the past with regard to Egypt and Syria. The classic dilemma would return: supplying arms to gain influence but thereby augmenting the possibility of war with its risk of Arab (Palestinian) defeat; the blow to Soviet prestige; the need for Soviet intervention, escalation, and superpower confrontation. Even if the new state pursued a moderate policy (whether or not because the Soviets gained greater control over this client than it did over Egypt in the past, for example), a problem would occur over the continued operations of dissident Palestinian groups. From this point of view the history of the Palestinian issue, and the apparent devotion of most PLO members to a state in all of Palestine, provides an almost built-in contradiction to the achievement of the Soviet-backed solution of the problem, rendering it a somewhat different character than that of other movements supported by the Soviets in the past.

This is not to say that the liabilities are so great that the Soviets would prefer *not* to see the creation of a Palestinian state. Nor is it even certain that Moscow itself has ever drawn up such a ledger of benefits versus liabilities or, for that matter, that any state conducts its foreign policies according to such rational calculations. If anything, the Soviets appear to act on an ad hoc basis with regard to the Palestinian problem, indicating keen awareness of the problems and risks involved, trying to minimize or change them through increased Soviet influence while trying to maximize the advantage, particularly tactical, that can be achieved. Thus one should neither exaggerate Soviet optimism with regard to the whole issue nor accept as given Moscow's confidence in—or commitment to—the creation of a Palestinian state.

Postscript

This chapter was prepared before the Israeli war in Lebanon in the summer of 1982, but the events of the war have borne out a number of hypotheses and trends already noted. The earlier Soviet reticence to assist PLO military activities from Lebanon because of concern that these actions might lead to an Israeli invasion became, during the war, almost total Soviet inaction on behalf of the PLO, lest the Soviet Union be dragged into the military arena. Thus the tactical nature of Moscow's interest in the PLO became blatantly clear.

Early in the war, Moscow used two separate channels to make the limits of its support understood to the PLO. In response to what the PLO radio termed an Arafat call to Moscow to "help stop the Israeli aggression," the PLO representative in Moscow, Muhammed ash-Sha'ir, issued a statement on June 8 that the Soviet Union would continue to send military supplies to the Palestinians but would send no troops, adding that no troops had been requested.[10] None of the above appeared in the Soviet version of the Sha'ir statement,[11] but this Soviet position presumably was also conveyed to PLO political-department chief Kaddumi in his talk with Gromyko at the United Nations the next day. Almost immediately, Abu Iyad, a critic of the Soviet Union in the past, publicly expressed the PLO's disappointment with the Soviets, saying that from the beginning the PLO had wanted the Soviets to adopt a more radical position, "but our Soviet brothers have their own way of acting."[12] Soviet sensitivity to such criticism—of which this was only the beginning—was one of the factors prompting the June 14 Soviet-government statement. Although its wording was to some degree the public expression of the note sent to Reagan a few days earlier (primarily from concern over Israeli-Syrian fighting), the tone and timing were clearly designed to restore the cease-fire, lest Israel take Beirut; but its warning to Israel lacked the strong threat expressed at critical times in previous Arab-Israeli wars (indeed, the PLO representative in the Persian Gulf was to make just this point, critical of Moscow, several days later).[13]

On the critical point of actual Soviet assistance to the Palestinians (or Syrians) the statement was vague, even defensive. It said only that "It is working to bring about the withdrawal of the aggressor from Lebanon."[14]

These efforts were limited to diplomatic actions, although Soviet propaganda broadcasts implied, by reference to past cases, that this also meant Moscow's role in the creation of Arab military strength.[15] Even this, however, said nothing of the present, prompting increasingly explicit Palestinian criticism over the following weeks. Moscow's ally, Hawatimah, calling on the Soviets to use "all possible means including military power," complained that Moscow was satisfying itself with diplomatic and political pressures, the effect of which was "limited, if not zero."[16] The Soviets were apparently no more forthcoming in the letter Brezhnev sent to Arafat sometime in the last week of June, for Abu Iyad said of the letter that "it contains pretty words, but they have no basis on the ground."[17] Abu Iyad had already termed Soviet "inactivity" as inexplicable.[18] Prior to his early July visit to Moscow, as part of the Arab League delegations designated to visit all the permanent members of the Security Council, Kaddumi was quoted as planning to ask the Soviets for "drastic action," saying that condemning Israel was not sufficient.[19] According to Arab sources, quoted in the West, Gromyko told Kaddumi (and the accompanying Moroccan and Kuwaiti foreign ministers) that Soviet military aid in the form of troops or combat ships was out of the question, refusing to change the Soviet position or increase its role in Lebanon in any way.[20] The Soviets offered little else in answer to the Palestinians' demands and criticism aside from protestations of how much the Soviet Union was doing, minimization of the Palestinians' losses (meaning that their own arms and training, like that of the Syrians, were well provided by Moscow), and the more frequent argument employed implicitly and later explicitly that the Arab states were supposed to be the Palestinians' greatest defenders. Citing help from their own allies, South Yemen and Syria, and their potential ally, Iran, the Soviets predictably tried to shift the criticism to the Arab world, citing its lack of unity and failure to act.[21]

While criticism of the Soviet Union came from almost every quarter of the PLO, particularly Fatah, the one surprising exception was George Habash. Once the most outspoken critic of Moscow, Habash's silence regarding Moscow during the war can only be an indication of how far Soviet-PFLP relations did indeed progress after Camp David and the degree of cooperation Habash apparently hoped to maintain with the Soviets in the future. While Habash's silence may not in fact have been significant, it is a strong possibility that one of the outcomes of the summer's conflict will be a strengthening of the radical wing of the PLO, as opposed to Arafat. In view of the Israeli government's choice of the military option, Arafat will have still greater difficulty in arguing that he was right to press for the political approach, the road of international pressures and state alliances, and the option of negotiations and implied compromise. The likelihood of the radicalization of the PLO, and its probable return to terrorism as its only means of operating, has already been perceived by the Soviets,[22] but it is not necessarily a positive development in Soviet eyes. There is a wide gap between Moscow's position and that of the radicals, not only on the issue of international terrorism but on the whole spectrum of questions related to an Arab-Israeli settlement—including the very idea of a settlement. Gromyko, in his press conference of June 22, reiterated this position, underlining the point of greatest conflict between Moscow and the radical Palestinians: Moscow's recognition of Israel's right to exist.[23]

The radicalization of the PLO is but one problem Moscow may have to face. A more serious problem for the Soviets may be that the United States will emerge from the whole conflict as the winner. This, in fact, was one of the major Soviet concerns from the beginning of the war, probably the major concern once the Syrian-Israeli hostilities viritually ceased and the period of negotiations set in. From its first announcements of the war, the Soviet Union sought to make it clear to the Arab world that the United States was as much to blame and as deeply involved as the Israeli attackers themselves. Moscow sought to exploit the conflict to hamper the United States, both by drawing a straight line between Camp David, the U.S.-Israeli strategic alliance, and the summer war and by encouraging the Arab states to employ the oil weapon against the United States. Thus, as early as June 8 the Soviets called on the Arab states to help the Palestinians; but this appeal was not a call for Arab military aid, rather it was for the safer, but more effective—from the Soviet point of view—use of the oil weapon.[24]

Beneath this perhaps far-fetched hope of achieving an active—and significant—anti-U.S. policy from the Arab states, which might even unite the more reactionary Arab states like Saudi Arabia with the more radical ones, the Soviets were most likely intent upon limiting U.S. exploitation of the crisis to improve further its position. The prominence of this global calculation in Soviet thinking was most apparent in the warning sent by Brezhnev to Reagan on July 8.[25] For weeks the PLO had been surrounded and bombarded in West Beirut, and there had been the daily threat of Israeli occupation and destruction of the PLO strongholds in the city. Yet during all this time the Soviets did little to nothing, choosing to respond only when a new element appeared: the possibility of U.S. marines being sent to Lebanon to assist in the evacuation of the PLO. The Soviet warning was couched mainly in terms of preventing an Israeli move on west Beirut, and it was relatively milder than the June 14 statement in that it omitted any reference to the proximity of the area to the Soviet Union. But it was quite clear in its opposition to any importation of U.S. forces into the area—a step the Soviets undoubtedly saw as a serious change in the superpower status quo in the area, reminiscent of the days of powerful U.S. intervention in the Middle East (Lebanon 1958) to prop up the regimes of its choice against the threat of pro-Soviet moves elsewhere in the area. The July 8 warning did not even mention Israeli withdrawal from Lebanon, an omission designed perhaps to lower the price necessary for U.S. agreement to desist from sending troops—a move obviously considered more threatening to Soviet interests than the continued presence of the Israeli army in Lebanon.

Although the U.S. troop threat was mitigated by its incorporation into a multilateral supervisory force, the problem of U.S. diplomatic victory remained. The Americans, having successfully mediated the solution to the PLO presence in Beirut, were also presented with the possibility of perhaps achieving a modus operandi with the organization. Having no diplomatic relations with Israel, and no patron-client relationship with Lebanon, the Soviets had no way of challenging the U.S.-conducted negotiations. According to a Saudi source, the Soviets refused a Palestinian request to send a Soviet negotiator on the grounds that the absence of Soviet-Israeli relations would be an obstacle to the success of such an effort.[26] For a certain period of time, it appeared that the Soviets encouraged the Palestinians and Syrians, or anyone else approached as a potential host for the PLO, to resist a settlement. The Soviets may have hoped thereby to prevent a U.S.-mediated solution, as well as to demonstrate that the Americans, after all, could offer the Arabs nothing. At best, the negotiations could be shifted to the UN or a multinational forum that would include the Soviet Union, a suggestion that was raised by the Soviets late in July.[27] When, however, Israeli preparedness to take west Beirut became more than apparent and tensions increased on the eastern (Israel-Syria) front, Syria and others suddenly changed their positions regarding a Palestinian evacuation. The sudden change, which included South Yemen's agreement to receive Palestinians, strongly suggests Soviet intervention, presumably because the Soviets became convinced that Israel had reached the limits of its patience and war was about to break out again full force.

There is always the possibility that the conflict in Lebanon strengthened those persons or forces in Moscow that were opposed to such massive Soviet involvement with the Palestinians, or in this area at all. It has been argued over the years that elements of the Soviet military opposed such involvement on the grounds that it was too risky, that the Arab clients were too unstable and uncertain, and that war, including confrontation with the United States (or at the very least loss of modern Soviet equipment), would be the result. Others were said to have opposed supporting non-Marxist groups, believing the investment to be worthless over the long run. Others may in fact have pressed for greater support as part of the Soviet-Chinese competition among the national liberation movements. Conversely, there were those who preferred only state-to-state relations as the cornerstone of Soviet policy, no matter how progressive or Marxist the nonruling client group.

There has also been some evidence of persons or groups favoring detente as distinct from those who seek every opportunity to denigrate the possibility of detente with the United States. In the Lebanese crisis, there actually was a divergence between the standard Soviet line and the comments of one journalist, *Izvestiia's* Middle East political expert, Bovin, who at least twice sought to dissociate the United States from responsibility for the Israeli action.[28] Bovin's name has been associated with that of new First Secretary Iurri Andropov, just as various personalities and institutions have been identified with each of the above views. It has been speculated that the lack of Soviet aid to the PLO at this time was evidence of a change in Soviet policy as a result of a shift among the power groups in the Kremlin, possibly in connection with the death of Suslov in 1982. Given the closed nature of the Soviet political system, all this is but speculation, but the Soviet-PLO relationship and Soviet behavior toward the PLO have been both clear and consistent over the years. Soviet behavior in this crisis was indeed totally consistent with, and the logical consequence of, the policies pursued by the Brezhnev regime over the past ten years, if not longer.

Notes

1. For different perspectives on this period, see Salah Dabagh, *The Soviet Union and the Problem of Palestine* (Beirut: PLO Research Center, 1968); Augustus R. Norton, "Moscow and the Palestinians, A New Tool of Soviet Policy in the Middle East," in Michael Curtis, et al., *The Palestinians* (New Brunswick, N.J.: Transaction Books, 1975); Aryeh Yodfat, "The USSR and the Palestinians," *New Outlook* 19 (June 1976):30; Oded Eran, *The Soviet Union and the Palestine Guerilla Organizations* (Tel Aviv: Tel Aviv University, 1971); Leon Romaniecki, *The Arab Terrorists in the Middle East and Soviet Union* (Jerusalem: Soviet and East European Research Centre of the Hebrew University of Jerusalem, 1973); and William Quandt, Fuad Jabber, and Ann Morley Lesch, *The Politics of Palestinian Nationalism* (Berkeley, Calif.: University of California Press, 1973).

2. For further considerations and analyses of Soviet-PLO relations, see Galia Golan, *The Soviet Union and the Palestine Liberation Organization: An Uneasy Alliance* (New York: Praeger, 1980), pp. 39-49. See also, Stephen P. Gilbert, "Wars of Liberation and Soviet Military Policy," *Orbis* 10 (Fall 1966):113-126.

3. For an example of Soviet concern over internal divisions within the PLO, see "Special Document: The Soviet Attitude to the Palestine Problem," *Journal of Palestine Studies* 2, no. 1 (1972):187-212; Victor Bukharov, "Palestine National Council Session," *New Times* (June 1974):12-13; V. Vladimirov, "A Peaceful Settlement in the Middle East,"

Mezhdunarodnaia zhizn' 10 (1974):109; and V. Bukharov, "The Palestine Movement Shapes Its Course," *New Times* (December 1976):26-27.

4. See John Cooley, "The Shifting Sands of Arab Communism," *Problems of Communism* 14, no. 2 (1975):22-42.

5. E. Dimitryev, "The Middle East: An Important Factor of Settlement," *Kommunist* (1976):99-105; E. Primakov, "Zionism and Israel Against the Arab People of Palestine," Part II *Aziia i Afrika Segodnia* (April 1977):10; "Interview With the Palestine National Front," *Palestine Digest* (Washington) 6 (October 1976):21; and Naim Ashab, "The Palestinian Aspect of the Middle East Crisis," *World Marxist Review* 17 (April 1974):29. See also Golan, *The Soviet Union and the Palestine Liberation Organization,* citations on pp. 75-76.

6. R. Landa, "The Contemporary Stage in the Struggle of the Palestinian Movement of Resistance," *Narody Azii i Afriki* (May 1976):24-25; and Y. Glukhov, "Arab Interests Betrayed," *International Affairs* (June 1979):83.

7. Robert Freedman, "Soviet Policy Towards International Terrorism," in Yonah Alexander, ed., *International Terrorism: National, Regional and Global Perspectives* (New York: Praeger, 1976):122; and Edward Weisband and Damir Roguly, "Palestinian Terrorism: Violence, Verbal Strategy, and Legitimacy," in Alexander, pp. 283-308. On training terrorists, see Baruch Gurevitz, "The Soviet Union and the Palestinian Organizations," in Y. Ro'i, ed., *The Limits to Power: Soviet Policy in the Middle East* (London: Croom Helm, 1979), pp. 270-271; Leonard Shapiro, "The Soviet Union and the PLO," *Survey* 23 (Summer 1977-1978):206; and Ran Merom, "The Soviet Concept of Guerilla Warfare and Retaliation, The Case of the Palestinian Guerillas and Israel," *International Problems* (Tel Aviv) 16, nos. 3-4 (1977):78-91.

8. See Golan, *The Soviet Union and the Palestine Liberation Organization,* pp. 143-179, for a detailed discussion of internal differences within the PLO.

9. On the possible configuration of such a state, see Avi Plascov, "A Palestinian State? Examining the Alternatives," Adelphi Paper no. 163 (Spring 1981).

10. WAFA, 9 June 1982.

11. See, for example, *Pravda,* 9 June 1982; and Radio Peace and Progress (in Arabic), 9 June 1982.

12. Radio Monte Carlo, 11 June 1982.

13. Qatar News Agency, 28 June 1982.

14. TASS, 14 June 1982.

15. Moscow radio in Arabic, 16 June 1982.

16. Reuters, 26 June 1982; AFP 26 June 1982. For still stronger criticism by Hawatimah, see AFP, 15 July 1982. The only PLO official to

visit Moscow in June was the Hawatimah organization's Yasir abd-Rbbu, a member of the PLO Executive. The Soviet media carried only his words of praise for the Soviet Union (for example, Moscow radio in Arabic, 28 June 1982). There were reports of a high-level Palestinian delegation meeting the Soviets in Moscow and in Damascus (AFP, 18 June 1982; and Radio Damacus, 19 June 1982, respectively).

17. Radio Monte Carlo, 26 June 1982.

18. *Le Monde,* 22 June 1982.

19. Kuwait News Agency and *al-Siyassah,* 4 July 1982.

20. *International Herald Tribune,* 7 July 1982.

21. *Sovetskaia Rossiia,* 10 June 1982; Soviet television, 11 June 1982 (Primakov); Moscow radio in Arabic, 2 July 1982; TASS, 24 and 25 June; and 1 and 2 July 1982; Moscow domestic radio, 4 July 1982.

22. See for example, *Pravda's* political commentator, Demchenko, on Moscow domestic radio, 4 July 1982.

23. *Pravda,* 23 June 1982.

24. Radio Peace and Progress (in Arabic), 8 June 1982.

25. TASS, 8 July 1982.

26. *Al-Riyadh,* 13 July 1982.

27. On June 20, radio foreign-affairs specialist Shishkin, in an argument with *Izvestiia* political expert Bovin, remarked that it was not now the time for an international conference, though this Soviet idea was a good one. This comment, and the fact that this conference idea was in fact only proposed a month later, suggests that these were differences of opinion on the issue in Moscow. Moscow domestic radio, 20 June 1982.

28. Soviet television, 8 June 1982; Moscow domestic radio, 20 June 1982; the latter contained the argument between Bovin and Shishkin.

10 Politics in the Yemens and the Horn of Africa: Constraints on a Superpower

Paul R. Viotti

It is the location of Ethiopia, Somalia, Djibouti, and the Yemens astride the Red Sea that makes these countries of such lasting importance to states outside of the region. Although possessing little mineral or other wealth themselves, much of the world's commerce passes by their shores. Nowadays it is the flow of oil by tanker through the Bab al-Mandab Straits, transiting the Red Sea and Suez Canal en route to European ports, that attracts the most attention. The route is important not only to the West (given its, especially European, dependency on a continuing supply of oil), but also to both Western and Soviet navies. The alternative route around the African continent adds cost in fuel and time that effectively reduces the flexibility of Soviet, U.S., British, and French naval units with military tasks in both the Mediterranean Sea and Indian Ocean.[1] Port facilities at Aden, Socotra, Hudaydah, Djibouti, and Berbera are also used to service various clients transiting the Indian Ocean—both naval traffic and commercial shipping. Finally, aircraft are able to make use of landing fields in the region.

The assumptions one makes about Soviet motives inevitably color interpretations of their behavior. One view is that Soviet policymakers are conservative and largely defensive in orientation, pursuing actions designed merely to provide greater security. Thus, establishment of bases in Ethiopian or South Yemeni territory is seen as an effort to assure continuing Soviet access to the region, especially to maintain freedom of navigation for both commercial and military purposes.[2]

An alternative view is that far from being defensive, Soviet policy is driven principally by expansionist motives. Whether based on a grand design or the result of what might be called *incremental opportunism*, the Soviet aim from this perspective is always to increase the scope of its influence on a global basis. Apart from messianic notions of being the principal agent for spreading Marxism-Leninism throughout the world, Soviet policy is also said to reflect a "drive for great power status."[3]

In any event, Soviet objectives in the Horn of Africa and across the Red Sea in the Yemens cannot be understood merely as abstract formulations

The views expressed here are those of the author and do not necessarily reflect those of the U.S. government.

made by Politburo members or their staffs any more than U.S. objectives are set in that fashion. At the very least, objectives are shaped (or constrained) by the political situation in any given country, relations among states within the region, and the play of other state actors external to the region such as the United States, France, and the United Kingdom.

Competing views within the Soviet hierarchy itself also play a part in determining what objectives will be sought. Unfortunately, given the absence of data on bureaucratic politics within the Kremlin on most issues, one must draw inferences concerning policy choices from observation of consistencies (or inconsistencies) in Soviet behavior. Moreover, superpower and other great power involvement as well as the politics of each country and region pose their own sets of opportunities and opposing constraints to Soviet decision makers.

One of the clearest statements of Soviet geopolitical interest in the region was made in 1978 by the press spokesman of the Soviet Foreign Ministry:

> The Horn of Africa is first and foremost of military, political and economic significance. The importance of the area lies in its location at the link-up of the two continents of Asia and Africa. There are a lot of good sea ports in the Persian Gulf and the Indian Ocean. Moreover, there are sea lanes which link oil-producing countries with America and Europe.[4]

Although it is relatively easy to establish Soviet interest in the region, it is much more difficult to define Soviet objectives with any degree of precision. Given uncertainty as to Soviet objectives (if even the Soviets have defined them precisely), a more productive focus is on the constraints they have and will continue to face.

The complexity of politics in the Yemens and the Horn of Africa can best be appreciated if one's examination takes explicit account of constraints posed by domestic or tribal aspects within each state, relations among regional states, and interactions with extraregional states to include the superpowers and such other "great" (or medium) powers as Britain, France, and Italy. Exclusive focus on either domestic, regional, or global dimensions without consideration of the other would result in a rather distorted image of politics in the area. Thus, each of these perspectives will be considered in the discussion that follows.

Constraints Stemming from International Competition

As superpowers the United States and the Soviet Union compete for influence on a global basis. Even though neither superpower has the capacity to control the actions of most other states, the influence of both is pervasive. Other states (for example, China, Britain, and France) may be in a position to assert influence in selected regions, but only the superpowers can do so on a global scale.[5]

It is a mistake to attribute superpower status merely to the possession of large numbers of nuclear weapons and their associated delivery systems. Even if nuclear weapons did not exist, the United States and Soviet Union would arguably remain classed as superpowers. The sheer magnitude of their economies and their nonnuclear military-force postures, dependent as both are on technological infrastructure, place the superpowers in a league well above that of any other state. Only an industrially developed and technologically more advanced China or a united Europe—a vision that appears increasingly remote[6]—would have the capacity to compete globally with the superpowers.

Each of the superpowers is constrained by the actions, reactions, or expected reactions of the other superpower. Thus, any attempt by one to upset the status quo would likely be met by moves undertaken by the other designed to preclude any loss of its position of influence. As a practical matter, neither superpower has exhibited intent to seek major alteration of the status quo since the shifts that took place after the Ethiopian revolution in the 1970s (when the USSR relinquished its position in Somalia following establishment of close ties with Ethiopia and the United States reduced its presence in Ethiopia, developing a new relationship with the Somali government). Instead, both have been content to accept separate spheres of influence.[7] On the other hand, both superpowers have been on their guard lest internal developments in the region beyond their direct control result in an alteration of the present strategic balance adverse to their separate interests.

Although the former colonial states—Britain, Italy, and France—retain interest in the area, only the French maintain a substantial presence in Djibouti sufficient to pose a significant counter to Soviet influence. For their part, Britain, Italy, Egypt, Saudi Arabia, and Jordan have given support on occasion to either North Yemen or Somalia, thus providing a pro-Western alternative to Soviet influence. By contrast, Soviet purposes have been aided by Cuban and Libyan support for Ethiopia and South Yemen.

Wars between Ethiopia and Somalia or between the two Yemens or insurgent movements they sponsor become particularly troublesome to outside powers because of their potential for destabilizing regional politics. Certainly any attempt by outside powers to provide assistance to either side that would lead to dramatic or major defeat of the other would violate the tacit rules of the superpower game. Accordingly, the experience of recent years has been a considerable degree of restraint by the superpowers and explicit avoidance of actions that would threaten their interests. The risks involved in seeking an alternative order have thus far seemed much greater than expected gains associated with such policies.

One reason the superpowers proceed with such caution is that neither has a clear military advantage over the other. An assessment of military capabilities suggests that "distance and Soviet force-structure considerations" are significant. Designed primarily for fighting a European war, the "further Soviet forces must operate from their borders the more significant Soviet constraints are and the more vulnerable Soviet forces come to interdiction and disruption."[8] True, the USSR is closer to the region than the United States, but even the Soviets are some two thousand miles from Aden. Bases in South Yemeni and Ethiopian territory reduce this logistics problem somewhat, but as Dunn notes, the "lack of guaranteed access to facilities and a general dislike and distrust for not only the Soviet Union, but also the communist system" raise serious questions about the reliability of these bases.[9]

In any event, neither the Soviet Union nor the United States has been willing to pursue courses of action in the region that would risk a major superpower confrontation. Both have been willing to pursue relatively modest aims, accepting a rough division of the area into separate spheres of influence.

Regional and Domestic Politics as Constraints

Both superpowers are constrained by the domestic politics and relations among states in the region. The most dramatic example of this was the necessity for the Soviets to cease support for both Somalia and the Eritrean secessionists as the price for securing its position of influence in Ethiopia. Unstable domestic politics in all of these states with the ever-present threat of coups and subsequent changes in policy line represent another problem with which outside powers must cope.

State boundaries in the area (as in so many other regions subjected to colonialism) were imposed by European states, often as arbitrary divisions of spheres of influence. The lines might have been redrawn later with some modifications, but they still bestow on the region a legacy of frontiers often bearing little relation to ethnic, tribal, or even geographic features.

Projection of the European state system throughout the globe culminated with independence movements following the two twentieth-century world wars. Establishment of mandates under the League of Nations and trusteeships under the United Nations (as half-way houses preparing the way to full independence) provided legitimacy for transforming global politics. The European model of a set of independent states each claiming a right to sovereign status became the world model.

An appreciation for this colonial legacy is essential to understanding contemporary politics in the Yemens and in the Horn of Africa. In this region as elsewhere, newly created states were left with an extremely difficult, seemingly insoluble problem, of establishing a sense of national unity in the presence of cultural, religious, language, tribal, and other ethnic divisions among the inhabitants of any given new state. In fact, politics in the new states typically perpetuated established divisions and patterns of interaction among the diverse tribal and ethnic groups. By no means could one speak of national unity, the sense of which is contained in the modern term *nation-state*. Not only were single *nations* as integral units virtually nonexistent in the new *states*, but the capacity of governing authorities to perform administrative functions, maintain order, and provide other values was also quite weak. Given these conditions, politics could be described, at best, as keeping an uneasy truce among rival elements and, at worst, as attempting to maintain patterns of dominance by one group over another with all of their potential for developing into civil war. That outside powers must deal essentially with tribal societies rather than modern states provides both opportunities and constraints that will be discussed here.

The Yemens

Soviet policy in southwest Arabia has proceeded along very cautious lines with Moscow rendering support to both Yemens.[10] Given hostility between the two, a strong Soviet position in the south has necessarily reduced whatever influence Moscow might have had in the north. In short, a regional conflict that has provided an opportunity for the Soviets has also constrained the exercise of that influence largely to one side or the other.

Surprisingly, the Soviets have not been as constrained as they might have been by the seeming incompatibility of their Marxist-Leninist ideology with local Islamic practice and belief. Extremely flexible, Marxism-Leninism posed more as a nationalist ideology in the south (an alternative to colonial exploitation) and thus gained legitimacy during the independence movement. In the absence of any such experience in the north, Marxism-Leninism remains suspect there, particularly since the ideology has become associated with the adversary regime in the south.

Even more important than ideology, Soviet policymakers have found opportunities, but have also been constrained by the realities of a tribal and highly personalized politics endemic to the region. Although the population of both Yemens is predominantly Arab, there is no real sense of national unity that would serve as a firm basis for integrating the two states. The political order in much of the Yemen Arab Republic (YAR) or North Yemen, for example, amounts to little more than a confederation of tribes. Maintaining some semblance of unity among the various tribal shaykhs is a major governmental task, as is also the case in the People's Democratic Republic of Yemen (PDRY) to the south.[11]

Not only are the two states deeply split, but the YAR is itself divided between Shi'i Muslim tribes of the north (the Zaydi) and the Sunni Muslim tribes to the south (the Shafii). Representing at most about half the population of the YAR, the Zaydi nevertheless dominate the government in Sana'a. Capitalizing on discontent in the south with the Sana'a regime, the National Democratic Front (NDF), supported by the predominantly Sunni PDRY, has made inroads along the frontier that divides the two countries. On the other hand, tactics pursued by the NDF in some villages have alienated a number of villagers, making them potentially more subject to influence by Sana'a.

The notion of a united Yemen may have roots in ancient history, but it certainly has no modern historical basis. Failure to achieve unity in talks initiated in 1972 and renewed in 1979 can be explained in part by tribal-religious cleavages already described. The colonial experience is also an important factor. Britain occupied Aden in 1839, gradually expanding its control both east and north. Meanwhile, North Yemen under the Imamate remained part of the Ottoman Empire until the end of World War I in 1918.[12]

Throughout much of the nineteenth and early twentieth centuries the Yemens were an object of competition between the British and Ottoman imperial realms. Given its strategic location on the sea route to India and the Far East, Britain gave particular attention to the port of Aden and the territory of southern Yemen where a protectorate was established. By contrast, the tribes to the north under the Imam at Sana'a were of less importance, especially since the Imamate was capable of maintaining order, thus precluding disruptions that might have been injurious to British interests.

Although the Imamate claimed historical right in the south as well as the north, as a practical matter its political sway was concentrated in the north. Even there, considerable tribal autonomy (especially in the far north) served to constrain the Imam. Following the defeat of the Ottomans in World War I and the subsequent establishment of Saudi Arabia as an independent state, delineation of the northern border was finally worked out between the Imam and the Saudis in 1934. Also in the same year the Imam signed a treaty with the British, ending claim to British areas in the south and largely confirming the earlier territorial division between British and Ottoman imperial realms.[13] This effectively legitimized separate Yemens—one in the north under the Imam at Sana'a and the other a protectorate in the south under British hegemony at Aden. Given this sociocultural and historical legacy, establishment of a separate south Yemeni state at independence in 1967 was hardly surprising. Three years later the Marxist-oriented regime in Aden adopted formally the name People's Democratic Republic of Yemen.

For its part, North Yemen experienced an eight-year civil war that began when the Imam was overthrown by army rebels in 1962.[14] The *republicans*, supported by Egypt,[15] fought *royalist* followers of the Imam, backed by Saudi Arabia and Jordan. After the defeat in the 1967 war with the Israelis, the Egyptians withdrew their troops from the YAR. Three years later reconciliation finally occurred between republican and royalist tribes and a loose confederation of tribes was reestablished. Saudi Arabia endorsed the arrangement, granting recognition to the new republican regime in Sana'a.

The Soviets, aided by Cuba, East German, and their own advisors,[16] exercise considerable influence in the PDRY—a country that provides them access to the region by both air and sea. Aden, long important to British security of the Red Sea and Indian Ocean trade routes as well as being a useful refueling stop,[17] serves the same purposes for the Soviet fleet as does the strategically located island of Socotra. Soviet use of air bases to facilitate the supply of arms to both the PDRY and Ethiopia and to conduct aerial reconnaisance throughout the region has also been documented.[18]

The more radical the Marxist regime in Aden, the more dependent it has become upon Soviet support against what are perceived to be hostile neighbors.[19] The Moscow-Aden link developed slowly in the aftermath of Moscow's recognition of South Yemen immediately after its independence from Britain in 1967. (In the late 1950s the Soviets had also given aid to the Sana'a regime but had not been very successful in their attempt to secure greater influence in the north.) Moving cautiously in the late 1960s, Soviet activity in the PDRY may well have been designed as much to compete with Chinese activity in the region as to establish a firm basis for Soviet power in the area. In any event, Moscow now gives aid to both Yemens, although the bulk of its support and its strongest ties are with the south.

Rubinstein argues that it was Aden's fear that the "neighboring conservative regimes in Saudi Arabia, the YAR, and Oman might seek to depose it" that drove the PDRY closer to the USSR. Failure in its support for the Dhufar rebellion in western Oman that culminated in defeat for the Dhufaris in 1976, coupled with failure to date in its support or sponsorship of the NDF against the YAR, have led the Aden regime to question the utility of its Moscow tie.[20]

Soviet fence straddling in the form of granting aid to both North and South Yemen keeps Moscow's options open, but it has not been well received in Aden. Although not all observers would agree, it may be that Soviet interest in improving relations with the Saudis has contributed to their willingness to maintain a stalemate between the Yemens. That the prospect of normalizing relations with Saudi Arabia could be damaged or destroyed by Soviet support for a successful PDRY campaign against the YAR may have constrained Soviet behavior somewhat, making Moscow more cautious in supporting its South Yemeni client.

Although the Soviet position remains dominant, the Aden regime has diversified its external support base to a slight degree in the form of a 1981 pact with two other Soviet clients, Libya and Ethiopia. Whether the support the PDRY receives from its new allies will continue to be more symbolic than real in terms of tangible benefit to the country is not entirely clear. To date, benefits have been primarily symbolic—a joint demonstration of their solidarity against so-called imperialist states.

South Yemeni ties with Ethiopia and Libya are certainly more acceptable to Moscow than if Aden were to turn toward the West. For example, Moscow must certainly be on guard against any reestablishment by Aden of close links with London. Given the almost inevitable diminution over time of anticolonial ardor, a phenomenon observed elsewhere and particularly in Africa, the prospect of improved relations with the United Kingdom as a possible South Yemeni counterweight to its Soviet tie cannot be entirely dismissed, however unlikely it may appear in the short run.

South Yemeni leaders would certainly approach such a shift in policy with great caution. Indeed, there is some indication (though no definitive proof) that the Soviets were at least indirectly involved in the 1977 overthrow of South Yemeni President Salim Rubayy' Ali who was, at the time, pursuing rapprochement with both Saudi Arabia and North Yemen.[21] Following the coup, the new government under Fattah Ismail signed a fifteen-year friendship and cooperation treaty with the USSR. The regime's successor (again by coup d'état in 1980) has maintained close ties with the Soviets.

Given the British colonial legacy, state institutions in the PDRY are somewhat stronger than in the YAR where support for the Sana'a regime stems from a loose coalition of tribal shaykhs who still exercise effective jurisdiction in much of the hinterland. Although tribal politics are also part of the South Yemeni scene, central governmental institutions in the south exercise somewhat greater sway over the countryside.

So long as the regime in Aden supports the Soviets, their position throughout the country will likely remain relatively secure. By contrast, the Soviet Union (or any other state) seeking a client in the YAR would necessarily be somewhat more constrained by the shifting and highly personal politics of intertribal relations.

U.S. and Saudi support for Sana'a is another counter to the Soviets who, as already noted, have also given aid to Sana'a. For example, in 1979 some $400 million worth of urgently needed U.S. arms were paid for by the Saudis and sent to the YAR to help in its struggle with the NDF and PDRY.[22] Meanwhile, Soviet arms transfers to the PDRY amounted to an average of about $240 million per year over the four year 1977-1980 time period.[23]

Ethiopia, Somalia, and Djibouti

The Ogaden War. Following the overthrow of Ethiopian emperor Haile Selassie in 1974,[24] the Soviets gradually established a position of influence in

Addis Ababa, signing a military-assistance agreement with Ethiopia in December 1976.[25] Ethiopian military ties with the United States were terminated four months later, although diplomatic relations were maintained.[26]

Fighting in the Ogaden desert between Ethiopia and Somalia broke out in the summer of 1977 when the Somalis attacked Ethiopian positions.[27] The Soviets responded by airlifting military supplies and Cuban troops to assist the Ethiopians in resisting the Somalis. Because of hostility between the two countries, Moscow could not maintain its position in both. Choosing the client that offered the greater potential for its own position in the region, Moscow was forced by the regime in Mogadishu to relinquish its position in Somalia.[28]

Indeed, Soviet support for Ethiopia led in November 1977 to Somali president Siad Barre's decision to abrogate the treaty of friendship and cooperation his regime had signed with the Soviets in 1974.[29] Having lost its position in Ethiopia to the Soviets, the United States reopened its aid program in Somalia in 1978.[30] This mutual exchange between the superpowers, accommodating to changes in the internal politics of the region, is more reminiscent of eighteenth- or nineteenth-century balance of power politics in Europe, when both loose coalitions and formal alliances were made and broken with greater facility than they are today.

Be that as it may, the Soviet move to exploit its Ethiopian opportunity should not be understood merely in terms of securing a position with a larger country with greater resources and potential than economically distraught Somalia. The relatively greater value of Ethiopia to the Soviets was underscored by the geographic location of Ethiopia not only as a Red Sea state with ports at Assab and Massawa but also as one providing access to the agricultural potential of the Sudan and to other countries in north-central Africa. At the same time that politics in Ethiopia offered Moscow this opportunity, the Soviets were also constrained by regional politics and had to surrender their position in Somalia.

The Ethiopia-Somalia conflict over the Ogaden is far more complex than being merely a territorial dispute involving Somali irredentism. Tribes loyal to the Somali regime of Siad Barre are prone to support Siad's view that all Somalis should be brought within the territorial control of the Mogadishu regime. As is true in southwest Arabia, the countries of the African Horn remain tribal societies. Gains by tribes controlling (or in positions of influence with) central governments are seen as losses by those tribes lacking such influence.

Tribal differences are indeed the principal differences among Somalis. Language, religious, and ethnic homogeneity would provide some basis for national unity were it not for these tribal rivalries. Thus, claims by the regime in Mogadishu to territory inhabited by Somalis in Kenya, Ethiopia, and Djibouti are seen by outlying tribes as attempts to subordinate them to the central government.[31] Anti-Siad Somali tribes thus represent fertile ground for political organization by Ethiopia. The Somali Democratic Salvation Front (SDSF) is such an Ethiopian- and Libyan-supported movement of Somalis opposed to the Siad regime.

Fighting continues as of this writing with the Ethiopians having launched the latest offensive. Now largely on the defensive, the Somalis have turned to the United States, Saudi Arabia, Italy, and other Arab and European states for assistance. Outside states are thus drawn into disputes in which they may have little or no direct interest. As they work to constrain local adventurism that would upset the status quo and threaten their own position, the superpowers and other outside states are, in effect, forced to aid local regimes as the price for maintaining their positions of influence.[32]

Distrust of the motives of the other superpower also motivates both to continue support for their respective clients. Pursuit of opportunities for continuing influence (and, conversely, denying expansion of influence by their opposite numbers) carries a price to the superpowers—a constraint on their freedom of policy choice. They may counsel moderation, but they must in the final analysis cope with the realities of local regional politics if they are to maintain their positions of influence. Indeed, neither has any assurance that the status quo will obtain indefinitely.

In sharp contrast to Somalia, Ethiopia is a polyglot state composed of numerous ethnic and tribal groups with at least seventy languages spoken.[33] Among the major ethnic groups are the Amharas in the central region (the dominant group within the country); the Gallas (or Oromos as they are also called) in the south and central areas; the Somalis (including the Issas or Ishaak tribes) in the east; and Tigrais, Sahos, and Afars in Eritrea along the Red Sea.[34] As one might expect, the country is beset by numerous secessionist movements resisting subordination to rule by the Amharas—the Tigrais, Somalis, Gallas, Afars, and Eritreans.

Eritrea. Aside from the conflict with Somalia over the Ogaden, Ethiopia's major security problem is in Eritrea province along the Red Sea.[35] An Italian colony since the 1880s, Eritrea became part of Ethiopia following World War II. The Eritrean claim rests partly on this colonial status as being separate from Ethiopia but even more importantly on the fact that much of the population in Eritrea is Arab and Muslim. Eritrea's importance to the Soviets and their Ethiopian clients is its location on the Red Sea and the ports of Assab and Massawa that it offers. Without Eritrea, Ethiopia would be a landlocked state.

Eritrean secession dates at least from the early 1960s. Given tribal and ideological divisions within Eritrea, the secessionist movement is also divided, but the leading force is the Marxist-oriented Eritrean Popular Liberation Front (EPLF). Colin Legum describes the EPLF as "undoubtedly the most sophisticated guerrilla movement spawned in Africa." He adds that "unlike others, it is technologically competent; most of its cadres, men and women, are highly educated."[36]

Since establishing ties with Addis Ababa, the Soviets have shifted from support for Eritrean secession much as it abandoned support for Somalia in the Ogaden. Early in 1977, Fidel Castro tried to effect reconciliation between Addis Ababa and the Eritreans as part of a so-called progressive alliance that would have included Djibouti, Eritrea, the PDRY, Ethiopia, and Somalia. Failing in that, the Cubans have been unwilling to commit troops to supporting Ethiopia's campaign against the secessionists, arguing that unlike the Ogaden, Eritrea is a political problem that should not be settled by armed force.[37]

Thus, the Ethiopian campaign against the Eritreans has been supported by the Soviets but has been fought by Ethiopians. Without Cuban troops, Ethiopian forces have had less success fighting in the rugged terrain of Eritrea than it has against Somalia where Cuban troops have supported the effort. For their part, the Eritreans have continued to receive some support from sympathetic Arab states.

Djibouti. Contiguous to Eritrea, French Somaliland (later known as the French Territory of Issas and Afars) became the independent state of Djibouti in 1976.[38] Connected by rail to Addis Ababa, the port of Djibouti has provided a useful alternative to Ethiopian ports in Eritrea. Djibouti remains dependent on French military support to include the continuing presence of more than two thousand troops.[39] The country is divided between ethnic Somalis (the Issas) and those with links to tribes in Eritrea and north-central Ethiopia (the Afars).[40] In the absence of the French (or other outside stabilizing power), Djibouti would undoubtedly be yet another battleground between both Somali and Ethiopian irredentist movements.

Conclusions

Much has been made in the international-relations literature of a global shift from U.S.-Soviet bipolarity in the years following World War II to what is variously called *multipolarity* (or impending multipolarity), *polycentrism, asymmetric multipolarity*, and even *bimultipolarity*. The continuing, pervasive influence of the superpowers throughout the world, however, does lead one to challenge whether multipolar images can be supported empirically. Kenneth Waltz takes issue with the popular view that the world has become multipolar. Part of the problem is the tendency "to identify power with control."[41] Because they are superpowers does not mean that the United States and the Soviet Union can control the actions of other states.

Their superpower status does mean, however, that their actions or policies are an important ingredient in the calculations of less powerful states throughout the world.

The pervasive influence of the superpowers is abundantly clear in any study of the countries in the African Horn and southwest Arabia. But neither superpower is in a controlling position in the region. Indeed, a principal focus of the discussion in this chapter is on the constraints imposed on a superpower. Having said this, it must also be added that the influence of either superpower cannot be ignored. What some states do is of little or no consequence to states outside of their spheres of influence. By contrast, what the superpowers do can be ignored only at the peril of other states. It is this reality that leads one to argue that the world remains essentially bipolar, notwithstanding the great complexity of international relations, and that in certain issues and certain regions the influence of other states may well rival that of the superpowers.

At the international level, politics in the African Horn and southwest Arabia involve two opposing loose coalitions of outside states. To be sure, each state pursues what it perceives to be its own interests, but there are two distinct communities of overlapping interests, two rival groupings generally consistent with global divisions among these states.

The Soviets, Cubans, and Libyans actively support Ethiopia and the PDRY. On the other hand, Somalia and the YAR receive support from the United States, Saudi Arabia, and such other moderate or conservative Arab states as Egypt, Jordan, and the Sudan, countries that have also been supportive of Eritrean insurgents in their secessionist struggle against the Ethiopians. Also loosely tied to this pro-Western coalition, the French maintain a relatively strong position in Djibouti and the Italians retain some influence in Somalia.

Of course, not all relations in the region follow such a Soviet-U.S. or East-West dichotomy. The British maintain diplomatic relations and a potential for greater influence with the South Yemenis and the Soviets have tried to woo the North Yemenis with offers of aid and other assistance; however, neither Britain nor the USSR have yet to establish strong influence in either the PDRY or YAR, given the ties these countries have with rival coalitions.

Unstable politics in the region provide opportunities to the superpowers and the two coalitions for an expansion of their separate spheres of influence. Because of the zero-sum (my gain is your loss) nature of the conflict, exploitation of such opportunities upsets the existing order and carries with it the potential for loss. The structure of conflict in the region thus contributes to stabilization of conflict relations—a stand-off between two loose coalitions, each recognizing that fundamental alteration of the status quo could work to its disadvantage. Moreover, the superpowers and their rival coalitions may try to influence the course of local or tribal politics within each country and of conflicts among regional states, but their policy choices seem always to be constrained by the course and outcomes of these continuing struggles.

The objectives both sides pursue thus appear to be relatively modest. As discussed earlier, the strategic location of countries in the region is the principal interest of outside states. Consistent with this principal strategic interest is the minimal objective of maintaining stability in the region that will assure safe passage of ships and aircraft transiting the area.

Alteration of established patterns of relations has occurred in the recent past (as when the superpowers and their coalitions exchanged positions in Ethiopia and Somalia) and may well occur in the coming years, whether in response to domestic or regional changes or provoked by the superpowers or other outside states. Nevertheless, there are strong incentives for both sides to maintain the status quo.

Notes

1. For a discussion of Soviet naval interest in the region, see Richard B. Remnek, "Soviet Policy in the Horn of Africa: The Decision to Intervene," in Robert H. Donaldson, ed., *The Soviet Union in the Third World: Successes and Failures* (Boulder: Westview Press, 1981), pp. 127-132.

2. The commercial importance of the region to the USSR is underscored by Friedgut who observes that "although it has only a little over 5 percent of the world's merchant shipping tonnage, the Soviet Union claims to be the leading civil user of the Suez Canal." Theodore H. Friedgut, "The Middle East in Soviet Global Strategy," *Jerusalem Journal of International Relations* 5, no. 1 (1980):75.

3. See the discussion in Henry Bienen, "Soviet Political Relations with Africa," *International Security*, (Spring 1982):153-154, 167-169.

4. New China News Agency, 14 March 1978, as cited by Colin Legum, "Angola and the Horn of Africa," in Stephen S. Kaplan, et al., *Diplomacy of Power: Soviet Armed Forces as a Political Instrument* (Washington, D.C.: The Brookings Institution, 1981), p. 610. Reprinted by permission of Xinhua News Agency.

5. The view expressed here is developed in greater detail by Kenneth N. Waltz, *Theory of International Politics* (Reading, Mass.: Addison-Wesley, 1979), pp. 129-131, 161-193.

6. For an explanation of why European integration has not proceeded further, see Ernest B. Haas, "Turbulent Fields and the Theory of Regional Integration," *International Organization* 30, no. 2 (Spring 1976):173-212.

7. Recent studies of superpower involvement in the region include Marina S. Ottaway, *Soviet and American Influence in the Horn of Africa* (New York: Praeger, 1982); and J.E. Peterson, *Conflict in the Yemens and Superpower Involvement* (Washington, D.C.: Georgetown University Center for Contemporary Arab Studies, 1981). Also see Robert F. Gorman, *Political Conflict on the Horn of Africa* (New York: Praeger, 1981); and Colin Legum and Bill Lee, *Conflict in the Horn of Africa* (New York: Africana, 1977).

8. Keith A. Dunn, "Constraints on the USSR in Southwest Asia: A Military Analysis," *Orbis* 25, no. 3 (Fall 1981):628. Reprinted with permission.

9. Ibid., p. 629.

10. On Soviet policy in the Yemens, see Nimrod Novik, "Between Two Yemens: The Soviet Challenge and U.S. Response," in Nimrod Novik and Joyce Starr, eds., *Challenges in the Middle East: Regional Dynamics and Western Security* (New York: Praeger, 1981). Other recent works on Yemen include J.E. Peterson, *Yemen: The Search for a Modern State* (Baltimore: The Johns Hopkins University Press, 1982); and Mohammed Ahmad Zabarah, *Yemen: Traditionalism versus Modernity* (New York: Praeger, 1982).

11. For a discussion of tribal and other politics, see Robert W. Stookey, "Social Structure and Politics in the Yemen Arab Republic," *Middle East Journal* 28, no. 3 (Summer 1974):248-260; and "Part II: The Political System," 28, no. 4 (Autumn 1974):409-418. See Stookey's *Yemen: The Politics of the Yemen Arab Republic* (Boulder: Westview Press, 1978). See also the discussion in Richard F. Nyrop et al., *Area Handbook for the Yemens* (Washington, D.C.: U.S. Government Printing Office, 1977), pp. 71-81, 94-106, 141-144, 163-164, 207-224.

12. The Yemeni monarchy and politics are discussed in Ulick Loring and Jeffrey Finestone, *The Yemeni Monarchy* (London: MPA Publications, 1977); Manfred W. Wenner, *Modern Yemen, 1918-1966* (Baltimore: Johns Hopkins University Press, 1967); and William Harold Ingrams, *The Yemens: Imans, Rulers and Revolutions* (London: Murray, 1963).

13. See Ann Williams, *Britain and France in the Middle East and North Africa, 1914-1967* (New York: St. Martin's Press, 1968), p. 50. See Roy E. Thoman, "Aden and South Arabia," *Current History* 58, no. 341 (January 1970):27-33, 49-50.

14. For more extensive treatment of the Yemeni civil war, see Edgar O'Ballance, *The War in Yemen* (London: Faber and Faber, 1971); Dana Adams Schmidt, *Yemen: The Unknown War* (London: Bodley Head, 1968); William R. Brown, "The Yemeni Dilemma," *Middle East Journal* 17, no. 4 (1963):349-367; and J. Bell, *South Arabia: Violence and Revolt* (London: Institute for the Study of Conflict, 1973).

15. For a discussion of Egypt's role in the area, see A.I. Dawisha, "Intervention in the Yemen: An Analysis of Egyptian Perceptions and Policies," *Middle East Journal* 29, no. 1 (1975):47-64.

16. Andrew J. Pierre, *Global Politics of Arms Sales* (Princeton: Princeton University Press, 1982), p. 187.

17. Williams, *Britain and France in the Middle East and North Africa*, p. 49.

18. See Alvin Z. Rubinstein, "The Soviet Presence in the Arab World," *Current History* 80, no. 9. 468 (October 1981):316.

19. See the discussion in Rubinstein, ibid., pp. 315-316. On aspects of Sino-Soviet competition mentioned later in this paragraph, see Charles T. Creekman, "Sino-Soviet Competition in the Yemens," *Naval War College Review* 32, no. 4 (1979):73-82.

20. Rubinstein, "The Soviet Presence in the Arab World," p. 316. On the Dhufar rebellion, see Fred Halliday, *Arabia without Sultans* (New York: Vintage, 1975); and J.E. Peterson, "Guerilla Warfare and Ideological Confrontation in the Arabian Peninsula: The Rebellion in Dhufar," *World Affairs* 139, no. 4 (1977):278-295.

21. Rubinstein, ibid., p. 316.

22. Pierre, *Global Politics of Arms Sales*, p. 187.

23. Ibid., p. 133. See *SIPRI Yearbook, 1981*, p. 198.

24. On the Ethiopian revolution, see Marina Ottaway and David Ottaway, *Ethiopia: Empire in Revolution* (New York: Africana Publications, 1978); Colin Legum, *Ethiopia: The Fall of Haile Selassie's Empire* (New York: Africana Publications, 1975); David Hamilton, *Ethiopia's Embattled Revolutionaries* (London: Institute for the Study of Conflict, 1977); and Robert O. Aliboni, "The Ethiopian Revolution: Stabilization," *Armed Forces and Society* 7, no. 3 (1981):423-444. On external policy, see Olusola Ojo, "Ethiopia's Foreign Policy Since the 1974 Revolution," *Horn of Africa* 3, no. 4 (1980/81):3-12.

25. See Gary D. Payton, "The Soviet-Ethiopian Liaison," *Air University Review* 31, no. 1 (1979):66-73.

26. For a discussion of U.S.-Ethiopian relations, see John H. Spencer, *Ethiopia, the Horn of Africa, and US Policy* (Cambridge, Mass.: Institute for Foreign Policy Analysis, 1977).

27. For related discussions, see Habte Selassie Bereket, *Conflict and Intervention in the Horn of Africa* (New York: Monthly Review Press, 1980); and Tom J. Farer, *War Clouds on the Horn of Africa: The Widening Storm*, 2d rev. ed. (New York: Carnegie Endowment for International Peace, 1979).

28. See Gary D. Payton, "Soviet Military Presence Abroad: The Lessons of Somalia," *Military Review* 59, no. 1 (1979):67-77.

29. See Brian Crozier, *The Soviet Presence in Somalia* (London: Institute for the Study of Conflict, 1975).

30. On the development of the US-Somali connection, see Abdi Sheikh-Abdi, "Somalia: A Litmus Paper for U.S. Foreign Policy in the 1980s," *Horn of Africa* 3, no. 2 (1980):34-43; and Raymond L. Thurston, "The United States, Somalia, and the Crisis in the Horn," *Horn of Africa* 1, no. 2 (1978):11-20.

31. See Janet Fraser, "The Somalian-Ethiopian-Kenyan Conflict, 1960-1964," in *The Control of Local Conflict* 3 (Washington, D.C.: 1967), pp. 457-506; and James Mayall, "The Battle for the Horn: Somali Irredentism and International Diplomacy," *The World Today* 34, no. 9 (1978):336-345.

32. On local and regional politics, see Jake C. Miller, "Ethiopia and Intra-African Politics," *Horn of Africa* 1, no. 2 (1978):41-47.

33. Harold D. Nelson and Irving Kaplan, *Ethiopia: A Country Study* (Washington, D.C.: U.S. Government Printing Office, 1981), p. 72. See John Markakis, *Ethiopia: Anatomy of a Traditional Polity* (Oxford: Clarendon Press, 1974).

34. See the discussion on ethnicity in Nelson and Kaplan, ibid., pp. 72-93.

35. A recent study of the Eritrean revolt is Richard Sherman, *Eritrea: The Unfinished Revolution* (New York: Praeger, 1980).

36. Colin Legum, "Eritrean Resistance Holds, With No End in Sight," *International Herald Tribune*, 27 September 1982. Reprinted with permission. Eritrean factions are discussed at length in Nelson and Kaplan, *Ethiopia: A Country Study*, pp. 265-268. See Colin Legum, "Angola and the Horn of Africa," in Kaplan, et al., *Diplomacy of Power*, p. 607.

37. Legum, "Angola and the Horn of Africa," pp. 611-612.

38. For further reading on this ministate, see Virginia Thompson and Richard Adloff, *Djibouti and the Horn of Africa* (Stanford: Stanford University Press, 1968); and Said Yusuf Abdi, "The Mini-Republic of Djibouti: Problems and Prospects," *Horn of Africa* 1, no. 2 (1978):35-40.

39. Legum, "Angola and the Horn of Africa," p. 606.

40. Nelson and Kaplan, *Ethiopia: A Country Study*, pp. 76-77.

41. Waltz, *Theory of International Politics*, pp. 191-192.

11 The Soviet Union and Iran since 1978

Malcolm E. Yapp

Readers of the *Memoirs of Sherlock Holmes* will recall the case of the racehorse, Silver Blaze, that mysteriously disappeared before the Wessex Cup. The diligent, but unimaginative policeman, Inspector Gregory, requested the help of Holmes and asked him if there was any point to which Holmes would like to draw attention. "To the curious incident of the dog in the nighttime," replied Holmes. But, objected Gregory, "The dog did nothing in the nighttime." "That," remarked Holmes, "was the curious incident." If we substitute *bear* for dog we have captured the essence of the Soviet attitude toward Iran since the Islamic revolution. The Soviet Union has done nothing and the purpose of this chapter is to inquire into the reasons for this curious inactivity.

It will be convenient first to examine some of the principal problems that have emerged in Soviet-Iranian relations since the revolution. The most prominent issues have been those concerning economic links between the two countries, Afghanistan, the Iran-Iraq war, and ideology.

During the last decade or more of the reign of Muhammad Riza Shah Pahlavi economic relations between Iran and the USSR blossomed: trade flourished; the Soviet Union took delivery of Iranian natural gas, hitherto wasted, at the rate of about ten billion cubic meters a year through a newly constructed gasline and planned to take much more through a second gasline scheduled for completion in 1981; and the Soviet Union built large industrial and communications projects for Iran, notably the Isfahan steel mills. The revolution greatly diminished this activity; trade fell off considerably although it picked up again in 1982; deliveries of natural gas were greatly reduced, partly because Iranian natural gas is a by-product of oil extraction and with a fall off in oil production there was less gas to sell but also because of a major disagreement between the two states about the price of the gas. In July 1979 Iran canceled the second gasline project and in March 1980 demanded five times more for her gas than the shah had received before 1978. The USSR would offer little more than three times the former sum.[1] During these negotiations the Soviet Union's demeanor was mild. While plainly trying to make the best bargain she could (and it was certain that Iran could sell her gas to no one else) the USSR did not retaliate in the manner to which Iran had become uncomfortably familiar during the reign of Riza Shah. The important transit routes through the USSR were kept open for Iranian trade with Europe and the Soviet Union strove patiently for a new agreement on trade. In fact, a trade agreement was concluded in June 1980 and a new transit agreement in September of the same year. Further negotiations followed and in February 1982 a new economic and scientific protocol was signed. Nevertheless, as the USSR made clear, it was felt that Iran was still dragging her feet on the development of economic cooperation.

Afghanistan

The Afghanistan issue made its first appearance in Soviet-Iranian relations soon after the April 1978 revolution in Afghanistan. Accusations of Soviet complicity in this revolution were made in Iran at the time and they continued to be voiced after the triumph of the Islamic revolution in February 1979. Following the disorders in Afghanistan and the flight of refugees from that country in consequence of the Taraki government's decision to press ahead with radical land reform, Iranian criticisms of Soviet involvement became stronger. The Soviet Union was accused by Ayattallah Khumayni and others of interfering in Afghanistan, and support was given to Afghan groups that opposed the revolutionary government in Afghanistan. The Soviet invasion of Afghanistan in December 1979 inevitably provided the USSR's Iranian critics with more ammunition to hurl at their northern neighbor. The Soviet invasion, however, occurred at a time when Iranian attention was focused on relations with the United States following the seizure of the U.S. Embassy in November 1979 and the beginning of the prolonged hostage crisis. The episode was an absolute boon to the Soviet Union and undoubtedly played an important part in deferring any substantial clash between the USSR and Iran because many Iranians were unwilling to provoke the USSR, which gave Iran general support over the issue while still asserting the principle of diplomatic immunity. It was noticeable that it was those Iranians who were opposed to the hostage takers and who sought an improvement of relations with the United States who were most vocal in their criticisms of Soviet actions in Afghanistan—in particular, the foreign minister, Sadiq Qutbzadah (executed for conspiracy by the Islamic Republic in September 1982) and the finance minister, soon to be president, Abulhasan Bani Sadr. These critics accused the USSR of aiming at a position from which it could dominate the Indian Ocean. In June 1980 Qutbzadah linked his criticism of Soviet designs in Afghanistan with the Soviet Union's invasion of Iran in 1941, noted that the former invasion was justified by reference to Articles 5 and 6 of the 1921 Soviet-Iranian Treaty, and pointed out that the USSR had refused to accept the unilateral abrogation of these articles by the Islamic Republic in 1979. He implied that the

USSR was reserving its right to attack Iran if the situation justified such an action, an implication that was doubtless just, although the action would be much more of a last resort than Qutbzadah indicated.[2]

On 27 December 1980, on the anniversary of the Soviet invasion of Afghanistan, there was a powerful and violent demonstration by Afghans outside the Soviet Embassy in Tehran. On that occasion the USSR abandoned its moderate line and roused itself to make it clear, in a note dated 28 December, that the Soviet Union would act to protect its own diplomats if the Iranian government could not keep demonstrators in check. In reply the prime minister of Iran, Muhammad Ali Raja'i, said that if the USSR would withdraw from Afghanistan, such incidents would not occur. The USSR then complained that Iran had done nothing to punish those guilty of damaging Soviet property. Raja'i rejected any Soviet right to interfere and in his turn complained, as Qutbzadah had done before him, that the USSR was behaving in the same way as the United States.[3] This charge was particularly wounding to the USSR, which has consistently gone to great pains to establish that there is a fundamental difference between its own principled behavior and that of the imperialist United States. On the Iranian side the charge is a key to sorting out attitudes within the Iranian system: on the one hand are those like Khumayni who have consistently argued that the United States is the major enemy and the USSR is a lesser evil and on the other hand those who have attempted to put them into the same category. The implications for the future direction of Iranian policy are clear although to date, the Khumayni line of the great and little Satans has triumphed.

The line taken by Raja'i concerning the Afghan issue was repeated by a number of Iranian spokesmen in the following months. In February 1981 an Iranian delegation to Uzbekistan, led by Jalal al-Din Farsi, criticized Soviet intervention in Afghanistan and other Soviet policies. In relation to the question of negotiations to settle the Afghan problem Iran took an uncompromising line, one much less flexible, indeed, than that of the Pakistan government. Iran refused to take part in any talks until the Soviet forces were withdrawn; and Iranian plans for Afghanistan, unveiled in November 1981, envisaged a pure Muslim state in Afghanistan, backed by a Muslim army.[4]

A large number of Afghan refugees (the number is uncertain but more moderate estimates range between one-quarter and one-half million) had fled to Iran mainly since the Soviet invasion of Afghanistan and were located principally in the eastern provinces of Iran. Several political and military groups were formed among these refugees and some of the Pakistan-based guerrilla groups also set up offices in Iran. The cause of the refugees was publicized on radio, television, and in the newspapers and, although there is no conclusive evidence, it is highly probable that the military groups used

Iranian territory as a base for military operations in Afghanistan, being permitted to pass virtually unhindered by Iranian frontier guards.

By contrast with the frequent violent attacks made on the Pakistan government for allegedly interfering in Afghanistan by aiding the guerrillas and for refusing to negotiate directly with the Karmal regime in Afghanistan, the attitude of the Soviet government to Iran's similar and even less conciliatory behavior has been extraordinarily mild. Indeed, the Karmal regime in Afghanistan (and it is reasonable to regard any statement emanating from the Afghan Foreign Ministry as being a Soviet production since neither in language nor in sentiment do such pronouncements ever deviate by a hair's breadth from the official Soviet line and are in contrast to internal announcements) has consistently lavished the most fulsome praise upon Khumayni at every opportunity. It is true that from time to time the Soviet press has complained about the activities of Afghan refugees in Iran—notably those of the Pakistan-based groups—(for example, Burhan al-Din Rabbani was accused of stirring up trouble in Sistan and Baluchistan) and has suggested that they were supported by "powerful figures in Iran."[5] Soviet sympathizers in the *Majlis* have been encouraged to ask for curbs to be placed on Afghan refugee activities and the Baku-based radio station, the National Voice of Iran, has warned that the refugees were being manipulated by the familiar demons of imperialism—the CIA, Mossad and company—and that they were being drawn into a plot against the Islamic Republic. But a scrutiny of these complaints shows that the Islamic Republic itself and Khumayni in particular are depicted as innocent parties in danger of being imposed upon by unscrupulous conspirators; the approach is quite unlike that adopted in the case of Pakistan and demonstrates once more the extreme caution the USSR has adopted in its dealings with Iran.

It is clear that there is in Iran both general and government support for the refugees, although there is also evidence, as there is in Pakistan, that in some areas where there are large concentrations of refugees there is friction between them and the local population. No doubt, as in Pakistan, there is a general wish that Iran should be relieved of this burden. The National Voice of Iran has attempted to exploit this feeling and has argued that Iran should accept what the Soviet Union would like to be the facts, namely that the Afghan revolution is irreversible; that neither the revolution nor the presence of Soviet troops in Afghanistan poses any threat to Iran; and that the sooner Iran accepts the situation the sooner it will be rid of the burdens of hostility.[6] So far Iran has proved quite impervious to these arguments; the refugees have been permitted to continue their activities; and Iran has come no nearer to negotiations than to agree to be a reluctant semiparticipant in the Geneva talks.

The Iran-Iraq War

The Iran-Iraq war, which broke out in September 1980, presented the Soviet Union with a difficult problem. The close relations between the USSR and Iraq had been cemented in 1972 by a treaty of friendship. During the 1970s trade between the two countries grew rapidly, and the USSR had been the major supplier of military equipment to Iraq. During the late 1970s, however, the warmth of these relations diminished for a variety of reasons, including Afghanistan, the treatment of Communists in Iraq, the Soviet unwillingness to supply Iraq with all the weapons requested, and the closer Soviet relations with Iraq's rival, Syria, which culminated in the Soviet-Syrian treaty of friendship of October 1980. Nevertheless, despite this relative coolness, Iraq, as a secular, modernizing state set upon the socialist road of development, looked to the USSR for support against an aggressive Muslim regime. Iraq did not receive that support. Instead the USSR adopted a policy of neutrality.[7]

The USSR found the Iran-Iraq war intensely embarrassing, since she wished for good relations with both countries. If she sided with Iran her position in the Arab world in general would be damaged; if she sided with Iraq she would incur the hostility of Iran, the possible consequences of which hostility will be considered below. But for the USSR the worst feature of the war was the threat that the resulting disorder in the region might drive other powers to seek shelter with the United States, which could return in even greater strength than before through the Rapid Deployment Force. So ill did the war serve Soviet interests that she could only conclude that it must be for the benefit of the United States—using the same type of facile and false reasoning that afflicts many Western analyses of regional problems. From concluding that the war could only benefit the United States it was an easy step to the further conclusion that the United States must have fostered the war, or at least it was found convenient to exhibit such a conviction to the world.[8]

Neutrality is a policy easier to enunciate than to execute. Since Iraq was far more dependent upon Soviet weaponry than was Iran, to stop supplies of weapons completely would be in effect to favor Iran. Although the evidence is deficient it seems likely that the USSR reduced shipments of arms to Iraq very considerably but maintained, through intermediaries, some supplies of replacements and spares. Iran frequently complained about Soviet arms deliveries to Iraq. Although there is again no certainty about the matter, it does not seem that the USSR has supplied weapons to Iran. In October 1980 Raja'i claimed that the USSR had offered Iran arms but that he had spurned the offer.[9] Too much should not, however, be made about the question of arms supplies. Since the business fell into the hands of governments it has become one of the most familiar techniques of black propaganda to claim that your enemy is receiving arms either from his enemy or yours or from some power fashionably obnoxious to the international community: one almost regrets the passing of Zakharov and his cosmopolitan arms-dealing colleagues; at least we could all hate them without disturbing the tranquility of interstate relations.

A major Iranian complaint against the USSR was that the USSR had failed to condemn Iraq as the aggressor, despite the fact that it was evident that Iraq had attacked Iran and had occupied large tracts of Iranian territory. The USSR refused to condemn Iraq, but Soviet policy was plainly influenced by the circumstance of Iraqi aggression. When the fortunes of war swung the other way and Iran expelled Iraqi forces from southwest Iran and mounted an offensive against Basra, it was reported that the Soviet Union had endeavored to persuade Iran not to cross into Iraqi territory.[10] After the failure of these endeavors the Soviet Union appeared to incline more toward support of Iraq without abandoning the general stance of neutrality. The attitude of the USSR in this matter reveals the familiar preference for upholding international law and the inviolability of state boundaries, the common posture of the defensive power from which the USSR departs only when convinced that it can do so with impunity.

Ideology

The last point that may be considered is that of ideology. How does the USSR categorize the Iranian revolution? The answer to that question is not easy to discover because in the serious Soviet journals there has been a marked absence of the usual type of analysis of such events. The standard description of the revolution employed by Soviet commentators is that it is antimonarchical and anti-imperialist. As far as it goes this description is unobjectionable: the revolution was plainly against the shah and, translating the word *imperialism* from its Soviet code use, the revolution was also certainly against the United States. But the description does not go very far. What, for example, do Soviet writers think the revolution was for? The answer to that is more or less silence. At the CPSU conference of 23 February 1981, President Brezhnev said that Islamic movements could be progressive or reactionary—"everything depends on the real and actual content of this or that movement." In the case of Iran the foreign-policy fruits were seemingly progressive—that is they were in accordance with the interests of the USSR—since the result of the revolution was to dislodge the United States from strong positions on the southern borders of the USSR. In relation to Afghanistan the progressive fruits were less visible.

With respect to internal developments, however, Soviet commentators found much more difficulty in identifying progressive fruits or in deciding what was the content of the Iranian revolution. In general Soviet reporting of events has been neutral. Soviet commentators remarked that there were no proposals the USSR would recognize as constituting major social or economic reforms—nor any suggested solution to the nationalities problem on which the USSR laid considerable stress. During the internal political crisis in Iran that occurred in the spring and early summer of 1981 and culminated in the dislodging of President Bani Sadr by the Islamic Republican party, there were hints that the USSR might be coming off the fence. One Soviet commentator did indicate a preference for the Bani Sadr party (despite its stronger opposition to Soviet policy) on the grounds that there was no evidence that the Islamic Republican party could run a modern state.[11] The USSR also criticized certain features of the revolution including the executions of the *Mujahhidin i-Khalq*. In 1982, Soviet criticisms of the way in which the revolution was developing became stronger. On 9 March *Pravda* published an important article on Iran, the first serious discussion of problems for a long period, in which Iran was warned that "right-wing groups" were jeopardizing relations between Iran and the USSR and in doing so were endangering Iran's economic prosperity, an apparently clear threat that Soviet economic sanctions might eventually be applied against Iran.

The best source for Soviet views of Iran is still, however, the National Voice of Iran. On 13 September 1982, this radio station broadcast a commentary concerning the difficulties of the revolution, alluded to the decline in production and employment and the increase of inflation, complained of mischief makers who equate the USSR with the United States and exploit anti-Sovietism, and demanded that the revolution should resume its anti-imperialist popular character and that critics of the USSR should be silenced.

The Iranian complaint about the Soviet attitude toward the revolution is that the USSR has missed its central feature, namely that the revolution is Islamic. The antimonarchical and anti-imperialist features, Iranian leaders assert, are only incidental. In a fascinating exchange that took place in the early part of 1981, Ali Raja'i complained that the USSR could not understand the Islamic revolution because it was not in the Soviet catalog of revolutions. He could extract from the Soviet ambassador only the Delphic statement that the Iranian revolution was "profound and peculiar."[12] Raja'i's observation was perfectly just. The USSR has no ideological way of accommodating the Islamic revolution. In the Marxist vision of human history secularization is bound up with progress; religion could be permitted to endure as a private activity but it had no public role. A revolution mounted with the object of giving religion a new, more prominent, place in public affairs was incomprehensible unless it could be seen as a temporary reactionary episode. All Soviet experience and ideology suggested that the next step from the rule of the shah should have been a national democratic revolution. An Islamic revolution was almost a contradiction in terms.

From this cursory examination of some leading features of Soviet-Iranian relations since 1978 a clear picture emerges. The Soviet Union was pleased to observe the dismissal of the United States from the Iranian scene but was dismayed at the prospect that opened up within Iran. It lacked any clear understanding of the revolution, was unable to discern the direction it would take, and was increasingly disturbed by developments during 1980-1982. On the foreign-policy front the revolution challenged Soviet policies in Afghanistan and, by destroying regional stability, threatened to strengthen ties between the Gulf states and the United States. The USSR had not liked the pre-1978 U.S. presence in the northern tier but it had grown accustomed to it and had worked out a reasonably successful policy of diminishing risks to itself by cultivating good relations with Turkey and Iran. The old familiar evil began to look, in the post-1978 situation, to be more comfortable than the new alternative of a U.S. military presence in the Gulf. On the internal front it seems probable that the USSR had thought it likely (as did many Western commentators) that Islamic fervor would soon subside after the triumph of the revolution, the *ulama* would return to their *madrassas*, a middle-class, leftist-inclined National Front government would emerge in Iran and create conditions in which the procommunist Tudeh party might hope to flourish. In fact the ulama have invaded government, the National Front has been virtually extinguished, the Bani Sadr group thrown out, and more recently the Tudeh party attacked, its leaders driven underground and its newspapers closed. Far from losing its peculiar Islamic character, the revolution, through the Committees, the Revolutionary Guards, and above all the dominance of Ayatallah Khumayni, has strengthened its Islamic element.

Soviet Caution

In the years since 1978 Soviet policy toward Iran has been characterized by great caution. The Soviet Union has played for time in the diminishing hope that the revolution would ultimately work to the advantage of the USSR. In the meantime Soviet policy has aimed at encouraging the Muslim revolutionaries to exhaust their strength in attacking the United States; in this context the long hostage crisis of November 1979 to January 1981 was a priceless boon to the USSR since it deflected anti-Soviet trends that had begun to emerge in Iran. Subsequently, U.S. policy in the Gulf and the Indian Ocean has provided the USSR a continuing basis for successful diversion of Iranian interest; Iran could not afford two mighty enemies and the constant rumblings made by the RDF has sufficed to convince most Iranian leaders that the United States is the real enemy. But it may not be possible to deflect criticism of the USSR indefinitely in this way. The Iran-Iraq war, Afghanistan, and other problems appear to be leading toward increasing tension between the USSR and Iran and growing criticism of Soviet policies in Iran, a marked feature of the second half of 1982. On the Soviet side also there have been recent signs that the USSR is finding it more difficult to maintain that silence about events in Iran that it found to be the most convenient device in the light of both its ideological incomprehension and tactical needs. The Soviet hope that the revolution would develop in the way Moscow wished has not been realized so far and while, in the long run, the revolution may yet take the formerly expected course, the long run is beginning to look an uncomfortable distance away. For the sake of its own prestige the USSR may soon be obliged to produce its own disturbing analysis of the Iranian revolution. The attitude of Mr. Micawber is not one that any superpower can adopt forever.

The Iranian Revolution

Unlike Marxism-Leninism, Western modernization theory does not have any major problem in accommodating the Iranian revolution. In traditional Iran the major political classes (apart from the monarchy and its immediate supporters) were the tribes, the landlords and the ulama. The Pahlavi revolution, conducted by father and son, remodeled the Iranian political scene. There was a great expansion of government activity at the expense of the power of nongovernmental institutions; the tribes were greatly reduced both as a proportion of the population and in their power; the landlords were deprived of a significant share in political power and their wealth was reduced; and the ulama were thrust out of their traditional preserves of law and education. As the White Revolution gathered force Iran seemed securely in the hands of a new middle class of civilians and army officers whose interests were closely linked to the Pahlavi program. If any threat to Pahlavi rule did emerge it was thought that it would come from this group: any coup could be likely to result in a republic, the partition of the Pahlavi share of the spoils among other men, and a continuation of the Pahlavi program of modernization without the shah.

Such forecasts were overturned by an unnoticed feature of the White Revolution, or rather a feature whose significance had been overlooked. Industrialization and urbanization had brought great numbers of immigrants from rural areas to the cities, especially to Tehran. The new immigrants resented the monopoly of power and wealth by the Westernized middle class. In opposition to the values of this class they asserted the values with which they themselves were most familiar, those of Islam. In other Muslim countries similar groups of immigrants threw out their own leaders, but in Iran they were able to draw upon the disaffected ulama. The old class of landed notables, now securely entrenched in business and the professions but still retaining its ancient hostility to the *parvenu* Pahlavis, went along with the tide, in the opportunistic hope that they could eventually master it. The consequence was the Islamic revolution.[13]

There is a major division between the ulama and their followers, involving both an ideological difference concerning whether it should be the so-called principles of Islam that should be applied or the letter of the *sharia* and also a difference about who should have power. Although so far the political ulama have secured their dominance, it is quite another question whether they can retain it indefinitely against those who want a very different type of program for the republic. In the long run the demands of the new immigrants may only be capable of satisfaction through a program that, in its essentials if not in its appearance, is very much closer to that formerly espoused by Muhammad Riza Shah. The question remains for Westerners as for the USSR: how long is the long run? And in the meantime, what will happen to Soviet-Iranian relations?

Explaining Soviet Policy: Aggressive Views

There are two broad views of Soviet policy in the northern tier/Indian Ocean area. One view holds that Soviet policy is aggressive: that the USSR aims at extending its power into the region and eventually dominating it. Several theories have been propounded to explain this movement: they include ideological arguments—the USSR aims to spread communism throughout the world by all means including force; economic reasons—the USSR aims to expand its trade with the region and gain control of supplies of Middle Eastern oil to supplement its own allegedly diminishing reserves; and strategic—the historical search for a warm-water port and the exigencies of superpower conflict. I have discussed these theories elsewhere and in this chapter will only repeat my conclusions.[14] The ideological theories run counter to the observed conduct of Soviet foreign policy; the USSR has no important economic stakes in the region, does not need oil, and has no wish to block Western supplies. And the historical argument is worthless—history shows that both czarist Russia and the USSR have always rejected policies aimed at the possession of a warm-water base on the Indian Ocean on the grounds that such a base would be a hostage to fortune. Only the superpower exigency theories have some merit. The Soviet Union does use the Indian Ocean and wishes to have a naval presence that will at least contest the Western claim to exclusive rights in the area. The Soviet Union is concerned with containing China and needs to be able to assist its clients, allies, and friends in the region, and the USSR does want political influence in Asia and Africa in order to compete with the West. Opportunities will arise to advance Soviet interests and the USSR wishes to be in a position to take advantage of them. Other things being equal, therefore, it may be said that superpower rivalry requires the USSR to seek a preponderant position in Iran that will make available Iranian resources to the USSR and enable her to operate with greater freedom and facility in the whole Indian Ocean region. But, of course, other things are not equal. There is a price to be paid for such a position and while no one can say what the future will bring the historical evidence suggests that the Soviet Union is very unwilling to divert the resources from Europe and the Far East to her southern frontier, which would be required to maintain such a position; one Afghanistan appears to be more than enough.

Defensive Views

The second view of Soviet policy in the Indian Ocean region stresses its defensive character and points to the requirements of border defense. The Soviet Union endeavors to protect all its frontiers with weak buffer states, preferably under its direct control, and to exclude the influence of its major international rivals from these regions. No doubt, in an ideal world the USSR would like to see on its southern frontier a satellite system comparable to that existing in Eastern Europe, although the problems of maintaining such a screen are not easy to solve. But in the state of affairs that has obtained since 1921, it has sought, with few exceptions, to maintain good relations with friendly regimes in Turkey, Iran, and Afghanistan. The departure from this pattern with the invasion of Afghanistan in December 1979 seems not to have been a change sought by the USSR.

Soviet Muslims and Events in Iran

To the usual problems associated with preserving secure frontiers a special problem presents itself on the Soviet Union's southern flank. This is the problem of the Soviet Muslims. Broadly speaking, the majority of peoples inhabiting the areas of the USSR contiguous with Iran are Muslim and speak Turkish and Iranian languages. A danger exists that these Soviet Muslims might become disaffected toward Soviet power as a result of the inspiration of events in Iran. In the West there has been much speculation concerning this possibility and there has also been some comment on the matter in the USSR. It may be helpful to offer some views on the question here.[15]

The most prominent fact about the Soviet Muslims is that their number is increasing much more rapidly than the number of other Soviet citizens, to the extent that by the end of the century one in every four Soviet citizens may be a Muslim (some demographers deny that this situation will occur and argue that the present high rate of natural increase among the Muslim population will soon begin to fall and that the reproduction rate of Soviet Muslims will conform to that of other Soviet groups). It is certain, however, that whatever the precise figures, the proportion of Muslims will increase substantially and, given also the increase of skills among them, various possibilities arise. First, because of the age distribution of the population a high proportion of the Soviet army will be composed of Muslims, who may not be content with their present lowly position in that institution. Second, there will be (and already are) demands for jobs for Muslims to be created by diverting an increasing amount of Soviet investment to the Muslim areas. Such a demand is not popular in non-Muslim areas but the alternative, of encouraging a transfer of Muslims to European Russian cities, seems to be even more unpopular among European Russians and Muslims alike. Third, in political terms a larger, more vocal Muslim population will demand a greater share in Soviet policymaking both in the Muslim-majority republics and at the Union level.

This line of argument assumes a clear distinction between the interests of Soviet Muslims and non-Muslims and Soviet writers deny that such a distinction exists. They argue that political divisions drawn on such lines are a product of capitalist society and do not exist in Soviet society. The Soviet author of a recent article on the subject denounced myths of a disintegrating Soviet empire and held that material advances, socialist ideas of internationalism, the Russian language, and other factors would bind the Soviet peoples together.[16]

Western writers have taken a different view. They point to the prevalent signs of cultural differences and presume that these will be developed into political divisions based on either religion or ethnicity. In relation to religion they point to the signs of the growing strength of Islam in the USSR. At the popular level there is extensive evidence of the activities of Sufi brotherhoods in the Caucasus, which appear to offer a parallel, nonofficial form of social organization. At the official level there is the much greater strength of organized Islam through the official bodies set up by the Soviet government. For various reasons the Soviet government has chosen to make extensive use of Islam in its relations with outside Muslim powers and in consequence has been obliged to create and staff an elaborate Muslim organization within the USSR. The personnel of this organization tend to be young, able, and well-trained men whose experience embraces both traditional Islam and modern culture. They could be formidable leaders of any Muslim opposition to Soviet control.

Despite these interesting indications it would not appear that the USSR has much to worry about at the moment. The Sufi brotherhoods flourish in the isolated and always distinctive Caucasus and there is little evidence that they enjoy anything like the same influence in the much more significant central Asian republics. And the official Muslim hierarchy appears to be the loyal supporter of Soviet power and could represent an important means of social control rather than lead any ebullient Muslim revival; in short, to act in the same way as the ulama have acted in most Muslim countries. Third, and more importantly, what appears to be an essential precondition of a Muslim revivalist movement does not exist in the USSR. This precondition is the existence of the sharia, the divinely ordained Muslim law, as a reference point. All revivalist movements have demanded the restoration of the sharia, although what they mean by this demand is not always clear. But in the USSR sixty years of Soviet rule has left the sharia apparently dead and buried. Soviet citizens live under Soviet law and there is no evidence of any wish to replace that law with the sharia. In this respect the Soviet Union conforms more nearly to the situation of Turkey, where no extensive revivalist movement exists. Without the sharia a Muslim revival looks to be impossible.

Ethnonationalism

The second possibility is that the Soviet Muslims may assert an ethnic identity; that is, adopt the type of nationalist program familiar in other regions. In this case there are two alternatives: first, there may be a revival of pan-Turkish ideas, such as existed during the first thirty years of the twentieth century; and second, there may emerge a nationalism based upon the Soviet-created republics of Uzbekistan, Tadzhikistan, and so forth. Of these two alternatives the latter seems the more likely. Pan-Turkism would be Uzbek-dominated and hence unlikely to be congenial to Turkmen, Kazakhs, Kirgiz, and Azeris—to say nothing of Persian-speaking Tadzhiks. Also, too many vested interests have been built into the existing republics that already possess the institutions that could shape and articulate any nationalist feeling. However, although one cannot exclude the possibility of a nationalist upsurge in the republics, it does not seem a likely eventuality in the foreseeable future. Quite apart from the existence of firm Soviet control through a variety of institutions, there is also the circumstance that the rural-urban relationship in the central Asian republics is not the same as that usually associated with a powerful nationalist drive. The factors that could alter this situation would be a rapid industrialization, causing a large movement to the towns, and an exodus of Russian and Ukrainian residents of the central Asian towns, a not impossible notion if there is insufficient investment in central Asia. Given the present rate of Muslim population increase neither of these two factors seem altogether unlikely during the next decade or so.

The conclusion of this very brief survey of the arguments concerning the Soviet Muslims is that the Soviet Muslim problem presents serious long-term dangers to the USSR but the perils are not such as to require in themselves short-term actions against Iran or Afghanistan to stifle any exhibition of Muslim assertiveness or nationalist determination such as might influence Soviet Muslims to try to emulate their neighbors. On the other hand, over a longer period, such exhibitions may produce the contemplated result unless Soviet Muslims can be persuaded that not only their best, but their only, future lies within the USSR.

Soviet Muslims may be persuaded that their best future lies within the USSR by convincing them that the Soviet system can secure them the highest standard of living. And indeed so far the Soviet system has done pretty well by the Soviet Muslims in this respect. Measured by all the usual criteria, they enjoy a better general standard of living than any of their Muslim neighbors, if one excludes the oil-rich Gulf states. But it is a very simple-minded view of politics that equates political contentment with a full belly; as a matter of observation the two move more commonly in the opposite direction; prosperity produces discontent and poverty resignation. Totalitarian states do better to try the other tack, namely to persuade people that their only future lies in acceptance of the status quo. The last proposition brings us to one of the most important dynamics of Soviet policy in the southern borderlands: the assertion of Soviet prestige, an activity that depends not only on the exhibition of Soviet power but the vindication of Soviet ideology.

Ideology and Soviet Fear of the Unknown

Earlier in this chapter I discounted the view that ideology was an important element in an expansionist Soviet policy. Ideology is, however, a very important element in a defensive Soviet policy. Ultimately, the Soviet Union is legitimized by a theory of history. History, said Marx and his successors, is moving in a certain direction and it is futile to resist its flow. History is also irreversible; there may be temporary setbacks but when a society has entered a new stage of development there is no turning back. If people can be persuaded of the truth of this foolish proposition then the Soviet Union is safe, for who but a few fanatics would think it worthwhile to oppose the juggernaut of history. No matter that the Soviet system is inefficient, unpleasant, and occasionally beastly so long as it is believed to be irresistible. For the Soviet Union the worst situation is that its peoples should be persuaded that there are different paths, that nothing is inevitable, and that movements are, after all, reversible. Once such ideas become established, Soviet strength is seen to rest mainly on coercion and when Soviet powers of coercion are diminished its influence may disappear and the Soviet state even begin to crumble.

The peculiar danger of recent events on the southern frontier of the USSR, therefore, is not only that they threaten the security of Soviet frontiers, or that they incite Soviet citizens to disobedience, but that they challenge the Soviet theory of history. The Islamic revolution in Iran is apparently a new and unforeseen direction of development and it challenges the Soviet concept of the proper course of development.

With reference to the Sherlock Holmes story, the inactivity of the bear in the nighttime may therefore be explained as the fear of the unknown. The USSR hopes and believes that ultimately Iran will revert to the orderly path of decreed development, that Islamic revolution will transpose into a familiar national democratic revolution, and that the peculiar Islamic features will be seen only as the transitory survivals of an older system. So far it has been willing to wait for this event although it may now be unhappy about the time it has to wait for the expected change to be accomplished. But as long as possible the Soviet Union will adopt a low profile, swallow the insults, extend the hand of friendship, and try to avoid disputes. But what if this strategy does not work? What other levers does the Soviet Union possess that may be used against Iran?

Economic. The first group of levers that could be used on Iran are economic. Before the Second World War there was little Iran could do in the face of Soviet economic pressure that was regularly applied; northern Iran was wholly dependent upon the Soviet market and on the transit routes to Europe that crossed Soviet territory. By closing the frontier the USSR could bring Iran to heel. It is doubtful whether such levers could have anything like the same effect today; the improvement of Iranian communications has made northern Iran virtually independent of trade with the USSR and Iran now has access to European markets by several routes.

Propaganda. The second lever is propaganda, mainly through the medium of radio. The National Voice of Iran has broadcast from Baku since 1948 and is extensively used to enunciate the Soviet view. But it had little effect when used extensively against Muhammad Riza Shah and it is difficult to see why it should be more useful today. Indeed, the reverse flow of propaganda might be more effective.

Intervention. The third lever is intervention in Iran's internal affairs either through direct action—threats, bribes, and such—or through the Tudeh party. The Tudeh party is in effect the Iranian Communist party and takes its orders from Moscow. During the 1940s and early 1950s it allegedly achieved a position of some power and influence, especially in the army, but the great purge of the mid-1950s crushed the organization. Indeed, one may doubt whether it was ever so powerful as it was claimed to be and speculate that it was, at that time, convenient to label as Tudeh party supporters or sympathizers men who were to be purged for a variety of reasons.

During the events of 1978-1979 the Tudeh party revived. In February 1979, Nur al-Din Kiyanuri, a veteran Iranian Communist who had long been resident in Paris, took over the leadership of the Tudeh party, which thereupon adopted a new line of complete support for Khumayni. In the following months the Tudeh party hardly deviated from the Islamic Republican line, save only in matters relating to executions, the treatment of nationalities, and policy toward the USSR. It has been alleged that Tudeh members supplied information that led to the arrest of several opponents of the Islamic regime. But the Tudeh's loyalty to the Islamic Republic did not pay off in popular support. In the Majlis elections the party received very few votes. The party itself attracted few members from the young, who were drawn either to the mujahhidin or to the Islamic Republican party, and some of its older members drifted away disgusted by the party's support of Islamic policies. During the course of 1982 the Tudeh party itself became the object of increasing attacks by the Islamic Republican party, especially after Iran's relations with the USSR deteriorated following the turn of the tide in the Iran-Iraq war. The Tudeh newspaper, *Payam i-Mardom,* was closed down and the leaders scattered. The Tudeh strategy of hanging on at all costs while its secular rivals were eliminated, in the hope that the party would become the only logical alternative to the Islamic Republican party when that body collapsed, seemed to have failed. It is difficult to believe that the Tudeh party could be a major lever for use by the USSR in the near future.

Ethnic Divisions. The fourth lever the USSR could use would be support of ethnic nationalist movements within Iran; for example, among the Azeris of Azerbaidzhan, the Kurds, the Turkmen, the Baluchis, the Arabs, or among the tribes. It is true that uneasy relations presently exist among several of these groups and there is much discontent against the Tehran government. In 1946 the USSR did play the ethnic card and supported separatist movements in Kurdistan and Azerbaidzhan apparently in the hope of influencing the Tehran government to accept Soviet demands. On that occasion matters went very badly for the USSR and it has avoided the ethnic policy ever since, preferring to seek good relations with stable governments in Tehran. The dangers of such a policy are no less clear today. Support for ethnic separatist movements would make any accommodation with Tehran impossible and would jeopardize relations with Iraq and Turkey. It would also invite the possibility of countervailing Western actions, which could result in the reestablishment of Western power and influence in the region in greater strength than before. Nevertheless, if the USSR ever found it necessary to resort to extreme measures against a hostile government in Tehran, support of ethnic movements in the northern provinces of Iran would seem to be a distinct possibility.

Invasion. When other possibilities are exhausted, the last option is a military invasion. In this event there is nothing that Tehran could do to oppose Soviet actions; but the Soviet Union must shrink from such an action, which would damage—even more than its action in Afghanistan has done—its position in the rest of the world. Also it would inevitably lead to Western action in the Gulf. Short of an Iranian violation of Soviet frontiers or a Western attack on southern Iran, the use of Soviet troops against Iran appears to be highly unlikely.

Conclusions

The possibilities of successful Soviet action against Iran do not seem promising, except at a very heavy price. The Soviet Union must hope that it does not become necessary to embark upon any such venture. It must yet strive to achieve good relations with some government in Tehran. And, if worse came to worse, the Soviet Union might prefer some form of joint action with other powers, even with the West, over unilateral action. Curiously enough, both sides would like to see similar types of government in Tehran. There is also a clear distinction to be made in Iran between the north, where Soviet interests are preponderate, and the south, where those of the West are greatest. In 1907 and 1941 the distinction of interests formed the basis of joint Anglo-Russian action in Iran. It does not seem wholly impossible that it might happen again.

Notes

1. Alvin Z. Rubinstein, "The Soviet Union and Iran Under Khomeini," *International Affairs* (Autumn 1981):599-617.
2. *USSR and Third World,* nos. 4, 5 and 6 (1980):91-92.
3. *USSR and Third World,* nos. 1, 2 (1981):25-26.
4. BBC, *Summary of World Broadcasts (SWB), Far East,* 3 and 12 November 1981.

5. *USSR and Third World,* nos. 3, 4 (1981):57.

6. BBC, *Summary of World Broadcasts (SWB), Middle East,* 12 October 1982.

7. Karen Dawisha, "Moscow and the Gulf War," *World Today* (January 1981).

8. For example, V. Viktorov, "The Persian Gulf: Washington's Imperial Ambitions," *International Affairs,* Moscow, 7 (1982):36.

9. *USSR and Third World,* nos. 4, 5, 6 (1980):90.

10. Radio Iran, 29 August 1982.

11. Alexander Blokin in *Izvestiia,* 13 June 1981.

12. *USSR and Third World,* nos. 1, 2 (1981):26-27.

13. For Western views of the Islamic revival, see the following: John L. Esposito, ed., *Islam and Development* (Syracuse: Syracuse University Press, 1980); G.H. Jansen, *Militant Islam* (London: Pan, 1979); A. Cudsi and Ali E. Hillal Dessouki, *Islam and Power* (London: Croom Helm, 1981); Mohammed Ayoob, ed., *The Politics of Islamic Reassertion* (London: Croom Helm, 1981); Michael Curtis, ed., *Religion and Politics in the Middle East* (Boulder: Westview Press, 1981); William Ochsenwald, "Saudi Arabia and the Islamic Revival," *International Journal of Middle Eastern Studies* 13 (1981):271-286; Metin Heper, "Islam, Polity and Society in Turkey: A Middle Eastern Perspective," *Middle East Journal* 35 (1981):345-363; Ruth McVey, "Islam Explained," *Pacific Affairs* 54, no. 2 (1981):260-287; and M.E. Yapp, "Contemporary Islamic Revivalism," *Asian Affairs* (June 1980):178-195. *Middle East Journal,* Summer 1982, contains a number of useful articles.

14. M.E. Yapp, "Soviet Relations with the Countries of the Northern Tier," in Adeed Dawisha and Karen Dawisha, eds., *The Soviet Union in the Middle East* (London: Heineman, 1982), pp. 24-44.

15. On the Soviet Muslim question, see the following: G. Wheeler, *The Modern History of Soviet Central Asia* (London: Weidenfeld and Nicolson, 1964); A. Bennigsen and C. Lemercier-Quelquejay, *Islam in the Soviet Union* (London: Pall Mall Press, 1967); E. Goldhagen, ed., *Ethnic Minorities in the Soviet Union* (New York: Praeger, 1968); E. Allworth, ed., *Soviet Nationality Problems* (New York: Columbia University Press, 1971); E. Allworth, *The Nationality Question in Soviet Central Asia* (New York: Praeger, 1973); R.A. Lewis, R.H. Rowland, and R.S. Clem, *Nationality and Population Change in Russia and the USSR* (New York: Praeger, 1976); R.A. Lewis and R.H. Rowland, *Population Redistribution in the USSR: Its Impact on Society 1897-1977* (New York: Praeger, 1979); Hélène Carrère D'Encausse, *Decline of an Empire* (New York: Newsweek Books, 1979); J.R. Azrael, ed., *Soviet Nationality Policies and Practices* (New York: Praeger, 1978); B.R. Bociurkiv and J.S. Strong, eds., *Religion and Atheism in the USSR and Eastern Europe* (Toronto: Toronto University

Press, 1975); and G.W. Simmonds, ed., *Nationalism in the USSR and Eastern Europe in the Era of Brezhnev and Kosygin* (Detroit: University of Detroit, 1977). *Soviet Studies* and *Problems of Communism* regularly publish valuable articles on this subject. For Soviet views see, for example, E. Bagramov, "The Soviet Nationality Policy and Bourgeois Falsifications," *International Affairs,* Moscow (June 1977); and V. Pravotorov, "Triumph of the Leninist Policy of Internationalism," *International Affairs,* Moscow (July 1982):54-64.

16. Pravotorov, ibid., pp. 54-64.

12

The Soviet Occupation of Afghanistan

Henning Behrens

The Soviet invasion of Afghanistan in the last days of 1979 and its resultant regional and global impact will be discussed in this chapter in the context of four questions:

1. What were the important historical developments prior to December 1979 that might help us to improve our understanding of the contemporary situation in Afghanistan?
2. Why has the USSR, in contradiction to western experts' predictions, transformed the long-standing Soviet-Afghan relationship into an example of international military aggression?
3. How has the situation in Afghanistan changed since the Soviet occupation and what have been the reverberations of the occupation throughout the region?
4. Why has the Afghanistan conflict not yet been resolved by what has been referred to as a *political solution?*

Historical Developments

Until the eighteenth century when its struggle for independence began, Afghanistan had not appeared as an independent political unit. The territory of contemporary Afghanistan had been for more than two-thousand years a transit area for Hellenistic, Persian, Buddhist, Arabic, and Mongol cultures and invaders in central Asia. The most prominent names in ancient Afghan history are Cyrus the Great (sixth century B.C.), Alexander the Great (328 B.C.), Genghis Khan (1220), and Timur-i-Lang (Tamerlane) (1381). In the sixteenth century one of the descendants of Genghis Khan, Shah Babur, made Kabul the center of his Mongol empire. The Mongols finally were defeated in 1739 by the last great horse nomad, Nadir Shah Ashari, who expanded Persia to the Indus. After Nadir Shah's assassination, the Pashtun leader Ahmad Shah Durrani made use of the chaos in the Persian army and rallied the Afghan tribes. He became the first king of Afghanistan, which in 1747 included the territory of contemporary Cashmir and Pakistan.

At least three lessons can be drawn from this early historical period. First, because of the diversity of cultural influences, there is considerable ethnic heterogeneity within contemporary Afghanistan. The major groups comprising the population consist of Pashtuns (50 percent), Tadzhiks (25 percent), Uzbeks (10 percent), and Turkmens (10 percent). Second, Afghan kings from the beginning have had to balance rivalries between the tribes to establish and maintain a central government. It was Amir Abdur Rahman Khan (1880-1901) who introduced the most important instruments for the nation-building process in Afghanistan: a standing army; a central bureaucracy with responsibilities such as weapons production, taxation, and jurisdiction; and the first steps toward integration of the Muslim clergy. Later kings who neglected these instruments experienced threats to Afghan unity, as for example King Amanullah whose reformist initiatives were criticized and who was forced to resign in 1929 by religious and tribal leaders on the grounds that he had paid insufficient attention to the standing army and the central bureaucracy.

A third lesson can be drawn from Afghan history, particularly of the nineteenth century. The nation-building process was at the same time accelerated and impeded by interference from outside. On the one hand, there was concern with Russian advances in central Asia. From 1734 to 1920, Russia expanded step by step toward the borders of Afghanistan. Between 1860 and the 1890s the czarist empire established control over Kazakhstan, Bukhara, Samarkand, Tashkent, Kokand, Khiva, Merv, and the Pamir. It was not until the Peace of Brest-Litovsk in 1918 that the Soviet Union finally acknowledged the independence of Afghanistan. On the other hand, Britain was heavily involved in the region as an aspect of its presence in India. British interference in Afghan affairs led to three British-Afghan wars (1838-1842, 1878-1880, 1919), the last of which ended with British acknowledgement of Afghan independence. The struggle to assert national identity and autonomy, therefore, was already an important concern for the Afghan people during the nineteenth century.[1]

Twentieth-century developments in Afghanistan are characterized by an important element of continuity but also by the growing importance of Soviet-Afghan relations. King Amanullah took the initiative to improve relations in 1919, the same year in which Afghanistan received a Soviet-constructed radio station as a gift. Treaties of friendship were signed in 1921, 1931, and 1978. The most recent one, the so-called Treaty of Friendship, Good Neighborliness, and Cooperation between the USSR and the Democratic Republic of Afghanistan, formed an important prelude to the events that will be discussed in the second section of this chapter. Since the 1950s a series of additional treaties indicated increasing levels of cooperation. In 1954 three credit agreements were signed and in 1956 both countries agreed on further technical and economic cooperation, which after 1967 led to Afghan gas exports to the USSR. From a postinvasion perspective, one should keep in mind that the USSR and Afghanistan initiated not less than twenty-nine treaties and agreements of a more or less concrete character during the period between April 1978 and December 1979.

In comparison with the continuous development of Soviet-Afghan relations, the domestic political situation in Afghanistan showed sharp discon-
tinuities. In 1973 Muhammad Daoud, former prime minister and cousin to
King Zahir, took over power in a bloodless coup, thus ending the constitutional monarchy in Afghanistan. Daoud had announced a radical political
and social program. But once in power, and to the disappointment of many
Afghans, he relied on a rather conservative inner-cabinet circle to buttress
his authority and drifted steadily to the right.[2] Frustrated by their exclusion
from the political mainstream and by Daoud's failure to produce mean-
ingful reforms, left-wing elements within Afghanistan became more assertive as the government's political base weakened.

Since its creation in 1965 the major left grouping in Afghanistan had
been the *Jamiyat-i-Demokratiki-yi Khalq-i-Afghanistan*, People's Democratic Party of Afghanistan (PDPA) or *Khalq* (Masses) faction, led by Nur
Muhammad Taraki and Hafizullah Amin. In 1967 a major split occurred
within the Khalq between the party's mainstream and an opposition faction led by Babrak Karmal, known after the name of its press organ as the
Parcham (Flag) faction. Personal, ethnic, and political differences occasioned the split and for ten years the two factions functioned independently,
but in 1977 both Khalq and Parcham agreed to form a united opposition to
the failing Daoud regime.

On 27 April 1978, in the wake of the murder of a popular Parcham activ-
ist, subsequent antigovernment demonstrations, and a wave of arrests of leftist leaders, Daoud was overthrown in a coup led by Taraki and Amin of the
Khalq in which Daoud and about one thousand other persons were killed.[3]
A thirty-five-member Revolutionary Council including both Khalq and Parcham leaders assumed power and a Democratic Republic of Afghanistan
was declared. The first Taraki government announced on May 1 consisted
of a cabinet with eleven Khalq and ten Parcham ministers, with Babrak
Karmal as vice president and Hafizullah Amin as foreign minister. Taraki
himself emerged as the dominant figure, simultaneously holding the positions of prime minister, chairman of the revolutionary council, commander
in chief of the armed forces, and secretrary general of the PDPA. The new
government announced a very ambitious program including land reform,
universal education, cultural development, tax reductions, and campaigns
against corruption, smuggling, and drugs. Political realities, however, looked
quite different. The proposed reforms alienated influential elements within
Afghan society and the new leadership could not overcome the traditional
rivalry between Parcham and Khalq within its own ranks.[4]

In July 1978 the dominant Khalq group was able to force key Parcham
leaders to leave the country by adopting a technique utilized in the past by
Daoud—assigning them to ambassadorial posts. Babrak Karmal, for example, became the Afghan ambassador in Prague.[5] Internal difficulties continued to mount, however, as it became obvious that the core program of

the revolution, the land reform, was a failure. The land-reform law, prom-
ulgated in November 1978, intended to reduce land ownership to a maximum of thirty *jerib* (six hectares) in a land where many families had owned
more than one hundred hectares.[6] Resistance to the reform program of the
PDPA, often inspired by Muslim-incited opposition to the secularization
programs, became stronger and stronger. This resistance was directed particularly against the land reforms, with the result that they could not be effectively implemented by the government. As early as September 1978,
Afghan *mujahhidin* ("holy warriors") declared the *jihad* or holy war
against their own government. From March 1979 onward military resistance
could be described as somewhat coordinated.[7]

Government shakeups occurred in August 1978 with the arrest of Parcham activists and the formal expulsion of Karmal and other exiled leaders
from the Revolutionary Council, and in March 1979 with Amin replacing
Taraki as prime minister (though the latter retained his other posts and remained the revolution's leading figure). New political alignments and increasing Soviet involvement could not, however, prevent the domestic situation from further deteriorating. Hundreds, thousands, and finally tens of
thousands of regular Afghan troops deserted and went over to the mujahhidin, often with all their equipment. Even Soviet personnel became victims, as for example during the confrontation at Herat in March 1979,
where at least twenty Soviet advisors were killed. In the springtime and late
summer of 1979, the Soviet Union sent military delegations to Afghanistan
to evaluate the military and political situation through on-the-spot in-
vestigations. The Soviet Union itself increased its presence in Afghanistan,
corresponding to the more threatening activities of the mujahhidin.

In September 1979 the Soviet Union appears to have sponsored an attempt to oust Amin from the leadership of the PDPA. The attempt failed
disastrously, resulting in the murder of Taraki and his family and an Amin-
dominated government. Despite increasingly severe measures, Amin was
unable to contain domestic unrest and resistance and the Soviet presence in
Afghanistan continued to grow. Shortly before Christmas 1979 more than
five thousand Soviet soldiers were stationed in Afghanistan and important
military facilities, including airfields, were under direct Soviet control.
After December 17 this was also the case for the Bagram military airport
near Kabul, and massive troop concentrations in the areas of Fergana,
Frunze, Tashkent and Samarkand indicated growing Soviet preparedness
for military intervention.

Military Intervention

Prior to December 1979 many analysts accepted a Soviet occupation of
Afghanistan as a theoretical possibility, but rejected it as unrealistic and im-

practical. Many counterarguments could indeed be produced asserting disincentives the Soviet Union would encounter when considering such an action. First of all, Peter the Great's dream of access to a warm-water port no longer seems a convincing motivation in explaining Soviet military intervention in Afghanistan. Today the Soviet Union has naval access from the Black Sea through the Dardanelles into the Mediterranean and through the Suez Canal into the Arabic Sea and Indian Ocean. The Soviet navy can use facilities in east Africa and at the southern end of the Arabic peninsula and permanently maintains a considerable warm-water presence that can easily be increased.

Two further arguments against the probability of Soviet military intervention in Afghanistan relate to Soviet-Third World relations and the global East-West conflict. Why should the USSR threaten the degree of influence it has managed to achieve, often at great expense, with the nonaligned countries and the Islamic states? Additionally, the Soviet Union could aggravate its own nationality and minority problems in the event, for example, of fraternization occurring between occupying Muslim troops from Soviet central Asian republics and the Muslims of Afghanistan. During the 1970s, the decade of detente, a military step of such dimensions could obviously be counterproductive. It would not only violate the code of conduct agreed upon by Nixon and Brezhnev, according to which the superpowers should in the future abstain from seeking unilateral advantage, but it could also cause friction or even drastically reduce the level of East-West trade and cooperation. Why should the Soviet Union threaten its economic and technological interaction with the West that enables this, in many respects, still-backward country to narrow the technological gap?

One is struck by the fact that in the autumn of 1979 the emphasis in Western analysis was not so much on justifications for a military intervention as upon excuses allowing the Soviet Union to leave the Khalq regime in Afghanistan alone. After all, the Soviet Union had virtually ignored the PDPA for most of its existence. The party had neither been invited to the Third World congress of Communist parties (1969) nor to the last three congresses of the CPSU (1966, 1971, 1976). In Moscow the Afghan Marxist party had retained the image of being unreliable and overly nationalistic. The PDPA's land-reform program was criticized in the Soviet media because land was being distributed directly to the peasants without even discussing possible forms of collectivization. The fundamental question of whether a preindustrial social and political system such as Afghanistan's, based mainly on tribal structures and feudal forms, was ripe for the socioeconomic and political reforms of the PDPA could easily have been answered in the negative. Finally, it was correctly stressed that superpower rivalry in no way necessitated an intervention. The United States had reduced its development aid for Afghanistan in 1979 and U.S. policy was defined more by a hands-off attitude than a search for expanding influence. U.S. ambassador Adolph Dubs had been killed in Kabul by *Setem-i-Meli* terrorists whose identity remained unknown,[8] and the Iran debacle was exerting an enormously paralyzing effect upon the entire Middle East policy of the Carter administration. But the Soviet military intervention made clear that there had been an academic dimension to the emphasis upon disincentives. Certainly many of the points raised here remain highly interesting and deserve further discussion, but the fact is simply that these themes failed to address the Soviet Union's central concerns as its aircraft and tanks poured into Afghanistan after Christmas 1979.

Using the rational actor model as summarized by Graham Allison,[9] I will attempt to present an overview of the most important hypotheses to be found in the literature addressing the problem of why the Soviet Union chose to occupy militarily Afghanistan.

1. Henry Kissinger, among others, interpreted the military intervention as a case of radical opportunism. Kissinger identified a U.S. loss of "will, capability, and credibility" that had become especially marked by 1979 in the Middle East. A first hypothesis can thus be formulated as follows: *The Soviet Union filled a power vacuum that was caused by the weaknesses of U.S. policies in the region.* This argument is very much in line with the diplomatic image of a rational, calculating, and risk-avoiding Soviet Union and with power-politics theory of which Adolf Berle's work is a good example.[10] History never allows a long-lasting power vacuum. To agree with this hypothesis, as I do, does not mean to assume that it provides a full-scale explanation of Soviet actions. Important additional dimensions, such as the specific situations of all actors and the domestic political contexts must be taken into account. Therefore quite a variety of additional hypotheses have been developed in the literature.

2. The USSR itself has developed three arguments in an attempt to legitimize the Soviet military intervention in Afghanistan: (a) The Afghan government, that is to say the Amin regime, is said to have requested Soviet assistance; (b) the Treaty of Friendship, Good Neighborliness, and Cooperation signed in 1978 obligated the Soviet Union to provide assistance; and (c) self-defense was a primary Soviet motive in accordance with Article 51 of the UN Charter.[11] A second hypothesis can thus be formulated: *Afghanistan's requests for help and a formal obligation to provide assistance induced the Soviet Union to intervene.* It is true that Afghan political leaders, especially after the April Revolution, asked quite frequently for Soviet aid in the form of weapons, development assistance, and such. But as it was succinctly phrased in a session of the Security Council by the representative of Singapore, it is unlikely that the Amin government "invited" Soviet troops to invade the country, to depose the leadership, and to murder Amin himself.[12] This argument hardly requires further comment.

Article 4 of the 1978 Friendship Treaty refers to the friendship treaties between the Soviet Union and Afghanistan of 1921 and 1931 in which independence, acknowledgement of sovereignty, and mutual noninterference are expressly mentioned. Article 51 of the UN charter is also not valid in this case because no armed intervention by a third power took place. The UN resolution of 14 January 1980, in which 104 out of the 152 member states requested the unconditional withdrawal of foreign troops from Afghanistan was but the first in a long series of international condemnations of an act of aggression that clearly defies international law.

3. One of the most frequently encountered hypotheses asserts that *the Afghanistan intervention was the consequence of a long-range Soviet strategy, seeking geostrategic advantages to obtain access to warm waters and to the oil reserves of the Gulf.* It can be granted that Soviet political leaders do have grand designs, an ideological orientation, and a dream of expanding global influence. But I also agree with those who, citing phenomena such as bureaucratic politics or incremental policies, warn us against evaluating every single political act in terms of grand designs, or as others have formulated it, to commit the mistake of so-called monocausal demonology. To discuss the third hypothesis, let us concentrate on the following two questions: what potential advantages might have prompted the Afghanistan intervention in the context of such a long-range strategy, and were these advantages worth the foreign-policy costs the Soviet Union has had to pay? The warm-water argument has already been rejected in this regard. The remaining arguments focus upon access to Gulf oil reserves and the use of Afghanistan as a center for geostrategic expansion in the directions of Iran, Iraq, Pakistan, the Gulf region, and southern Asia.

The geostrategic importance of Afghanistan has been discussed under three headings: (a) Soviet rule in Afghanistan offers the chance for more direct political and military pressure in connection with subversive activities toward Iran and Pakistan; (b) via Afghanistan the Soviet Union is in closer geographic proximity to India; and (c) the central geostrategic argument that Afghanistan can be used as a base for airlifts to other bases in Africa and southern Asia.[13] In reference to points (a) and (b), it is true that the Soviet occupation of Afghanistan, however insecure it may be, must be taken into account as a new power factor in this region of the Middle East. This is especially true for neighboring countries because it demonstrates the willingness of the Soviet Union to make use of military power in situations that allow for opportunism. To make such a statement does not imply that the occupation has been a success. On the contrary, the military stalemate in Afghanistan and the very limited ability of the Soviet Union to assert control over the country have not increased, but rather decreased, Soviet potential for further expansion. The intervention into Afghanistan has presented the Soviets not only opportunities but also liabilities and dilemmas. The refugee problems in Iran and Pakistan and the fact that a nonaligned country has been attacked are additional burdens for relations with nonaligned countries, of which India is a prominent leader. In reference to point (c), it is also true that airbases in Afghanistan can be used for strategic purposes and the further plans of the Soviet Union will without any doubt be to expand and consolidate their military infrastructure in Afghanistan.[14] On the other hand, the reduced distance to the Strait of Hormuz is no longer a very important factor—with the Soviet Union capable of utilizing long-range Backfire bombers. Why didn't the Soviet Union use its strong, if not dominant, relationship with Afghanistan prior to 1979 to build such a military infrastructure? Even if we suppose that because of misperceptions elements of the Soviet leadership failed to calculate all of the disadvantages that an occupation would induce (in terms of economic costs, resentment, and distrust in the Third World; a stronger presence of the United States in the region; setbacks for detente; and so on), the slight potential geostrategic advantages do not at all match even those manifest disadvantages it would have been impossible to ignore.

4. After the Soviet Union discovered that the Afghanistan situation could not be resolved via a blitzkrieg strategy, it is interesting to note that in the media the Soviet population began to be reminded of historical cases such as those of Mongolia, Tadzhikistan, and other central Asian republics now bordering Afghanistan where absorption into the Russian and Soviet spheres of influence occurred as a long-term process. The fourth hypothesis to be found in the literature can be formulated as follows: *The Soviet treatment of Mongolia serves as a historical precedent.*[15] the Soviet Union sent soldiers into Mongolia in 1921 after a Soviet-created Provisional People's Government of Mongolia had requested help. Soviet forces did not leave until 1925, and not before Outer Mongolia had been transformed into a Soviet protectorate. The case of Mongolia is also posed as an ideological model, proving that a preindustrial country with a feudalistic social structure can begin, without a capitalist transition phase, a process of socialist construction.

5. Years before the Soviet Afghanistan intervention in a speech to the Twenty-fifth Party Congress in February 1976, Brezhnev posed some of the problems related to such an occupation in a discussion of the fate of the Allende government in Chile. According to his speech, the "tragedy of Chile" has demonstrated that a revolution must be in a position to defend itself.[16] Peaceful coexistence does not exclude the possibility of involvement by the Soviet Union in the affairs of other countries to insure that the "world revolutionary process" can develop in a favorable manner. This assertion, that Communist revolutions (in our case the April Revolution of 1978 in Kabul) must be irreversible, led to Brezhnev's statement in *Pravda* on 13 January 1980, asserting that Afghanistan must never become a "second

Chile.'' We may thus formulate as a fifth hypothesis that *the Soviet intervention was designed to prevent the reversal of a socialist revolution by counterrevolutionary forces.*

6. An additional hypothesis may be formulated in the following manner: *the Soviet Union's intervention in Afghanistan was a consequence of Afghan domestic problems and a series of mistakes and miscalculations on the part of Soviet policy toward Afghanistan.*

The *Times* of 2 January 1980 described the Soviet intervention in Afghanistan as a "defensive aggression," and Theo Sommer has reduced the Soviet decision to the simple desire to put an end to the chaos across its southern borders.[17] These statements imply that the Soviet goal in Afghanistan was mainly of a so-called negative-defensive nature. The USSR did not intend an improvement beyond the status quo but sought to avoid a deterioration in the region that could not only bring an end to the traditionally positive Soviet-Afghan relationship but also provoke unrest within the Soviet Union's own Islamic Soviet republics. It is questionable whether the Islamic problem was a primary concern of the Soviet leadership at the time it was contemplating intervention. It remains true, nevertheless, that the Soviet Union has not yet succeeded in finding a more moderate political strategy that could provide Afghanistan with space for independent development as well as provide the prerequisites for a more constructive and cooperative relationship with the USSR. As the historical section of this chapter attempted to demonstrate, by 1979 the Soviet Union had reached a point of decision and was required to choose, to cite Brezhnev, either "to help friendly Afghanistan" or to risk the loss of the entire experiment in Soviet-Afghan cooperation.[18]

Our brief discussion of these six hypotheses may be summarized as follows:

The Soviet Union did perceive a power vacuum in the region and, according to Kissinger's formula of *radical opportunism,* the risks of military intervention could be calculated to be at a comparatively low level.

Given the decreasing importance of access to warm waters, the high risk of a superpower confrontation in the Gulf region, the relatively small advantage to be gained by the use of an occupied Afghanistan as a geostrategic base, and keeping in mind the high foreign-policy costs intervention implied, expansion in the context of a long-term Soviet strategy may be rejected as a primary goal of the Afghanistan intervention.

Ideological and operational parallels indicate that the Soviet Union is striving in the long run to achieve a status for Afghanistan that may be described as *Mongolization.*

The formula *Afghanistan must not become a second Chile* is not in contradiction with the Soviet definition of peaceful coexistence and bears important elements of face-saving with respect to the Third World.

The Afghanistan intervention had as a primary goal the avoidance of a deterioration of the status quo. It was a *defensive aggression* undertaken in order not to risk the entire experiment of Soviet-Afghan cooperation.

The Impact of the Occupation

After nearly three years of warfare in Afghanistan the military situation seems to be more or less at a stalemate despite the presence of approximately 120,000 Soviet soldiers. Several factors may be mentioned to help explain why the Soviet Union, with the resources of a superpower, has not been able to solve its Afghanistan problem via a quick military victory.

Soviet forces are trained primarily for nuclear, chemical, and conventional warfare, not for guerilla warfare in an area such as the Hindu Kush mountains. One military expert has compared the Soviet occupation forces to a "blind giant with a big stick" trying to "knock down" the mujahhidin from the mountains.[19] Other sources have noted tactical miscalculations, particularly excessive reliance upon unwieldy forays by tanks and other armored vehicles preceded by air assaults from MiG fighters and helicopter gunships. Such assaults have caused enormous destruction but have not tended to achieve substantial tactical advantages. When Soviet and Afghan forces withdraw from an area it may be reoccupied by the mujahhidin. Permanent control is not etablished and Soviet forces continue to be exposed to mines, booby traps, and sniper fire. The Soviets fight defensively from within armored vehicles and aircraft, and their raids do little to change the military status quo.

The Soviets have attempted to alter their tactics. Lighter tanks and more light mobilized units have been introduced, guerrilla training for soldiers has been instituted, command has been decentralized into seven military districts, and increasing reliance has been placed upon the Mi-24 helicopter. In spite of such measures, however, Soviet military control has remained very limited. Prior to 27 December 1979 the Amin government and the Afghan regular army were able to control about 30 percent of Afghanistan's national territory. After nearly three years of occupation it may be estimated that the Soviets together with the Afghan regular army, operating from bases in the half-dozen largest cities, are able to control not much more than 10 percent of the national territory. This means very little effective control in a nation like Afghanistan where the majority of the population lives in the countryside.

One major change that has certainly worked to the disadvantage of the Soviets has been the shrinking number of regular Afghan troops. They have declined from 80,000 to about 35,000 within less than one year of the occupation. The Afghan regular army consisted of thirteen divisions (three tank and ten infantry divisions) and a number of specialized brigades, plus an air force utilizing about 170 tactical aircraft. Aircraft, weapons, and military vehicles had been overwhelmingly imported from the Soviet Union. There were a great number of Soviet military advisors, and Afghan officers had been trained in Soviet military doctrine and tactics. But for many soldiers, Islamic roots outweighed the order to fight for a pro-Soviet government. The effects of the mass desertions were magnified by the fact that many deserters brought their weapons with them, thus placing them at the disposal of the mujahhidin (including the Soviet AK-47 rifle, the anti-tank weapon RPG-7, and even SAM-7s). According to estimates by the mujahhidin, about 90 percent of their weapons are either captured or brought by deserters. Recent measures reducing the age for military service, instituting forced recruitment, raising pay levels, and declaring a general mobilization for all reservists under thirty-five (according to the general mobilization order issued by Babrak Karmal in September 1981) indicate that the government is trying by all means to reverse the trend of a shrinking Afghan army.

An additional disappointment for the Soviets was the behavior of Muslim troops from the central Asian republics of the USSR. Rather than providing the Afghan population with an example of how Soviet power, national identity, and Islam could coexist, these soldiers demonstrated an even lower morale than the average Soviet soldier. They have been especially reluctant to fight. Some are reported to have offered their gun for a *Qur'an,* and many have sympathized with the mujahhidin or even deserted. The Soviets seem to have learned a lesson and sent most of them back home.[20]

The most dramatic change the war has wrought in Afghanistan has been the destructive impact upon the population. This would include civilian victims, the casualties of the mujahhidin, and an exodus of roughly 4 million refugees now living in camps (about 2.5 million in Pakistan and 1.5 million in Iran). This is a reflection of general resistance to the Soviet occupation. There is no doubt that the Soviet intervention has rallied very heterogenous mujahhidin groupings under the general banner of a holy war. But it should not be overlooked that the Afghan resistance also consists of religious groups (orthodox and progressive), national-democratic groups (civil servants, industrialists, students), and a group of non-Moscow-oriented Marxists and Communists. All are operating to some extent from Pakistan, but have not yet been amalgamated into a common organization. Effective coordination of resistance efforts, therefore, has not been achieved. One should also keep in mind that the political solutions proffered by these different groups vary widely, including constitutional monarchy, Western democracy, Islamic republic, and communism à la Mao. Underlying political, philosophical, and tactical disagreements is Afghanistan's traditional tribal heterogeneity, which has certainly not disappeared.

It is not surprising that the domestic political situation in Afghanistan has been stagnating. The aims of the revolution, especially the land-reform and literacy programs, cannot be effectively implemented due to lack of control over the countryside. Most ministries and administrations lack adequately trained personnel and cannot function properly. The exodus of medical doctors, scientists, teachers, and technicians since 1978 has not been compensated for by an infusion of experts from East-bloc countries. In spite of the unpopularity of Babrak Karmal as head of a Soviet puppet government, some Afghans have been ready to concede that his government tries to avoid repression and social provocation as much as possible. There have nevertheless been repeated rumors reporting Karmal's imminent ouster by the Soviets. Moscow has not been successful in its attempts to integrate the two left factions in Afghanistan, the Khalq and Parcham. The creation of the National Fatherland Front in June 1981 did not lead to the kind of progress in unifying diverse groups within Afghanistan that had been desired. Furthermore, the appointment in 1981 of Sultan Ali Keshtmand as prime minister, with Karmal remaining leader of the PDPA and head of state, indicates an ongoing rivalry between the two factions that inhibits and destabilizes an already weak regime. Both Keshtmand and Karmal are stalwarts of the Parcham, and Keshtmand was imprisoned and tortured during the Taraki-Amin period by order of Assadullah Sarwari, now leader of the Khalq.[21]

In contrast to military and political immobility, steady progress has been made with Afghan-Soviet development projects seeking to improve the country's economic infrastructure and to exploit more effectively its energy resources. In 1982 a bridge over the Amu Darya and an enlarged river-harbor facility were completed. But the fact that the Soviet Union is now importing virtually all of the Afghan natural-gas production (with the result that the Afghan petrochemical and electric plants in the area of Mazar-i-Sharif are being forced to switch to coal) indicates that Afghan-Soviet development projects are not in all respects well balanced.[22]

Moving briefly to the regional level, John C. Campbell has correctly noted that the Soviet invasion of Afghanistan put the problems of the entire Middle East in a new light.[23] If we focus on three critical regional dilemmas—the problem of security in the Gulf region and access to Gulf oil, the conflict between Israel and the Arab states, and the conflict between India and Pakistan—it becomes evident that the Soviet occupation of Afghanistan has had substantial, though differing, effects. In regard to the Gulf security problem, one form of Western reaction to the occupation has been increased interest in elaborating the infrastructure of an effective rapid-deployment force. This would include a build-up of bases and facilities in southern Asia and possibly in the Gulf region itself. As far as the Arab-Israel conflict is concerned, an attempt has been made to use the Arab reaction to the occupation to structure a regional strategic consensus focused on Soviet expansionism. This has not been successful. For most Arab states the conflict with Israel has remained the number-one problem in the Middle East. Israel's actions in Lebanon in 1982 simply reaffirmed this priority. Even in the case of Pakistan, the country most severely affected by the Soviet occupation, the traditional conflict with India has continued to dominate security considerations. The West has expressed interest in moving to strengthen this militarily weak country and to bolster its politically shaky regime, but it is probable that India will view such moves primarily in terms of the classic Pakistan-India conflict and not in terms of a larger Soviet threat to the region.[24] It has been argued that because the Afghan resistance is organized mainly in Pakistan, a limited military build-up of Pakistan might be perceived as serving India's interests. Two reasons have been given. First of all, Pakistan is the last buffer state between a Soviet-occupied Afghanistan and India. Second, it has been argued that a conventionally weak and irredentist Pakistan might be tempted to develop nuclear weapons and this would actually pose the greatest threat to Indian security. In spite of such arguments, it remains to be seen whether Western assistance can effectively serve to stabilize the domestic situation in Pakistan.[25] Similarly it is questionable as to whether military assistance will actually function to contain Soviet expansion in and beyond Afghanistan or simply fuel a new India-Pakistan arms race. The Soviet occupation therefore has served to sharpen regional contradictions and dilemmas and to heighten a sense of wariness on the part of the West. It has not given rise to anything approaching a regional consensus identifying the Soviet Union as the primary threat to the area.

Prospects for a Political Solution

Several organizations have attempted to construct peace proposals allowing for a negotiated end to the Soviet Union's Afghanistan involvement. One of the more significant has been proposed by the European Economic Community (EEC).[26] In Moscow during July 1981, then British Foreign Minister Lord Carrington made a formal proposal on behalf of the EEC including the following salient points: (a) official talks between the permanent members of the UN Security Council, Pakistan, India, Iran, the secretary general of the UN, and the Group of Islamic States; and (b) a second round of talks including representatives of the Democratic Republic of Afghanistan with the goal of achieving a consensus on the proposals developed during the first round.

The Soviet Union immediately condemned the EEC plan, terming it an "intolerable maneuver" and "unrealistic," as the plan's ultimate aim was the neutralization of Afghanistan. The West Europeans, who had a special interest in resolving the Afghanistan conflict as soon as possible to avoid the disintegration of detente, were particularly criticized by the Soviets because they had included China (as a permanent member of the UN Security Council) in the first round of talks at the same time that Afghanistan itself was excluded. Carrington stressed the point that the Soviet complaints about "interference from outside" tended to ignore their own blatant intervention.[27] The EEC plan, which sought to integrate the international, regional, and internal aspects of the Afghanistan problem, has not, up to now, led to more than a vague agreement among EEC members to remain in contact on the Afghanistan issue.

A very different mix of proposals has been articulated by the Islamic Conference Organization (ICO). Its resolutions assert the right of the Afghan people to determine their own form of government as well as their own economic and social system "without interference and force from outside." In addition to the principles of independence, sovereignty, and nonalignment, the preservation of "Islamic identity" is mentioned.[28] A special commission of the ICO consisting of the foreign ministers of Iran, Pakistan, and the secretary of the ICO has developed a more detailed program consisting of the following key points: (a) talks between the various resistance groups within Afghanistan that are opposing the Soviet occupation; and (b) negotiations between the resistance groups, the PDPA, and the Soviet Union mediated by the United Nations.

The Soviet Union, primarily interested in obtaining formal recognition for the Karmal regime, has pursued its own diplomatic initiatives on a double track. On the one hand it has attempted to place the Afghanistan problem in the larger context of security concerns within the entire Gulf region. On the other hand it has authorized the Karmal regime to pursue bilateral negotiations with its immediate neighbors with the condition that discussion of Afghan internal affairs be strictly excluded.

The Soviet Union's own Gulf security plan consists of five points: (a) exclusion of foreign military bases and atomic weapons from the Persian Gulf; (b) exclusion of the use of force against the states of the region and of interference in their internal affairs; (c) respect for the nonaligned status of the Gulf states; (d) respect for the sovereign right of the Gulf states to control their own natural resources; and (e) no interference with the normal flow of trade and with utilization of sea lanes.[29] The United States and China, which together with Japan and the USSR were to guarantee this arrangement, condemned it in turn as "ironic" and "hypocritical."[30] Without a prior withdrawal of Soviet troops from Afghanistan, it was asserted, such an agreement would remain untrustworthy. The Soviet Union was accused of seeking to make the Gulf region, and not Afghanistan, the central issue for negotiations. The proposal is in fact probably best interpreted as the maximum Soviet position that foresees a neutralization of the entire region. Aside from the Gulf, the area would also include Iran, Pakistan, the Indian Ocean with the approaches to the Persian Gulf, and by implication, Afghanistan. The guarantors would be the Soviet, U.S., Chinese, Pakistani, and Iranian governments.[31]

Babrak Karmal himself has put forward a series of prerequisites for a solution to the Afghanistan problem including: (a) an end to all outside interference in Afghanistan's internal affairs; (b) negotiations and normalization of relations with Pakistan and Iran; (c) if required, the mediation of the UN Secretary General; (d) guarantees preventing any future outside interference in Afghanistan's internal affairs; (e) withdrawal of the "Soviet limited military contingents"; (f) discussion of the Afghanistan issue in the context of the Gulf region; and (g) exclusion from the negotiating process of discussions on the character of the Afghan regime and other Afghan internal affairs.[32]

These various plans represent just a selection of many proposals that have been offered. Up to now such plans have revealed more about the narrow interests of their respective originators than anything else. What have been lacking are more realistic approaches on both sides. To initiate a phase of sincere negotiations addressing the Afghanistan problem, at least three main issues will have to be dealt with: (a) The Soviet Union can be attracted to negotiations only in a situation of military stalemate. What can be offered the USSR to enhance its interest in a withdrawal? (b) The United States, its allies, the nonaligned countries, and the Islamic states have an interest in negotiations only if the status of the present Afghan regime is not excluded from discussions. Under whose auspices could supervised elections take place in Afghanistan? (c) In the event that positive answers could be found to the aforementioned problems, other difficulties remain. Who could effectively mediate between the PDPA and the mujahhidin, and where is the Afghan political leader who could possibly integrate the rivaling Afghan tribes and groups that have remained divided even as they struggle for survival? Under the best of circumstances constructive answers to these questions will be extremely difficult to find.

Notes

1. For historical and cultural background see Louis Dupree, *Afghanistan* (Princeton: Princeton University Press, 1973); Dietrich Geyer, *Der russische Imperialismus: Studien über den Zusammenhang von innerer und auswärtiger Politik, 1860-1914* (Göttingen: Vandenhoeck and Ruprecht, 1977); and Richard S. Newell, *The Politics of Afghanistan* (Ithaca: Cornell University Press, 1972).

2. It has been suggested that Daoud's increasing conservatism was in part the result of a growing involvement by Iran in Afghanistan's internal affairs. See Selig Harrison, "The Shah, Not Kremlin, Touched off Afghan Coup," *Washington Post*, 13 May 1979.

3. Gerd Linde, "Afghanistan und der Nachbar im Norden," in Heinrich Vogel, ed., *Die sowjetische Intervention in Afghanistan: Entstehung und Hintergründe einer weltpolitischen Krise* (Baden-Baden: Nomos, 1980), pp. 67-92.

4. For additional accounts of the April 1978 coup and of factional divisions within the PDPA see Louis Dupree, "Afghanistan Under the *Khalq*," *Problems of Communism* (July/August 1979):34-50; Fred Halliday, "Revolution in Afghanistan," *New Left Review* (November/December 1978):3-44; Hannah Negaran (pseud.), "The Afghan Coup of April 1978," *Orbis* (Spring 1979):93-113; and Winfried F. Wiegandt, *Afghanistan: Nicht aus heiterem Himmel* (Zurich: Fuessli, 1980).

5. Karmal and other *Parcham* leaders soon abandoned their diplomatic assignments and apparently spent considerable time thereafter consulting with Soviet emissaries in Moscow and elsewhere. See Karl-Heinrich Rudersdorf, *Afghanistan, eine Sowjetrepublik?* (Reinbek bei Hamburg: Rowohlt, 1980).

6. Decree Number 8 on Land Reforms in Afghanistan, dated 28 November 1978, in Afghan Ministry of Information and Culture, *Decrees of the Democratic Republic of Afghanistan* (Kabul), pp. 20-29.

7. The call to holy war was raised by the religious leader Sayyid Ahmad Gailani in Kabul. Resistance groups sprang up chaotically and by the spring of 1979 no less than ten distinct organizations could be identified. For details see Henning Behrens, *Die Afghanistan-Intervention der UdSSR* (Munich: tuduv, 1982), p. 49.

8. The *Setem-i-Meli* ("Against National Oppression") is an ultraleft faction that split from the PDPA in 1969. See the postscript in Dupree, *Afghanistan*.

9. Graham T. Allison, *Essence of Decision* (Boston: Little, Brown, and Co., 1971).

10. Adolf A. Berle, *Macht: die treibende Kraft der Geschichte* (Hamburg: Hoffmann und Campe, 1973).

11. See the text of Brezhnev's *Pravda* interview of 13 January 1980 in *Neues Deutschland*, 14 January 1980; and the interview with Babrak Karmal in *Der Spiegel*, 31 March 1980, p. 144.

12. Cited in Dieter Heinzig, "Eine neue Qualität sowjetischer Aussenpolitik?," *Information für die Truppe* 5 (1980):38.

13. Jürgen Heuchling, "Afghanistan-strategische Bedeutung zwischen gestern und morgen," *Europäische Wehrkunde* (June 1980):278-281.

14. Wolfgang Berner, "Der kampf um Kabul: Lehren und Perspektiven der sowjetischen Militärintervention in Afghanistan," *Berichte des Bundesinstituts für ostwissenschaftliche und internationale Studien* 14 (1980):51.

15. Ibid., pp. 4-6. See also Alvin Z. Rubinstein, "Embraced by the Bear," *Orbis* (Spring 1982):135-153.

16. Helmut Dahm, "Das Unternehmen Afghanistan als Lehrstück der politischen und militärischen Doktrin Sowjetrusslands," *Berichte des Bundesinstituts für ostwissenschaftliche und internationale Studien* 9 (1980):17.

17. Theo Sommer, "Der Kreml glaubt den Tränen nicht," *Die Zeit,* 28 March 1980, p. 3.

18. A. Petrov [pseud.], in *Pravda,* 1 March 1980.

19. Edgar O'Ballance, "Die sowjetische Besetzung Afghanistans," *Europäische Wehrkunde* 11 (1980):551.

20. The inhibiting effect of the Polish crisis upon Soviet options should also be noted. See K. Wafadar (pseud.), "Afghanistan in 1980: The Struggle Continues," *Asian Survey* (February 1981):179.

21. See Behrens, *Die Afghanistan-Intervention der UdSSR,* pp. 179-180. According to a high-level defector, tension between *Parcham* and *Khalq* functionaries led to an August 1982 shoot out in the presidential palace in Kabul in which at least six people were killed. See *Le Monde,* 12/13 September 1982, p. 4.

22. See the three-part series by Olaf Ihlau, "Afghanistan," *Süddeutsche Zeitung,* 12/13, 18, and 21 December 1981, pp. 3.

23. John C. Campbell, "Soviet Policy in the Middle East," *Current History* (January 1981):1-4.

24. Rodney W. Jones, "Mending Relations with Pakistan," *Washington Quarterly* (Spring 1981):26.

25. Zalmay Khalilzad, "The Struggle for Afghanistan," *Survey* (Spring 1980):209.

26. *International Herald Tribune,* 20 February and 25 June 1980.

27. *Archiv der Gegenwart,* 6 July 1981, pp. 24719-24720.

28. *Süddeutsche Zeitung,* 7 July 1981.

29. *Archiv der Gegenwart,* 22 May 1980, pp. 23564-23565.

30. Ibid., 8 January 1981, pp. 24175-24179.

31. *Süddeutsche Zeitung,* 13 December 1980.

32. For critical and sympathetic commentary upon Kabul's original proposals see the *Economist,* 17-23 May 1980, p. 35; and Dmitry Volsky, "The Kabul Programme and the Manoeuvres of its Opponents," *New Times* 23 (1980):12-13.

13

The Superpowers in the Middle East: The Dynamics of Involvement

Richard Ned Lebow
with *Jonathan Cooper*

Since 1945 the superpowers have been drawn into the vortex of Middle Eastern politics for a number of political, economic, strategic, historical, and geographical reasons. The most outstanding feature of their involvement has been a negative one. Despite their intense and continuous involvement in the region they have been relatively unable to shape the course of events in the Middle East. Moreover, what was in the past a qualified observation about their impotence in the area has in the course of the last decade become something of a critical paradox. For both the United States and the USSR recently have shown themselves to be even more eager than before to define and defend their interests in the Middle East. At the same time, they have been more often thwarted and commensurably less able to exert political influence to serve their chosen ends. This concluding chapter will attempt to describe the sets of countervailing forces that in the past few years have pulled the superpowers into the region but have also stymied their attempts to consolidate and expand their respective political footholds.

1. Drawing forces:
   a. Cold-war competition for influence.
   b. Importance of raw materials.
   c. Domestic political pressures.
   d. Strategic factors.
2. Stymieing forces:
   a. Indigenous instability.
   b. Antisuperpower feeling.
   c. Regional cleavages.
   d. Burden of past actions.
   e. Ideological incompatibility.
   f. Alliance problems.

Drawing Forces

Cold-War Competition for Influence

A perennial and integral feature of any superpower-client state relationship in a regional area is its relevance to the wider context of the U.S.-USSR bipolar balance. Post-World War II experience has shown that a regional presence by one superpower almost inevitably provokes some reciprocal involvement by the other, exclusive of any specific set of interests that might draw the latter independently into the region. The cold-war paranoia that first fed, for example, the Soviet urge to gain the A-bomb in the late 1940s, or later the U.S. need to bridge the apocryphal missile gap in the 1950s, expressed a type of reciprocal mentality that has been reproduced in every sphere of superpower competition. In both cases the USSR and the United States reacted from a fear of deprivation; there arose a so-called superpower need to gain at all costs what its opponent had, and what it lacked itself, even though the consequences of that mentality might lead to spiraling dangers of confrontation.

This logic now extends to superpower competition for client-states throughout the Third World. In its simplest form it is power politics in its crudest form; influence being a sine qua non of power. Each superpower has attempted to extend its sphere of influence over any state or region it can as such an extension, by definition, deprives its opponent of similar influence in the given sphere. However, that very deprivation nourishes the opponent's resolve to expand its own influence in the same region. Within the infernal machine of bipolar politics global equilibrium has become a facile readiness to respond to every challenge the antagonist makes, wherever it is made. The contest may sometimes be muted for fear of escalation to direct confrontation but the incentives to become involved are generally perceived within a reciprocal perspective.

The extent of mutual superpower involvement obviously depends on the political sensibility of the region in question. Latin America and Eastern Europe are areas where superpower interests are so well-defined and consolidated to make reciprocal involvement a very high-risk operation, yet even they are regarded as vulnerable to at least ideological overtures (and by proxy sometimes more) from the adversary. The Middle East, where the stakes are high but where neither Moscow nor Washington is dominant, has understandably become the principal focus of their rivalry.

The relative ascendancy of the U.S. presence in the core area of the Middle East has excluded the Soviet Union from the Arab-Israeli negotiating process for the time being, but it has not dampened Soviet resolve to counterbalance that U.S. predominance. On the contrary, it must be seen as a factor contributing to Soviet determination. Of course, the Soviet Union does have separate and specific interests in the Middle East; it would be simplistic to assume that Soviet foreign policy is driven solely by a need to meet an established U.S. position. In strategic terms, by simple reason of its geographical proximity, the Middle East has long been a region vital to Soviet security. After the Second World War her attempts to influence the politics of northern Iran and Turkey were the antecedents of efforts in the 1950s and 1960s to harness embryonic Arab nationalism and anti-Western sentiment to the Communist wagon.

However, the Soviet's "loss" of Egypt, and the rise of detente, viewed within the SALT framework as a formalization of superpower parity, contributed in the 1970s to a new dynamic of Cold War reciprocity in the Middle East. For, while detente laid the foundations for a recognized global equilibrium, the Middle East seemed to confound Soviet desires for this to be reflected regionally. The dominant U.S. role in negotiating an Egyptian-Israeli settlement became an embarrassment to Soviet prestige and damaged her integrity as a superpower equal.

Soviet efforts since the October 1973 war, and especially her overtures to the PLO, have been aimed toward proving her indispensability to radical Arab demands. Many of these demands are, in fact, an anathema to her own ideology and long-term interests. It is a tactical arrangement, designed to undermine the U.S. position. The apparent inadequacy of U.S. half-way steps to Middle Eastern peace as represented by the Camp David accords are the basis upon which the Soviets wish to promote their alternative prescriptions. By supporting extreme Arab demands the Soviets signal to the United States that they are determined to work against any negotiated peace that excludes their participation. The Cold War logic preempts any settlement initiated from a U.S. position of strength; the Soviet Union will not desist from interfering while the United States monopolizes the negotiating role.

Ironically, the inability of the United States to construct a framework for a lasting peace settlement has further heightened the competition. Bound by the zero-sum conviction that "he who supplants his rival's influence will thereby gain," both superpowers are petrified by the possibility that any diminution of their influence in the region will be interpreted by the opposing side as a weakness to be exploited. Rather than accept the reality that their influence is definitively limited by other factors, they are moved to act tougher than ever in the vain hope of increasing credibility in the rival's eyes. The global implications of Middle Eastern involvement were dramatically expressed by the Soviet threat to intervene during the October War and the consequent U.S. decision to alert her conventional strategic forces. By contrast, the Iranian revolution in 1978 and the Soviet invasion of Afghanistan in 1979 were two events that, in their separate ways, emphasized the parameters of prior involvement in the region. Nonetheless, they contributed to a cyclical process of *challenge-response* that helped to scupper SALT II, endanger the stability of European and global detente, and provoke greater perceptions of both sides' *need* to expand their influence as preventive measure against the other.

Importance of Raw Materials

While competition for influence may of itself be a spur to push the superpowers into the Middle East, it is also a feature heightened by other more specific interests. The most significant of these interests in recent years has been the growing importance of the region as a source of raw materials, most especially of course, energy.

Since the October 1973 war, the problem of ensuring a constant supply of oil to the industrialized West has been well documented. Economic security has been a by-word of the Western democratic system since World War II and the 1970s oil crisis underlined the vulnerability of the Western economies in this regard. That the largest part of the West's imported oil arrives from the Middle East automatically defines the area as one of vital interest. Because Middle Eastern peace is the best guarantee of reliable supply, it follows that the West cannot but involve itself in the settlement process.

For the Soviet Union the importance of the Middle East as an energy source has, until recently, been a peripheral consideration. Two factors during the 1970s have altered this conception. As the world's largest oil producer the Soviet Union turned economic entrepreneur in the mid-'70s to take best advantage of the OPEC price rises. Not only did the USSR reap the economic benefits of an inflow of extra petrodollars from sales to the West, but she also gained some political kudos in India, for example, where she supplied oil at prices below the revised OPEC rates. The gas pipeline to Iran, commissioned in 1970 and operational before the 1978 revolution, also paved the way for the gas deal with Western Europe. By servicing her industries in the southeastern regions of the Soviet Union with Iranian gas, the USSR hoped to feed Western Europe with gas from her own fields in western Siberia.

The second factor that kindled the Soviet drive for Middle Eastern energy sources was a related one, based upon the recognition of an imminent decline in her own exports in the next two decades. Moscow is eager to maintain a secure supply of her own energy to Western markets to guarantee the hard currency and technology transfer needed to exploit the scarcely tapped energy potential from its relatively inaccessible fields east of the Urals for its longer-term needs. In so doing, however, the USSR may be unable to meet, in the interim period at least, East European energy requirements without a supplementary source from the Middle East.

Few aspects of Soviet-Middle Eastern cooperation on energy issues can be viewed in isolation from the political implications of the wider bipolar balance. Here, again, we are led to the qualified conclusion that the thrust of superpower attraction to Middle Eastern politics largely stems from the perceived utility of such involvement to the European sphere. The political experience of superpower presence in the Middle East fundamentally is framed by the threats and opportunities it presents within the European theater.

The 1973 energy crisis deepened rifts already developing in the Western Alliance. Western economic interdependence had been challenged by the crumbling Bretton Woods system, and fears of U.S. parochialism had placed Western Europe firmly on the defensive as regards its Atlantic neighbor's economic policy. Western Europe's particular vulnerability to the oil weapon exposed the structural problems that had been anticipated in the early 1970s with the dollar weakened and free trade threatened. Western Europe's immediate preoccupation during the crisis with economic security was seen from the U.S. perspective as obstructing her own political attempts to resolve the deeper rooted Arab-Israeli confrontation. The difference in perception generated intra-alliance mistrust that the Soviet Union was swift to recognize and make use of. Her interests are clearly served by perpetuating and intensifying, if possible, a divisive issue whose repercussions are felt so keenly in the West.

As we have already noted, an exploitation of regional conflict for wider purposes, if perceived as such by the adversary, may well produce an iron-fist reciprocation—a resort to firmer measures than before in order to retain one's influence. The difference in economic vulnerability between the United States and Western Europe to the caprices of OPEC policy pointed to an achilles heel that Washington appreciated and that hardened its commitment and resolve in the late 1970s as regards the flow of oil. The energy crisis touched upon the frangibility of the very alliance. During the unpredictable 1970s the persistent NATO quandary of how to forge a credible political-military alliance spanning three continents was amplified by the increasingly divisive issue of economic security. As one consequence of the sensitivity to alliance politics of Middle Eastern energy the United States reacted more aggressively in the region. Oil has become a symbol of alliance credibility—the template of the West's ability and will to defend a regional interest whose political impact reaches far beyond its geographical locality. However, differing U.S. and European perceptions on how best to secure a steady flow of oil has intensified intra-alliance tensions. Disjunction in the Western Alliance is, of course, regarded by the USSR as an opportunity to be exploited, and if energy is an issue that might promote this, then more aggressive, forceful U.S. posturing in the Middle East will result to counter the potential advantages that trans-Atlantic divisions might provide for the Soviets. To some extent, this is already apparent.

Domestic Political Pressures

The strength of the Jewish lobby in the United States has long been recognized as an important consideration in Middle Eastern policy assessment for successive U.S. governments. Even more important and generally overlooked has been the strength of non-Jewish public opinion, sympathetic to Israel since its creation. It may, however, be premature to regard this as a permanent factor in U.S. politics. The Reagan administration alienated much of its previous Jewish support with the conclusion of the AWACS deal to Saudi Arabia; and this, combined with the resignation of Secretary of State Haig and the general unease over the Israeli invasion of Lebanon, might have colored popular conceptions of the merit of U.S. support for the Israeli cause. This is not to say that a different perspective on the conflict will lead to less U.S. involvement or concern for the Middle East. It might actually increase pressure on Washington to exert its influence in the region. Waning U.S. support for Israel might also act to unite Jewish opinion, currently divided by the hard line of Menahem Begin's policies.

Not bound by the limitations of democratic public opinion, the Soviet Union has not felt the same constraints of domestic ethnic lobbies. Nevertheless, the USSR's substantial and growing Muslim population in her southern provinces constitutes a potential danger to the impermeability of centralized decision making. The Islamic revolution could creep further north. Whether or not the religious zeal of the Soviet Muslims, muffled since 1917 by the orthodoxy of state socialism, would be roused to the same degree as that of their brothers in the Gulf states, is a moot point. However, Soviet attempts to stem the tide of Muslim fundamentalism by greater involvement in the region might have ironically had the opposite effect by heightening the Islamic consciousness of the Muslims in her southern provinces.

Strategic Factors

Much to superpower dismay the credo that posits political influence as an automatic adjunct to military strength does not always stand up to close scrutiny in the case of their involvement in the Middle East. The Soviets, for example, have found the task of imposing their political will by means of military coercion a difficult one in Afghanistan. Alternatively, the threatening presence of the U.S. fleet in the Arabian Sea during the Iranian hostage crisis did nothing to expedite the release of the American hostages from the Tehran embassy.

This again underlines divided perceptions of political reality in the Middle East, which—rather than warn them off—tend to draw the superpowers deeper into the arena. At one level their military presence is a direct response to the indigenous instability of the region. At another level it is a function of the reciprocal Cold War logic we have already mentioned. The failure to consolidate political goals at the first level, as in the examples of Afghanistan or the hostage crisis, does not deter the superpowers from further involvement, but becomes instead the motivation at the second level for greater commitment. It is a formidable cycle from which to break away.

This cycle has promoted the increasing militarization of U.S. policies in the area. Frustrated U.S. efforts to manage the course of the Iranian revolution were reshaped thereafter into a more audible military signal to both regional and bipolar ears. President Carter's State of the Union speech laid the political foundations for the Reagan administration to shore up U.S. military presence in the Middle East. According to this logic, the Gulf states' reluctance to welcome the United States as a strong ally is rooted not in the complexities of regional politics but in the decline of a strong U.S. presence, ergo credibility, in the region. Washington believes that a greater military presence would perform three functions: it would defend the vital interest of oil, and access to it; it would be a bipolar signal to the Soviet Union of U.S. resolve; and it would be a regional signal (especially to Saudi Arabia) confirming U.S. commitment. Reagan's arms sales, his determination to operationalize the Rapid Deployment Force, the increased naval deployment in the Indian Ocean, and most recently military aid to hard-pressed Somalia are all indications of this policy.

The step-up in U.S. military resolve is also, of course, a response to the Soviet military build-up. Though the combat capability of the Soviet navy, for example, may be questioned, its increased size and mobility forewarns a greater deployment into forward positions in the Indian Ocean that the Americans do not believe they can ignore. Similarly, the Afghanistan invasion gave the United States the opportunity to play at geopolitical opportunism; finding themselves sharing some common interests over the issue, China and the United States were both vociferous in their condemnation of it. Yet geopolitical "two-upsmanship" is only likely to increase paranoid Soviet resolve to maintain a presence in buffer-state Afghanistan and to deploy still more ships in the Indian Ocean to ensure that her routes to the maritime provinces are not endangered by threats from the East, the West—or the Soviet nightmare—both of them together.

The irony of this increased build-up is that it does not serve the long-term objectives of either superpower. Post-shah anti-Westernism is not going to diminish with the threat of Rapid Deployment Force activity ready to impose so-called stability in the region. But neither can the USSR translate that into Soviet benefit. The invasion of Afghanistan was condemned by Islam. Could the United States channel those anti-Soviet energies? No, since Islam is also unconvinced by the U.S. preoccupation with Israel, Egypt, and efforts for a separate peace. The quagmire of Middle Eastern politics threatens to overwhelm the superpowers: the harder they struggle the deeper they seem to sink.

Both superpowers have been thwarted in many attempts to control the direction of Middle Eastern politics. What are the factors that stymie their efforts?

Stymieing Forces

Indigenous Instability

As illustrated by the case of Iran, the political infrastructure of many Arab states is built on shifting sands. One of the pitfalls of superpower involvement is that their perceptions of Middle Eastern instability have often underestimated the force of such structural turmoil. In the 1950s and 1960s, the traditional authority structures of the Arab states were often buried by a popular fervor for nationalism and industrialization. However, the new Arab leaders aroused expectations that for the most part they were unable to fulfill. Domestic failure led to the familiar search for scapegoats, and Israel provided a convenient foil for their inability to achieve internal goals. For Nasir's Egypt, for Syria and Iraq, hostility to Israel became an important source of domestic legitimacy. Furthermore, conservative, status quo Arab states like Jordan and Saudi Arabia were lured into the conflict since their leaders were so insecure as to fear that their own survival might be threatened should they alienate nationalist opinion in their own countries. Perhaps Israel, whose existence many Arabs now feel they have to accept, and with whom Egypt has actually made peace, is now at least temporarily eclipsed by militant, Islamic Iran as a cause for regional insecurity and domestic instability. There are few areas of the globe so prone to changes of alignment as the Middle East, and the fear that the Iranian thrust for regional domination could wreak similar havoc in other polities as did the Khumayni revolution upon the Peacock Throne in 1978 may again be pushing the Middle East toward new associations.

If the weakness of a state's political system can be identified as a reason for an aggressive foreign policy, and thereby a source of regional instability, the causes of such weakness have proved relatively impervious to treatment. It is an uncomfortable dilemma for the superpowers. Insufficient and uneven economic development has always been an important source of unsympathetic Arab nationalism in the 1950s and 1960s, but where, as in the case of Iran, the pace of economic modernization outstripped the ability of traditional authority structures to adapt to it, the consequences were even more dramatic and destabilizing. The only certainty in Middle Eastern politics seems to be that governments will continue to be overthrown, and new political alignments established.

The policy implications for the superpowers with regard to Middle Eastern client-states should be cautionary:

1. Too large an investment is a risk since one's influence is almost certain to diminish when domestic political circumstances change. The USSR should have learned this lesson in Egypt, and the United States in Iran following the fall of the shah.
2. Too close an involvement may preclude doing business with a successor regime. The United States confronts this problem in Iran. Before that it faced it in Greece when the colonels were overthrown.
3. Too large an investment with a regime that is later overthrown loses face vis-à-vis one's superpower adversary. The humiliation attendant upon this may require intervention to preserve the vestiges of diminishing influence. The Soviet invasion of Afghanistan appears to be motivated by such a concern and may yet prove analogous to the U.S. debacle in Vietnam.

Antisuperpower Feeling

A colonial past has left the West with a difficult inheritance. Initial Arab suspicions of the United States, acting as the agent of the excolonial powers, were founded on the mistrust of a fundamental aim of U.S. foreign policy in the immediate postwar era: that of providing the new Israeli state with the means of defending herself successfully against Arab aggression. Within the matrix of Arab nationalism this has always curbed the will or desire of Arab states to be influenced by either the United States or her European allies. However, while Moscow views the weakness of Arab ties to the West as a potential asset to her own Middle East policy, it has only been partially successful in translating anti-Western sentiment into Soviet benefit despite its identification with the Arab cause. Even so-called client-states like Syria and Iraq, heavily dependent upon Soviet military and economic aid, have pursued quite independent foreign policies, at times embarrassing to Moscow.

Muslim fundamentalism, and its concommitant anti-Westernism, has erected a further barrier to superpower influence in the region. It is an autonomous, local force, virulently anticommunist and anticapitalist. Its influence has spread beyond those states, like Iran, in which Muslim fundamentalism is the dominant political force, to more moderate states whose leaders are concerned about not antagonizing a growing fundamentalist constituency. The attack on Mecca and later the assassination of Anwar al-Sadat provided a vivid demonstration of the disruptive potential possessed by even a small but fanatic coterie of fundamentalists. Events like these have made all Arab leaders just that much more cautious about too open and close ties with either superpower.

Regional Cleavages

While regional cleavages may be exploited as tools of superpower entry into local politics, they have also restricted their room for further maneuver. This can be seen in three ways:

1. Local hostility stunts initiatives for regional alliance building. Neither superpower can hope to spread its influence through the entire area in the absence of some reconciliation of the numerous and serious cleavages in the region. The Arab-Israeli conflict is merely the most obvious of these. Other important cleavages divide Egypt and Libya, Iraq and Syria, Syria and Saudi Arabia, Iran and Iraq, and further afield, Morocco and Algeria or Somalia and Ethiopia. Strong superpower backing of any one of these countries is invariably perceived as a threat by its local adversary and often prompts it to turn to the other superpower for support.

2. The price of backing one side of a contentious dyad is obvious: the more associated with one state or grouping a superpower is, the less able it is to deal with its rivals. U.S. support for Israel, prior to the Sadat initiative in 1977, contributed to Egyptian intransigence and reluctance to negotiate through the Americans. It still makes U.S. relations with many other Arab states strained. The Soviets have also paid the price of regional division, in one instance by virtue of an effort to establish close relations with both sides of a regional conflict. In their efforts to supplant U.S. influence in Ethiopia they antagonized her adversary, Somalia, where Moscow had already built up a commanding presence. The Soviets were expelled from Somalia and lost their most important strategic air and naval base in the Indian Ocean. More recently, the Iran-Iraq war has caused Moscow some difficult moments, as it would prefer to maintain as close a relationship as possible with both countries. Moscow's failure to provide massive military aid to Iraq led to a decline in her relations with that country. Moreover, it is by no means clear that Soviet moderation has led to an improvement in her relations with Iran.

3. The intensity of regional conflicts illustrates one very important way in which local interests differ from superpower interests. Regional powers usually make overtures to superpowers as a means of gaining political leverage against their regional foes, or even friends. But superpower support often allows the recipient to use military force against its regional adversary. If the other superpower is backing that adversary it raises the

spectre of superpower conflict. This risks the most harrowing scenario, a direct superpower confrontation, such as nearly came about in October 1973. Passivity, however, at the other end of the scale, risks the loss of superpower prestige that accompanies a client-state's defeat.

Burden of Past Actions

Over thirty-five years of inconsistent policymaking has tarnished the credibility of both superpowers in dealings with their clients at the heart of the Arab-Israeli conflict. Rather than having consolidated their positions in the Middle East, past duplicity or inconstancy has bred mistrust of the United States on the part of the Israelis, and of the USSR by the Arabs.

The U.S. commitment to Israel, in the long term in both country's interests, has often generated short-term frictions. These have become more acute in recent years. Israeli political and military policies under Begin have frequently proven embarrassing to Washington and counterproductive to her own expectations in the region. Begin's outburst at U.S. criticism to the annexation of the Golan Heights in December 1981 is a case in point. Having been embarrassed—if secretly delighted—by Israel's attack on the Iraqi nuclear-reactor plant, or the Israeli air strikes on the PLO in Beirut in 1981, the White House seems to have convinced itself that the strategic agreement reached between the two countries late in the year would reinforce the United State's uncertain capacity to bridle the more hawkish policies of the Israeli leader. Begin's, "Are we a vassal state, Are we a banana republic?" rhetoric that followed the U.S. criticism demonstrated otherwise. It made quite clear the difference in perceptions that has existed, as well as the limits of restraint that U.S. policy has had upon Israel's behavior.

The differences between Israel and the United States became even more apparent during the recent war in Lebanon and led U.S. leaders for the first time to speculate openly about the possibility of an arms embargo directed against Israel. From Jerusalem's perspective, her relationship with the United States, while essential, is equally frustrating. Israelis, and not only supporters of Begin, see the United States as unpredictable, only partially reliable, and generally pursuing unrealistic goals. Dealing with the Reagan administration has been particularly difficult for Israelis as they never have been certain about who in that administration is ultimately responsible for Middle Eastern policy.

In contrast, the USSR's approach to the Arab states has been more reliable, if also more heavy-handed, but no more successful. In a region where local turbulence makes alliance-building difficult at the best of times, the USSR's clumsy dealing with Iran, Iraq, the Horn of Africa, and of course Egypt, have labeled her as an arrogant and self-interested patron, keen to establish her own foothold in order to counterbalance the United States rather than to serve local interests, or even the Communist ideal. The result of her frustrations and failures within the core of the Arab world has led her to turn toward geographically peripheral states. This should be recognized in the West as an ill-disguised, second-best option, not as some clever policy based on the belief that the peripheral areas are of primary strategic importance. Even here, the Soviets have met with only marginal success.

Ideological Incompatibility

U.S. problems with traditional authority structures in the Middle East have already been mentioned and have been most clearly manifest in the experience in Iran. Washington may now be courting another disaster in Saudi Arabia, where it has been making a similar political-military investment.

Ideological incompatibility is a problem Moscow faces as well. The anti-Western denominator that provided a link between Marx and Islam after the Second World War has proven to be a shallow foundation upon which communism might have built a power base in the Middle East. The failure of Arab socialism to provide the social and economic reconstruction it promised has possibly pushed communism still further away as an alternative ideology. The rise of fundamentalism in the last decade, which has confounded U.S. aspirations, is by no means a cause for Soviet rejoicing. It might even have closed the door on Marxist influence for the foreseeable future.

Alliance Problems

A major threat to Western security in the late 1970s arose not from the Eastern bloc, but from centrifugal forces within the structure of the Atlantic relationship itself. A changing international economy, creeping protectionism, and industrial recession contributed to a general erosion of the tenets of Atlantic cooperation upon which the Western Alliance depends for its credibility. As we have noted, the oil crisis exacerbated rifts that were already present if muted. Europe's greater vulnerability to changes in the supply of oil from the Middle East prompted her to look for short-run solutions that were interpreted in the United States as complicating the U.S. efforts to negotiate a long-term Middle Eastern settlement. European reluctance to commit itself wholeheartedly to the Camp David process again underlined their separate desire not to damage commercial links with the Arab oil producers.

Toward the end of the decade NATO bickering within the European arena was magnified by a further divergence of interests over Middle Eastern policy. The Reagan administration's commitment to a Rapid Deployment Force and the determination to reassert a U.S. regional presence after the Iran debacle gave strength to the conviction of many in the European peace movement that the United States rather than the USSR was the superpower most threatening to world peace. Although Europe has remained the geographical focus of NATO policy, the significance of the Middle East to NATO interests requires some redefinitions of the scope and interests of the alliance in the 1980s. It is doubtful that European defense and European security are any longer completely synonymous. Extra-European problems, not only in the Middle East, loom increasingly important to European security. The problems that this creates for the alliance demand a careful analysis and policy reappraisal.

For the Soviet Union the difficulty is only relatively less acute. The invasion of Afghanistan clearly had an impact upon the Warsaw Pact. Soviet attention to Middle Eastern developments makes Warsaw Pact cohesion all the more important to her. However, her intervention in Afghanistan has hardly been reassuring to her Eastern European allies, as was indicated by Rumania's abstention in the UN vote on Afghanistan. Developments in Eastern Europe may also influence Soviet Middle East policy. The delicate and still unresolved Polish situation could conceivably temper the prospect of Soviet military involvement in Asia and the Middle East in the 1980s.

Policy Implications

This brief sketch of forces that limit superpower influence should indicate a corresponding degree of caution and reserve in Moscow and Washington despite the obvious attractions for an even-deeper involvement. In this regard, three general policy conclusions emerge from the preceding discussion.

1. For a variety of reasons superpower influence in the Middle East is destined to be highly qualified. Any assumption that influence is an automatic by-product of involvement has to be reviewed. Even the heaviest of investment in terms of economic or military aid—the Soviet Union in Egypt in the late 1960s, the United States in Iran, Saudi Arabia, or even Israel—does not pay the anticipated dividends. A host of autonomous, regional forces seem fated to frustrate superpower aspirations. At the same time, the costs, actual and potential, rise precipitously as superpower involvement deepens. Experience shows that a large investment in a regime does not alter the ineluctable fact of political change in the Middle East. Too large an investment only makes the superpower more vulnerable to that

change and its costs; it guarantees little else. The U.S. experience in Iran and that of the Soviets in Afghanistan are both illustrative of this problem. Neither investment paid off. Iran has excluded the United States from foreseeable involvement, while the USSR is engaged in a debilitating and protracted war of attrition.

2. It is a common misapprehension in Washington that the Arab-Israeli dispute is the only major obstacle standing in the way of the spread of U.S. influence throughout at least the Arab part of the Middle East. Camp David, a notable achievement in its own right, is, of course, inadequate in Palestinian eyes. But even the successful conclusion of an Arab-Israeli settlement, not that that is likely, would lift only one of the storm clouds from the region. The resolution of the Palestinian problem and the acceptance of Israel's existence and borders by neighboring Arab states are necessary ingredients for Middle Eastern peace, but they are not sufficient. The Middle East, as we have seen, is marked by numerous acute, and in many cases, long-standing rivalries based on religious, ideological, and territorial differences. These conflicts would continue to poison relations among the states of the area, making it impossible for either superpower to forge an effective regional alliance. Beyond this, superpower influence would continue to be limited by the variety of domestic political considerations we have noted that make it in the interest of most local leaders to keep at least some distance between themselves and outside powers.

3. The U.S. tendency to exaggerate the extent and danger of Soviet influence in the area is not necessarily in her interest. Politically, the Soviet Union faces at least the same barriers that confound attempts by the United States to influence events. Her record in the area reveals weaknesses not strengths. Technically, her aid, economic and military, is second-rate compared to the United States; ideologically, communism is antipathetic to the Islamic dynamic; militarily, her heavy-handedness reached its ugliest peak in Afghanistan where the invasion set a precedent that her neighbors will watch with circumspect curiosity. That the Afghani rebels have resisted the Soviets so successfully makes the realization of any grand-design theory that posits a military drive south to the warm-water ports of the Gulf most unlikely. It is also important to realize that it is not, after all, a Western presence that is tying Soviet hands in Afghanistan, but the resistance of the indigenous population. And the USSR would meet no less resistance in Iran. The greatest deterrent to Soviet expansionism in the Middle East remains the local forces and local nationalism.

Seen in this context, the utility of a Rapid Deployment Force has to be carefully reconsidered. President Jimmy Carter's reaction to Afghanistan represented a kind of cognitive flip-flop; one simplistic and relatively benign notion of Soviet intentions was abandoned for another simplistic, but extreme, one. Had the RDF been available during the Iranian crisis the pressures on the president to have used it would have been enormous. Such a force may preclude inaction in an acute crisis, but in the Middle East, inaction may at times be the most sensible policy alternative. For this reason among others, there are merits to a *small* RDF as a deterrent element against the USSR. Such a force would also have some capability against local military forces. Even so, the RDF could prove more trouble than it is worth.

Looking back upon the past several years, it is apparent that the super-powers have suffered major, even humiliating, setbacks in the Middle East. It is an unfortunate feature of great power status that humiliation often leads to a grimmer determination to respond to future challenges. Yet stymieing forces augur badly for the ability of either superpower to do this. The involvement-influence equation seems even less promising that it did a decade ago. However, a neurotic preoccupation on the part of both Moscow and Washington with the way in which weaknesses are perceived and acted upon continues to fuel a self-defeating instinct to respond to every opportunity or challenge as though it were a major one. It is a perilous process. Some recognition of both the meager rewards and great costs of in-volvement and with it, greater superpower caution, would be in the interests not only of the United States and the Soviet Union but of the indigenous countries of the region as well.

Index

Abduh, Muhammad, 113
Aden, South Yemen, 45, 138, 168, 211, 216, 217
Afars (Ethiopia), 220, 221
Afghanistan, 23, 42, 247-250; and U.S., 251-252; and USSR, 1, 2, 4, 13, 15, 20, 22, 43, 49, 50, 57, 60, 72-97 *passim*, 125, 129, 134, 135, 136, 145 n.15, 159, 181, 193, 195, 228-230, 247-263 *passim*, 267, 273, 277, 278
Ahmad Shah Durrani, 247
Airborne Warning and Control Systems (AWACs), 3, 76, 84, 86, 94, 96, 97, 99, 101, 139, 144 n.12, 160, 164, 270
Ajami, Fouad, 61
Albania, 44
Alexander Hamilton (USS), 44
Algeria, 85, 114, 168; and Morocco, 72, 101-102, 274; and PLO refugees, 35, 37; and Steadfastness and Confrontation Front, 14, 25, 35, 73, 77, 101; and U.S. hostage crisis, 77, 80; and USSR, 17, 57, 74, 79, 80, 101; and Western Sahara dispute, 13, 80
Ali, Muhammad, 167
Allende government (Chile), 254
Allison, Graham, 252
Amanullah, King (Afghanistan), 248
Amharas (Ethiopia), 220
Amin, Hafizullah, 249, 250, 251, 256
Anatolia, 42
Andreasian, Reuben, 97
Andropov, Iurii, 61, 208
Ansar, al-, 193
Aqabah, Jordan, 35
Arab Deterrent Force, 31, 27
Arab-Israeli conflict, 1, 4, 13, 14-15, 17, 25-26, 36, 42, 58-59, 60, 74, 78, 81, 85, 101, 132, 149, 159, 160, 175-176, 258-259, 272, 274, 275, 278
Arab-Israel peace negotiations, 20-21; Camp David Agreement, 2, 16, 17, 36, 59-60, 73-83 *passim*, 94-102 *passim*, 132, 171, 175-176, 191, 193, 267, 276, 278; Fahd plan, 99-100;

Soviet plan, 58, 72, 78, 80, 81, 82, 84, 93, 95, 96, 99, 101, 191-192
Arab-Israeli wars: 1956, 20, 24, 169; 1967, 20, 99, 117-118, 169, 173; 1969-1970, 17, 20, 37, 173; 1973, 5, 14, 17, 21, 25, 35, 38, 59, 72, 73, 129, 170, 173, 267, 268, 275
Arab League, 14, 20, 23-25, 26, 31, 118, 160, 175, 205
Arab Liberation Front, 193
Arab states, 2, 32, 37, 81-102, 103 n.9, 106 n.49, 202, 272; and U.S., 3, 21, 73, 86, 89, 101, 107 n.75, 274; and USSR, 3, 31, 56, 72, 73-74, 157-158, 251, 275-276
Arab unity, 23-24, 56, 73, 76, 84, 86, 100, 118
Arabian Sea, 18, 138, 139
Arafat, Yasir, 27, 95, 109 n.100, 189, 190-191, 192, 194, 195, 196, 198, 201, 204, 205
Arms transfers, 4, 17, 18, 19, 25, 38, 55, 133, 158, 182
Asad, Hafiz al- (Syria), 30, 32, 35, 84
Assab, Ethiopia, 219, 220
Aswan Dam (Egypt), 72, 95
Ataturk, 62 n.7
Australia, 138
Azerbaidzhan (Iran), 42, 43, 130, 140, 242
Azeris, 48, 239, 242
Azhar, al-, 114
Azrael, Jeremy, 65 n.35

B-52 bombers, 98, 138
Bab al-Mandab Straits, 45, 47, 60, 211
Babur, Shah, 247
Backfire bomber (USSR), 138, 254
Baghdad Conference (1978), 74, 82
Baghdad Pact (1955), 19-20, 23, 44
Bahashti, Ayatollah Muhammad, 91
Bahrain, 32, 33, 74, 76, 148, 151, 161 n.3
Baktiar (Iranian prime minister), 91
Baku Conference (1920), 43
Baluchis, 135, 242
Baluchistan, 230

About the Contributors

Henning Behrens is assistant professor at the Geschwister-Scholl-Institut, University of Munich. His publications include *Die Afghanistan-Intervention der UdSSR* (1982) and, with Paul Noack, *Theorien der Internationalen Politik* (1983).

Jonathan Cooper is a graduate of the Johns Hopkins University School of Advanced International Studies, Bologna Center, and is employed with the Atomic Energy Commission, Vienna.

Robert O. Freedman is professor of political science and dean of the Graduate School, Baltimore Hebrew College. His publications include *Soviet Policy toward the Middle East Since 1970* (1982) and numerous other articles and monographs on Soviet Middle Eastern policy.

Galia Golan is Darwin Professor of Soviet and East European Studies, Hebrew University of Jerusalem. Her publications include *Yom Kippur and After: The Soviet Union and the Middle East Crisis* (1977), and *The Soviet Union and the Palestine Liberation Organization: An Uneasy Alliance* (1980).

Kenneth Hunt, formerly deputy director of the International Institute for Strategic Studies, is visiting professor of international relations, University of Surrey. He is specialist advisor to the Defense Committee of the British House of Commons.

J.C. Hurewitz is director of the Middle East Institute, Columbia University. He is a leading scholar of Middle Eastern affairs and author and editor of numerous publications including *Middle East Politics: The Military Dimension* (1974).

Mamoun Kurdi is director of the Saudi Arabian Economic Research Unit, London.

Richard Ned Lebow is professor of strategy, the Johns Hopkins University School of Advanced International Studies, Bologna Center. Recent publications include *Between Peace and War: The Nature of International Crisis* (1981).

Mohammed Anis Salem is a former employee of the Egyptian Foreign Ministry and is currently a research associate with the International Institute for Strategic Studies, London.

Udo Steinbach is director of the Deutsches Orient-Institut, Hamburg, and a leading European specialist of Middle Eastern affairs. His publications include *Kranker Wächter am Bosporus: Die Turkei als Riegel zwischen Ost und West* (1979).

Paul R. Viotti is professor of political science, U.S. Air Force Academy. His most recent publication, coedited with Douglas J. Murray, is *The Defense Policies of Nations* (1982).

Malcolm E. Yapp is senior lecturer in the history of the Near and Middle East at the School of Oriental and African Studies, University of London. He is the author of numerous articles on the modern history of the Middle East and South Asia, and his recent book, *Strategies of British India* (1980) won the Trevor Reese Memorial Prize awarded for the best work in the field of imperial history.

About the Editors

Mark V. Kauppi is assistant professor of political science, University of Colorado at Colorado Springs. His current research interest involves Soviet activity in the Third World.

R. Craig Nation is assistant professor, University of Southern California, School of International Relations, and specializes in Soviet foreign relations.